Copyright © 2021 -All rights reserved.

No part of this book may be reproduced or transmitted in any form or by any means, electronic or mechanical, including photocopying and recording, or by any information storage and retrieval system, without permission in writing from the publisher. This is a work of fiction. Names, places, characters and incidents are either the product of the author's imagination or are used fictitiously, and any resemblance to any actual persons, living or dead, organizations, events or locales is entirely coincidental. The unauthorized reproduction or distribution of this copyrighted work is ilegal.

Please note the information contained within this document is for educational and entertainment purposes only. All effort has been executed to present accurate, up to date, reliable, complete information. No warranties of any kind are declared or implied. Readers acknowledge that the author is not engaged in the rendering of legal, financial, medical, or professional advice. The content within this book has been derived from various sources. Please consult a licensed professional before attempting any techniques outlined in this book. By reading this document, the reader agrees that under no circumstances is the author responsible for any losses, direct or indirect, that are incurred as a result of the use of the information contained within this document, including, but not limited to, errors, omissions, or inaccuracies.

INTRODUCTION

A plant-based diet is a diet based primarily on whole plant foods. It is identical to the regular diet we're used to already, except that it leaves out foods that are not exclusively from plants. Hence, a plant-based diet does away with all types of animal-sourced foods, hydrogenated oils, refined sugars, and processed foods. A whole food plant-based diet comprises not just fruits and vegetables; it also consists of unprocessed or barely-processed oils with healthy monounsaturated fats (like extra-virgin olive oil), whole grains, legumes (essentially lentils and beans), seeds and nuts, as well as herbs and spices.

What makes a plant-based meal (or any meal) fun is the manner with which you make them; the seasoning process; and the combination process that contributes to a fantastic flavor and makes every meal unique and enjoyable. There are lots of delicious recipes (all plant-centered), which will prove helpful in when you intend making mouthwatering, healthy plant-based dishes for personal or household consumption. Provided you're eating these plant-based foods regularly, you'll have very problems with fat or diseases that result from bad dietary habits, and there would be no need for excessive calorie tracking.

Plant-based diet recipes are versatile; they range from colorful Salads to Lentil Stews, and Bean Burritos. The recipes also draw influences from around the globe, with Mexican, Chinese, European, Indian cuisines all part of the vast array of plant-based recipes available to choose from.

Why You Ought to Reduce Your Intake of Processed and Animal-Based Foods

You have likely heard over and over that processed food has adverse effects on your health. You might have also been told repeatedly to stay away from foods with lots of preservatives; nevertheless, nobody ever offered any genuine or concrete facts about why you ought to avoid these foods and why they are unsafe. Consequently, let us properly dissect it to help you properly comprehend why you ought to stay away from these healthy eating offenders.

1. They have massive habit-forming characteristics

Humans have a predisposition towards being addicted to some specific foods; however, the reality is that the fault is not wholly ours.

Every one of the unhealthy treats we relish now and then triggers the dopamine release in our brains. This creates a pleasurable effect in our brain, but the excitement is usually short-lived. The discharged dopamine additionally causes an attachment connection gradually, and this is the reason some people consistently go back to eat certain unhealthy foods even when they know it's unhealthy and unnecessary. You can get rid of this by taking out that inducement completely.

2. They are sugar-laden and plenteous in glucose-fructose syrup

Animal-based and processed foods are laden with refined sugars and glucose-fructose syrup which has almost no beneficial food nutrient. An ever-increasing number of studies are affirming what several people presumed from the start; that genetically modified foods bring about inflammatory bowel disease, which consequently makes it increasingly difficult for the body to assimilate essential nutrients. The disadvantages that result from your body being unable to assimilate essential nutrients from consumed foods rightly cannot be overemphasized. Processed and animal-based food products contain plenteous amounts of refined carbohydrates. Indeed, your body requires carbohydrates to give it the needed energy to run body capacities.

In any case, refining carbs dispenses with the fundamental supplements; in the way that refining entire grains disposes of the whole grain part. What remains, in the wake of refining, is what's considered as empty carbs or empty calories. These can negatively affect the metabolic system in your body by sharply increasing your blood sugar and insulin quantities.

3.   They contain lots of synthetic ingredients

At the point when your body is taking in non-natural ingredients, it regards them as foreign substances. Your body treats them as a health threat. Your body isn't accustomed to identifying synthetic compounds like sucralose or these synthesized sugars. Hence, in defense of your health against this foreign "aggressor," your body does what it's capable of to safeguard your health. It sets off an immune reaction to tackle this "enemy" compound, which indirectly weakens your body's general disease alertness, making you susceptible to illnesses. The concentration and energy expended by your body in ensuring your immune system remain safe could instead be devoted somewhere else.

4.   They contain constituent elements that set off an excitable reward sensation in your body

A part of processed and animal-based foods contain compounds like glucose-fructose syrup, monosodium glutamate, and specific food dyes that can trigger some addiction. They rouse your body to receive a benefit in return whenever you consume them. Monosodium glutamate, for example, is added to many store-bought baked foods. This additive slowly conditions your palates to relish the taste. It gets mental just by how your brain interrelates with your taste sensors. This reward-centric arrangement makes you crave it increasingly, which ends up exposing you to the danger of over consuming calories.

For animal protein, usually, the expression "subpar" is used to allude to plant proteins since they generally have lower levels of essential amino acids as against animal-sourced protein. Nevertheless, what the vast majority don't know is that large amounts of essential amino acids can prove detrimental to your health. Let me break it down further for you.

5.   Animal-Sourced Protein has no Fiber

In their pursuit to consume animal protein increasingly, the vast majority wind up dislodging the plant protein that was previously available in their body. Replacing the plant proteins with its animal variant is wrong because, in contrast to plant protein, animal proteins typically have fiber deficiency, phytonutrients, and antioxidant properties. Fiber insufficiency is a regular feature across various regions and societies on the planet. In America, for example, according to the National Academy of Medicine, the typical adult takes in roughly 15 grams of dietary fiber daily rather than the recommended daily quantity of 25 to 30 grams. A deficiency in dietary fiber often leads to a heightened risk of breast and colorectal cancers, in addition to constipation, inflammatory bowel disease, and cardiovascular disease.

6.   Animal Protein Leads to a Jump in IGF-1 Levels

Insulin-like growth factor 1 (IGF-1) is a vital growth hormone identical in molecular geometry to insulin which contributes significantly to the growth of children and impacts adults in an anabolic manner. It fuels cell division and development, which may seemingly seem positive; however, it correspondingly triggers the development of cancer cells. Hence, an increased level of IGF-1 in the blood is connected to a heightened risk of cancer, malignant tumor, and spread.

7.   Animal protein brings about an upsurge in Phosphorus levels in the body

Animal protein has significant levels of Phosphorus. Our bodies stabilize these plenteous amounts of Phosphorus by producing and discharging a hormone known as fibroblast growth factor 23 (FGF23). Studies have shown that this hormone is dangerous to our veins. FGF23 also causes asymmetrical expansion of heart muscles – a determinant for congestive heart failure and even mortality in some advanced cases.

Having discussed the many problems associated with animal protein, it becomes more apt to replace its "high quality" perception with the tag, "highly hazardous." In contrast to caffeine, which has a withdrawal effect if it's discontinued abruptly, you can stop taking processed and animal-based foods right away without any withdrawals. Possibly the only thing that you'll give up is the ease of some meals taking little-to-no time to prepare.

BREAKFAST RECIPES

Gingerbread Waffles

Preparation Time: 30 minutes
Cooking Time: 20 minutes
Servings: 6
Ingredients:
- 1 cup spelt flour
- 2 teaspoon baking powder
- ¼ teaspoon salt
- 1 tablespoon ground flax seeds
- 1 ½ teaspoon ground cinnamon
- 2 teaspoon ground ginger
- 4 tablespoon coconut sugar
- ¼ teaspoon baking soda
- 1½ tablespoon olive oil
- 1 cup non-dairy milk
- 1 tablespoon apple cider vinegar
- 2 tablespoon blackstrap molasses

Directions:
1. Take a waffle iron, oil generously, and preheat.
2. Take a large bowl and add the dry ingredients. Stir well together.
3. Put the wet ingredients into another bowl and stir until combined.
4. Stir the dry and wet together until combined.
5. Pour the mixture into the waffle iron and cook on a medium temperature for 20 minutes.
6. Open carefully and remove.
7. Serve and enjoy.

Nutrition: calories 173 fat 5 carbs 29 protein 3

Blueberry French Toast Breakfast Muffins

Preparation Time: 20 minutes
Cooking Time: 25 minutes
Servings: 12
Ingredients:
- 1 cup unsweetened plant milk
- 1 tablespoon ground flaxseed
- 1 tablespoon almond meal
- 1 tablespoon maple syrup
- 1 teaspoon vanilla extract
- 1 teaspoon cinnamon
- 2 teaspoons nutritional yeast
- ¾th cup frozen blueberries
- 9 slices soft bread
- ¼th cup oats
- 1/3rd cup raw pecans
- ¼th cup of coconut sugar
- 3 tablespoons coconut butter, at room temperature
- 1/8th teaspoon sea salt
- 9 slices bread, each cut into 4

Directions:
1. Preheat your oven to 370°F and grease a muffin tin. Pop to one side.
2. Find a medium bowl and add the flaxseeds, almond meal, nutritional yeast, maple syrup, milk, vanilla, and cinnamon.
3. Mix well using a fork then pop into the fridge.
4. Grab your food processor and add the topping ingredients (except the coconut butter.) Whizz to combine.
5. Add the butter then whizz again.
6. Grab your muffin tin and add a teaspoon of the flax and cinnamon batter to the bottom of each space.
7. Add a square of the bread then top with 5-6 blueberries.
8. Sprinkle with 2 teaspoons of the crumble then top with another piece of bread.
9. Place 5-6 more blueberries over the bread, sprinkle with more of the topping then add the other piece of bread.
10. Add a tablespoon of the flax and cinnamon mixture over the top and add a couple of blueberries on the top.
11. Pop into the oven and cook for 20-25 minutes until the top begins to brown.
12. Serve and enjoy.

Nutrition: calories 132 fat 5 carbs 14 protein 3

Greek Garbanzo Beans on Toast

Preparation Time: 25 minutes
Cooking Time: 5 minutes
Servings: 2
Ingredients:
- 2 tablespoons olive oil
- 3 small shallots, finely diced
- 2 large garlic cloves, finely diced
- ¼ teaspoon smoked paprika
- ½ teaspoon sweet paprika
- ½ teaspoon cinnamon
- ½ teaspoon salt
- ½-1 teaspoon sugar, to taste
- Black pepper, to taste
- 1 x 14 oz. can peel plum tomatoes
- 2 cups cooked garbanzo beans
- 4-6 slices of crusty bread, toasted
- Fresh parsley and dill
- Pitted Kalamata olives

Directions:
1. Pop a skillet over medium heat and add the oil.
2. Add the shallots to the pan and cook for five minutes.
3. Add the garlic and cook until ready then add the other spices to the pan.
4. Stir well then add the tomatoes.
5. Lower the heat and simmer on low until the sauce thickens.
6. Add the garbanzo beans and warm through.
7. Season with the sugar, salt, and pepper, then serve and enjoy.

Nutrition: calories 709 fat 12 carbs 23 protein 19

Easy Hummus Toast

Preparation Time: 10 minutes
Cooking Time: 10 minutes
Servings: 1
Ingredients:
- 2 slices sprouted wheat bread
- ¼ cup hummus
- 1 tablespoon hemp seeds
- 1 tablespoon roasted unsalted sunflower seeds

Directions:
1. Start by toasting your bread.
2. Top with the hummus and seeds then eat!

Nutrition: calories 316 fat 16 carbs 13 protein 18

No-Bake Chewy Granola Bars

Preparation Time: 10 minutes
Cooking Time: 10 minutes
Servings: 8
Ingredients:
- ¼ teaspoon cinnamon
- ¼ teaspoon salt
- ½ teaspoon cardamom
- ¼ cup of coconut oil
- 1 cup oats
- 1 teaspoon vanilla extract
- ½ cup raw almonds, sliced
- ¼ cup sunflower seeds
- ½ cup pumpkin seeds
- 1¼ teaspoon nutmeg
- 1 tbsp chia seeds
- ¼ cup honey
- 1 cup dried figs, chopped

Directions:
1. Line a 6" x 8" baking dish with parchment paper and pop to one side.
2. Grab a saucepan and add the salt, honey, oil, and spices.
3. Pop over medium heat and stir until it melts together.
4. Reduce the heat, add the oats, and stir.
5. Add the dried fruit, seeds, and nuts, and stir through again.
6. Cook for 10 minutes.
7. Remove from the heat and transfer the oat mixture to the pan.
8. Press down until it's packed firm.
9. Leave to cool completely then cut into 8 bars.
10. Serve and enjoy.

Nutrition: calories 308 fat 14 carbs 35 protein 6

Tasty Oatmeal and Carrot Cake

Preparation Time: 5 minutes
Cooking Time: 10 minutes
Servings: 2
Ingredients:
- 1 cup of water
- ½ teaspoon of cinnamon
- 1 cup of rolled oats
- Salt
- ¼ cup of raisins
- ½ cup of shredded carrots
- 1 cup of non-dairy milk
- ¼ teaspoon of allspice
- ½ teaspoon of vanilla extract

Toppings:
- ¼ cup of chopped walnuts
- 2 tablespoons of maple syrup
- 2 tablespoons of shredded coconut

Directions:
1. Put a small pot on low heat and bring the non-dairy milk, oats, and water to a simmer.
2. Now, add the carrots, vanilla extract, raisins, salt, cinnamon, and allspice. You need to simmer all the ingredients, but do not forget to stir them. You will know that they are ready when the liquid is fully absorbed into all the ingredients (in about 7-10 minutes).
3. Transfer the thickened dish to bowls. You can top them with coconut or walnuts.
4. This nutritious bowl will allow you to kickstart your day.

Nutrition: calories 210 fat 11 carbs 42 protein 4

Almond Butter Banana Overnight Oats

Preparation Time: 5 minutes
Cooking Time: 10 minutes
Servings: 2
Ingredients:
- ½ cup rolled oats
- 1 cup almond milk
- 1 tablespoon chia seeds
- ¼ teaspoon vanilla extract
- ½ teaspoon ground cinnamon
- 1 tablespoon honey or maple syrup
- 1 banana, sliced
- 2 tablespoons natural almond butter

Directions:
1. Take a large bowl and add the oats, milk, chia seeds, vanilla, cinnamon, and honey.
2. Stir to combine then divide half of the mixture between two bowls.
3. Top with the banana and peanut butter then add the remaining mixture.
4. Cover then pop into the fridge overnight.
5. Serve and enjoy.

Nutrition: calories 227 fat 11 carbs 35 protein 7

Peach & Chia Seed Breakfast Parfait

Preparation Time: 5 minutes
Cooking Time: 10 minutes
Servings: 4
Ingredients:
- ¼ cup chia seeds
- 1 tablespoon pure maple syrup
- 1 cup of coconut milk
- 1 teaspoon ground cinnamon
- 3 medium peaches, diced small
- 2/3 cup granola

Directions:
1. Find a small bowl and add the chia seeds, maple syrup, and coconut milk.

2.	Stir well then cover and pop into the fridge for at least one hour.
3.	Find another bowl, add the peaches and sprinkle with the cinnamon. Pop to one side.
4.	When it's time to serve, take two glasses, and pour the chia mixture between the two.
5.	Sprinkle the granola over the top, keeping a tiny amount to one side to use to decorate later.
6.	Top with the peaches and the reserved granola and serve.
Nutrition: calories 260 fat 13 carbs 22 protein 6

Avocado Toast with White Beans

Preparation Time: 5 minutes
Cooking Time: 6 minutes
Servings: 4
Ingredients:
* ½ cup canned white beans, drained and rinsed
* 2 teaspoons tahini paste
* 2 teaspoons lemon juice
* ½ teaspoon salt
* ½ avocado, peeled and pit removed
* 4 slices whole-grain bread, toasted
* ½ cup grape tomatoes, cut in half

Directions:
1.	Grab a small bowl and add the beans, tahini, ½ the lemon juice, and ½ the salt. Mash with a fork.
2.	Take another bowl and add the avocado and the remaining lemon juice and salt. Mash together.
3.	Place your toast onto a flat surface and add the mashed beans, spreading well.
4.	Top with the avocado and the sliced tomatoes then serve and enjoy.
Nutrition: calories 140 fat 5 carbs 13 protein 5

Oatmeal & Peanut Butter Breakfast Bar

Preparation Time: 10 minutes
Cooking Time: 0 minutes
Servings: 8
Ingredients:
* 1 ½ cups date, pit removed
* ½ cup peanut butter
* ½ cup old-fashioned rolled oats

Directions:
1.	Grease a baking tin and pop to one side.
2.	Grab your food processor, add the dates, and whizz until chopped.
3.	Add the peanut butter and the oats and pulse.
4.	Scoop into the baking tin then pop into the fridge or freezer until set.
5.	Serve and enjoy.
Nutrition: calories 232 fat 9 carbs 32 protein 8

Chocolate Chip Banana Pancake

Preparation Time: 15 minutes
Cooking Time: 3 minutes
Servings: 6
Ingredients:
* 1 large ripe banana, mashed
* 2 tablespoons coconut sugar
* 3 tablespoons coconut oil, melted
* 1 cup of coconut milk
* 1 ½ cups whole wheat flour
* 1 teaspoon baking soda
* ½ cup vegan chocolate chips
* Olive oil, for frying

Directions:
1.	Grab a large bowl and add the banana, sugar, oil, and milk. Stir well.
2.	Add the flour and baking soda and stir again until combined.
3.	Add the chocolate chips and fold through then pop to one side.
4.	Put a skillet over medium heat and add a drop of oil.
5.	Pour ¼ of the batter into the pan and move the pan to cover.
6.	Cook for 3 minutes then flip and cook on the other side.
7.	Repeat with the remaining pancakes then serve and enjoy.
Nutrition: calories 105 fat 13 carbs 23 protein 5

Avocado and 'Sausage' Breakfast Sandwich

Preparation Time: 15 minutes
Cooking Time: 10 minutes
Servings: 1
Ingredients:
* 1 vegan sausage patty
* 1 cup kale, chopped
* 2 teaspoons extra virgin olive oil
* 1 tablespoon pepitas
* Salt and pepper, to taste
* 1 tablespoon vegan mayo
* 1/8 teaspoon chipotle powder
* 1 teaspoon jalapeno chopped
* 1 English muffin, toasted
* ¼ avocado, sliced

Directions:
1.	Place a sauté pan over high heat and add a drop of oil.
2.	Add the vegan patty and cook for 2 minutes.
3.	Flip the patty then add the kale and pepitas.
4.	Season well then cook for another few minutes until the patty is cooked.
5.	Find a small bowl and add the mayo, chipotle powder, and the jalapeno. Stir well to combine.
6.	Place the muffin onto a flat surface, spread with the spicy mayo then top with the patty.
7.	Add the sliced avocado then serve and enjoy.
Nutrition: calories 573 fat 23 carbs 36 protein 21

Cinnamon Rolls with Cashew Frosting

Preparation Time: 25 minutes
Cooking Time: 25 minutes
Servings: 12
Ingredients:
* 3 tablespoons vegan butter
* ¾ cup unsweetened almond milk
* ½ teaspoon salt

- 3 tablespoons caster sugar
- 1 teaspoon vanilla extract
- ½ cup pumpkin puree
- 3 cups all-purpose flour
- 2 ¼ teaspoons dried active yeast
- 3 tablespoons softened vegan butter
- 3 tablespoons brown sugar
- ½ teaspoon cinnamon
- ½ cup cashews
- ½ cup icing sugar
- 1 teaspoon vanilla extract
- 2/3 cup almond milk

Directions:
1. Soak the cashews for 1 hour in boiling water.
2. Grease a baking sheet and pop to one side.
3. Find a small bowl, add the butter, and pop into the microwave to melt.
4. Add the sugar and stir well then set aside to cool.
5. Grab a large bowl and add the flour, salt, and yeast. Stir well to mix.
6. Place the cooled butter into a jug, add the pumpkin puree, vanilla, and almond milk. Stir well together.
7. Pour the wet ingredients into the dry and stir well to combine.
8. Tip onto a flat surface and knead for 5 minutes, adding extra flour as needed to avoid sticking.
9. Pop back into the bowl, cover with plastic wrap, and pop into the fridge overnight.
10. Remove the dough from the fridge and punch down with your fingers.
11. Using a rolling pin, roll to form an 18" rectangle then spread with butter.
12. Find a small bowl and add the sugar and cinnamon. Mix well then sprinkle with the butter.
13. Roll the dough into a large sausage then slice into sections.
14. Place onto the greased baking sheet and leave in a dark place to rise for one hour.
15. Preheat the oven to 350°F.
16. Drain the cashews and put them to your blender. Whizz until smooth.
17. Add the sugar and the vanilla then whizz again.
18. Add the almond milk until it reaches your desired consistency.
19. Pop into the oven and bake for 20 minutes until golden.
20. Pour the glaze over the top then serve and enjoy.

Nutrition: calories 243 fat 9 carbs 34 protein 4

Vegan Variety Poppy Seed Scones

Preparation Time: 5 minutes
Cooking Time: 10 minutes
Servings: 12.
Ingredients:
- 1 cup white sugar
- 2 cups flour
- Juice from 1 lemon
- Zest from 1 lemon
- 4 teaspoon baking powder
- ½ teaspoon salt
- 1 cup Earth Balance or vegan butter
- 2 tablespoon poppy seeds
- ½ cup soymilk
- 1/3 cup water

Directions:
1. Begin by preheating the oven to 400 degrees Fahrenheit.
2. Next, mix the sugar, the flour, the powder, and the salt in a big mixing bowl. Add the vegan butter to the mixture and cut it up until you create a sand-like mixture. Next, add the lemon juice, the lemon zest, and the poppy seeds. Add the water and the soy milk, and stir the ingredients well.
3. Portion the batter out over a baking sheet in about ¼ cup portions. Allow the scones to bake for fifteen minutes and let them cool before serving. Enjoy.

Nutrition: calories 205 fat 3 carbs 12 protein 6

Sweet Pomegranate Porridge

Preparation Time: 5 minutes
Cooking Time: 20 minutes
Servings: 4
Ingredients:
- 2 Cups Oats
- 1 ½ Cups Water
- 1 ½ Cups Pomegranate Juice
- 2 Tablespoons Pomegranate Molasses

Directions:
1. Pour all ingredients into the instant pot and mix well.
2. Seal the lid, and cook on high pressure for four minutes.
3. Use a quick release, and serve warm.

Nutrition: calories 177 fat 6 carbs 23 protein 8

Apple Oatmeal

Preparation Time: 5 minutes
Cooking Time: 20 minutes
Servings: 4
Ingredients:
- ¼ Teaspoon Sea Salt
- 1 Cup Cashew Milk
- 1 Cup Strawberries, Halved & Fresh
- 1 Tablespoon Brown Sugar
- 2 Cups Apples, Diced
- 3 Cups Water
- ¼ Teaspoon Coconut Oil
- ½ Cup Steel Cut Oats

Directions:
1. Start by greasing your instant pot with oil, and add everything to it except for the milk and berries.
2. Lock the lid and cook on high pressure for ten minutes. Allow for a natural pressure release, and then add in your milk and strawberries. Mix well, and serve warm.

Nutrition: calories 435 fat 7 carbs 34 protein 8

Breakfast Cookies

Preparation Time: 10 minutes
Cooking Time: 6 minutes
Servings: 24-32
Ingredients:
Dry **Ingredients:**
- ½ teaspoon baking powder
- 2 cups rolled oats
- ½ teaspoon baking soda

Wet **Ingredients:**
- 1 teaspoon pure vanilla extract
- 2 flax eggs (2 tablespoons ground flaxseed and around 6 tablespoons of water, mix and put aside for 15 minutes)
- 2 tablespoons melted coconut oil
- 2 tablespoons pure maple syrup
- ½ cup natural creamy peanut butter
- 2 ripe bananas

Add-in **Ingredients:**
- ½ cup finely chopped walnuts
- ½ cup raisins

Optional Topping:
- 2 tablespoons chopped walnuts
- 2 tablespoons raisins

Directions:
1. Preheat the oven to 325 degrees F, and then use parchment paper to line a baking sheet and put aside.
2. Add the bananas in a large bowl, and then use a fork to mash them until smooth. Add in the other wet ingredients and mix until well incorporated.
3. Add the dry ingredients and then use a rubber spatula to stir and fold them into the dry ingredients until well mixed. Stir in the walnuts and raisins.
4. Scoop the cookie dough onto the prepared baking sheet making sure that you leave adequate space between the cookies.
5. Bake in the preheated oven for around 12 minutes. Once ready, let the cookies cool on the baking sheet for around 10 minutes.
6. Lift the cookies carefully from the baking sheet onto a cooling rack to further cool.
7. Store the cookies in an airtight container in the fridge or at room temperature for up to one week.
Nutrition: calories 565 fat 6 carbs 32 protein 8

Vegan Breakfast Biscuits

Preparation Time: 10 minutes
Cooking Time: 10 min
Servings: 6
Ingredients:
- cups Almond Flour - quantity not mentioned
- 1 tbsp Baking Powder
- ¼ teaspoon Salt
- ½ teaspoon Onion Powder
- ½ cup Coconut Milk
- ¼ cup Nutritional Yeast
- 2 tbsp Ground Flax Seeds
- ¼ cup Olive Oil

Directions:
1. Preheat oven to 450F.

2. Whisk together all ingredients in a bowl.
3. Divide the batter into a pre-greased muffin tin.
4. Bake for 10 minutes.
Nutrition: calories 432 fat 5 carbs 13 protein 8

Orange French Toast

Preparation Time: 5 minutes
Cooking Time: 30 minutes
Servings: 8 servings
Ingredients:
- 2 cups of plant milk (unflavored)
- Four tablespoon maple syrup
- 11/2 tablespoon cinnamon
- Salt (optional)
- 1 cup flour (almond)
- 1 tablespoon orange zest
- 8 bread slices

Directions:
1. Turn the oven and heat to 400 degree F afterwards.
2. In a cup, add **Ingredients:** and whisk until the batter is smooth.
3. Dip each piece of bread into the paste and permit to soak for a couple of seconds.
4. Put in the pan, and cook until lightly browned.
5. Put the toast on the cookie sheet and bake for ten to fifteen minutes in the oven, until it is crispy.
Nutrition: Calories: 129 Fat: 1.1g Carbohydrates: 21.5g Protein: 7.9g

Chocolate Chip Coconut Pancakes

Preparation Time: 5 minutes
Cooking Time: 30 minutes
Servings: 8 servings
Ingredients:
- 11/4 cup oats
- 2 teaspoons coconut flakes
- 2 cup plant milk
- 11/4 cup maple syrup
- 11/3 cup of chocolate chips
- 2 1/4 cups buckwheat flour
- 2 teaspoon baking powder
- 1 teaspoon vanilla essence
- 2 teaspoon flaxseed meal
- Salt (optional)

Directions:
1. Put the flaxseed and cook over medium heat until the paste becomes a little moist.
2. Remove seeds.
3. Stir the buckwheat, oats, coconut chips, baking powder and salt with each other in a wide dish.
4. In a large dish, stir together the retained flax water with the sugar, maple syrup, vanilla essence.
5. Transfer the wet mixture to the dry **Ingredients:** and shake to combine
6. Place over medium heat the nonstick grill pan.
7. Pour 1/4 cup flour onto the grill pan with each pancake, and scatter gently.

8. Cook for five to six minutes, before the pancakes appear somewhat crispy.
Nutrition: Calories: 198 Fat: 9.1g Carbohydrates: 11.5g Protein: 7.9g

Chickpea Omelet

Preparation Time: 10 minutes
Cooking Time: 30 minutes
Servings: 3 servings
Ingredients:
- 2 cup flour (chickpea)
- 11/2 teaspoon onion powder
- 11/2 teaspoon garlic powder
- 1/4 teaspoon pepper (white and black)
- 1/3 cup yeast
- 1 teaspoon baking powder
- 3 green onions (chopped)

Directions:
1. In a cup, add the chickpea flour and spices.
2. Apply 1 cup of sugar, then stir.
3. Power medium-heat and put the frying pan.
4. On each omelets, add onions and mushrooms in the batter while it heats.
5. Serve your delicious Chickpea Omelet.
Nutrition: Calories: 399 Fat: 11.1g Carbohydrates: 11.5g Protein: 7.9g

Apple-Lemon Bowl

Preparation Time: 5 minutes
Cooking Time: 15 minutes
Servings: 1-2 servings
Ingredients:
- 6 apples
- 3 tablespoons walnuts
- 7 dates
- Lemon juice
- 1/2 teaspoon cinnamon

Directions:
1. Root the apples, then break them into wide bits.
2. In a food cup, put seeds, part of the lime juice, almonds, spices and three-quarters of the apples. Thinly slice until finely ground.
3. Apply the remaining apples and lemon juice and make slices.
Nutrition: Calories: 249 Fat: 5.1g Carbohydrates: 71.5g Protein: 7.9g

Breakfast Scramble

Preparation Time: 10 minutes
Cooking Time: 30 minutes
Servings: 6 servings
Ingredients:
- 1 red onion1 to
- 2 tablespoons soy sauce
- 2 cups sliced mushrooms
- Salt to taste
- 11/2 teaspoon black pepper
- 11/2 teaspoons turmeric
- 1/4 teaspoon cayenne
- 3 cloves garlic
- 1 red bell pepper
- 1 large head cauliflower

- 1 green bell pepper

Directions:
1. In a small pan, put all vegetables and cook until crispy.
2. Stir in the cauliflower and cook for four to six minutes or until it smooth.
3. Add spices to the pan and cook for another five minutes.
Nutrition: Calories: 199 Fat: 1.1g Carbohydrates: 14.5g Protein: 7.9g

Brown Rice Breakfast Pudding

Preparation Time: 5 minutes
Cooking Time: 15 minutes
Servings: 4 servings
Ingredients:
- 2 cups almond milk
- 1 cup dates (chopped)
- 1 apple (chopped)
- Salt to taste
- 1/4 cup almonds (toasted)
- 1 cinnamon stick
- Ground cloves to taste
- 3 cups cooked rice
- 1 tablespoon raisins

Directions:
1. Mix the rice, milk, cinnamon stick, spices and dates in a small saucepan and steam when the paste is heavy.
2. Take the cinnamon stick down. Stir in the fruit, raisins, salt and blend.
3. Serve with almonds bread.
Nutrition: Calories: 299 Fat: 1.1g Carbohydrates: 71.5g Protein: 7.9g

Black Bean and Sweet Potato Hash

Preparation Time: 10 minutes
Cooking Time: 30 minutes
Servings: 4 servings
Ingredients:
- 1 cup onion (chopped)
- 1/3 Cup vegetable broth
- 2 garlic (minced)
- 1 cup cooked black beans
- 2 teaspoons hot chili powder
- 2 cups chopped sweet potatoes

Directions:
1. Put the onions in a saucepan over medium heat and add the seasoning and mix.
2. Add potatoes and chili flakes, then mix.
3. Cook for around 12 minutes more until the vegetables are cooked thoroughly.
4. Add the green onion, beans, and salt
5. Cook for more 2 minutes and serve.
Nutrition: Calories: 239 Fat: 1.1g Carbohydrates: 71.5g Protein: 7.9g

Apple-Walnut Breakfast Bread

Preparation Time: 15 minutes
Cooking Time: 60 minutes
Servings: 8 servings
Ingredients:
- 11/2 cups apple sauce

- 1/3 cup plant milk
- 2 cups all-purpose flour
- Salt to taste
- 1 teaspoon ground cinnamon
- 1 tablespoon flax seeds mixed with 2 tablespoons warm water
- 3/4 cup brown sugar
- 1 teaspoon baking powder
- 1/2 cup chopped walnuts

Directions:
1. Preheat to 375 degree Fahrenheit.
2. Combine the apple sauce, sugar, milk, and flax mixture in a jar and mix.
3. Combine the flour, baking powder, salt, and cinnamon in a separate bowl.
4. Simply add dry **Ingredients:** into the wet **Ingredients:** and combine to make slices.
5. Bake for 25 minutes until it becomes light brown.

Nutrition: Calories: 309 Fat: 9.1g Carbohydrates: 16.5g Protein: 6.9g

Vegan Salmon Bagel

Preparation Time: 10 minutes
Cooking Time: 30 minutes
Servings: 2 servings
Ingredients:
- 4 cups of water
- 11/2 red onion
- Vegan cream cheese
- Salt, pepper
- 4 bagels
- 11/2 cup of apple cider vinegar
- 7 carrots

Directions:
1. Preheat to 200 degree Celsius.
2. Slice the carrots.
3. In a mixer to mix, combine sugar, vinegar, and ground pepper.
4. Put the carrot strips in a stir fry bowl, apply the marinade and stir.
5. Cover the carrots with foil and bake for twenty minutes, then switch heat down to 210°F and cook for 40 minutes more.

Nutrition: Calories: 232 Fat: 9.1g Carbohydrates: 71.5g Protein: 7.9g

Mint Chocolate Green Protein Smoothie

Preparation Time: 5 minutes
Cooking Time: 10 minutes
Servings: 1 servings
Ingredients:
- 1 scoop chocolate powder
- 1 tablespoon flaxseed
- 1 banana
- 1 mint leaf
- 3/4 cup almond milk
- 3 tablespoons dark chocolate (chopped)

Directions:
1. Blend all the **Ingredients:** except the dark chocolate.
2. Garnish dark chocolate when ready.

Nutrition: Calories: 300 Fat: 19.1g Carbohydrates: 21.5g Protein: 27.9g

Dairy-Free Coconut Yogurt

Preparation Time: 5 minutes
Cooking Time: 10 minutes
Servings: 2 servings
Ingredients:
- 1 can coconut milk
- 4 vegan probiotic capsules

Directions:
1. Shake coconut milk with a whole tube.
2. Remove the plastic of capsules and mix in.
3. Cut a 12-inch cheesecloth until stirred.
4. Freeze or eat immediately.

Nutrition: Calories: 219 Fat: 10.1g Carbohydrates: 1.5g Protein: 7.9g

Vegan Green Avocado Smoothie

Preparation Time: 5 minutes
Cooking Time: 10 minutes
Servings: 2 servings
Ingredients:
- 1 banana
- 1 cup water
- 1/2 avocado
- 1/2 lemon juice
- 1/2 cup coconut yoghurt

Directions:
1. Blend all **Ingredients:** until smooth.

Nutrition: Calories: 299 Fat: 1.1g Carbohydrates: 1.5g Protein: 7.9g

Sun-Butter Baked Oatmeal Cups

Preparation Time: 10 minutes
Cooking Time: 35 minutes
Servings: 12 cups
Ingredients:
- 1/4 cup coconut sugar
- 11/2 rolled oats
- 2 tablespoon chia seeds
- 1/4 teaspoon salt
- 1 teaspoon cinnamon
- 1/2 cup non-dairy milk
- 1/2 cup Sun-Butter
- 1/2 cup apple sauce

Directions:
1. Preheat oven to 350°F.
2. Mix all **Ingredients:** and blend well.
3. Add in muffins and Insert extra toppings.
4. Bake 25 minutes, or until golden brown.

Nutrition: Calories: 129 Fat: 1.1g Carbohydrates: 1.5g Protein: 4.9g

Chocolate Peanut Butter Shake

Preparation Time: 5 minutes
Cooking Time: 5 minutes
Servings: 2 servings
Ingredients:
- 2 bananas
- 3 Tablespoons peanut butter
- 1 cup almond milk
- 3 Tablespoons cacao powder

Directions:
1.   Combine **Ingredients:** in a blender until smooth.
Nutrition: Calories: 149 Fat: 1.1g Carbohydrates: 1.5g Protein: 7.9g

Berries and Banana Smoothie Bowl

Preparation Time: 5 minutes
Cooking Time: 0 minutes
Servings: 4
Ingredients:
For the Smoothie:
- 4 cups frozen mixed berries
- 4 small frozen banana, sliced
- 4 scoops of vanilla protein powder
- 12 tablespoons almond milk, unsweetened

For the Toppings:
- 4 tablespoons chia seeds
- 4 tablespoons shredded coconut, unsweetened
- 4 tablespoons hemp seeds
- ½ cup Granola
- Fresh strawberries, sliced, as needed

Directions:
1.   Add mixed berries into a food processor along with banana and then pulse at low speed for 1 to 2 minutes until broken.
2.   Add remaining ingredients for the smoothie and then pulse again for 1 minute at low speed until creamy, scraping the sides of the container frequently.
3.   Distribute the smoothie among four bowls, then top with chia seeds, coconut, hemp seeds, granola, and strawberries and serve.
Nutrition: 214 Cal 2.5 g Fat 1.6 g Saturated Fat 47.5 g Carbohydrates 8.8 g Fiber 26 g Sugars 2.8 g Protein;

Kale and Peanut Butter Smoothie

Preparation Time: 5 minutes
Cooking Time: 0 minutes
Servings: 4
Ingredients:
- 4 frozen banana, sliced
- 2 cups kale
- ½ cup peanut butter
- 2 2/3 cups coconut milk, unsweetened

Directions:
1.   Add all the ingredients in the order into a food processor or blender and then pulse for 1 to 2 minutes until blended, scraping the sides of the container frequently.
2.   Distribute the smoothie among glasses and then serve.
Nutrition: 390 Cal 19 g Fat 2.5 g Saturated Fat 42 g Carbohydrates 7 g Fiber 22 g Sugars 15 g Protein;

Mint Chocolate Protein Smoothie

Preparation Time: 5 minutes
Cooking Time: 0 minutes
Servings: 4
Ingredients:
- 4 tablespoons ground flaxseed

- 4 cups fresh spinach
- 4 frozen banana, sliced
- 4 scoops of chocolate protein powder
- 4 tablespoons chopped dark chocolate, vegan
- ½ cup melted dark chocolate
- 1 teaspoon peppermint extract, unsweetened
- 4 tablespoons honey
- 3 cups almond milk, unsweetened
- 1 cup ice cubed

Directions:
1.   Add all the ingredients in the order into a food processor or blender and then pulse for 1 to 2 minutes until blended, scraping the sides of the container frequently.
2.   Distribute the smoothie among glasses and then serve.
Nutrition: 480.5 Cal 20.3 g Fat 8.4 g Saturated Fat 45.6 g Carbohydrates 9.7 g Fiber 22.5 g Sugars 31.2 g Protein;

Berry Breakfast Smoothie

Preparation Time: 5 minutes
Cooking Time: 0 minutes
Servings: 4
Ingredients:
- 1 cup of frozen mixed berries
- 1 cup quick oats
- 1 frozen banana
- 2 cups vanilla almond milk, unsweetened

Directions:
1.   Add all the ingredients in the order into a food processor or blender and then pulse for 1 to 2 minutes until blended, scraping the sides of the container frequently.
2.   Distribute the smoothie among glasses and then serve.
Nutrition: 138.5 Cal 2.5 g Fat 0.3 g Saturated Fat 25.6 g Carbohydrates 3.6 g Fiber 6.6 g Sugars 3.5 g Protein;

Sunrise Smoothie

Preparation Time: 5 minutes
Cooking Time: 0 minutes
Servings: 4
Ingredients:
- 4 tablespoons chia seed
- 2 frozen banana
- 2 lemon, peeled
- 2 cups diced carrots
- 4 clementine, peeled
- 4 cups frozen strawberries, unsweetened
- 12 tablespoons pomegranate tendrils
- 2 cup almond milk, unsweetened

Directions:
1.   Add all the ingredients in the order into a food processor or blender and then pulse for 1 to 2 minutes until blended, scraping the sides of the container frequently.
2.   Distribute the smoothie among glasses and then serve.

Nutrition: 274 Cal 5.4 g Fat 0.5 g Saturated Fat 57.3 g Carbohydrates 13.3 g Fiber 33.8 g Sugars 0.5 g Protein;

Sunshine Orange Smoothie

Preparation Time: 5 minutes
Cooking Time: 0 minutes
Servings: 4
Ingredients:
- 2 medium oranges, zested, juiced
- 4 frozen bananas
- 4 tablespoons goji berries
- ½ cup hemp seeds
- 1 teaspoon grated ginger
- 1 cup almond milk, unsweetened
- ½ cup of ice cubes

Directions:
1. Add all the ingredients in the order into a food processor or blender and then pulse for 1 to 2 minutes until blended, scraping the sides of the container frequently.
2. Distribute the smoothie among glasses and then serve.

Nutrition: 131 Cal 2.3 g Fat 0.3 g Saturated Fat 26.7 g Carbohydrates 4.4 g Fiber 11 g Sugars 2.6 g Protein;

Chocolate and Hazelnut Smoothie

Preparation Time: 5 minutes
Cooking Time: 0 minutes
Servings: 4
Ingredients:
- 1 frozen banana
- 1 cup hazelnuts, unsalted, roasted
- 8 teaspoons maple syrup
- 4 tablespoons cocoa powder, unsweetened
- 1/2 teaspoon hazelnut extract, unsweetened
- 2 cups almond milk, unsweetened
- 1 cup of ice cubes

Directions:
1. Add all the ingredients in the order into a food processor or blender and then pulse for 1 to 2 minutes until blended, scraping the sides of the container frequently.
2. Distribute the smoothie among glasses and then serve.

Nutrition: 198 Cal 12 g Fat 1 g Saturated Fat 21 g Carbohydrates 5 g Fiber 12 g Sugars 5 g Protein;

Blueberry Oatmeal Smoothie

Preparation Time: 5 minutes
Cooking Time: 0 minutes
Servings: 4
Ingredients:
- 2 cups frozen blueberries
- 1 cup old-fashioned oats
- 2 teaspoons cinnamon
- 2 tablespoons maple syrup
- 1 cup spinach
- 2 cup almond milk, unsweetened
- 8 ice cubes

Directions:

1. Add all the ingredients in the order into a food processor or blender and then pulse for 1 to 2 minutes until blended, scraping the sides of the container frequently.
2. Distribute the smoothie among glasses and then serve.

Nutrition: 194 Cal 5 g Fat 3 g Saturated Fat 34 g Carbohydrates 5 g Fiber 15 g Sugars 5 g Protein;

Cookie Dough Smoothie

Preparation Time: 5 minutes
Cooking Time: 0 minutes
Servings: 4
Ingredients:
- 4 frozen banana
- 8 tablespoons hemp seeds
- 8 tablespoons chocolate chips, vegan
- 4 scoops of salted caramel protein
- 2 teaspoons cinnamon
- 8 teaspoons honey
- 8 tablespoons peanut butter powder
- 4 cups almond milk, unsweetened
- 4 cups of ice cubes

Directions:
1. Add all the ingredients in the order into a food processor or blender and then pulse for 1 to 2 minutes until blended, scraping the sides of the container frequently.
2. Distribute the smoothie among glasses and then serve.

Nutrition: 442 Cal 19.5 g Fat 4 g Saturated Fat 41.3 g Carbohydrates 8 g Fiber 22.2 g Sugars 31.2 g Protein;

Coffee Smoothie

Preparation Time: 5 minutes
Cooking Time: 0 minutes
Servings: 4
Ingredients:
- 4 cups baby spinach
- 4 tablespoons hemp hearts
- 12 Medjool dates, pitted
- 4 tablespoons cashew butter
- 2 cup brewed coffee, chilled
- 6 cups of ice cubes

Directions:
1. Place pitted dates in a medium bowl, cover with hot water and let them soak for 15 minutes.
2. Drain the dates, add them into a food processor along with the remaining ingredients, and then pulse for 1 to 2 minutes until blended, scraping the sides of the container frequently.
3. Distribute the smoothie among glasses and then serve.

Nutrition: 391 Cal 15 g Fat 2 g Saturated Fat 60 g Carbohydrates 6 g Fiber 47 g Sugars 10 g Protein;

Breakfast Muesli

Preparation Time: 5 minutes
Cooking Time: 0 minutes
Servings: 4
Ingredients:
- 2 bananas, peeled, sliced
- 1 cup raspberries
- 2 cups sliced strawberries
- 1 cup blueberries

- 4 tablespoons crushed pistachios
- 4 tablespoons hemp seeds
- 4 tablespoons chia seeds
- 4 teaspoons honey
- 2 cups of coconut yogurt
- 2 cups muesli, unsweetened
- Mint leaves as needed for garnish

Directions:
1.   Take a large bowl, place yogurt in it, and then add muesli.
2.   Top with raspberries, strawberries, blueberries, and banana slices, drizzle with honey and then sprinkle with pistachios.
3.   Garnish with mint, hemp seeds, and chia seeds and then serve.

Nutrition: 411 Cal 18 g Fat 8 g Saturated Fat 53 g Carbohydrates 12 g Fiber 17 g Sugars 8 g Protein;

Banana Cream Pie and Chia Pudding

Preparation Time: 1 hour and 10 minutes
Cooking Time: 0 minutes
Servings: 4
Ingredients:
- 2 bananas, peeled, mashed
- 2 bananas, peeled, chopped
- 1/2 cup chia seeds
- 2 teaspoons cinnamon
- 4 tablespoons coconut flakes
- 1 cup coconut milk, unsweetened
- 2 tablespoons maple syrup
- 1 cup almond milk, unsweetened

Directions:
1.   Take a large bowl, add chia seeds and mashed bananas, add maple syrup and cinnamon, pour in almond and coconut milk and then whisk until well combined.
2.   Cover the bowl with lid, and then place it in the refrigerator for a minimum of 1 hour until firm.
3.   When ready to eat, distribute pudding evenly among 4 bowls, top with chopped banana, and sprinkle with coconut flakes and then serve.

Nutrition: 350 Cal 17 g Fat 4 g Saturated Fat 37 g Carbohydrates 12 g Fiber 19 g Sugars 5 g Protein;

Brown Rice Breakfast Pudding

Preparation Time: 5 minutes
Cooking Time: 15 minutes
Servings: 4
Ingredients:
- 1 tart apple, cored, chopped
- 1 cup Medjool dates, pitted, chopped
- 3 cups cooked brown rice
- 1/8 teaspoon salt
- ¼ teaspoon ground cloves
- 1 cinnamon stick
- ¼ cup raisins
- ¼ cup slivered almonds, toasted
- 2 cups almond milk, unsweetened

Directions:
1.   Take a medium saucepan, place it over medium-low heat, add rice, dates, cloves, and cinnamon, pour in milk, stir until mixed and cook for 12 minutes until thickened.

2.   Then remove and discard cinnamon stick, add apple and raisins and then stir in salt.
3.   Remove pan from heat, distribute pudding among four bowls and top with almonds.
4.   Serve straight away.

Nutrition: 391 Cal 4.8 g Fat 0.6 g Saturated Fat 81.1 g Carbohydrates 5.7 g Fiber 24.8 g Sugars 6 g Protein;

Oats with Chia

Preparation Time: 6 hours and 10 minutes
Cooking Time: 0 minutes
Servings: 4
Ingredients:
- 3 cups rolled oats
- 4 tablespoons chia seeds and more for topping
- 4 tablespoons maple syrup
- 1 teaspoon cinnamon
- 1 teaspoon vanilla extract, unsweetened
- 1 cup almond milk, unsweetened
- 2 cups of water
- 1 cup sliced strawberries

Directions:
1.   Take a large container, add oats and chia seeds in it, add cinnamon, vanilla extract, and maple syrup, then pour in water and almond milk and stir until mixed.
2.   Cover the bowl with lid, and then place it in the refrigerator for a minimum of 6 hours.
3.   When ready to eat, distribute oats and chia mixture evenly among 4 bowls, top with some chia seeds and sliced strawberries, and then serve.

Nutrition: 351.8 Cal 7.4 g Fat 1.1 g Saturated Fat 62.4 g Carbohydrates 10.3 g Fiber 14.6 g Sugars 8.8 g Protein;

Carrot Cake Oats

Preparation Time: 6 hours and 10 minutes
Cooking Time: 0 minutes
Servings: 4
Ingredients:
- ¼ cup shredded carrot
- 1/3 cup rolled oats
- 2 tablespoons chopped pineapple
- 1 tablespoon shredded coconut, unsweetened and more for topping
- 1 tablespoon ground flaxseed
- 1 tablespoon raisins and more for topping
- 2 tablespoons maple syrup and more for topping
- 1/8 teaspoon ground nutmeg
- ¼ teaspoon ground cinnamon and more for topping
- ¼ teaspoon vanilla extract, unsweetened
- 1 tablespoon chopped walnuts and more for topping
- ½ cup almond milk, unsweetened

Directions:
1.   Take a large bowl, place all the ingredients in it, and stir until well mixed.
2.   Cover the bowl with lid, and then place it in the refrigerator for a minimum of a minimum of 6 hours.

3.   When ready to eat, distribute oats mixture evenly among 4 bowls, top with some shredded coconut, raisins, and walnuts, sprinkle with cinnamon, drizzle with maple syrup and then serve.
Nutrition: 242 Cal 9 g Fat 2 g Saturated Fat 35 g Carbohydrates 6 g Fiber 12 g Sugars 7 g Protein;

Toast with Avocado and Berries

Preparation Time: 10 minutes
Cooking Time: 10 minutes
Servings: 4
Ingredients:
- 1 cup sliced strawberries
- 2 large avocados, peeled, pitted, sliced
- 4 tablespoons honey
- 4 slices of whole-grain bread
- 4 ounces block of vegan cheddar cheese, thinly sliced

Directions:
1.   Take a skillet pan, place it over medium heat and when hot, toast bread slices for 2 to 3 minutes until toasted.
2.   Peel the avocados, remove the pit, cut the flesh in slices, place into a bowl, and then mash with a fork.
3.   Spread mashed avocado on one side of the toasted slices, then top with berries and cover with cheese slices.
4.   Drizzle with honey and then serve.
Nutrition: 379 Cal 21 g Fat 6 g Saturated Fat 35 g Carbohydrates 10 g Fiber 9 g Sugars 18 g Protein;

Chocolate Chip and Coconut Pancakes

Preparation Time: 10 minutes
Cooking Time: 40 minutes
Servings: 8
Ingredients:
- 1¼ cups buckwheat flour
- 1 tablespoon flaxseeds
- 2 tablespoons coconut flakes, unsweetened
- ¼ cup rolled oats
- 1/8 teaspoon sea salt
- 1 tablespoon baking powder
- 1/3 cup mini chocolate chips, vegan
- ¼ cup maple syrup
- 1 teaspoon vanilla extract, unsweetened
- ½ cup applesauce, unsweetened
- 1 cup almond milk, unsweetened
- ½ cup of water
- 2 bananas, peeled, sliced

Directions:
1.   Take a small saucepan, place it over medium heat, add flaxseeds, pour in water, and then cook for 4 to 5 minutes until sticky mixture comes together.
2.   Strain the flaxseeds mixture immediately into a cup, discard the seeds, and set aside the collected flax water until required.
3.   Take a large bowl, add buckwheat flour and oats in it, and then stir in salt, baking powder, and coconut until mixed.
4.   Take a medium bowl, add 2 tablespoons of reserved flax water along with maple syrup and

vanilla, pour in applesauce and milk, and whisk until combined.
5.   Pour the milk mixture into the flour mixture, whisk well until thick batter comes together, and then fold in chocolate chips.
6.   Take a griddle pan, place it over medium-low heat, spray it with oil and when hot, pour in 1/3 cup of the prepared batter, spread it gently and cook for 5 to 7 minutes until the bottom turns golden brown; pour in more batter if there is a space on the pan.
7.   Flip the pancake, continue cooking for 5 minutes, and when done, transfer pancake to a plate and then repeat with the remaining batter.
8.   Serve pancakes with sliced bananas.
Nutrition: 190 Cal 14 g Fat 6 g Saturated Fat 8 g Carbohydrates 2 g Fiber 4 g Sugars 8 g Protein;

Chocolate Pancakes

Preparation Time: 15 minutes
Cooking Time: 30 minutes
Servings: 12
Ingredients:
- 1¼ cups whole-grain flour
- 1 tablespoon baking powder
- 1 tablespoon ground flaxseed
- 1 tablespoon mini chocolate chips, vegan
- 2 tablespoons cocoa powder, unsweetened
- ¼ teaspoon of sea salt
- 1 tablespoon maple syrup
- 1 tablespoon apple cider vinegar
- 1 teaspoon vanilla extract, unsweetened
- ¼ cup applesauce, unsweetened
- 1 cup almond milk, unsweetened

Directions:
1.   Take a medium bowl, place whole-grain flour in it, and then whisk in flaxseed, baking powder, cocoa powder, salt, and chocolate chips until well combined.
2.   Take a small bowl, add vinegar, maple syrup, vanilla, and almond milk and whisk until combined.
3.   Pour the milk mixture into the flour mixture, whisk well until incorporated, and then let the batter stand for 10 minutes until thickened and doubled in size.
4.   Then take a large skillet pan, place it over medium heat, spray with oil and when hot, pour in one-twelfth of the batter into the pan, spread it gently and cook for 2 to 3 minutes until the bottom turn golden brown; pour in more batter if there is a space on the pan.
5.   Flip the pancake, continue cooking for 2 minutes, and when done, transfer pancake to a plate and then repeat with the remaining batter.
6.   Serve straight away.
Nutrition: 251.5 Cal 1 g Fat 0.3 g Saturated Fat 58.7 g Carbohydrates 3 g Fiber 5.7 g Sugars; 7 g Protein;

Blueberry and Lemon French Toast

Preparation Time: 15 minutes
Cooking Time: 30 minutes
Servings: 4
Ingredients:
- 2 tablespoons ground flaxseed

- 1 teaspoon ground cinnamon
- 1/8 teaspoon sea salt
- 1/2 teaspoon ground nutmeg
- 1/2 of a lemon, zested, juiced
- 2 tablespoons maple syrup
- 1 teaspoon vanilla extract, unsweetened
- 1 cup soymilk
- 1/4 cup hot water
- 1 cup frozen blueberries
- 8 slices of whole-grain bread

Directions:
1. Take a medium bowl, add flaxseeds in it, pour in hot water, stir until just mixed and let the mixture stand for 5 minutes until thickened.
2. Then add salt, all the spices and vanilla extract, whisk until combined, and whisk in soymilk until incorporated.
3. Take a large frying pan, place it over low heat, spray with oil and wait until hot.
4. Then soak each bread slice into prepared batter, place it into the frying pan and cook for 4 to 5 minutes per side until crispy and nicely brown on all sides; add more soaked slices if there is a space in the pan.
5. While toasts are being cooked, prepared blueberry syrup, and for this, place a medium heatproof bowl, add blueberries in it, lemon juice and zest, and maple syrup, stir until mixed and then microwave for 2 minutes until softened.
6. Serve toasts with prepared blueberry syrup.
Nutrition: 530 Cal 9 g Fat 0.5 g Saturated Fat 92 g Carbohydrates 19 g Fiber 23 g Sugars 21 g Protein;

Delicious Quiche made with Cauliflower & Chickpea

Total time: 45 minutes
Ingredients
- ½ teaspoon of salt
- 1 cup of grated cauliflower
- 1 cup of chickpea flour
- ½ teaspoon of baking powder
- ½ zucchini, thinly sliced into half moons
- 1 tablespoon of flax meal
- 1 cup of water
- 1 freshly chopped sprig of fresh rosemary
- ½ teaspoon of Italian seasoning
- ½ freshly sliced red onion
- ¼ teaspoon of baking powder

Directions
1. In a bowl, combine all the dry ingredients.
2. Chop the onion and zucchini.
3. Grate the cauliflower so that it has a rice-like consistency, and add it to the dry ingredients. Now, add the water and mix well.
4. Add the zucchini, onion, and rosemary last. You will have a clumpy and thick mixture, but you should be able to spoon it into a tin.
5. You can use either a silicone or a metal cake tin with a removable bottom. Now put the mixture in the tin and press it down gently.
6. The top should be left messy to resemble a rough texture.

7. Bake at 350o F for about half an hour. You will know your quiche is ready when the top is golden.
8. You can serve the quiche warm or cold, as per your preference.

Tasty Oatmeal and Carrot Cake

Total time: 20 minutes
Ingredients
- 1 cup of water
- ½ teaspoon of cinnamon
- 1 cup of rolled oats
- Salt
- ¼ cup of raisins
- ½ cup of shredded carrots
- 1 cup of non-dairy milk
- ¼ teaspoon of allspice
- ½ teaspoon of vanilla extract

Toppings:
- ¼ cup of chopped walnuts
- 2 tablespoons of maple syrup
- 2 tablespoons of shredded coconut

Directions
1. Put a small pot on low heat and bring the non-dairy milk, oats, and water to a simmer.
2. Now, add the carrots, vanilla extract, raisins, salt, cinnamon and allspice. You need to simmer all of the ingredients, but do not forget to stir them. You will know that they are ready when the liquid is fully absorbed into all of the ingredients (in about 7-10 minutes).
3. Transfer the thickened dish to bowls. You can drizzle some maple syrup on top or top them with coconut or walnuts.
4. This nutritious bowl will allow you to kickstart your day.

Go-Green Smoothie

Total time: 10 minutes
Ingredients
- 2 tablespoons of natural cashew butter
- 1 ripe frozen banana
- 2/3 cup of unsweetened coconut, soy, or almond milk
- 1 large handful of kale or spinach

Directions
1. Put everything inside a powerful blender.
2. Blend until you have a smooth, creamy shake.
3. Enjoy your special green smoothie.

Tasty Oatmeal Muffins

Total time: 30 minutes
Ingredients
- ½ cup of hot water
- ½ cup of raisins
- ¼ cup of ground flaxseed
- 2 cups of rolled oats
- ¼ teaspoon of sea salt
- ½ cup of walnuts
- ¼ teaspoon of baking soda
- 1 banana
- 2 tablespoons of cinnamon
- ¼ cup of maple syrup

Directions

1. Whisk the flaxseed with water and allow the mixture to sit for about 5 minutes.
2. In a food processor, blend all the ingredients along with the flaxseed mix. Blend everything for 30 seconds, but do not create a smooth substance. To create rough-textured cookies, you need to have a semi-coarse batter.
3. Put the batter in cupcake liners and place them in a muffin tin. As this is an oil-free recipe, you will need cupcake liners. Bake everything for about 20 minutes at 350 degrees.
4. Enjoy the freshly-made cookies with a glass of warm milk.

Glory Muffins

Total time: 30 minutes

Ingredients

- 1¾ cups flour
- ½ teaspoon baking powder
- ½ cup sugar
- 2 teaspoons cinnamon
- ½ teaspoon ground ginger
- 3 flax eggs
- 1 cup plant-based milk
- ½ cup maple syrup
- 1 teaspoon vanilla extract
- 1 apple, shredded
- 2 carrots, shredded
- 1 teaspoon baking soda
- ⅓ cup walnuts, chopped
- ½ teaspoon salt

Directions

1. The oven should be preheated at 350 degrees F.
2. Mix flaxseed with water in a bowl and leave for 10 minutes.
3. In a bowl, mix flour, sugar, ginger, cinnamon, baking soda, salt, and baking powder.
4. Stir in vanilla, maple syrup, and milk along with flaxseed mix.
5. Mix well to make a batter then fold in apple, nuts, and carrots.
6. Line a muffin tin with 6 muffin cups and divide the carrot batter evenly between the cups.
7. Bake for 20 minutes then serve.

Amazing Almond & Banana Granola

Total time: 75 minutes

Ingredients:

- 2 peeled and chopped ripe bananas
- 8 cups of rolled oats
- 1 teaspoon of salt
- 2 cups of freshly pitted and chopped dates
- 1 cup of slivered and toasted almonds
- 1 teaspoon of almond extract

Directions

1. Preheat the oven to 275o F.
2. Line two 13 x 18-inch baking sheets with parchment paper.
3. In a medium saucepan, add 1 cup of water and the dates, and bring to a boil. On medium heat, cook them for about 10 minutes. The dates will be soft and pulpy. Keep on adding water to the saucepan so that the dates do not stick to the pan.
4. After removing the dates from the heat, allow them to cool before you blend them with salt, almond extract, and bananas.
5. You will have a smooth and creamy puree.
6. Add this mixture to the oats, and give it a thorough mix.
7. Divide the mixture into equal halves and spread over the baking sheets.
8. Bake for about 30-40 minutes, stirring every 10 minutes or so.
9. You will know that the granola is ready when it becomes crispy.
10. After removing the baking sheets from the oven, allow them to cool. Then, add the slivered almonds.
11. You can store your granola in an airtight container and enjoy it whenever you are hungry.

Pomegranate Overnight Oats

Total time: 10 minutes

Ingredients

- ½ cup rolled oats
- ½ cup almond milk
- ½ cup pomegranate seeds
- 1 tablespoon ground flax seeds
- 1 tablespoon cocoa nibs

To Garnish:

- ¼ cup pomegranate seeds
- 2 teaspoon coconut shreds

Directions

1. In a sealable container, add everything and mix well.
2. Seal the container and refrigerate overnight.
3. Serve with coconut shreds and pomegranate seeds on top.

Almond Chia Pudding

Total time: 10 minutes

Ingredients

- 3 tablespoons almond butter
- 2 tablespoons maple syrup
- 1 cup almond milk
- ¼ cup plus 1 tablespoon chia seeds

Directions

1. In a sealable container, add everything and mix well.
2. Seal the container and refrigerate overnight.
3. Serve with a splash of almond milk.

Breakfast Parfait Popsicles

Total time: 10 minutes

Ingredients

- 1 cup soy yogurt
- 1 cup berries
- 1 cup granola

Directions

1. In a popsicle mold, divide the berries.
2. Add yogurt to the molds and gently mix the berries using a stick.
3. Sprinkle granola on top and place the popsicle sticks in the mixture.
4. Freeze overnight.
5. Serve.

Apple Chia Pudding

Total time: 15 minutes
Ingredients
Chia Pudding:
- 4 tablespoons chia seeds
- 1 cup almond milk
- ½ teaspoon cinnamon

Apple Pie Filling:
- 1 large apple, peeled, cored and chopped
- ¼ cup water
- 2 teaspoons maple syrup
- Pinch cinnamon
- 2 tablespoons golden raisins

Directions
1. In a sealable container, add cinnamon, chia seeds and almond milk, mix well.
2. Seal the container and refrigerate overnight.
3. In a medium pot, combine all apple pie filling ingredients and cook for 5 minutes.
4. Serve the chia pudding with apple filling on top.
5. Enjoy.

Pumpkin Spice Bites

Total time: 10 minutes
Ingredients
- ½ cup pumpkin puree
- ½ cup almond butter
- ¼ cup maple syrup
- 1 teaspoon pumpkin pie spice
- 1⅓ cup rolled oats
- ⅓ cup pumpkin seeds
- ⅓ cup raisins
- 2 tablespoons chia seeds

Directions
1. In a sealable container, add everything and mix well.
2. Seal the container and refrigerate overnight.
3. Roll the mixture into small balls.
4. Serve.

Chive Waffles with Mushrooms

Total time: 35 minutes
Ingredients
- 2 cups soymilk
- 1 teaspoon apple cider vinegar
- 2 tablespoon rapeseed oil
- ⅓ cup cooked, mashed sweet potato
- 5 ounces polenta
- 5 ounces plain flour
- 1 tablespoon baking powder
- 1 small bunch chives, chopped
- 1 tablespoon maple syrup
- 2 teaspoons light soy sauce
- 6 large mushrooms, sliced
- Olive oil, for frying
- Soy yogurt, to serve

Directions
1. Preheat your waffle iron.
2. Meanwhile, sauté mushrooms with salt and black pepper in a suitable pan.
3. Keep the mushrooms aside ready to serve.
4. In a bowl, mash sweet potato and stir in the rest of the ingredients.
5. Mix it well to make the waffle batter.
6. Pour batter into the waffle iron until it is filled and close it to cook for 5 minutes.
7. Make 5 more waffles using this batter.
8. Serve with the sautéed mushrooms and yogurt on top.

Lemon Spelt Scones

Total time: 28 minutes
Ingredients
- 1¾ cups spelt flour
- 1¼ cup whole spelt
- ⅔ cup coconut sugar
- 2 teaspoons baking powder
- ½ teaspoon salt
- 3 tablespoons lemon zest
- ½ cup coconut oil
- 1 cup coconut cream
- 2 tablespoons almond milk
- 2 cups frozen raspberries

Directions
1. Preheat your oven to 425 degrees F.
2. Whisk dry ingredients in a stand mixer using whisk attachment.
3. Freeze the dry mixture for 10 minutes then place it back on the mixer.
4. Using the paddle attachment, stir in coconut oil, coconut cream, and almond milk then beat until smooth.
5. Fold in frozen raspberries and mix again, divide the dough into two parts.
6. Spread each part into a thick disk and cut each into 6 wedges of equal size.
7. Line a suitable baking sheet with parchment paper and place the wedges on the tray.
8. Bake for 18 minutes then serve.

Veggie Breakfast Scramble

Total time: 24 minutes
Ingredients
- 1 cup yellow onions, chopped
- 1 cup red bell peppers, diced
- 1½ cups zucchini, sliced
- 3 cups cauliflower florets
- 1 tablespoon garlic, minced
- 1 tablespoon tamari
- 2 tablespoons vegetable broth
- 2 tablespoons nutritional yeast
- 1 (15 ounce) can chickpeas, drained
- 2 cups baby spinach, chopped

Spice Mix:
- 1 teaspoon onion powder
- 1 teaspoon garlic powder
- 1 teaspoon dried minced onions
- ¾ teaspoon dried ground mustard powder
- 1 teaspoon dried thyme leaves
- 1 teaspoon smoked paprika
- ¼ teaspoon turmeric
- ¾ teaspoon salt
- ¼ teaspoon black pepper

Directions

1.	In a suitable pan, add cooking oil and all the vegetables.
2.	Cook while stirring for 7 minutes on medium heat.
3.	Toss in the chickpeas and all the spices.
4.	Continue sautéing for another 7 minutes.
5.	Serve warm.

Strawberry Smoothie Bowl

Total time: 30 minutes
Ingredients
- Smoothie bowl:
- 1 banana frozen
- 1½ cups frozen strawberries
- ½ cup coconut milk
Toppings:
- Fresh strawberries sliced
- Fresh bananas sliced
- Chia seeds

Directions
1.	In a blender jug, puree all the ingredients for the smooth bowl.
2.	Pour the smoothie in the serving bowl.
3.	Add strawberries, banana and chia seeds on top.
4.	Chill well then serve.

Peanut Butter Granola

Total time: 57 minutes
Ingredients
- Nonstick spray
- 4 cups oats
- ⅓ cup of cocoa powder
- ¾ cup peanut butter
- ⅓ cup maple syrup
- ⅓ cup avocado oil
- 1½ teaspoons vanilla extract
- ½ cup cocoa nibs
- 6 ounces dark chocolate, chopped

Directions
1.	Preheat your oven to 300 degrees F.
2.	Spray a baking sheet with cooking spray.
3.	In a medium saucepan add oil, maple syrup, and peanut butter.
4.	Cook for 2 minutes on medium heat, stirring.
5.	Add the oats and cocoa powder, mix well.
6.	Spread the coated oats on the baking sheet.
7.	Bake for 45 minutes, occasionally stirring.
8.	Garnish with dark chocolate, cocoa nibs, and peanut butter.
9.	Serve.

Sweet Potato Toasts

Total time: 20 minutes
Ingredients
- 2 large sweet potatoes, sliced into ¼ inch thick slices
- 1 tablespoon avocado oil
- 1 teaspoon salt
- ½ cup guacamole
- ½ cup tomatoes, sliced

Directions
1.	Preheat your oven to 425 degrees F.
2.	Cover a baking sheet with parchment paper.
3.	Rub the potato slices with oil and salt and place them on a baking sheet.
4.	Bake for 5 minutes in the oven, then flip and bake again for 5 minutes.
5.	Top the baked slices with guacamole and tomatoes.
6.	Serve.

Tofu Scramble Tacos

Total time: 20 minutes
Ingredients
- 1 package tofu
- ¼ cup nutritional yeast
- 2 teaspoons garlic powder
- 2 teaspoons cumin
- 2 teaspoons chili powder
- ½ teaspoon turmeric
- 1 teaspoon salt
- ½ teaspoon pepper
- 1 tablespoon avocado oil
- Warm corn tortillas

Directions
1.	In a pan, add avocado oil and tofu.
2.	Sauté and crumble the tofu on medium heat.
3.	Stir in all the remaining spices and yeast.
4.	Mix and cook for 2 minutes.
5.	Serve on tortillas.

Omelet with Chickpea Flour

Total time: 30 minutes
Ingredients
- ½ teaspoon of onion powder
- ¼ teaspoon of black pepper
- 1 cup of chickpea flour
- ½ teaspoon of garlic powder
- ½ teaspoon of baking soda
- ¼ teaspoon of white pepper
- 1/3 cup of nutritional yeast
- 3 finely chopped green onions
- 4 ounces of sautéed mushrooms

Directions
1.	In a small bowl, mix the onion powder, white pepper, chickpea flour, garlic powder, black and white pepper, baking soda, and nutritional yeast. Add 1 cup of water and create a smooth batter.
2.	On medium heat, put a frying pan and add the batter just like the way you would cook pancakes. On the batter, sprinkle some green onion and mushrooms. Flip the omelet and cook evenly on both sides.
3.	Once both sides are cooked, serve the omelet with spinach, tomatoes, hot sauce, and salsa. Enjoy a guilt-free meal.

A Toast to Remember

Total time: 25 minutes
Ingredients
- 1 can of black beans
- Pinch of sea salt
- 2 pieces of whole-wheat toast
- ¼ teaspoon of chipotle spice
- Pinch of black pepper
- 1 teaspoon of garlic powder

- 1 freshly juiced lime
- 1 freshly diced avocado
- ¼ cup of corn
- 3 tablespoons of finely diced onion
- ½ freshly diced tomato
- Fresh cilantro

Directions

1.	Mix the chipotle spice with the beans, salt, garlic powder, and pepper. Stir in the lime juice. Boil all of these until you have a thick and starchy mix.

2.	In a bowl, mix the corn, tomato, avocado, red onion, cilantro, and juice from the rest of the lime. Add some pepper and salt.

3.	Toast the bread and first spread the black bean mixture followed by the avocado mix.

4.	Take a bite of wholesome goodness!

Onion & Mushroom Tart with a Nice Brown Rice Crust

Total time: 65 minutes

Ingredients

- 1 ½ pounds of mushrooms: button, portabella, or shiitake
- 1 cup of short-grain brown rice
- 2 ¼ cups of water
- ½ teaspoon of ground black pepper
- 2 teaspoons of herbal spice blend
- 1 sweet large onion
- 7 ounces of extra-firm tofu
- 1 cup of plain non-dairy milk
- 2 teaspoons of onion powder
- 2 teaspoons of low-sodium soy or tamari sauce
- 1 teaspoon of molasses
- ¼ teaspoon of ground turmeric
- ¼ cup of white wine or cooking sherry
- ¼ cup of tapioca or arrowroot powder

Directions

1.	Cook the brown rice and put it aside for later use.

2.	Slice the onions into thin strips and sauté them in water until they are soft. Then, add the molasses, and cook them for a few minutes.

3.	Next, sauté the mushrooms in water with the herbal spice blend. Once the mushrooms are cooked and they are soft, add the white wine or sherry. Cook everything for a few more minutes.

4.	In a blender, combine milk, tofu, arrowroot, turmeric, and onion powder till you have a smooth mixture

5.	On a pie plate, create a layer of rice, spreading evenly to form a crust. The rice should be warm and not cold. It will be easy to work with warm rice. You can also use a pastry roller to get an even crust. With your fingers, gently press the sides.

6.	Take half of the tofu mixture and the mushrooms and spoon them over the tart dish. Smooth the level with your spoon.

7.	Now, top the layer with onions followed by the tofu mixture. You can smooth the surface again with your spoon.

8.	Sprinkle some black pepper on top.

9.	Bake the pie at 350o F for about 45 minutes. Toward the end, you can cover it loosely with tin foil. This will help the crust to remain moist.

10.	Allow the pie crust to cool down, so that you can slice it. If you are in love with vegetarian dishes, there is no way that you will not love this pie.

Perfect Breakfast Shake

Total time: 10 minutes

Ingredients

- 3 tablespoons of raw cacao powder
- 1 cup of soy/almond milk
- 2 frozen bananas
- 3 tablespoons of natural peanut butter

Directions

1.	Use a powerful blender to combine all the ingredients.

2.	Process everything until you have a smooth shake.

3.	Enjoy a hearty shake to kickstart your day.

Perfect Polenta with a Dose of Cranberries & Pears

Total time: 15 minutes

Ingredients

- 2 pears freshly cored, peeled, and diced
- 1 batch of warm basic polenta
- ¼ cup of brown rice syrup
- 1 teaspoon of cinnamon
- 1 cup of dried or fresh cranberries

Directions

1.	Warm the polenta in a medium-sized saucepan. Then, add the cranberries, pears, and cinnamon powder.

2.	Cook everything, stirring occasionally. You will know that the dish is ready when the pears are soft.

3.	The entire dish will be done within 10 minutes.

4.	Divide the polenta equally among 4 bowls. Add some pear compote as the last finishing touch.

5.	Now you can dig into this hassle-free breakfast bowl full of goodness.

Breakfast Burritos

Total time: 20 minutes

Ingredients

- 2 (15 oz) cans black beans, drained and rinsed
- ½ cup of water
- 4 whole-wheat tortillas
- 8 leaves romaine lettuce
- 2 tomatoes, sliced
- 2 avocados, peeled, pitted, and sliced
- 1 ½ cups salsa

Seasonings:

- 1 tbsp garlic powder
- 1 tbsp onion powder
- 1 tbsp chili powder
- 1 tsp dried cumin
- 1 tsp dried oregano

Directions

1.   In a medium-sized pot, add the beans, water, and seasonings. Allow boiling over medium heat and then simmer for 10 minutes. Drain the beans after.
2.   Onto the whole wheat tortillas, add one or two leaves of romaine lettuce, tomatoes, and avocado.
3.   Add the black beans on top and then, the salsa.
4.   Serve the burritos immediately.

Gingerbread Chia Porridge

Total time: 25 minutes
Ingredients
- ¼ cup Chia Seeds
- Pinch of Clove, grounded
- ¾ cup Soymilk, unsweetened
- ¼ tsp. Cinnamon, grounded
- 1 tbsp. Maple Syrup
- Dash of Sea Salt
- ¼ tsp. Ginger, grounded

For garnishing:
- 1 tbsp. Raisins

Directions
1.   Start by combining all the ingredients needed to make the oatmeal in a mason jar.
2.   Place the Mason jar in the refrigerator for 8 hours.
3.   Stir once the porridge before keeping it for refrigeration.
4.   Now, garnish it with raisins.
5.   Serve and enjoy.

Protein Granola

Total time: 25 minutes
Ingredients
- 2 tbsp. Flax Seed, grounded
- 1/3 cup Chocolate Chips
- ¼ cup Almond Butter
- 1 tsp. Vanilla Extract
- 1 tsp. Cinnamon
- ¼ cup Agave Nectar
- ¼ tsp. Salt
- 2 cups Rolled Oats

Directions
1.   For making this healthy granola, you first need to preheat the oven to 325°F.
2.   After that, melt almond butter and honey together in a small saucepan over medium-low heat.
3.   Then, spoon in the agave nectar to it. Mix well.
4.   Now, remove the pan from the heat. Spoon in the oats, cinnamon, flax seeds, and salt to it. Tip: Mix the mixture well so that the butter honey mixture coats the oats well.
5.   Next, transfer the oats mixture to a parchment paper-lined baking sheet and spread it across evenly.
6.   Bake for 8 minutes. Once eight minutes is up, pull out the sheet from the oven and stir it well.
7.   After stirring, keep the pan in the oven and bake for further 8 minutes or until lightly golden.
8.   Allow the mixture to cool completely. Spoon in the chocolate chips.
9.   Serve and enjoy.

Almond Teff Porridge

Total time: 25 minutes
Ingredients
- ¼ tsp. Cinnamon, grounded
- 1 cup Whole Grain Teff
- ¼ cup Almonds, crushed
- 1 ½ cup Water
- ¼ tsp. Sea Salt
- 1 ½ cup Almond Milk, unsweetened
- 1 Banana, sliced
- 1 tbsp. Extra Virgin Olive Oil

Directions
1.   First, place teff, banana slices, almond milk, sea salt, water, cinnamon, and coconut oil in a deep saucepan over medium heat.
2.   Stir well and bring the teff mixture to a boil.
3.   Once it starts boiling, lower the heat to low.
4.   Then, cover the pan with a lid.
5.   Next, allow the teff mixture to simmer for 15 to 20 minutes. Tip: Make sure to stir it continuously so that the teff doesn't stick to the bottom of the pan.
6.   Take the saucepan from the heat once the teff gets cooked.
7.   Finally, transfer to the serving bowl and enjoy.

Raspberry Overnight Oats

Total time: 5 minutes
Ingredients
- 1 tsp. Maple Syrup
- ¼ cup White Beans
- ¼ cup Raspberries
- ½ cup Rolled Oats
- 10 Almonds, raw & chopped
- 1 tsp. Chia Seeds
- 1 tsp. Maple Syrup
- 2/3 cup Soymilk

Directions
1.   To start with, place the beans in a large mason jar and mash it with a fork.
2.   Next, stir in all the remaining ingredients to the Mason jar. Mix well.
3.   Now, keep the jar in the refrigerator overnight.
4.   In the morning, keep the Mason jar out of the refrigerator and mix well.
5.   Serve immediately and enjoy it.

Coconut Buckwheat Porridge

Total time: 20 minutes
Ingredients
- 1 cup Water
- 2 tsp. Vanilla Extract
- 1 cup Buckwheat Grouts
- Dash of Salt
- ¼ cup Chia Seeds
- ¼ tsp. Cinnamon
- 3 cups Coconut Milk, unsweetened
- Dash of Salt

Directions
1.   For making this high-protein oatmeal, you need to mix all the ingredients in a large mixing bowl until combined well.

2.   Then, cover the bowl with plastic cling and place it in the refrigerator overnight.
3.   Next morning, transfer the contents to a deep saucepan over medium heat.
4.   Cook for 10 minutes or until thickened. Tip: Make sure to stir it continuously.
5.   Serve it hot or warm.

Chickpea Scramble Bowl

Total time: 20 minutes
Ingredients
- ¼ of 1 Onion, diced
- 15 oz. Chickpeas
- 2 Garlic cloves, minced
- ½ tsp. Turmeric
- ½ tsp. Black Pepper
- ½ tsp. Extra Virgin Olive Oil
- ½ tsp. Salt

Directions
1.   Begin by placing the chickpeas in a large bowl along with a bit of water.
2.   Soak for few minutes and then mash the chickpeas lightly with a fork while leaving some of them in the whole form.
3.   Next, spoon in the turmeric, pepper, and salt to the bowl. Mix well.
4.   Then, heat oil in a medium-sized skillet over medium-high heat.
5.   Once the oil becomes hot, stir in the onions.
6.   Sauté the onions for 3 to 4 minutes or until softened.
7.   Then, add the garlic and cook for further 1 minute or until aromatic.
8.   After that, stir in the mashed chickpeas. Cook for another 4 minutes or until thickened.
9.   Serve along with micro greens. Place the greens at the bottom, followed by the scramble, and top it with cilantro or parsley.

Maple Flavoured Oatmeal

Total time: 30 minutes
Ingredients
- 2 tbsp. Maple Syrup
- 1 cup Oatmeal
- ½ tsp. Cinnamon
- 2 ½ cup Water
- 2/3 cup Soymilk
- 1 tsp. Earth Balance or Vegan Butter

Directions
1.   To start with, place oatmeal and water in a medium-sized saucepan over medium-high heat.
2.   Bring the mixture to a boil.
3.   Next, lower the heat and cook for further 13 to 15 minutes while keeping the pan covered. Tip: At this point, all the water should get absorbed by the grains.
4.   Now, remove the pan from the heat and fluff this mixture with a fork.
5.   Cover the pan again. Set it aside for 5 minutes.
6.   Then, stir in all the remaining ingredients to the oatmeal mixture until everything comes together.
7.   Serve and enjoy.

Chocolate Chip Cookie Dough

Total time: 10 minutes
Ingredients
- ½ tsp. Sea Salt
- 2 cups Chickpeas, cooked & drained
- ¼ cup Maple Syrup
- 1/3 cup Coconut Oil, melted
- 3 tbsp. Coconut Flour
- 2 tsp. Vanilla Extract

Directions
1.   To make this delightful cookie dough, first blend the chickpeas in a high-speed blender for a minute or until smooth.
2.   Spoon in the oil, sea salt, maple syrup, and vanilla extract. Blend for a further minute or until combined.
3.   Next, stir in the coconut flour and blend again. Scrape the sides.
4.   Now, transfer the mixture to a medium-sized bowl and place in the refrigerator for 2 hours.
5.   Serve on its own or with crackers.

Banana Strawberry Oats

Total time: 30 minutes
Ingredients
- 1 tbsp. Almonds, sliced
- ½ cup Oats
- ½ tsp. Cinnamon
- 1 cup Zucchini, shredded
- ½ of 1 Banana, mashed
- 1 cup Water
- ½ cup Strawberries, sliced
- Dash of Sea Salt
- 1 tbsp. Flax Meal
- ½ scoop of Protein Powder

Directions
1.   First, combine oats, salt, water, and zucchini in a large saucepan.
2.   Cook the mixture over medium-high heat and cook for 8 to 10 minutes or until the liquid is absorbed.
3.   Now, spoon in all the remaining ingredients to the mixture and give everything a good stir.
4.   Finally, transfer the mixture to a serving bowl and top it with almonds and berries.
5.   Serve and enjoy.

LUNCH RECIPES

Tahini Broccoli

Preparation Time: 5 Minutes
Cooking Time: 15 Minutes
Servings: 4
Ingredients:
- Toasted sesame seeds (.25 c.)
- Minced green onions
- Broccoli slaw (1 bag)
- Soy sauce (2 teaspoon.)
- Sesame oil (1 Tablespoon.)
- Rice vinegar (1 Tablespoon.)
- White miso (2 Tablespoon.)
- Tahini (.25 c.)

Directions:
1. Take out a bowl and whisk together the soy sauce, oil, vinegar, miso, and tahini.
2. Add in the sesame seeds, green onions, and broccoli slaw. Set aside for 20 minutes and then serve.
Nutrition: Calories: 135 Carbs: 37g Fat: 0g Protein: 23g

Steamed Cauliflower

Preparation Time: 5 Minutes
Cooking Time: 15 Minutes
Servings: 4
Ingredients:
- Red pepper flakes (1 teaspoon.)
- Salt (.5 teaspoon.)
- Water (1 c.)
- Cauliflower (1 head)

Directions:
1. Take the leaves off the cauliflower and then slice into florets.
2. Bring out a pan and bring some water to a boil. Add the steamer basket over it and then add in the salt and florets.
3. Cover and let this steam for a bit. After five minutes, this should be nice and tender.
4. In a bowl, toss this with the red pepper flakes and then serve.
Nutrition: Calories: 35 Carbs: 7g Fat: 0g Protein: 3g

Cauliflower Tacos

Preparation Time: 10 Minutes
Cooking Time: 30 Minutes
Servings: 8
Ingredients:
For the roasted cauliflower
- Chili powder (1 teaspoon.)
- Smoked paprika (2 teaspoon.)
- Nutritional yeast (2 Tablespoon.)
- Flour (2 Tablespoon.)
- Olive oil (1 Tablespoon.)
- Cauliflower (1 head)
For the tacos
- Lime wedges (
- Corn tortillas (8)
- Guacamole (.5 c.)
- Mango salsa (.5 c.)
- Grated carrots (
- Quartered cherry tomatoes (2 c.)
- Shredded lettuce (2 c.)

Directions:
1. Turn on the oven and let it heat up to 350 degrees. Prepare a baking tray and set it to the side.
2. Toss the cauliflower with the oil and, in another bowl, mix all of the seasonings before adding it to the cauliflower.
3. Spread this onto the baking tray and add to the oven. After 20 minutes, this will be done, and you can take it out of the oven.
4. When the cauliflower is cooked, you can use those and the rest of the **Ingredients:** to assemble the tacos.
Nutrition: Calories: 198 Carbs: 32g Fat: 6g Protein: 7g

Sweet Potatoes

Preparation Time: 10 Minutes
Cooking Time: 35 Minutes
Servings: 4
Ingredients:
- Salt (.5 teaspoon.)
- Garlic powder (.5 teaspoon.)
- Dried thyme (.5 teaspoon.)
- Dried oregano (.5 teaspoon.)
- Smoked paprika (.5 teaspoon.)
- Cayenne pepper (.5 teaspoon.)
- Olive oil (2 teaspoon.)
- Sweet potatoes (2 lbs.)

Directions:
1. Turn on the oven and let it heat up to 400 degrees. Prepare a baking sheet with some parchment paper.
2. Wash the potatoes and then cube up. Move to a bowl and add the oil and potatoes together.
3. Combine the seasonings into another bowl and then sprinkle on top of the potatoes. Add this to the baking sheet and into the oven.
4. After 30 minutes of baking, take out of the oven and then serve warm.
Nutrition: Calories: 219 Carbs: 46g Fat: 3g Protein: 4g

Smoky Meal

Preparation Time: 5 Minutes
Cooking Time: 10 Minutes
Servings: 6
Ingredients:
- Chipotle powder (.25 teaspoon.)
- Smoked paprika (.25 teaspoon.)
- Pepper (.25 teaspoon.)
- Salt (.5 teaspoon.)
- Plain vegan yogurt (3 Tablespoon.)
- Rice vinegar (.25 c.)
- Mayo (.33 c.)
- Shredded cabbage (1 lb.)

Directions:

1. Bring out a big bowl and add the shredded cabbage inside. In another bowl, combine the chipotle powder, paprika, pepper, salt, sugar, yogurt, vinegar, and mayo.
2. Pour this over the cabbage and then mix it all up. Divide up and serve.
Nutrition: Calories: 73 Carbs: 8g Protein: 1g Fat: 4g

Mediterranean Pizza

Preparation Time: 5 Minutes
Cooking Time: 25 Minutes
Servings: 2
Ingredients:
- Cheesy sprinkle (4 Tablespoon.)
- Classic hummus (.5 c.)
- Pizza crusts (
- Olive oil
- Chopped olives (2 Tablespoon.)
- Halved cherry tomatoes (1 c.)
- Sliced red onion
- Sliced zucchini

Directions:
1. Turn on the oven to 400 degrees. Place the vegetables in a bowl and sprinkle on the salt and oil and toss around.
2. Layout the two crusts on a baking tray and spread half the hummus on each one.
3. Top with the vegetable mixture and some of the cheesy mixture before adding to the oven.
4. After 20 minutes, take these out and then serve.
Nutrition: Calories: 500 Carbs: 58g Fat: 25g Protein: 19g

Red Lentil and Chickpea Bowl

Preparation Time: 5 Minutes
Cooking Time: 25 Minutes
Servings: 4
Ingredients:
- Salt (1 teaspoon.)
- Curry powder (.5 teaspoon.)
- Garam masala seasoning (2 teaspoon.)
- Drained chickpeas (15 oz.)
- Diced Roma tomatoes
- Water (1 c.)
- Vegetable broth (2 c.)
- Vegan milk (1 c.)
- Dried red lentils (1.5 c.)
- Diced onion (.5 c.)
- Chopped carrots (

Directions:
1. To start this recipe, take out a pot and start boiling some water and carrots on the stove. After 5 minutes, you can drain these and set it to one side.
2. As the carrots are boiling, you can heat up a bit of oil in a frying pan and cook the onion for a bit. It will take about ten minutes.
3. In a big pan, add in the chickpeas, carrots, milk, water, vegetable broth, lentils, and onion along with the seasonings and spices.
4. Bring all of this to a boil before reducing the heat and letting it simmer for a bit.

5. After twenty minutes of cooking, you can take it off the heat before serving and enjoying it.
Nutrition: Calories: 189 Carbs: 22g Fat: 11g Protein: 16g

Curry Wraps

Preparation Time: 5 Minutes
Cooking Time: 22 Minutes
Servings: 5
Ingredients:
- Chapatis (8)
- Sliced garlic cloves
- Sliced onions
- Olive oil (2 Tablespoon.)
- Tandoori curry paste (2 Tablespoon.)
- Cubed tofu (600g)
- Mint sauce (3 Tbs.)
- Yogurt (4 Tablespoon.)
- Shredded red cabbage head
- Quartered lime

Directions:
1. We can start this out by taking out a bowl and mix the yogurt, cabbage, and mint sauce then set it to the side.
2. Toss the tofu and the tandoori paste into a frying pan with some of the oil. Then cook this for a bit on each side to make it all golden brown. Take out of the heat when you are done with this.
3. Next, we can add the garlic and onions into the same pan and cook those for a bit. After ten minutes, add the tofu back in and cook a bit longer.
4. Heat up the chapatis using the **Directions:** on the package and then fill them up with the tandoori tofu and the sauce that you made. Serve with the lime quarters.
Nutrition: Calories: 211 Carbs: 22g Fat: 7g Protein: 19g

One Pan Spicy Rice

Preparation Time: 5 Minutes
Cooking Time: 25 Minutes
Servings: 5
Ingredients:
- Yogurt to serve
- Cashew nuts (1 handful)
- Spinach (2 c.)
- Raisins (1 handful)
- Chickpeas, rinsed and drained (15 oz.)
- Vegetable stock (2 c.)
- Basmati rice, rinsed (1.5 c.)
- Curry paste (2 Tablespoon.)
- Crushed garlic cloves 9
- Sunflower oil (1 Tablespoon.)

Directions:
1. Take out a pan and heat up some oil inside. When it is hot, you can add in the curry paste and garlic to cook and heat up for a minute.
2. When this is done, add the pepper, salt, chickpeas, raisins, vegetable stock, and rice into the pan and stir it around well.
3. Reduce the heat for a bit and let this cook. After 15 minutes, all of the liquid should be gone, and

the rice should be tender. Add the cashew nuts and the spinach as well.

4.   Serve with some of the natural yogurts and enjoy it.

Nutrition: Calories: 170 Carbs: 16g Fat: 2g Protein: 5g

Chickpea Sunflower Sandwich

Preparation Time: 15 minutes
Cooking Time: 10 minutes
Servings: 2
Ingredients:
For The Sandwich:
- 1 ¾ cup cooked chickpeas
- 1/4 cup chopped red onion
- 1/4 cup roasted sunflower seeds, unsalted
- ½ teaspoon salt
- ¼ teaspoon ground black pepper
- 1 tablespoon maple syrup
- 1/2 teaspoon Dijon mustard
- 3 tablespoons vegan mayonnaise
- 2 tablespoons fresh dill
- 4 pieces of rustic bread

For The Garlic Herb Sauce:
- 1 teaspoon minced garlic
- 1/2 of lemon, juiced
- ½ teaspoon of sea salt
- 1 teaspoon dried dill
- ¼ dried dill
- 1/4 cup hummus
- ¼ cup almond milk, unsweetened

For Topping:
- 1 avocado, pitted, sliced
- 1 medium white onion, peeled, sliced
- ½ cup chopped lettuce
- 1 medium tomato, sliced

Directions:
1.   Prepare the garlic herb sauce and for this, take a medium bowl, place all of its ingredients and whisk until combined, set aside until combined.

2.   Take a medium bowl, add chickpeas in it, and then mash by using a fork until broken.

3.   Then add onion, dill, sunflower seeds, salt, black pepper, mustard, maple syrup, and mayonnaise and stir until well combined.

4.   Take a medium skillet pan, place it over medium heat, add bread slices, and cook for 3 minutes per side until toasted.

5.   Spread chickpea mixture on one side of two bread slices, top with prepared garlic herb sauce, avocado, onion, tomato, and lettuce and cover with the other two slices.

6.   Serve straight away.

Nutrition: 532 Cal 30 g Fat 4 g Saturated Fat 52 g Carbohydrates 14 g Fiber 8 g Sugars 17 g Protein;

White Bean and Artichoke Sandwich

Preparation Time: 15 minutes
Cooking Time: 10 minutes
Servings: 4
Ingredients:
- 1 ¼ cooked white beans
- ½ cup cashew nuts
- 6 artichoke hearts, chopped
- ¼ cup sunflower seeds, hulled
- 1 clove of garlic, peeled
- ¼ teaspoon salt
- ¼ teaspoon ground black pepper
- 1 teaspoon dried rosemary
- 1 lemon, grated
- 6 tablespoons almond milk, unsweetened
- 8 pieces of rustic bread

Directions:
1.   Soak cashew nuts in warm water for 10 minutes, then drain them and transfer into a food processor.

2.   Add garlic, salt, black pepper, rosemary, lemon zest, and milk and then pulse for 2 minutes until smooth, scraping the sides of the container frequently.

3.   Take a medium bowl, place beans in it, mash them by using a fork, then add sunflower seeds and artichokes and stir until mixed.

4.   Pour in cashew nuts dressing, stir until coated, and taste to adjust seasoning.

5.   Take a medium skillet pan, place it over medium heat, add bread slices, and cook for 3 minutes per side until toasted.

6.   Spread white beans mixture on one side of four bread slices and then cover with the other four slices.

7.   Serve straight away.

Nutrition: 220 Cal 8 g Fat 1 g Saturated Fat 28 g Carbohydrates 8 g Fiber 2 g Sugars 12 g Protein;

Sabich Sandwich

Preparation Time: 10 minutes
Cooking Time: 10 minutes
Servings: 4
Ingredients:
- 1/2 cup cooked white beans
- 2 medium potatoes, peeled, boiled, ½-inch thick sliced
- 1 medium eggplant, destemmed, ½-inch cubed
- 4 dill pickles, ¼-inch thick sliced
- ¼ teaspoon of sea salt
- 2 tablespoons olive oil
- 1/4 teaspoon harissa paste
- 1/2 cup hummus
- 1 tablespoon mayonnaise
- 4 pita bread pockets
- 1/2 cup tabbouleh salad

Directions:
1.   Take a small frying pan, place it over medium-low heat, add oil and wait until it gets hot.

2.   Season eggplant pieces with salt, add to the hot frying pan and cook for 8 minutes until softened, and when done, remove the pan from heat.

3.   Take a small bowl, place white beans in it, add harissa paste and mayonnaise and then stir until combined.

4.   Assemble the sandwich and for this, place pita bread on clean working space, smear generously with hummus, then cover half of each pita bread with potato slices and top with a dill pickle slices.

5. Spoon 2 tablespoons of white bean mixture on each dill pickle, top with 3 tablespoons of cooked eggplant pieces and 2 tablespoons of tabbouleh salad and then cover the filling with the other half of pita bread.
6. Serve straight away.
Nutrition: 386 Cal 13 g Fat 2 g Saturated Fat 56 g Carbohydrates 7 g Fiber 3 g Sugars 12 g Protein;

Tofu and Pesto Sandwich

Preparation Time: 10 minutes
Cooking Time: 15 minutes
Servings: 4
Ingredients:
- 2 blocks of tofu, firm, pressed, drain
- 8 slices of tomato
- 8 leaves of lettuce
- 1 ½ teaspoon dried oregano
- ½ cup green pesto
- 2 tablespoons olive oil
- 8 slices of sandwich bread

Directions:
1. Switch on the oven, then set it to 375 degrees F and let it preheat.
2. Cut tofu into thick slices, place them in a baking sheet, drizzle with oil and sprinkle with oregano, and bake the tofu pieces for 15 minutes until roasted.
3. Assemble the sandwich and for this, spread pesto on one side of each bread slice, then top four slices with lettuce, tomato slices, and roasted tofu and then cover with the other four slices.
4. Serve straight away.
Nutrition: 277 Cal 9.1 g Fat 1.5 g Saturated Fat 33.1 g Carbohydrates 3.6 g Fiber 12.7 g Sugars 16.1 g Protein;

Chickpea and Mayonnaise Salad Sandwich

Preparation Time: 10 minutes
Cooking Time: 0 minutes
Servings: 4
Ingredients:
For the mayonnaise:
- 1/3 cup cashew nuts, soaked in boiling water for 10 minutes
- ½ teaspoon ground black pepper
- 1 teaspoon salt
- 6 teaspoons apple cider vinegar
- 2 teaspoon maple syrup
- 1/2 teaspoon Dijon mustard
For the chickpea salad:
- 1 small bunch of chives, chopped
- 1 ½ cup sweetcorn
- 3 cups cooked chickpeas
To serve:
- 4 sandwich bread
- 4 leaves of lettuce
- ½ cup chopped cherry tomatoes

Directions:
1. Prepare the mayonnaise and for this, place all of its ingredients in a food processor and then pulse for 2 minutes until smooth, scraping the sides of the container frequently.

2. Take a medium bowl, place chickpeas in it, and then mash by using a fork until broken.
3. Add chives and corn, stir until mixed, then add mayonnaise and stir until well combined.
4. Assemble the sandwich and for this, stuff sandwich bread with chickpea salad, top each sandwich with a lettuce leaf, and ¼ cup of chopped tomatoes and then serve.
Nutrition: 387 Cal 19 g Fat 5 g Saturated Fat 39.7 g Carbohydrates 7.2 g Fiber 4.6 g Sugars 10 g Protein;

Mushrooms Sandwich

Preparation Time: 10 minutes
Cooking Time: 5 minutes
Servings: 4
Ingredients:
- 8 cherry tomatoes, halved
- 2 ounces of baby spinach
- 20 ounces of oyster mushrooms
- 2/3 teaspoon salt
- 1/3 teaspoon ground black pepper
- 2 tablespoons olive oil
- 4 tablespoons of barbecue sauce
- 8 slices of bread, toasted

Directions:
1. Take a griddle pan, place it over medium-high heat, grease it with oil and let it preheat.
2. Cut mushroom into thin strips, add to the hot griddle pan, drizzle with oil and cook for 5 minutes until done.
3. Transfer grilled mushrooms into a medium bowl, season with salt and black pepper, add barbecue sauce and toss until mixed.
4. Spread prepared mushroom mixture evenly on four bread slices, top with spinach and cherry tomatoes, then cover with the other four slices and serve.
Nutrition: 350 Cal 11 g Fat 3 g Saturated Fat 46 g Carbohydrates 9 g Fiber 7.2 g Sugars 12.1 g Protein;

Rainbow Taco Boats

Preparation Time: 10 minutes
Cooking Time: 0 minutes
Servings: 4
Ingredients:
- 1 head romaine lettuce, destemmed
For the Filling:
- 1/2 cup alfalfa sprouts
- 1 medium avocado, peeled, pitted, cubed
- 1 cup shredded carrots
- 1 cup halved cherry tomatoes
- 3/4 cup sliced red cabbage
- 1/2 cup sprouted hummus dip
- 1 tablespoon hemp seeds
For the Sauce:
- 1 tablespoon maple syrup
- 1/3 cup tahini
- 1/8 teaspoon sea salt
- 2 tablespoons lemon juice
- 3 tablespoons water

Directions:

1. Prepare the sauce and for this, take a medium bowl, add all the ingredients in it and whisk until well combined.

2. Assemble the boats and for this, arrange lettuce leaves in twelve portions, top each with hummus, and the remaining ingredients for the filling.

3. Serve with prepared sauce.

Nutrition: 314 Cal 23.6 g Fat 4 g Saturated Fat 23.2 g Carbohydrates 9.3 g Fiber 6.2 g Sugars 8 g Protein;

Eggplant Sandwich

Preparation Time: 10 minutes
Cooking Time: 25 minutes
Servings: 4
Ingredients:
For the Sandwich:
- 2 ciabatta buns
- 1 medium eggplant, peeled, sliced, soaked in salted water
- 1 medium tomato, sliced
- 1/2 of a medium cucumber, sliced
- 1/2 cup arugula
- 4 tablespoons mayo

For the Marinade:
- 1 teaspoon agave syrup
- 1/4 teaspoon salt
- 1/4 teaspoon ground black pepper
- 1 teaspoon smoked paprika
- 1 tablespoon soy sauce
- 1 tablespoon olive oil

Directions:
1. Switch on the oven, then set it to 350 degrees F and let it preheat.

2. Prepare the marinade and for this, take a small bowl, place all the ingredients in it and whisk until combined.

3. Drain the eggplant slices, pat dry with a kitchen towel, brush with prepared marinade, arrange them on a baking sheet and then bake for 20 minutes until done.

4. Assemble the sandwich and for this, slice the bread in half lengthwise, then spread mayonnaise in the bottom half of the bun and top with baked eggplant slices, tomato, and cucumber slices, and sprinkle with salt and black pepper.

5. Top with arugula leaves, cover with the top half of the bun, and then cover with aluminum foil.

6. Preheat the grill over medium-high heat setting and when hot, place prepared sandwiches and grill for 3 to 5 minutes until toasted.

7. Cut each sandwich through the foil into half and serve.

Nutrition: 688 Cal 15 g Fat 2 g Saturated Fat 118 g Carbohydrates 7 g Fiber 7 g Sugars 21 g Protein;

Lentil, Cauliflower and Grape Salad

Preparation Time: 10 minutes
Cooking Time: 25 minutes
Servings: 4
Ingredients:
- For the Cauliflower:

- 1 medium head of cauliflower, cut into florets
- 1/4 teaspoon sea salt
- 1 1/2 tablespoons curry powder
- 1 1/2 tablespoons melted coconut oil

For the Tahini Dressing:
- 2 tablespoons tahini
- 1/8 teaspoon salt
- 1.8 teaspoon ground black pepper
- 4 1/2 tablespoons green curry paste
- 1 tablespoon maple syrup
- 2 tablespoons lemon juice
- 2 tablespoons water

For the Salad:
- 1 cup cooked lentils
- 4 tablespoons chopped cilantro
- 1 cup red grapes, halved
- 6 cups mixed greens

Directions:
1. Switch on the oven, then set it to 400 degrees F and let it preheat.

2. Prepare the cauliflower and for this, take a medium bowl, place cauliflower florets in it, drizzle with oil, season with salt and curry powder, toss until mixed.

3. Take a baking sheet, line it with parchment sheet, spread cauliflower florets in it, and then bake for 25 minutes until tender and nicely golden brown.

4. Meanwhile, prepare the tahini dressing and for this, take a medium bowl, place all of its ingredients and whisk until combined, set aside until required.

5. Assemble the salad and for this, take a large salad bowl, add roasted cauliflower florets, lentils, grapes, and mixed greens, drizzle with prepared tahini dressing and toss until well combined.

6. Serve straight away.

Nutrition: 420 Cal 14 g Fat 5 g Saturated Fat 37.6 g Carbohydrates 9.8 g Fiber 12.8 g Sugars 10.8 g Protein;

Loaded Kale Salad

Preparation Time: 10 minutes
Cooking Time: 30 minutes
Servings: 4
Ingredients:
- 1 ½ cup cooked quinoa

For The Vegetables:
- 1 whole beet, peeled, sliced
- 4 large carrots, peeled, chopped
- 1/2 teaspoon curry powder
- 1/8 teaspoon sea salt
- 2 tablespoons melted coconut oil

For The Dressing:
- ¼ teaspoon of sea salt
- 2 tablespoons maple syrup
- 3 tablespoons lemon juice
- 1/3 cup tahini
- 1/4 cup water

For the Salad:
- 1/2 cup sprouts
- 1 medium avocado, peeled, pitted, cubed

- 1/2 cup chopped cherry tomatoes
- 8 cups chopped kale
- 1/4 cup hemp seeds

Directions:

1. Switch on the oven, then set it to 375 degrees F and let it preheat.
2. Take a baking sheet, place beets and carrots on it, drizzle with oil, season with curry powder and salt, toss until coated, and then bake for 30 minutes until tender and golden brown.
3. Meanwhile, prepare the dressing and for this, take a small bowl, place all the ingredients in it and whisk until well combined, set aside until required.
4. Assemble the salad and for this, take a large salad bowl, place kale leaves in it, add remaining ingredients for the salad along with roasted vegetables, drizzle with prepared dressing and toss until combined.
5. Serve straight away.

Nutrition: 472 Cal 22.8 g Fat 3.8 g Saturated Fat 58.7 g Carbohydrates 12.5 g Fiber 9.2 g Sugars 14.6 g Protein;

Black Bean and Quinoa Salad

Preparation Time: 35 minutes
Cooking Time: 20 minutes
Servings: 4
Ingredients:
For the Salad:

- 1 cup of corn
- 1 ½ cup cooked black beans
- 1 cup quinoa
- 1/2 cup minced red onion
- 2 medium tomatoes, chopped
- 4 tablespoons chopped cilantro
- 2 cups of water

For The Dressing:

- 4 tablespoons lime juice
- 2 tablespoons lime zest
- ¼ teaspoon of sea salt
- 2 tablespoons olive oil

Directions:

1. Take a medium saucepan, place it over medium heat, pour in water, add quinoa, and bring it to a boil.
2. Then switch heat to the low level and cook the quinoa for 15 minutes until all the water has been absorbed and quinoa has cooked.
3. While quinoa cooks, prepare the dressing, and for this, take a small bowl, place all of its ingredients in it and then whisk until combined, set aside until required.
4. When quinoa has cooked, fluff it with a fork, then transfer it into a medium bowl and chill in the refrigerator for 30 minutes.
5. Add remaining ingredients for the salad into the quinoa, drizzle with the dressing and then toss until well mixed.
6. Serve straight away.

Nutrition: 229 Cal 10 g Fat 2 g Saturated Fat 27 g Carbohydrates 3 g Fiber 2 g Sugars 6 g Protein;

Garden Pasta Salad

Preparation Time: 10 minutes
Cooking Time: 12 minutes
Servings: 4
Ingredients:
For the Salad:

- 1 cup chopped kale
- 1/4 cup chopped basil
- 2 cups of sliced yellow cherry tomatoes
- 16 ounces tri-colored pasta

For the Dressing:

- 1/2 teaspoon sea salt
- ¼ teaspoon ground black pepper
- 1 teaspoon dried Italian seasoning
- 1/2 cup white wine vinegar
- 3 tablespoons lemon juice
- 1 teaspoon olive oil

Directions:

1. Cook the pasta, and for this, take a large pot half full with salty water, place it over medium heat and bring it to a boil.
2. Add pasta, cook for 10 to 12 minutes until tender, and then drain well into a colander.
3. While pasta cooks, prepare the dressing, and for this, take a small bowl, place all of its ingredients in it and whisk until combined.
4. Transfer pasta into a large bowl, add remaining ingredients for the salad in it, drizzle with prepared dressing and then toss until well combined.
5. Serve straight away.

Nutrition: 424 Cal 3 g Fat 0 g Saturated Fat 46 g Carbohydrates 5 g Fiber 8 g Sugars 13 g Protein;

Roasted Vegetables and Tofu Salad

Preparation Time: 10 minutes
Cooking Time: 25 minutes
Servings: 4
Ingredients:

- For the salad:
- 2 cups chopped tofu, firm, pressed, drained
- 2 cups cooked chickpeas
- 4 cups spinach
- 2 cups broccoli floret
- 2 cups chopped sweet potato, peeled
- 2 cups Brussel sprout, halved
- 4 teaspoons ground black pepper
- 4 teaspoons salt
- 4 tablespoons red chili powder
- 1 cup olive oil
- For the dressing:
- 2 teaspoons salt
- 2 teaspoons ground black pepper
- 4 teaspoons dried thyme
- 4 tablespoons lemon juice
- 4 tablespoons olive oil
- 2 teaspoons water
- ½ cup hummus

Directions:

1. Switch on the oven, then set it to 400 degrees F and let it preheat.

2.	Take a large baking sheet, grease it with oil, and spread broccoli florets in one-fifth of the portion, reserving few florets for later use.
3.	Add sprouts, sweet potatoes, tofu, and chickpeas as an individual pile on the baking sheet, drizzle with oil, season with salt, black pepper, and red chili powder and then bake for 25 minutes until the tofu has turned nicely golden brown and vegetables are softened, tossing halfway.
4.	While vegetables, grains, and tofu are being roasted, prepare the dressing and for this, take a medium jar, add all of its ingredients in it, stir until well combined, and then divide the dressing among four large mason jars.
5.	When vegetables, grains, and tofu has been roasted, distribute evenly among four mason jars along with reserved cauliflower florets and shut with lid.
6.	When ready to eat, shake the Mason jar until salad is coated with the dressing and then serve.
Nutrition: 477 Cal 24 g Fat 5 g Saturated Fat 52 g Carbohydrates 16 g Fiber 11 g Sugars 21 g Protein;

Farro and Lentil Salad

Preparation Time: 10 minutes
Cooking Time: 0 minutes
Servings: 4
Ingredients:
For the Salad:
- 1 cup grape tomato, halved
- ½ cup diced yellow bell pepper
- 1 cup diced cucumber,
- ½ cup diced red bell pepper
- 1 cup fresh arugula
- 1/3 cup chopped parsley
- 1 ½ cups lentils, cooked
- 3 ½ cups farro, cooked

For the Dressing:
- ½ teaspoon minced garlic
- ½ teaspoon salt
- ¼ teaspoon ground black pepper
- 1 teaspoon Italian seasoning
- 1 teaspoon Dijon mustard
- 2 tablespoons red wine vinegar
- 2 tablespoons lemon juice
- 1/3 cup olive oil

Directions:
1.	Take a large bowl, place all the ingredients for the salad in it except for arugula and then toss until combined.
2.	Prepare the dressing and for this, take a medium bowl, add all of its ingredients in it and then stir whisk until well combined.
3.	Pour the dressing over the salad, toss until well coated, then distribute salad among four bowls and top with arugula.
4.	Serve straight away.
Nutrition: 379 Cal 10 g Fat 2 g Saturated Fat 63.5 g Carbohydrates 11 g Fiber 2.5 g Sugars 12.5 g Protein;

Greek Zoodle Bowl

Preparation Time: 10 minutes
Cooking Time: 0 minutes

Servings: 4
Ingredients:
- ½ cup chopped artichokes
- 14 cherry tomatoes, chopped
- 1 medium red bell peppers, cored, chopped
- 4 medium zucchini
- 1 medium yellow bell pepper, cored, chopped
- 6 tablespoons hemp hearts
- 1 English cucumber
- 6 tablespoons chopped red onion
- 2 tablespoons chopped parsley leaves
- 2 tablespoons chopped mint

For the Greek Dressing:
- 2 tablespoons chopped mint
- 1 teaspoon garlic powder
- ½ teaspoon salt
- ¼ teaspoon dried oregano
- 2 teaspoons Italian seasoning
- 3 tablespoons red wine vinegar
- 1 tablespoon olive oil

Directions:
1.	Prepare zucchini and cucumber noodles and for this, spiralize them by using a spiralizer or vegetable peeler and then divide evenly among four bowls.
2.	Top zucchini and cucumber noodles with artichokes, tomato, bell pepper, hemp hearts, onion, parsley, and mint and then set aside until required.
3.	Prepare the dressing and for this, take a small bowl, add all the ingredients for the dressing in it and whisk until combined.
4.	Add the prepared dressing evenly into each bowl, then toss until the vegetables are well coated with the dressing and serve.
Nutrition: 250 Cal 14 g Fat 3 g Saturated Fat 19 g Carbohydrates 5 g Fiber 9 g Sugars 13 g Protein;

Roasted Vegetables and Quinoa Bowls

Preparation Time: 10 minutes
Cooking Time: 20 minutes
Servings: 4
Ingredients:
- 3 cups cooked quinoa

For the Broccoli:
- 2 teaspoons minced garlic
- 4 cups broccoli florets
- ½ teaspoon salt
- ¼ teaspoon ground black pepper
- 4 teaspoons olive oil

For the Chickpeas:
- 4 teaspoons sriracha
- 3 cups cooked chickpeas
- 2 teaspoons olive oil
- 4 teaspoons soy sauce

For the Roasted Sweet Potatoes:
- 2 teaspoons curry powder
- 2 small sweet potatoes, peeled, ¼-inch thick sliced
- 1/8 teaspoon salt
- 2 teaspoons sriracha
- 2 teaspoons olive oil

For the Chili-Lime Kale:
- 1/2 of a lime, juiced
- 4 cups chopped kale
- 1/8 teaspoon salt
- 1/8 teaspoon ground black pepper
- 1 teaspoon red chili powder
- 2 teaspoons olive oil

Directions:
1. Switch on the oven, then set it to 400 degrees F and let it preheat.
2. Prepare broccoli florets and for this, take a large bowl, place all of its ingredients in it, toss until well coated, then take a baking sheet lined with parchment paper and spread florets in a one-third portion of the sheet in a row.
3. Add chickpeas into the bowl, add its remaining ingredients, toss until well mixed and spread them onto the baking sheet next to the broccoli florets.
4. Add sweet potatoes into the bowl, add its remaining ingredients, toss until well mixed and spread them onto the baking sheet next to the chickpeas.
5. Place the baking sheet containing vegetables and chickpeas into the oven and then bake for 20 minutes until vegetables have turned tender and chickpeas are slightly crispy, turning halfway.
6. Meanwhile, prepare the kale and for this, take a large skillet pan, place it over medium heat, add 1 teaspoon oil and when hot, add kale and cook for 5 minutes until tender.
7. Then season kale with salt, black pepper, and red chili powder, toss until mixed and continue cooking for 3 minutes, set aside until required.
8. Assemble the bowl and for this, distribute quinoa evenly among four bowls, top evenly with broccoli, chickpeas, sweet potatoes, and kale and then serve.

Nutrition: 415 Cal 17 g Fat 2 g Saturated Fat 54 g Carbohydrates 8 g Fiber 5 g Sugars 16 g Protein;

Sweet Potato and Quinoa Bowl

Preparation Time: 5 minutes
Cooking Time: 20 minutes
Servings: 4
Ingredients:
- 2 cups quinoa
- 1 cup diced red onion
- 2 cups diced sweet potato
- 1 1/2 cup raisins
- 1 cup sunflower seeds, shelled, unsalted
- 2 cups vegetable broth

Directions:
1. Take a medium pot, place it over high heat, add quinoa, and sweet potatoes, pour in vegetable broth, stir until mixed and bring it to a boil.
2. Then switch heat to medium-low level, cover pot with the lid, and cook for 20 minutes until the quinoa has cooked.
3. When done, remove the pot from heat and fluff quinoa by using a fork.

4. Add onion, raisins, and sunflower seeds, stir until mixed and transfer into a large bowl.
5. Let it chill in the refrigerator for 30 minutes and then serve.

Nutrition: 204 Cal 7 g Fat 3 g Saturated Fat 31 g Carbohydrates 3 g Fiber 11 g Sugars 3 g Protein;

Chickpea Salad Bites

Preparation Time: 15 minutes
Cooking Time: 0 minutes
Servings: 4
Ingredients:
For the Bread:
- 2 tablespoons chopped parsley
- 1 small green chili pepper
- 1/3 cup of raisins
- 1 teaspoon garlic powder
- ½ teaspoon salt
- 1/3 teaspoon ground black pepper
- ½ teaspoon smoked paprika
- ½ tablespoon maple syrup
- ½ teaspoon cayenne pepper
- 2 tablespoons balsamic vinegar
- 1 1/2 cups crumbled rye bread, whole-grain

For the Salad:
- 2 scallions, chopped
- 1/3 cup chopped pickles
- 2 tablespoons chopped chives and more for topping
- ½ teaspoon minced garlic
- 1 ½ cup cooked chickpeas
- 1 lemon, juiced
- ½ teaspoon salt
- ¼ teaspoon ground black pepper
- 1 tablespoons poppy seeds
- 1 teaspoon mustard paste
- 1/3 cup coconut yogurt

Directions:
1. Prepare the bread, and for this, place all of its ingredients in a food processor and then pulse for 1 minute until just combined; don't overmix.
2. Then make bites of the bread mixture and for this, take a 2.3-inch round cookie cutter, add 2 tablespoons of the bread mixture, press it into the cutter, and gently lift it out, repeat with the remaining batter to make seven more bites.
3. Prepare the salad and for this, take a large bowl, add chickpeas in it, then add chives, scallion, pickles, and garlic and then mash chickpeas by using a fork until broken.
4. Add remaining ingredients for the salad and stir until well mixed.
5. Assemble the bites and for this, top each prepared bread bite generously with prepared salad, sprinkle with chives and poppy seeds, and then serve.

Nutrition: 210 Cal 4 g Fat 1 g Saturated Fat 36 g Carbohydrates 6 g Fiber 4 g Sugars 7 g Protein;

Avocado and Chickpeas Lettuce Cups

Preparation Time: 10 minutes
Cooking Time: 0 minutes
Servings: 4

Ingredients:
- 2 small avocados, peeled, pitted, diced
- 8 ounces hearts of palm
- ¾ cup cooked chickpeas
- 1/2 cup cucumber, diced
- 1 tablespoon minced shallots
- 2 cups mixed greens
- 1 tablespoon Dijon mustard
- 1 lime, zested, juiced
- 2 tablespoons chopped cilantro and more for topping
- 2/3 teaspoon salt
- 1/3 teaspoon ground black pepper
- 1 tablespoon apple cider vinegar
- 2 ½ tablespoons olive oil

Directions:
1. Take a medium bowl, add shallots and cilantro in it, stir in salt, black pepper, mustard, vinegar, lime juice, and zest until just mixed and then slowly mix in olive oil until combined.
2. Add cucumber, hearts of palm and chickpeas, stir until mixed, fold in avocado and then top with some more cilantro.
3. Distribute mixed greens among four plates, top with chickpea mixture and then serve.
Nutrition: 280 Cal 12.6 g Fat 1.5 g Saturated Fat 32.8 g Carbohydrates 9.3 g Fiber 1.2 g Sugars 7.6 g Protein;

Pesto Quinoa with White Beans

Preparation Time: 5 minutes
Cooking Time: 15 minutes
Servings: 4
Ingredients:
- 12 ounces cooked white bean
- 3 ½ cups quinoa, cooked
- 1 medium zucchini, sliced
- ¾ cup sun-dried tomato
- ¼ cup pine nuts
- 1 tablespoon olive oil

For the Pesto:
- 1/3 cup walnuts
- 2 cups arugula
- 1 teaspoon minced garlic
- 2 cups basil
- ¾ teaspoon salt
- ¼ teaspoon ground black pepper
- 1 tablespoon lemon juice
- 1/3 cup olive oil
- 2 tablespoons water

Directions:
1. Prepare the pesto, and for this, place all of its ingredients in a food processor and pulse for 2 minutes until smooth, scraping the sides of the container frequently and set aside until required.
2. Take a large skillet pan, place it over medium heat, add oil and when hot, add zucchini and cook for 4 minutes until tender-crisp.
3. Season zucchini with salt and black pepper, cook for 2 minutes until lightly brown, then add tomatoes and white beans and continue cooking for 4 minutes until white beans begin to crisp.

4. Stir in pine nuts, cook for 2 minutes until toasted, then remove the pan from heat and transfer zucchini mixture into a medium bowl.
5. Add quinoa and pesto, stir until well combined, then distribute among four bowls and then serve.
Nutrition: 352 Cal 27.3 g Fat 5 g Saturated Fat 33.7 g Carbohydrates 5.7 g Fiber 4.5 g Sugars 9.7 g Protein;

Green Bean Casserole

Preparation Time: 5 minutes
Cooking Time: 40 minutes
Servings: 4
Ingredients:
- 6 ounces fried onions
- 1 ½ cups cremini mushrooms, diced
- 16 ounces frozen green beans
- ½ cup diced white onion
- 1 tablespoon minced garlic
- 3 ½ tablespoons all-purpose flour
- 1/3 teaspoon ground black pepper
- ½ teaspoon dried oregano
- 3 ½ tablespoons olive oil
- 2 cups vegetable broth, hot

Directions:
1. Switch on the oven, then set it to 400 degrees F and let it preheat.
2. Take a medium saucepan, place it over medium heat, add oil and when hot, add onion and mushrooms, stir in garlic and cook for 4 minutes until tender.
3. Stir in flour until the thick paste comes together and then cook for 2 minutes until golden.
4. Stir in vegetable broth, bring it to a simmer, then stir in black pepper and oregano, whisk well and cook for 15 minutes until gravy thickened to the desired level.
5. Add green beans, stir until mixed, remove the pan from heat, top beans with fried onions and bake for 15 minutes.
6. Serve straight away.
Nutrition: 191 Cal 10 g Fat 2 g Saturated Fat 22 g Carbohydrates 3.3 g Fiber 2.5 g Sugars 4.1 g Protein;

Pumpkin Risotto

Preparation Time: 5 minutes
Cooking Time: 20 minutes
Servings: 4
Ingredients:
- 1 cup Arborio rice
- ½ cup cooked and chopped pumpkin
- 1/2 cup mushrooms
- 1 rib of celery, diced
- ½ of a medium white onion, peeled, diced
- ½ teaspoon minced garlic
- ½ teaspoon salt
- 1/3 teaspoon ground black pepper
- 1 tablespoon olive oil
- ½ tablespoon coconut butter
- 1 cup pumpkin puree
- 2 cups vegetable stock

Directions:

1.   Take a medium saucepan, place it over medium heat, add oil and when hot, add onion and celery, stir in garlic and cook for 3 minutes until onions begin to soften.
2.   Add mushrooms, season with salt and black pepper and cook for 5 minutes.
3.   Add rice, pour in pumpkin puree, then gradually pour in the stock until rice soaked up all the liquid and have turned soft.
4.   Add butter, remove the pan from heat, stir until creamy mixture comes together, and then serve.
Nutrition: 218.5 Cal 5.2 g Fat 1.5 g Saturated Fat 32.3 g Carbohydrates 1.3 g Fiber 3.8 g Sugars 6.3 g Protein;

Brown Rice and Vegetable Stir-Fry

Preparation Time: 5 minutes
Cooking Time: 50 minutes
Servings: 4
Ingredients:
- 16-ounce tofu, extra-firm, pressed, drained, cut into ½-inch cubes
- 1 cup of brown rice
- 1 cup frozen broccoli florets
- 1 medium red bell pepper, cored, diced
- 1 small white onion, peeled, diced
- 1 tablespoon minced garlic
- ½ teaspoon salt
- 1/3 teaspoon ground black pepper
- 1 tablespoon olive oil
- 2 cups vegetable broth

Directions:
1.   Take a medium pot, place it over high heat, add brown rice, pour in vegetable broth, and bring it to a boil.
2.   Switch heat to medium-low level, cover the pot with the lid and cook for 40 minutes, and when done, remove the pot and set aside until required.
3.   Then take a large skillet pan, place it over medium-high heat, add oil and when hot, add tofu pieces, onion, broccoli, and bell pepper, season with salt and black pepper and cook for 5 minutes until sauté.
4.   Add cooked rice, stir until mixed and continue cooking for 5 minutes.
5.   Serve straight away.
Nutrition: 281.9 Cal 11.7 g Fat 1.7 g Saturated Fat 31.1 g Carbohydrates 9.7 g Fiber 2.1 g Sugars 20.1 g Protein;

Tomato Basil Spaghetti

Preparation Time: 5 minutes
Cooking Time: 20 minutes
Servings: 4
Ingredients:
- 15-ounce cooked great northern beans
- 10.5-ounces cherry tomatoes, halved
- 1 small white onion, peeled, diced
- 1 tablespoon minced garlic
- 8 basil leaves, chopped
- 2 tablespoons olive oil
- 1-pound spaghetti

Directions:

1.   Take a large pot half full with salty water, place it over medium-high heat, bring it to a boil, add spaghetti and cook for 10 to 12 minutes until tender.
2.   Then drain spaghetti into a colander and reserve 1 cup of pasta liquid.
3.   Take a large skillet pan, place it over medium-high heat, add oil and when hot, add onion, tomatoes, basil, and garlic and cook for 5 minutes until vegetables have turned tender.
4.   Add cooked spaghetti and beans, pour in pasta water, stir until just mixed and cook for 2 minutes until hot.
5.   Serve straight away.
Nutrition: 147 Cal 5 g Fat 0.7 g Saturated Fat 21.2 g Carbohydrates 1.5 g Fiber 5.4 g Sugars 3.8 g Protein;

Jamaican Jerk Tofu Wrap

Preparation Time: 1 hour and 15 minutes
Cooking Time: 16 minutes
Servings: 4
Ingredients:
- 28 ounces tofu, firmed, pressed, drain, ½-inch long sliced

For the Marinade:
- 2 small scotch bonnet pepper, deseeded, minced
- 2 teaspoons minced garlic
- 2 1/2 teaspoons sea salt
- 4 teaspoons allspice
- 2 teaspoon ground black pepper
- 4 teaspoons cinnamon
- 4 teaspoons maple syrup
- 4 teaspoons nutmeg
- 4 tablespoons apple cider vinegar
- 2 teaspoon avocado oil and more for cooking
- ½ cup of soy sauce
- 2 tablespoon tomato paste

For the Wrap:
- 4 cups baby spinach leaves
- 2 small tomato, deseeded, diced
- 2 medium yellow bell pepper, deseeded, cut into strips
- 4 tablespoons Sriracha sauce
- 4 tortillas, whole-grain

Directions:
1.   Take a large bowl, place all the ingredients for the marinade in it, whisk until combined, then add tofu pieces, toss until well coated, and let it marinate for a minimum of 1 hour, turning halfway.
2.   Then take a large skillet pan, place it over medium-high heat, add some of the avocado oil, and when hot, add tofu pieces in a single layer and cook for 8 minutes per side until caramelized.
3.   Assemble the wrap and for this, place a tortilla on clean working space, top with 1 cup of spinach, half of each diced tomatoes and pepper strips, then top with 4 strips of tofu, drizzle with Sriracha sauce and wrap tightly.
4.   Repeat with the remaining tortilla, then cut each tortilla in half and serve.
Nutrition: 250 Cal 6 g Fat 1 g Saturated Fat 40 g Carbohydrates 7 g Fiber 11 g Sugars 9 g Protein;

Bean and Rice Burritos

Preparation Time: 10 minutes
Cooking Time: 20 minutes
Servings: 6
Ingredients:

- 32 ounces refried beans
- 2 cups cooked rice
- 2 cups chopped spinach
- 1 tablespoon olive oil
- 1/2 cup tomato salsa
- 6 tortillas, whole-grain, warm
- Guacamole as needed for serving

Directions:
1. Switch on the oven, then set it to 375 degrees F and let it preheat.
2. Take a medium saucepan, place it over medium heat, add beans, and cook for 3 to 5 minutes until softened, remove the pan from heat.
3. Place one tortilla on clean working space, spread some of the beans on it into a log, leaving 2-inches of the edge, top beans with spinach, rice and salsa, and then tightly wrap the tortilla to seal the filling like a burrito.
4. Repeat with the remaining tortillas, place these burritos on a baking sheet, brush them with olive oil and then bake for 15 minutes until golden.
5. Serve burritos with guacamole.
Nutrition: 421 Cal 9 g Fat 2 g Saturated Fat 70 g Carbohydrates 11 g Fiber 3 g Sugars 15 g Protein;

Chickpea Curry Soup

Preparation Time: 5 minutes
Cooking Time: 12 minutes
Servings: 4
Ingredients:

- 2 cups cooked chickpeas
- 1/4 of a medium white onion, peeled, chopped
- 1 tablespoon minced garlic
- 1 teaspoon ground coriander
- ¼ teaspoon cayenne pepper
- 1 tablespoon yellow curry powder
- 1 teaspoon turmeric
- ½ of a lime, juiced
- 1 tablespoon olive oil
- 2/3 cup coconut cream
- 2 cups vegetable broth
- 2 tablespoons pumpkin seeds

Directions:
1. Take a medium saucepan, place it over medium-high heat, add oil and when hot, add onion and garlic and cook for 1 minute until fragrant.
2. Add chickpeas, sprinkle with all the spices, stir until mixed and continue cooking for 5 minutes.
3. Pour in vegetable broth, simmer for 5 minutes, then stir in cream, lime juice and remove the pan from heat.
4. Ladle soup into bowls, top with pumpkin seeds, and then serve.
Nutrition: 154 Cal 8 g Fat 1 g Saturated Fat 16.5 g Carbohydrates 4 g Fiber 3 g Sugars 4.5 g Protein;

Roasted Green Beans

Preparation Time: 5 minutes
Cooking Time: 25 minutes
Servings: 2
Ingredients:

- ½ pound green beans
- ½ cup grated parmesan cheese
- 3 tablespoons coconut oil
- ½ teaspoon garlic powder

Extra:

- 1/3 teaspoon salt
- 1/8 teaspoon ground black pepper

Directions:
1. Switch on the oven, then set it to 425 degrees F, and let preheat.
2. Take a baking sheet, line green beans on it, and set aside until required.
3. Prepare the dressing, and for this, place remaining ingredients in a bowl, except for cheese and whisk until combined.
4. Drizzle the dressing over green beans, toss until well coated, and then bake for 20 minutes until green beans are tender-crisp.
5. Then sprinkle cheese on top of beans and continue roasting for 3 to 5 minutes or until cheese melts and nicely golden brown.
6. Serve straight away.
Nutrition: calories 119 fat 5 carbs 3 protein 8

Vegan Alfredo Fettuccine Pasta

Preparation Time: 15 minutes
Cooking Time: 15 minutes
Servings: 1
Ingredients:

- White potatoes - 2 medium
- White onion - ¼
- Italian seasoning - 1 tablespoon
- Lemon juice - 1 teaspoon
- Garlic - 2 cloves
- Salt - 1 teaspoon
- Fettuccine pasta - 12 ounces
- Raw cashew - ½ cup
- Nutritional yeast (optional) - 1 teaspoon
- Truffle oil (optional) - ¼ teaspoon

Directions:
1. Start by placing a pot on high flame and boiling 4 cups of water.
2. Peel the potatoes and cut them into small cubes. Cut the onion into cubes as well.
3. Add the potatoes and onions to the boiling water and cook for about 10 minutes.
4. Remove the onions and potatoes. Keep aside. Save the water.
5. Take another pot and fill it with water. Season generously with salt.
6. Toss in the fettuccine pasta and cook as per package instructions.
7. Take a blender and add in the raw cashews, veggies, nutritional yeast, truffle oil, lemon juice, and 1 cup of the saved water. Blend into a smooth puree.
8. Add in the garlic and salt.

9.	Drain the cooked pasta using a colander. Transfer into a mixing bowl.
10.	Pour the prepared sauce on top of the cooked fettuccine pasta. Serve.
Nutrition: calories 884 fat 13 carbs 15 protein 6

Spinach Pasta in Pesto Sauce

Preparation Time: 20 minutes
Cooking Time: 15 minutes
Servings: 1
Ingredients:
- Olive oil - 1 tablespoon
- Spinach - 5 ounces
- All-purpose flour - 2 cups
- Salt - 1 tablespoon plus ¼ teaspoon (keep it divided)
- Water - 2 tablespoons
- Roasted vegetable for serving
- Pesto for serving
- Fresh basil for serving

Directions:
1.	Take a large pot and fill it with water. Place it over a high flame and bring the water to a boil. Add one tablespoon of salt
2.	While the water is boiling, place a large saucepan over medium flame. Pour in the olive oil and heat it through.
3.	Once the oil starts to shimmer, toss in the spinach and sauté for 5 minutes.
4.	Take a food processor and transfer the wilted spinach. Process until the spinach is fine in texture.
5.	Add in the flour bit by bit and continue to process to form a crumbly dough.
6.	Further, add ¼ teaspoon of salt and 1 tbsp of water while processing to bring the dough together. Add the remaining 1 tbsp of water if required.
7.	Remove the dough onto a flat surface and sprinkle with flour. Knead well to form a dough ball.
8.	Use a rolling pin to roll out the dough. The dimensions of the rolled dough should be 18 inches long and 12 inches wide. The thickness should be about ¼ - inch thick.
9.	Cut the rolled dough into long and even strips using a pizza cutter. Make sure the strips are ½ - inch wide.
10.	The strips need to be rolled into evenly sized thick noodles.
11.	Toss in the prepared noodles and cook for about 4 minutes. Drain using a colander.
12.	Transfer the noodles into a large mixing bowl and add in the roasted vegetables, pesto. Toss well to combine.
13.	Garnish with basil leaves.
Nutrition: calories 591 fat 8 carbs 42 protein 16

Creamy Curry Noodles

Preparation Time: 19 minutes
Cooking Time: 10 minutes
Servings: 4
Ingredients:
Creamy Curry Sauce
- Apple cider vinegar, two tablespoons
- Water, one-quarter of one cup
- Avocado oil, two tablespoons
- Turmeric, ground, one teaspoon
- Black pepper, one half teaspoon
- Tahini, one-quarter of one cup
- Coriander, ground, one- and one-half teaspoons
- Cumin, ground, one teaspoon
- Salt, one teaspoon
- Curry powder, two teaspoons
- Ginger, ground, one quarter teaspoon

Noodle Bowl
- Cilantro, fresh, chopped small, one half cup
- Bell pepper, red, one cleaned and diced
- Zucchini noodles, one sixteen-ounce pack
- Carrots, two, peeled and cut in julienne strips
- Kale, two cups packed
- Cauliflower, one half of one head chopped small

Directions:
1.	Cover the zucchini noodles with two cups of boiling water in a medium-sized bowl and set them off to the side. After leaving the noodles in the water for five minutes, drain off the water and place the noodles back into the bowl. Prep all of the veggies and then toss them into the bowl with the noodles. Toss the ingredients in the bowl gently, but well.
2.	Divide the leaves of kale onto four serving plates. Mix the list of ingredients for the Creamy Curry Sauce and blend them until they are smooth and creamy. When the sauce is well mixed, then pour it over the ingredients in the bowl and toss the ingredients well until all are covered with the sauce.
3.	Then divide the noodles over the kale on the four plates and serve.
Nutrition: calories 192 fat 15 carbs 5 protein 8

Roasted Vegetables

Preparation Time: 10 minutes
Cooking Time: 20 minutes
Servings: 4
Ingredients:
- Cilantro, chopped, one-quarter of one cup
- Green onion, diced, one half of one cup

Masala Seasoning
- Black pepper, one half teaspoon
- Turmeric, one quarter teaspoon
- Chili powder, ground, one half teaspoon
- Tomato puree, one half of one cup
- Garam masala, one quarter teaspoon
- Salt, one half teaspoon
- Garlic, minced, one tablespoon
- Olive oil, two tablespoons
- Ginger, ground, two teaspoons

Veggies
- Cauliflower, one cup in small pieces
- Mushrooms, sliced one half of one cup
- Green beans, three-fourths of one cup

Directions:

1.   Heat the oven to 400. Place the rack in the oven in the middle. Use aluminum foil or parchment paper to completely cover a baking sheet. Chop the veggies if they are not already chopped. Use a medium-sized bowl to mix the chili powder, ginger, garam masala, garlic, pepper, salt, and the tomato puree, making sure the ingredients are all mixed well.
2.   Then mix in the olive oil. Place the chopped veggies into this mixture and mix them in well. Then place the coated veggies onto the covered baking sheet in one single layer.
3.   Roast the veggies in the heated oven for thirty to forty minutes or until the veggies are cooked in a manner in which you like them.
Nutrition: calories 105 fat 10 carbs 13 protein 3

Green Pea Fritter

Preparation Time: 10 minutes
Cooking Time: 20 minutes
Servings: 10
Ingredients:
- Frozen peas, two cups
- Olive oil, one tablespoon + one tablespoon
- Onion, one diced
- Garlic, three tablespoons
- Chickpea four, one- and one-half cups
- Baking soda, one teaspoon
- Salt, one quarter teaspoon
- Rosemary, one teaspoon
- Thyme, one half teaspoon
- Marjoram, one teaspoon
- Lemon juice, two tablespoons

Directions:
1.   Heat the oven to 350. Use spray oil to spray a baking sheet. Boil the peas for five minutes.
2.   Pour one tablespoon of olive oil in a skillet and fry the garlic and onion for five minutes.
3.   Pour the garlic and onion with the olive oil in a bowl and add the cooked peas, mashing them until they make a thick paste. Blend in the marjoram, thyme, rosemary, salt, baking soda, and chickpea flour.
4.   Dampen your hands and form the mash into ten equal-sized patties. Brush the patties with the other tablespoon of olive oil.
5.   Bake them for eighteen minutes in the oven, turning them over after nine minutes.
Nutrition: calories 224 fat 3 carbs 14 protein 6

Roasted Mushrooms and Shallots

Preparation Time: 10 minutes
Cooking Time: 20 minutes
Servings: 4
Ingredients:
- Mushrooms, fresh, one-pound cut into bite-size pieces
- Shallots, two cups sliced thick
- Olive oil, two tablespoons
- Thyme, dried, one teaspoon
- Salt, one quarter teaspoon
- Black pepper, one quarter teaspoon
- Red wine vinegar, one third cup

Directions:

1.   Heat your oven to 450.
2.   Place the shallots and mushrooms in a large bowl and add in the salt, pepper, thyme, and olive oil and toss the ingredients together to thoroughly coat the shallots and mushrooms.
3.   Roast the veggies on a baking sheet for fifteen minutes. Pour the red wine vinegar over the veggies and bake for five more minutes.
Nutrition: calories 178 fat 7 carbs 23 protein 5

Garlic Chili Roasted Kohlrabi

Preparation Time: 5 minutes
Cooking Time: 12 minutes
Servings: 1
Ingredients:
- Olive oil, two tablespoons
- Garlic, minced, one tablespoon
- Chili pepper, one teaspoon
- Salt, one quarter teaspoon
- Kohlrabi, one and one-half pounds, peel and cut into one half inch wedges
- Cilantro, fresh, chopped, two tablespoons

Directions:
1.   Heat your oven to 450. Mix in a large bowl, the pepper, salt, chili pepper, garlic, and olive oil. Put in the kohlrabi and toss well to coat the kohlrabi.
2.   Bake the coated kohlrabi for twenty minutes, stirring it around when you are about halfway done with cooking. Sprinkle on the cilantro and serve.
Nutrition: calories 185 fat 5 carbs 7 protein 3

Vegetarian Nachos

Preparation Time: 15 minutes
Cooking Time: 0 minutes
Servings: 6
Ingredients:
- Pita chips, whole wheat, three cups
- Nutritional yeast, one half cup
- Oregano, dried, one tablespoon minced
- Romaine lettuce, one cup chopped
- Grape tomatoes, one-half cup cut in quarters
- Olive oil, two tablespoons
- Lemon juice, one tablespoon
- Hummus, one-third cup prepared
- Black pepper, one half teaspoon
- Red onion, two tablespoons minced
- Tofu, one-half cup cut into small crumbles
- Black olives, two tablespoons chopped

Directions:
1.   Mix the hummus, pepper, olive oil, and lemon juice in a mixing bowl. Spread a layer of the pita chips on a serving platter.
2.   Drizzle three-fourths of the hummus mix over the pita chips. Use the lettuce, red onion, tomatoes, and olives to garnish the hummus.
3.   Make a small mound of the leftover hummus in the middle of the chips, then garnish all with the oregano and the nutritional yeast.
Nutrition: calories 159 fat 10 carbs 13 protein 4

VEGAN Macaroni and Cheese

Preparation Time: 15 minutes
Cooking Time: 20 minutes
Servings: 4
Ingredients:
- Elbow macaroni, whole grain, eight ounces, cooked
- Nutritional yeast, one quarter cup
- Garlic, minced, two tablespoons
- Apple cider vinegar, two teaspoons
- Broccoli, one head with florets cut into bite-sized pieces
- Water, one cup (more if needed)
- Garlic powder, one half teaspoon
- Avocado oil, two tablespoons
- Red pepper, flakes, one eighth teaspoon
- Onion, yellow, chopped, one cup
- Salt, one half teaspoon
- Russet potato, peeled and grated, one cup (about two small potatoes)
- Dry mustard powder, one half teaspoon
- Onion powder, one half teaspoon

Directions:
1. Cook the broccoli for five minutes in boiling water. Add the cooked broccoli to the cooked pasta in a large mixing bowl.
2. Cook the onion in the avocado oil for five minutes, then stir in the red pepper flakes, garlic, salt, mustard powder, garlic powder, grated potato, and onion powder. Cook this for three minutes and then pour in the water and mix well. Cook this for eight to ten minutes or until the potatoes are soft.
3. Pour all of this mixture carefully into a blender and add in the nutritional yeast and the vinegar and then blend. When this is creamy and smooth, then pour it into the mixing bowl and mix well with the broccoli and pasta.
Nutrition: calories 506 fat 22 carbs 67 protein 18

Cilantro Lime Coleslaw

Preparation Time: 5 minutes
Cooking Time: 0 minutes
Servings: 5
Ingredients:
- Avocados, two
- Garlic, minced, one tablespoon
- Coleslaw, ready-made in a bag, fourteen ounces
- Cilantro, fresh leaves, one-quarter cup minced
- Salt, one half teaspoon
- Lime juice, two tablespoons
- Water, one quarter cup

Directions:
1. Except for the slaw mix, put all of the ingredients that are listed into a blender. Blend these ingredients well until they are creamy and smooth.
2. Mix the coleslaw mix in with this dressing and then toss it gently to mix it well.
3. Keep the mixed coleslaw in the refrigerator until you are ready to serve.
Nutrition: calories 119 fat 3 carbs 3 protein 3

Delicious Broccoli

Preparation Time: 15 minutes
Cooking Time: 15 minutes
Servings: 8
Ingredients:
- 2 oranges, sliced in half
- 1 lb. broccoli rabe
- 2 tablespoons sesame oil, toasted
- Salt and pepper to taste
- 1 tablespoon sesame seeds, toasted

Directions:
1. Pour the oil into a pan over medium heat.
2. Add the oranges and cook until caramelized.
3. Transfer to a plate.
4. Put the broccoli in the pan and cook for 8 minutes.
5. Squeeze the oranges to release juice in a bowl.
6. Stir in the oil, salt, and pepper.
7. Coat the broccoli rabe with the mixture.
8. Sprinkle seeds on top.
Nutrition: calories 432 fat 1 carbs 24 protein 12

Spicy Peanut Soba Noodles

Preparation Time: 7 minutes
Cooking Time: 17 minutes
Servings: 1
Ingredients:
- 5 ounces uncooked soba noodles
- ½ tablespoon low sodium soy sauce
- 1 clove garlic, minced
- 4 teaspoons water
- 1 small head broccoli, cut into florets
- ½ cup carrot
- ¼ cup finely chopped scallions
- 3 tablespoons peanut butter
- 1 tablespoon honey
- 1 teaspoon crushed red pepper flakes
- 2 teaspoons vegetable oil
- 4 ounces button mushrooms, discard stems
- 3 tablespoons peanuts, dry roasted, unsalted

Directions:
1. Cook soba noodles following the directions on the package.
2. Add peanut butter, honey, water, soy sauce, garlic, and red pepper flakes. Whisk until well combined.
3. Place a skillet over medium heat. Add oil. When the oil is heated, add broccoli and sauté for a few minutes until crisp as well as tender.
4. Add mushrooms and sauté until the mushrooms are tender. Turn off the heat.
5. Add the sauce mixture and carrots and mix well.
6. Crush the peanuts by rolling with a rolling pin.
7. Divide the noodles into bowls. Pour sauce mixture over it. Sprinkle scallions and peanuts on top and serve.
Nutrition: calories 512 fat 11 carbs 20 protein 8

Grilled AHLT

Total time: 15 minutes

Ingredients

- ¼ cup Classic Hummus
- 2 slices whole-grain bread
- ¼ avocado, sliced
- ½ cup lettuce, chopped
- ½ tomato, sliced
- Pinch sea salt
- Pinch freshly ground black pepper
- 1 teaspoon olive oil, divided

Directions

1. Spread some hummus on each slice of bread. Then layer the avocado, lettuce, and tomato on one slice, sprinkle with salt and pepper, and top with the other slice.
2. Heat a skillet to medium heat, and drizzle ½ teaspoon of the olive oil just before putting the sandwich in the skillet. Cook for 3 to 5 minutes, then lift the sandwich with a spatula, drizzle the remaining ½ teaspoon olive oil into the skillet, and flip the sandwich to grill the other side for 3 to 5 minutes. Press it down with the spatula to seal the vegetables inside.
3. Once done, remove from the skillet and slice in half to serve.

Loaded Black Bean Pizza

Total time: 30 minutes

Ingredients

- 2 prebaked pizza crusts
- ½ cup Spicy Black Bean Dip
- 1 tomato, thinly sliced
- Pinch freshly ground black pepper
- 1 carrot, grated
- Pinch sea salt
- 1 red onion, thinly sliced
- 1 avocado, sliced

Directions

1. Preheat the oven to 400°F.
2. Lay the two crusts out on a large baking sheet. Spread half the Spicy Black Bean Dip on each pizza crust. Then layer on the tomato slices with a pinch pepper if you like.
3. Sprinkle the grated carrot with the sea salt and lightly massage it in with your hands. Spread the carrot on top of the tomato, then add the onion.
4. Pop the pizzas in the oven for 10 to 20 minutes, or until they're done to your taste.
5. Top the cooked pizzas with sliced avocado and another sprinkle of pepper.
6. Options: Try having this as a fresh unbaked pizza. Just toast a pita or bake the crust before loading it up, and perhaps use scallions instead of red. Bonus points—and flavor—if you top it with fresh alfalfa sprouts.

Falafel Wrap

Total time: 70 minutes

Ingredients

For the Falafel Patties

- 1 (14-ounce) can chickpeas, drained and rinsed, or 1½ cups cooked
- 1 zucchini, grated
- 2 scallions, minced
- ¼ cup fresh parsley, chopped
- 2 tablespoons black olives, pitted and chopped (optional)
- 1 tablespoon tahini, or almond, cashew, or sunflower seed butter
- 1 tablespoon lemon juice, or apple cider vinegar
- ½ teaspoon ground cumin
- ¼ teaspoon paprika
- ¼ teaspoon sea salt
- 1 teaspoon olive oil (optional, if frying)

FOR THE WRAP

- 1 whole-grain wrap or pita
- ¼ cup Classic Hummus
- ½ cup fresh greens
- 1 baked falafel patty
- ¼ cup cherry tomatoes, halved
- ¼ cup diced cucumber
- ¼ cup chopped avocado, or Guacamole
- ¼ cup cooked quinoa, or Tabbouleh Salad (optional)

Directions

For the Falafel

1. Use a food processor to pulse the chickpeas, zucchini, scallions, parsley, and olives (if using) until roughly chopped. Just pulse—don't purée. Or use a potato masher to mash the chickpeas in a large bowl and stir in the grated and chopped veggies.
2. In a small bowl, whisk together the tahini and lemon juice, and stir in the cumin, paprika, and salt. Pour this into the chickpea mixture, and stir well (or pulse the food processor) to combine. Taste and add more salt, if needed. Using your hands, form the mix into 6 patties.
3. You can either panfry or bake the patties. To panfry, heat a large skillet to medium, add 1 teaspoon of olive oil, and cook the patties about 10 minutes on the first side. Flip, and cook another 5 to 7 minutes. To bake them, put them on a baking sheet lined with parchment paper and bake at 350°F for 30 to 40 minutes.

Directions for the wrap

1. Lay the wrap on a plate and spread the hummus down the center. Then lay on the greens and crumble the falafel patty on top. Add the tomatoes, cucumber, avocado, and quinoa.
2. Fold in both ends, and wrap up as tightly as you can. If you have a sandwich press, you can press the wraps for about 5 minutes. This will travel best in a reusable lunch box, or reusable plastic lunch wrap.

Pad Thai Bowl

Total time: 20 minutes

Ingredients

- 7 ounces brown rice noodles
- 1 teaspoon olive oil, or 1 tablespoon vegetable broth or water
- 2 carrots, peeled or scrubbed, and julienned
- 1 cup thinly sliced napa cabbage, or red cabbage
- 1 red bell pepper, seeded and thinly sliced
- 2 scallions, finely chopped

- 2 to 3 tablespoons fresh mint, finely chopped
- 1 cup bean sprouts
- ¼ cup Peanut Sauce
- ¼ cup fresh cilantro, finely chopped
- 2 tablespoons roasted peanuts, chopped
- Fresh lime wedges

Directions
1. Put the rice noodles in a large bowl or pot, and cover with boiling water. Let sit until they soften, about 10 minutes. Rinse, drain, and set aside to cool.
2. Heat the oil in a large skillet to medium-high, and sauté the carrots, cabbage, and bell pepper until softened, 7 to 8 minutes. Toss in the scallions, mint, and bean sprouts and cook for just a minute or two, then remove from the heat.
3. Toss the noodles with the vegetables, and mix in the Peanut Sauce.
4. Transfer to bowls, and sprinkle with cilantro and peanuts. Serve with a lime wedge to squeeze onto the dish for a flavor boost.
5. Options: To enjoy an even more nutrient-dense version of this bowl, leave out the rice noodles and peel or spiralize a zucchini or carrot into long "noodles."

Curry Spiced Lentil Burgers

Total time: 80 minutes
Ingredients
- 1 cup lentils
- 2½ to 3 cups water
- 3 carrots, grated
- 1 small onion, diced
- ¾ cup whole-grain flour (see Options for gluten-free below)
- 1½ to 2 teaspoons curry powder
- ½ teaspoon sea salt
- Pinch freshly ground black pepper

Directions
1. Put the lentils in a medium pot with the water. Bring to a boil and then simmer for about 30 minutes, until soft.
2. While the lentils are cooking, put the carrots and onion in a large bowl. Toss them with the flour, curry powder, salt, and pepper.
3. When the lentils are cooked, drain off any excess water, then add them to the bowl with the veggies. Use a potato masher or a large spoon to mash them slightly, and add more flour if you need to get the mixture to stick together. The amount of flour depends on how much water the lentils absorbed, and on the texture of the flour, so use more or less until the mixture sticks when you form it into a ball. Scoop up ¼-cup portions and form into 12 patties.
4. You can either panfry or bake the burgers. To panfry, heat a large skillet to medium, add a tiny bit of oil, and cook the burgers about 10 minutes on the first side. Flip, and cook another 5 to 7 minutes. To bake them, put them on a baking sheet lined with parchment paper and bake at 350°F for 30 to 40 minutes.
5. Options: For the whole-grain flour, use whatever flour you like. Sorghum, rice, oat, buckwheat, and even almond meal would work and make these gluten-free. The flour in this recipe is just a binding agent, so it can be any type.

Black Bean Taco Salad Bowl

Total time: 20 minutes
Ingredients
For the Black Bean Salad
- 1 (14-ounce) can black beans, drained and rinsed, or 1½ cups cooked
- 1 cup corn kernels, fresh and blanched, or frozen and thawed
- ¼ cup fresh cilantro, or parsley, chopped
- Zest and juice of 1 lime
- 1 to 2 teaspoons chili powder
- Pinch sea salt
- 1½ cups cherry tomatoes, halved
- 1 red bell pepper, seeded and chopped
- 2 scallions, chopped
For 1 Serving of Tortilla Chips
- 1 large whole-grain tortilla or wrap
- 1 teaspoon olive oil
- Pinch sea salt
- Pinch freshly ground black pepper
- Pinch dried oregano
- Pinch chili powder
For 1 Bowl
- 1 cup fresh greens (lettuce, spinach, or whatever you like)
- ¾ cup cooked quinoa, or brown rice, millet, or other whole grain
- ¼ cup chopped avocado, or Guacamole
- ¼ cup Fresh Mango Salsa
- Directions for the black bean salad
- Toss all the ingredients together in a large bowl.

Directions
1. for the tortilla chips
2. Brush the tortilla with olive oil, then sprinkle with salt, pepper, oregano, chili powder, and any other seasonings you like. Slice it into eighths like a pizza. Transfer the tortilla pieces to a small baking sheet lined with parchment paper and put in the oven or toaster oven to toast or broil for 3 to 5 minutes, until browned. Keep an eye on them, as they can go from just barely done to burned very quickly.
Directions for the bowl
1. Lay the greens in the bowl, top with the cooked quinoa, ⅓ of the black bean salad, the avocado, and salsa.
2. Make ahead: The black bean mixture tastes better if you make it in advance, so the flavors have time to mix and mingle. Keep leftovers in the fridge in an airtight container.

Bibimbap Bowl

Total time: 30 minutes
Ingredients
- ½ cup cooked chickpeas
- 2 tablespoons tamari or soy sauce, divided
- 1 tablespoon plus 2 teaspoons toasted sesame oil, divided

- ¾ cup cooked brown rice, or quinoa, millet, or any other whole grain
- 1 teaspoon olive oil, or 1 tablespoon vegetable broth or water
- 1 carrot, scrubbed or peeled, and julienned
- 2 garlic cloves, minced, divided
- Pinch sea salt
- ½ cup asparagus, cut into 2-inch pieces
- ½ cup chopped spinach
- ½ cup bean sprouts
- 3 tablespoons hot pepper paste (the Korean version is gochujang)
- 1 tablespoon toasted sesame seeds
- 1 scallion, chopped

Directions

1. In a small bowl, toss the chickpeas with 1 tablespoon tamari and 1 teaspoon toasted sesame oil. Set aside to marinate.
2. Put the cooked brown rice in a large serving bowl, so that you'll be ready to add the vegetables as they cook.
3. Heat the olive oil a large skillet over medium heat, and start by sautéing the carrot and 1 garlic clove with the salt. Once they've softened, about 5 minutes, remove them from the skillet and put them on top of the rice in one area of the bowl.
4. Next, sauté the asparagus, adding a bit more oil if necessary, and when soft, about 5 minutes, place next to the carrots in the bowl.
5. Add a bit of water to the skillet and quick steam the spinach with the other garlic clove, just until the spinach wilts. Drizzle with the remaining 1 tablespoon tamari and 1 teaspoon toasted sesame oil. Lay the spinach on the other side of the carrots in the bowl.
6. You could lightly sauté the bean sprouts if you wish, but they're nice raw. However you prefer them, add them to the bowl.
7. 7.Place the marinated chickpeas in the final area of the bowl.
8. In a small bowl, mix together the hot pepper paste with 1 tablespoon sesame oil. Scoop that into the middle of the bowl. Sprinkle with sesame seeds and scallions, then mix it all together and enjoy!

Cashew-Ginger Soba Noodle Bowl

Total time: 25 minutes
Ingredients
For the Bowls
- 7 ounces soba noodles
- 1 carrot, peeled or scrubbed, and julienned
- 1 bell pepper, any color, seeded and thinly sliced
- 1 cup snow peas, or snap peas, trimmed and sliced in half
- 2 tablespoons chopped scallions
- 1 cup chopped kale, spinach, or lettuce
- 1 avocado, thinly sliced
- 2 tablespoons cashews, chopped
For the Dressing
- 1 tablespoon grated fresh ginger
- 2 tablespoons cashew butter, or almond or sunflower seed butter
- 2 tablespoons rice vinegar, or apple cider vinegar
- 2 tablespoons tamari, or soy sauce
- 1 teaspoon toasted sesame oil
- 2 to 3 tablespoons water (optional)

Directions

1. Boil a medium pot of water and add the noodles. Keep it at a low boil, turning down the heat and adding cool water if necessary to keep it just below a rolling boil. The soba will take 6 to 7 minutes to cook, and you can stir occasionally to make sure they don't stick to each other or the bottom of the pot. Once they're cooked, drain them in a colander and rinse with hot or cold water, depending on whether you want a hot or cold bowl.
2. You can have the vegetables raw, in which case you just need to cut them up. If you'd like to cook them, heat a skillet to medium-high, and sauté the carrot with a little water, broth, olive oil, or sesame oil. Once the carrot has softened slightly, add the bell pepper. Then add the peas and scallions, to warm for a minute, before turning off the heat.
3. Make the dressing by squeezing the grated ginger for its juice, then whisking together all the ingredients, or puréeing in a small blender, adding 2 to 3 tablespoons of water as needed to make a creamy consistency. Set aside.
4. Arrange your bowl, starting with a layer of chopped kale or spinach (for hot noodles) or lettuce (for cold noodles), then the noodles drizzled with some extra tamari, then the vegetables.
5. Top with the dressing, sliced avocado, and a sprinkle of chopped cashews.
6. Make ahead: Cooked and rinsed soba noodles keep well in the fridge, so make a whole package and keep them on hand for quick weeknight bowls or lunches to go.

Mediterranean Hummus Pizza

Total time: 40 minutes
Ingredients
- ½ zucchini, thinly sliced
- ½ red onion, thinly sliced
- 1 cup cherry tomatoes, halved
- 2 to 4 tablespoons pitted and chopped black olives
- Pinch sea salt
- Drizzle olive oil (optional)
- 2 prebaked pizza crusts
- ½ cup Classic Hummus, or Roasted Red Pepper Hummus
- 2 to 4 tablespoons Cheesy Sprinkle

Directions

1. Preheat the oven to 400°F.
2. Place the zucchini, onion, cherry tomatoes, and olives in a large bowl, sprinkle them with the sea salt, and toss them a bit. Drizzle with a bit of olive oil (if using), to seal in the flavor and keep them from drying out in the oven.

3.	Lay the two crusts out on a large baking sheet. Spread half the hummus on each crust, and top with the veggie mixture and some Cheesy Sprinkle.
4.	Pop the pizzas in the oven for 20 to 30 minutes, or until the veggies are soft.
5.	Make Ahead: For a shortcut, lightly sauté the veggies before putting them on the pizza, so you only have to bake it for a few minutes until warmed through. You could even use some leftover sautéed vegetables.

Maple Dijon Burgers

Total time: 50 minutes
Ingredients
- 1 red bell pepper
- 1 (19-ounce) can chickpeas, rinsed and drained, or 2 cups cooked
- 1 cup ground almonds
- 2 teaspoons Dijon mustard
- 2 teaspoons maple syrup
- 1 garlic clove, pressed
- Juice of ½ lemon
- 1 teaspoon dried oregano
- ½ teaspoon dried sage
- 1 cup spinach
- 1 to 1½ cups rolled oats

Directions
1.	Preheat the oven to 350°F. Line a large baking sheet with parchment paper.
2.	Cut the red pepper in half, remove the stem and seeds, and put on the baking sheet cut side up in the oven. Roast in the oven while you prep the other ingredients.
3.	Put the chickpeas in the food processor, along with the almonds, mustard, maple syrup, garlic, lemon juice, oregano, sage, and spinach. Pulse until things are thoroughly combined but not puréed. When the red pepper is softened a bit, about 10 minutes, add it to the processor along with the oats and pulse until they are chopped just enough to form patties.
4.	If you don't have a food processor, mash the chickpeas with a potato masher or fork, and make sure everything else is chopped up as finely as possible, then stir together.
5.	Scoop up ¼-cup portions and form into 12 patties, and lay them out on the baking sheet.
6.	Put the burgers in the oven and bake until the outside is lightly browned, about 30 minutes.

Cajun Burgers

Total time: 55 minutes
Ingredients
For the Dressing
- 1 tablespoon tahini
- 1 tablespoon apple cider vinegar
- 2 teaspoons Dijon mustard
- 1 to 2 tablespoons water
- 1 to 2 garlic cloves, pressed
- 1 teaspoon dried basil
- 1 teaspoon dried thyme
- ½ teaspoon dried oregano
- ½ teaspoon dried sage
- ½ teaspoon smoked paprika
- ¼ teaspoon cayenne pepper
- ¼ teaspoon sea salt
- Pinch freshly ground black pepper

For the Burgers
- 2 cups water
- 1 cup kasha (toasted buckwheat)
- Pinch sea salt
- 2 carrots, grated
- Handful fresh parsley, chopped
- 1 teaspoon olive oil (optional)

Directions
For the Dressing
1.	In a medium bowl, whisk together the tahini, vinegar, and mustard until the mixture is very thick. Add 1 to 2 tablespoons water to thin it out, and whisk again until smooth.
2.	Stir in the rest of the ingredients. Set aside for the flavors to blend.

For the Burgers
1.	Put the water, buckwheat, and sea salt in a medium pot. Bring to a boil and let boil for 2 to 3 minutes, then turn down to low, cover, and simmer for 15 minutes. Buckwheat is fully cooked when it is soft and no liquid is left at the bottom of the pot. Do not stir the buckwheat while it is cooking.
2.	Once the buckwheat is cooked, transfer it to a large bowl. Stir the grated carrot, fresh parsley, and all the dressing into the buckwheat. Scoop up ¼-cup portions and form into patties.
3.	You can either panfry or bake the burgers. To panfry, heat a large skillet to medium, add 1 teaspoon olive oil, and cook the burgers about 5 minutes on the first side. Flip, and cook another 5 minutes. To bake them, put them on a baking sheet lined with parchment paper and bake at 350°F for about 30 minutes.

Grilled Seitan in Barbeque Sauce

Total time: 10 minutes
Ingredients
- 8 oz of seitan (thinly sliced or chopped in 1" chunks)
- ½ cup of barbecue sauce
- Cubed vegetable of your choice (blanch)

Directions
1.	To start, make sure to soak the skewers in the water to prevent burning.
2.	Put seitan in a plastic bag or cover well with barbecue sauce in a
3.	deep pan. Mix and allow marinating for at least an hour; much better if longer.
4.	Heat a grill to medium-high temperature.
5.	Meanwhile, thread the seitan and vegetables on the skewers alternately. Grill the skewers on both sides until the seitan is cooked and golden brown on both sides while brushing with barbecue sauce.
6.	Dish with the food and serve.

Tofu Wraps Curried

Total time: 25 minutes
Ingredients
- ½ cup garden greens of your choice (shredded)

- 3 tbsp of mint sauce
- 4 tbsp of yogurt (non- dairy, heaped)
- 3 pcs of 200g of tofu (cut in 15 cubes)
- 2 tbsp of tandoori curry paste
- 2 tbsp of oil
- 2 large cloves of garlic (sliced)
- 2 small size of onions (sliced)
- 8 chapatis (whole-wheat)
- 2 pcs of limes (cut into quarters)

Directions

1. In a medium bowl, combine the garden greens, mint sauce and yogurt, and set aside.
2. In a medium bowl, mix the tofu, tandoori paste, and oil.
3. Heat a skillet over medium temperature and cook the tofu until cooked within. Stir in the garlic, onions, and cook for 3 more minutes. Turn the heat off.
4. Toast the chapatis in a preheated grill pan until golden brown and lay on a flat surface.
5. Spoon in the garden green mixture, top with the tofu mix, wrap, and serve warm.

Tempeh Quesadillas

Total time: 15 minutes

Ingredients

For marinating

- 8 oz tempeh (pasteurized and chopped)
- 1 tbsp of tamari sauce
- 1 tsp of pure maple syrup
- ½ tsp of ginger (grated)
- 1 tbsp of chipotle avocado
- ½ clove of garlic

For assembling

- 2 tbsp of grape seed oil (divided)
- 4 tbsp of cashew cheese (divided)
- 2 corn or tortilla (whole wheat)
- 2 tbsp of shallot (minced, divided)

Directions

1. In a medium bowl, mix all the marinating ingredients and allow the tempeh to sit for 30 minutes.
2. Heat some olive oil in a medium skillet and cook the tempeh on all sides until golden brown, 10 minutes. Transfer to a plate and set aside.
3. Working in batches, heat some oil in a medium skillet and lay in a tortilla.
4. Spread some cashew cheese on top and add the shallots and tempeh. Cover with the other tortilla.
5. Cook until the bottom part of the tortilla is golden brown, then carefully flip and cook the other side until golden brown, 10 minutes.
6. Transfer to a plate, slice into 4 pieces and serve warm.

Baked Squash topped with Beans

Total time: 30 minutes

Ingredients

- 2 tbsp of oil
- 6 cloves of garlic (minced)
- 2 small size onion (diced)
- 2 small size of mild chili (diced finely)
- 700 g of butternut squash (cut into 1cm diced)
- Salt and pepper to taste
- 2 tsp of paprika (smoked)
- ½ tsp of hot chili powder
- ½ tsp of cumin (ground)
- ½ tsp of coriander (ground)
- 800g of chopped tomatoes
- 800g of black beans (rinsed, drained)
- 50g of cheddar cheese (vegan, grated)

Directions

1. In a large frying pan, heat the oil and add the garlic, onion, chili, squash and pepper. Season well and cook for 5-10 minutes over medium heat until the onion is quite tender.
2. Add the spices, chopped tomatoes and black beans, and combine gently.
3. Cover with a lid, heat for another 5-10 minutes until the butternut squash is thoroughly cooked.
4. Place the grated cheese on top and allow melting.
5. Serve warm.

Mexican Lentil Soup

Total time: 55 minutes

Ingredients

- 2 tbsp of olive oil (extra virgin)
- 2 carrots (peeled, diced)
- 1 yellow onion (diced)
- 1 red bell pepper (diced)
- 2 celery stalks (diced)
- 1 tbsp of cumin
- 3 cloves of garlic (minced)
- 2 cups of green lentils (rinsed, picked over)
- 2 cups of tomatoes (diced) and the juice
- 8 cups of vegetable broth
- ½ tsp of salt
- 2 cans of green chile (diced)
- ¼ tsp of smoked paprika
- 1 tsp of oregano
- 1 avocado (peeled, pitted, diced and for garnish)
- Cilantro (fresh, for garnish)
- Hot sauce (optional and for serving)

Directions

1. In a large pot, heat the olive oil over medium heat and cook in the carrots, onion, bell pepper and celery until soften, 5 minutes. Season with the cumin, garlic, pepper and cook for another minute.
2. Mix in the lentils, tomatoes, broth, salt and green chilies. Bring to a boil, cover the lid, and simmer until the lentils soften, 10 to 15 minutes.
3. Adjust the taste with salt, black pepper, and dish the soup.
4. Top with the avocado, cilantro and hot sauce.

Black Bean and Quinoa Balls

Total time: 60 minutes

Ingredients

For black beans and quinoa balls

- ½ cup of quinoa
- 1 can of beans (black)
- ¼ cup of seeds (sesame)

- ½ tbsp of Sriracha
- ¼ cup of flour (oat) / bread crumbs
- 2 tbsp of tomato paste
- 2 tbsp of nutritional yeast
- 1 tsp of garlic (powder)
- 1/2 tbsp of fresh herbs (oregano or basil)

For sun- dried tomato sauce
- ½ cup of cherry tomatoes (halved)
- ½ cup of tomatoes (sun-dried)
- 1 tbsp apple cider vinegar (ACV)
- 1 clove garlic
- 2 tbsp of pine nuts (toasted)
- 2 tbsp of nutritional yeast
- fresh basil
- 1 tsp of oregano
- Salt and pepper to taste

For serving
- ½ cup of cherry tomatoes (halved)
- Fresh basil

Directions
1. Quinoa balls and black beans
2. In a dish, add quinoa and a cup of water, and boil until softens and the water absorbs, 15 minutes. Fluff and allow cooling.
3. Meanwhile, mash the black beans in a medium bowl using a fork and mix in the sesame seeds, Sriracha, quinoa, crumbs of bread or oat flour, tomato paste, spices and nutritional yeast and combine together until even dough forms.
4. Dig up about 2 tbsp of dough and roll into balls (approximately 22-25 total). Line a baking sheet with parchment paper and arrange the balls on top.
5. Cook in the oven for at 380 F until golden brown, 35 to 40 minutes.
6. For the sun- dried tomato sauce
7. Put all the sauce ingredients in a food processor or blender and process until creamy texture forms.
8. Serve the quinoa and black beans balls with the sauce and whole-wheat sauce.

Teriyaki Tempeh Tacos

Total time: 40 minutes
Ingredients
- Teriyaki Tacos
- 1 batch of tempeh
- 6 pcs of taco shells (gluten free)
- Asian Slaw
- 1 cup of cabbage (green, shredded)
- 1 cup of cabbage (red, shredded)
- 1 cup of carrots (grated)
- 3 of scallions (chopped)
- Dressing
- ¼ cup of apple cider vinegar (ACV)
- 2 tbsp of olive oil (extra virgin)
- 1 tbsp of lime juice
- ½ tbsp of tamari sauce
- 1 tbsp of pure maple syrup
- 1 tbsp of mustard (Dijon)
- 1 tbsp of sriracha or hot sauce
- ¼ tsp of salt and pepper to taste

Directions

1. Heat the olive oil in a medium skillet over medium heat and fry the tempeh in batches on both sides until golden brown, 10 minutes. Set aside.
2. In a medium bowl, mix all the ingredients for the Asian slaw and set aside.
3. In another bowl, mix the dressing's ingredients.
4. On each taco shell, divide the tempeh, slaw, and dressing.
5. Serve immediately.

Green Pea Fritters

Total time: 40 minutes
Ingredients
- Fritters
- 2 cups of fresh canned peas
- 1 tbsp of olive oil (divided)
- 3 cloves of garlic (minced)
- 1 large size of white onion (diced)
- 1 tsp of soda (bicarbonate)
- 2 tbsp herbs (dried, chopped finely)
- 1 ½ cups of chickpea flour
- Salt and pepper to taste
- Herby yoghurt dipping sauce
- 1 cup of yoghurt (soy)
- herbs (dried, chopped finely)
- 1 lemon (squeezed)

Directions
1. Set the oven to 350 F and use a baking paper to line a baking sheet.
2. In heated olive oil, sauté the garlic and onion until softened.
3. In a medium bowl, mash and mix the peas with the garlic and onion mixture, bicarbonate soda, herbs, chickpeas, salt and pepper until coarsely smooth mixture forms. Wet your hands and form 2-inch patties from the mixture and arrange on the baking tray.
4. Bake in the oven until golden brown and compacted.
5. Serve with the dipping sauce.
6. Dipping sauce
7. In a medium bowl, mix all the sauce's ingredients and serve immediately with the fritters.

Hearty Black Lentil Curry

Total time: 6 hours 35 minutes
Ingredients
- 1 cup of black lentils, rinsed and soaked overnight
- 14 ounces of chopped tomatoes
- 2 large white onions, peeled and sliced
- 1 1/2 teaspoon of minced garlic
- 1 teaspoon of grated ginger
- 1 red chili
- 1 teaspoon of salt
- 1/4 teaspoon of red chili powder
- 1 teaspoon of paprika
- 1 teaspoon of ground turmeric
- 2 teaspoons of ground cumin
- 2 teaspoons of ground coriander
- 1/2 cup of chopped coriander
- 4-ounce of vegetarian butter
- 4 fluid of ounce water

- 2 fluid of ounce vegetarian double cream

Directions:
1. Place a large pan over an average heat, add butter and let heat until melt.
2. Add the onion along with garlic and ginger and let cook for 10 to 15 minutes or until onions are caramelized.
3. Then stir in salt, red chili powder, paprika, turmeric, cumin, ground coriander, and water.
4. Transfer this mixture to a 6-quarts slow cooker and add tomatoes and red chili.
5. Drain lentils, add to slow cooker and stir until just mix.
6. Plug in slow cooker; adjust cooking time to 6 hours and let cook on low heat setting.
7. When the lentils are done, stir in cream and adjust the seasoning.
8. Serve with boiled rice or whole wheat bread.

Flavorful Refried Beans

Total time: 8 hours 15 minutes
Ingredients
- 3 cups of pinto beans, rinsed
- 1 small jalapeno pepper, seeded and chopped
- 1 medium-sized white onion, peeled and sliced
- 2 tablespoons of minced garlic
- 5 teaspoons of salt
- 2 teaspoons of ground black pepper
- 1/4 teaspoon of ground cumin
- 9 cups of water

Directions:
1. Using a 6-quarts slow cooker, place all the ingredients and stir until it mixes properly.
2. Cover the top, plug in the slow cooker; adjust the cooking time to 6 hours, let it cook on high heat setting and add more water if the beans get too dry.
3. When the beans are done, drain them and reserve the liquid.
4. Mash the beans using a potato masher and pour in the reserved cooking liquid until it reaches your desired mixture.
5. Serve immediately.

Chunky Black Lentil Veggie Soup

Total time: 4 hours 35 minutes
Ingredients
- 1 1/2 cups of black lentils, uncooked
- 2 small turnips, peeled and diced
- 10 medium-sized carrots, peeled and diced
- 1 medium-sized green bell pepper, cored and diced
- 3 cups of diced tomatoes
- 1 medium-sized white onion, peeled and diced
- 2 tablespoons of minced ginger
- 1 teaspoon of minced garlic
- 1 teaspoon of salt
- 1/2 teaspoon of ground coriander
- 1/2 teaspoon of ground cumin
- 3 tablespoons of unsalted butter

- 32 fluid ounce of vegetable broth
- 32 fluid ounces of water

Directions:
1. Using a medium-sized microwave, cover the bowl, place the lentils and pour in the water.
2. Microwave lentils for 10 minutes or until softened, stirring after 5 minutes.
3. Drain lentils and add to a 6-quarts slow cooker along with remaining ingredients and stir until just mix.
4. Cover with top, plug in slow cooker; adjust cooking time to 6 hours and let cook on low heat setting or until carrots are tender.
5. Serve straight away.

Exotic Butternut Squash and Chickpea Curry

Total time: 6 hours 15 minutes
Ingredients
- 1 1/2 cups of shelled peas
- 1 1/2 cups of chickpeas, uncooked and rinsed
- 2 1/2 cups of diced butternut squash
- 12 ounces of chopped spinach
- 2 large tomatoes, diced
- 1 small white onion, peeled and chopped
- 1 teaspoon of minced garlic
- 1 teaspoon of salt
- 3 tablespoons of curry powder
- 14-ounce of coconut milk
- 3 cups of vegetable broth
- 1/4 cup of chopped cilantro

Directions:
1. Using a 6-quarts slow cooker, place all the ingredients into it except for the spinach and peas.
2. Cover the top, plug in the slow cooker; adjust the cooking time to 6 hours and let it cook on the high heat setting or until the chickpeas get tender.
3. 30 minutes to ending your cooking, add the peas and spinach to the slow cooker and let it cook for the remaining 30 minutes.
4. Stir to check the sauce, if the sauce is runny, stir in a mixture of a tablespoon of cornstarch mixed with 2 tablespoons of water.
5. Serve with boiled rice.

Lovely Parsnip & Split Pea Soup

Total time: 5 hours 10 minutes
Ingredients
- 1 tablespoon of olive oil
- 2 large parsnips, peeled and chopped
- 2 large carrots, peeled and chopped
- 1 medium-sized white onion, peeled and diced
- 1 1/2 teaspoon of minced garlic
- 2 1/4 cups of dried green split peas, rinsed
- 1 teaspoon of salt
- 1/2 teaspoon of ground black pepper
- 1 teaspoon of dried thyme
- 2 bay leaves
- 6 cups of vegetable broth
- 1 teaspoon of liquid smoke

Directions:

1. Place a medium-sized non-stick skillet pan over an average pressure of heat, add the oil and let it heat.
2. Add the parsnip, carrot, onion, garlic and let it cook for 5 minutes or until it is heated.
3. Transfer this mixture into a 6-quarts slow cooker and add the remaining ingredients.
4. Stir until mixes properly and cover the top.
5. Plug in the slow cooker; adjust the cooking time to 5 hours and let it cook on the high heat setting or until the peas and vegetables get soft.
6. When done, remove the bay leaf from the soup and blend it with a submersion blender or until the soup reaches your desired state.
7. Add the seasoning and serve.

Incredible Tomato Basil Soup

Total time: 6 hours 10 minutes
Ingredients
- 1 cup of chopped celery
- 1 cup of chopped carrots
- 74 ounces of whole tomatoes, canned
- 2 cups of chopped white onion
- 2 teaspoons of minced garlic
- 1 tablespoon of salt
- 1/2 teaspoon of ground white pepper
- 1/4 cup of basil leaves and more for garnishing
- 1 bay leaf
- 32 fluid ounce of vegetable broth
- 1/2 cup of grated Parmesan cheese
Directions:
1. Using an 8 quarts or larger slow cooker, place all the ingredients.
2. Stir until it mixes properly and cover the top.
3. Plug in the slow cooker; adjust the cooking time to 5 hours and let it cook on the high heat setting or until the vegetables are tender.
4. Blend the soup with a submersion blender or until soup reaches your desired state.
5. Garnish it with the cheese, basil leaves and serve.

Sizzling Vegetarian Fajitas

Total time: 2 hours 25 minutes
Ingredients
- 4 ounces of diced green chilies
- 3 medium-sized tomatoes, diced
- 1 large green bell pepper, cored and sliced
- 1 large red bell pepper, cored and sliced
- 1 medium-sized white onion, peeled and sliced
- 1/2 teaspoon of garlic powder
- 1/4 teaspoon of salt
- 2 teaspoons of red chili powder
- 2 teaspoons of ground cumin
- 1/2 teaspoon of dried oregano
- 1 1/2 tablespoon of olive oil
Directions:
1. Take a 6-quarts slow cooker, grease it with a non-stick cooking spray and add all the ingredients.
2. Stir until it mixes properly and cover the top.

3. Plug in the slow cooker; adjust the cooking time to 2 hours and let it cook on the high heat setting or until cooks thoroughly.
4. Serve with tortillas.

Rich Red Lentil Curry

Total time: 8 hours 10 minutes
Ingredients
- 4 cups of brown lentils, uncooked and rinsed
- 2 medium-sized white onions, peeled and diced
- 2 teaspoons of minced garlic
- 1 tablespoon of minced ginger
- 1 teaspoon of salt
- 1/4 teaspoon of cayenne pepper
- 5 tablespoons of red curry paste
- 2 teaspoons of brown sugar
- 1 1/2 teaspoon of ground turmeric
- 1 tablespoon of garam masala
- 60-ounce of tomato puree
- 7 cups of water
- 1/2 cup of coconut milk
- 1/4 cup of chopped cilantro
Directions:
1. Using a 6-quarts slow cooker, place all the ingredients except for the coconut milk and cilantro.
2. Stir until it mixes properly and cover the top.
3. Plug in the slow cooker; adjust the cooking time to 5 hours and let it cook on the high heat setting or until the lentils are soft.
4. Check the curry during cooking and add more water if needed.
5. When the curry is cooked, stir in the milk, then garnish it with the cilantro and serve right away.

Smoky Red Beans and Rice

Total time: 5 hours 10 minutes
Ingredients
- 30 ounces of cooked red beans
- 1 cup of brown rice, uncooked
- 1 cup of chopped green pepper
- 1 cup of chopped celery
- 1 cup of chopped white onion
- 1 1/2 teaspoon of minced garlic
- 1/2 teaspoon of salt
- 1/4 teaspoon of cayenne pepper
- 1 teaspoon of smoked paprika
- 2 teaspoons of dried thyme
- 1 bay leaf
- 2 1/3 cups of vegetable broth
Directions:
1. Using a 6-quarts slow cooker place all the ingredients except for the rice, salt and cayenne pepper.
2. Stir until it mixes properly and then cover the top.
3. Plug in the slow cooker; adjust the cooking time to 4 hours and let it steam on a low heat setting.
4. Then pour in and stir the rice, salt, cayenne pepper and continue cooking for an additional 2 hours at a high heat setting.
5. Serve straight away.

Spicy Black-Eyed Peas

Total time: 8 hours 20 minutes
Ingredients
- 32-ounce black-eyed peas, uncooked
- 1 cup of chopped orange bell pepper
- 1 cup of chopped celery
- 8-ounce of chipotle peppers, chopped
- 1 cup of chopped carrot
- 1 cup of chopped white onion
- 1 teaspoon of minced garlic
- 3/4 teaspoon of salt
- 1/2 teaspoon of ground black pepper
- 2 teaspoons of liquid smoke flavoring
- 2 teaspoons of ground cumin
- 1 tablespoon of adobo sauce
- 2 tablespoons of olive oil
- 1 tablespoon of apple cider vinegar
- 4 cups of vegetable broth

Directions:
1. Place a medium-sized non-stick skillet pan over an average temperature of heat; add the bell peppers, carrot, onion, garlic, oil and vinegar.
2. Stir until it mixes properly and let it cook for 5 to 8 minutes or until it gets translucent.
3. Transfer this mixture to a 6-quarts slow cooker and add the peas, chipotle pepper, adobo sauce and the vegetable broth.
4. Stir until mixes properly and cover the top.
5. Plug in the slow cooker; adjust the cooking time to 8 hours and let it cook on the low heat setting or until peas are soft.
6. Serve right away.

Vegan Spinach Ricotta Lasagna

Total time: 75 minutes
Ingredients
- Cashew ricotta cheese
- 2 cups of cashews (raw)
- ¾ cups of water
- 1 lemon (squeezed)
- 2 cloves of garlic (grated)
- ½ tsp onion (powder)
- ½ tsp of garlic (powder)
- ½ tsp of sea salt
- Lasagna
- ½ onion (diced)
- 1 lb. mushrooms (sliced)
- 6 cups of baby spinach
- 4 ½ cups of tomato sauce
- 12 oz of lasagna noodles (no boil lentil)
- 6 oz of vegan smoked Gouda cheese slices
- 1 large heirloom tomato (sliced)
- 1/3 cup of basil leaves (garnish)
- A pinch of red pepper (flakes)

Directions
1. Cashew Ricotta
2. Wash the cashews thoroughly for 20 minutes, drain and blend in a food processor until smooth. Set aside in the refrigerator until needed.
3. Preparing the oven
4. In a large saucepan, steam the onion with a teaspoon of water. Add the mushrooms and simmer for 10 minutes. Season with salt to taste.

5. Pour another teaspoon of water in the same pan and cook in the spinach until wilted. Drain and set aside.
6. Spread 1 ½ cups of tomato sauce in a medium baking pan and lay in half of the noodles.
7. Spread a third of the ricotta cashew on top, add a third of the spinach mixture and repeat the layering process two more times making sure to top finally with the ricotta cashew cheese.
8. Layer the vegan smoked gouda layer on top and the sliced tomatoes on top.
9. Cover with foil and bake in the oven for 45 to 60 minutes or until the cheeses melt.
10. Remove from the oven, allow cooling for 5 minutes, top with the basil, slice and serve.

Spice- crusted Tofu with Kumquat Radish Salad

Total time: 5 minutes
Ingredients
- 200g of tofu (firm)
- 2 tbsp of sesame seeds
- 1 tbsp spice mix (Japanese shichimi togarashi)
- ½ tbsp of cornflour
- 1 tbsp of vegetable oil
- 200g of broccoli (Tender stem)
- 100g of sugar
- 5 radishes (sliced)
- 2 spring onions (chopped)
- 2 kumquats (sliced)
- 1 tbsp of sesame oil

For the dressing
- 2 tbsp of tamari sauce
- 2 tbsp of lime juice
- 1 tsp of golden caster sugar
- 1 small shallot (diced finely)
- 1 tsp of ginger (grated)

Directions
1. Cut the tofu in two and press with parchment paper. Cut into chunky slices.
2. In a cup, mix the sesame seeds, also mix the Japanese spice mix and corn flour. Slather the mixture and get it covered.
3. Heat the olive oil in a large skillet and fry the tofu on both sides, 10 minutes. Set aside in a large salad bowl.
4. Steam the broccoli and snap peas in a microwave until softened, 2 to 3 minutes.
5. In the salad bowl, add the broccoli, snap peas, radishes, spring onion and kumquats.
6. Mix the dressing's ingredients in a medium bowl and serve with the salad.

Mongolian Seitan

Total time: 30 minutes
Ingredients
For seitan
- 1 ½ tbsp of vegetable oil
- 1 lb. of seitan (cut into 1-inch pcs)
- For the Mongolian sauce
- 2 tsp of oil (vegetable)
- 3 cloves of garlic (minced)
- 1/2 tsp of ginger (minced)

- 1/3 tsp of five spice (optional)
- 1/3 tsp of red pepper (flakes)
- 1/2 cup of tamari sauce
- 1/2 cup + 2 tbsp sugar (coconut)
- 2 tbsp of cold water
- 2 tsp of cornstarch

For serving
- sesame seeds (toasted, optional)
- scallions (sliced, optional)

Directions

For the seitan

Heat the vegetable oil in a saucepan in a medium - high heat and cook in the seitan until golden brown on both sides, 10 minutes.

For the sauce:
1. Meanwhile, as the seitan cooks, warm the vegetable oil over medium heat in a pan.
2. Sauté the garlic, ginger, five spice (optional) and red pepper flakes until fragrant, 30 seconds.
3. Mix in the tamari sauce, coconut sugar and cook over low heat until the sugar melts.
4. In a small bowl, mix the cornstarch and cold water, and mix into the sauce. Cook for 1 minute.
5. Mix in the seitan, cook for 1 minute, and top with the sesame seeds and scallions.
6. Dish the food and serve warm.

Red Lentil Quinoa Fritters

Total time: 45 minutes

Ingredients
- Red lentil quinoa fritters
- ½ cup of red lentils
- 1 ½ cup of quinoa
- 4 cups of water
- 2 tsp of turmeric (ground)
- ½ lemon (squeezed)
- 1 tsp of cumin
- ½ tsp of salt and pepper to taste
- ¼ tsp of cinnamon (ground)
- ¼ cup of chickpea flour
- ¼ cup or cornmeal
- ¼ cup of fresh parsley (chopped)
- ¼ cup of tahini
- 1 tbsp of mustard (Dijon)
- Tahini yogurt sauce
- 1 cup plant-based yogurt
- 3 tbsp tahini
- juice of 1 lemon
- 2 minced garlic cloves
- 1 tbsp chopped fresh dill
- 1/4 tsp salt (or to taste)

Directions

For the fritters:
1. Set the oven for 400F and line a baking tray with parchment paper.
2. Wash and flush the lentils and quinoa. In a medium saucepan, boil lentils and quinoa for 15 minutes. Mix/stir well intermediary to avoid burning. Reserve to cool.
3. In a large mixing container, mix the turmeric, lemon juice, cumin, salt, and cinnamon until well combined.
4. Incorporate the chickpea flour and cornmeal into the mixture until moist dough forms.

Mold 1-inch patties from the mixture and arrange on the baking tray.
5. Bake in the oven for 15 minutes while flipping halfway until the patties are golden brown and well compacted.
6. Serve with the tahini yogurt sauce.

For the tahini yogurt sauce:
While still cooking the fritters, combine all the ingredients for the tahini yogurt sauce. Reserve until serving time.

Easy Vegan Chili Sin Carne

Total time: 30 minutes

Ingredients
- 2 tbsp of olive oil
- 1 large size of red onion (slice thinly)
- 3 cloves of garlic (minced)
- 2 medium size carrots (peeled, chopped finely)
- 2 small size red pepper (chopped roughly)
- 2 celery stalks (chopped finely)
- 1 tsp of chili powder
- Salt and pepper to taste
- 1 tsp of cumin (ground)
- 400g of red kidney beans (rinsed and drained)
- 800g of chopped tomatoes (tinned)
- 100g of red lentils (split)
- 250ml of vegetable stock
- 400g of soy mince (frozen)

Directions
1. Heat the olive oil in a large saucepan over medium heat.
2. Cook in the onion, garlic, carrots, pepper and celery until softened, 5 minutes.
3. Mix in the chili powder, salt, pepper, and cumin powder.
4. Add the kidney beans, tomatoes, lentils, vegetable stock and thin soy. Cook for 15 minutes and adjust the taste with salt and black pepper.
5. Dish the food and serve with cooked quinoa.

Fall Farro Protein Bowl

Total time: 45 minutes

Ingredients
- 1 cup of carrots (1/2 inch diced)
- 1 cup of sweet potato (1/2 inch diced)
- 2 tsp of organic oil (divided)
- Salt and pepper to taste (divided)
- 15oz of chickpeas (rinsed and drained)
- 4oz of smoky tempeh strips
- ½ cup of farro (uncooked)
- 1 ¼ cups of water
- 2 cups of mixed greens
- ¼ cup of hummus
- 2 tbsp of roasted almonds
- 4 slices of lemon (wedges)

Directions
1. Heat the oven to 375 F and prepare a large baking tray.
2. In a large mixing bowl, mix the carrots and sweet potatoes with 1 tsp of cooking oil and a pinch of salt and pepper. Spread the mixture on the baking sheet.

3.	In the same mixing container, place the chickpeas and a tsp of oil, a pinch of salt and 1/8 tsp of pepper, and mix well.
4.	Spread the mixture on the vegetables and top with the tempeh strips.
5.	Bake in the oven for until the sweet potatoes are tender, 30 minutes. Remove the food from the oven and set aside.
6.	Meanwhile as the vegetables baked, cook the farro in a slightly salted water in a medium pot over medium heat until softened and the water absorbs, 10 to 15 minutes.
7.	To serve, divide the farro and mixed greens between four bowls. Share the tempeh mixture likewise as well as the other ingredients.
8.	Serve warm.

Stir- fried Sprout with Green Beans, Lemon and Pine Nuts

Total time: 10 minutes
Ingredients
- 	300g of Brussels sprouts (trimmed, cut in quarter)
- 	300g of green beans
- 	1 tbsp of olive oil
- 	1 small lemon (zest and squeezed)
- 	2 tbsp of pine nuts (toasted)

Directions
1.	In a pan of boiling salted water, cook the sprouts and beans for 3 minutes, then drain well afterwards.
2.	Heat the olive oil in a medium skillet over medium heat and stir-fry the vegetables.
3.	Mix in the lemon zest, lemon juice, and pine nuts. Cook for 3 minutes and turn the heat off.
4.	Dish the food and serve warm.

Potato Tofu Quiche

Total time: 90 minutes
Ingredients
For the crust
- 	1 ½ medium size potatoes (grated)
- 	1 tbsp of sea salt and pepper
- 	1 tbsp of melted vegan butter
For the filling
- 	½ cup of chopped broccoli
- 	1 ½ cloves of garlic (chopped)
- 	1 medium size of leeks (sliced thinly)
- 	1 tbsp melted vegan butter
- 	1 tbsp of nutritional yeast
- 	Sea salt and pepper to taste
- 	1 ½ tbsp of hummus
- 	6 oz of tofu (extra- firm silken, dried)
- 	3 cups of cherry tomatoes (halves)

Directions
1.	Set the oven to 450 degrees F and gently dab a 9.5-inch baking pan with non-stick spray.
2.	Spread the potatoes on the baking sheet and season with the salt, pepper, and butter.
3.	In another baking sheet, mix the broccoli, garlic, leeks, and season with salt, black pepper, and drizzle the vegan butter on top.
4.	Place both sheets in the oven and bake until the vegetables are tender and golden brown, 25 to 30 minutes.
5.	Transfer the vegetables to a food processor and top with the remaining ingredients. Process until coarsely combined.
6.	Pour the mixture into a pre-greased loaf pan and bake in the oven until golden brown and compacted, 30 to 40 minutes.
7.	Remove the pan from the oven, allow cooling for 3 minutes and invert the quiche onto a flat surface.
8.	Slice and serve.

Black bean and Seitan Stir- fry

Total time: 25 minutes
Ingredients
- 	400g of black beans (drained, rinsed)
- 	75g of pure date sugar
- 	3 cloves of garlic
- 	2 tbsp of tamari sauce
- 	1 tsp of five- spice (powder)
- 	2 tbsp of wine vinegar
- 	1 tbsp of peanut butter (smooth)
- 	1 small size red chili (chopped finely)
- 	350g of marinated seitan (piece)
- 	1 small size shallots (chopped)
- 	1 tbsp of corn flour
- 	2 to 3 tbsp of vegetable oil
- 	1 small size red bell pepper (sliced)
- 	2 small size spring onions (sliced)
- 	300g of pak choi (chopped)

Directions
1.	Begin by preparing the sauce. In a food processor, add the black beans, date sugar, garlic, tamari sauce, five-spice powder, wine vinegar, peanut butter, and red chili. Process until smooth and pour the mixture into a medium pot. Heat the mixture over medium heat until thickened, 5 minutes.
2.	Wash and drain the seitan using a paper towel. Add the seitan in a container together with the corn flour and reserve for later. Warm your saucepan to a high temperature, heat in some oil and fry the seitan until golden brown on both sides, 10 minutes. Transfer to a plate and set aside.
3.	Heat a teaspoon of oil in the pot and sauté the shallots, peppers, spring onion, and pak choi until softened, 3 minutes.
Mix in the seitan, top with the sauce, toss well, and serve immediately

DINNER RECIPES

Black Bean Burgers

Preparation Time: 10 minutes
Cooking Time: 15 minutes
Servings: 6
Ingredients:
- 1 Onion, diced
- ½ cup Corn Nibs
- 2 Cloves Garlic, minced
- ½ teaspoon Oregano, dried
- ½ cup Flour
- 1 Jalapeno Pepper, small
- 2 cups Black Beans, mashed & canned
- ¼ cup Breadcrumbs (Vegan)
- 2 teaspoons Parsley, minced
- ¼ teaspoon cumin
- 1 tablespoon Olive Oil
- 2 teaspoons Chili Powder
- ½ Red Pepper, diced
- Sea Salt to taste

Directions:
1. Set your flour on a plate, and then get out your garlic, onion, peppers and oregano, throwing it in a pan. Cook over medium-high heat, and then cook until the onions are translucent. Place the peppers in, and sauté until tender.
2. Cook for two minutes, and then set it to the side.
3. Use a potato masher to mash your black beans, then stir in the vegetables, cumin, breadcrumbs, parsley, salt, and chili powder, and then divide it into six patties.
4. Coat each side, and then cook until it is fried on each side.

Nutrition: Calories: 357 kcal Protein: 17.93 g Fat: 5.14 g Carbohydrates: 61.64 g

Dijon Maple Burgers

Preparation Time: 20 minutes
Cooking Time: 30 minutes
Servings: 12
Ingredients:
- 1 Red Bell Pepper
- 19 ounces Can Chickpeas, rinsed & drained
- 1 cup Almonds, ground
- 2 teaspoons Dijon Mustard
- 1 teaspoon Oregano
- ½ teaspoon Sage
- 1 cup Spinach, fresh
- 1 – ½ cups Rolled Oats
- 1 Clove Garlic, pressed
- ½ Lemon, juiced
- 2 teaspoons Maple Syrup, pure

Directions:
1. Get out a baking sheet. Line it with parchment paper.
2. Cut your red pepper in half and then take the seeds out. Place it on your baking sheet, and roast in the oven while you prepare your other ingredients.
3. Process your chickpeas, almonds, mustard, and maple syrup together in a food processor.
4. Add in your lemon juice, oregano, sage, garlic, and spinach, processing again. Make sure it's combined, but don't puree it.
5. Once your red bell pepper is softened, which should roughly take ten minutes, add this to the processor as well. Add in your oats, mixing well.
6. Form twelve patties, cooking in the oven for a half-hour. They should be browned.

Nutrition: Calories: 96 kcal Protein: 5.28 g Fat: 2.42 g Carbohydrates: 16.82 g

Hearty Black Lentil Curry

Preparation Time: 30 minutes
Cooking Time: 6 hours and 15 minutes
Servings: 4
Ingredients:
- 1 cup of black lentils, rinsed and soaked overnight
- 14 ounce of chopped tomatoes
- 2 large white onions, peeled and sliced
- 1 1/2 teaspoon of minced garlic
- 1 teaspoon of grated ginger
- 1 red chili
- 1 teaspoon of salt
- 1/4 teaspoon of red chili powder
- 1 teaspoon of paprika
- 1 teaspoon of ground turmeric
- 2 teaspoons of ground cumin
- 2 teaspoons of ground coriander
- 1/2 cup of chopped coriander
- 4-ounce of vegetarian butter
- 4 fluid of ounce water
- 2 fluid of ounce vegetarian double cream

Directions:
1. Place a large pan over moderate heat, add butter and let heat until melt.
2. Add the onion and garlic and ginger and cook for 10 to 15 minutes or until onions are caramelized.
3. Then stir in salt, red chili powder, paprika, turmeric, cumin, ground coriander, and water.
4. Transfer this mixture to a 6-quarts slow cooker and add tomatoes and red chili.
5. Drain lentils, add to slow cooker, and stir until just mix.
6. Plugin slow cooker; adjust cooking time to 6 hours and let cook on low heat setting.
7. When the lentils are done, stir in cream and adjust the seasoning.
8. Serve with boiled rice or whole wheat bread.

Nutrition: Calories: 299 kcal Protein: 5.59 g Fat: 27.92 g Carbohydrates: 9.83 g

Flavorful Refried Beans

Preparation Time: 15 minutes
Cooking Time: 8 hours
Servings: 8
Ingredients:

- 3 cups of pinto beans, rinsed
- 1 small jalapeno pepper, seeded and chopped
- 1 medium-sized white onion, peeled and sliced
- 2 tablespoons of minced garlic
- 5 teaspoons of salt
- 2 teaspoons of ground black pepper
- 1/4 teaspoon of ground cumin
- 9 cups of water

Directions:
1. Using a 6-quarts slow cooker, place all the ingredients and stir until it mixes properly.
2. Cover the top, plug in the slow cooker, adjust the cooking time to 6 hours, let it cook on the high heat setting, and add more water if the beans get too dry.
3. When the beans are done, drain it then reserve the liquid.
4. Mash the beans using a potato masher and pour in the reserved cooking liquid until it reaches your desired mixture.
5. Serve immediately.

Nutrition: Calories: 268 kcal Protein: 16.55 g Fat: 1.7 g Carbohydrates: 46.68 g

Smoky Red Beans and Rice

Preparation Time: 15 minutes
Cooking Time: 6 minutes
Servings: 6
Ingredients:
- 30 ounce of cooked red beans
- 1 cup of brown rice, uncooked
- 1 cup of chopped green pepper
- 1 cup of chopped celery
- 1 cup of chopped white onion
- 1 1/2 teaspoon of minced garlic
- 1/2 teaspoon of salt
- 1/4 teaspoon of cayenne pepper
- 1 teaspoon of smoked paprika
- 2 teaspoons of dried thyme
- 1 bay leaf
- 2 1/3 cups of vegetable broth

Directions:
1. Using a 6-quarts slow cooker, place all the ingredients except for the rice, salt, and cayenne pepper.
2. Stir until it mixes properly and then cover the top.
3. Plug in the slow cooker, adjust the cooking time to 4 hours, and steam on a low heat setting.
4. Then pour in and stir the rice, salt, cayenne pepper and continue cooking for an additional 2 hours at a high heat setting.
5. Serve straight away.

Nutrition: Calories: 791 kcal Protein: 3.25 g Fat: 86.45 g Carbohydrates: 9.67 g

Spicy Black-Eyed Peas

Preparation Time: 12 minutes
Cooking Time: 8 hours and 8 minutes
Servings: 8
Ingredients:

- 32-ounce black-eyed peas, uncooked
- 1 cup of chopped orange bell pepper
- 1 cup of chopped celery
- 8-ounce of chipotle peppers, chopped
- 1 cup of chopped carrot
- 1 cup of chopped white onion
- 1 teaspoon of minced garlic
- 3/4 teaspoon of salt
- 1/2 teaspoon of ground black pepper
- 2 teaspoons of liquid smoke flavoring
- 2 teaspoons of ground cumin
- 1 tablespoon of adobo sauce
- 2 tablespoons of olive oil
- 1 tablespoon of apple cider vinegar
- 4 cups of vegetable broth

Directions:
1. Place a medium-sized non-stick skillet pan over an average temperature of heat; add the bell peppers, carrot, onion, garlic, oil, and vinegar.
2. Stir until it mixes properly and let it cook for 5 to 8 minutes or until it gets translucent.
3. Transfer this mixture to a 6-quarts slow cooker and add the peas, chipotle pepper, adobo sauce, and the vegetable broth.
4. Stir until mixed properly and cover the top.
5. Plug in the slow cooker, adjust the cooking time to 8 hours, and let it cook on the low heat setting or until peas are soft.
6. Serve right away.

Nutrition: Calories: 1071 kcal Protein: 5.3 g Fat: 113.65 g Carbohydrates: 18.51 g

Creamy Artichoke Soup

Preparation Time: 5 minutes
Cooking Time: 40 minutes
Servings: 4
Ingredients:
- 1 can artichoke hearts, drained
- 3 cups vegetable broth
- 2 tbsp. lemon juice
- 1 small onion, finely cut
- 2 cloves garlic, crushed
- 3 tbsp. olive oil
- 2 tbsp. flour
- ½ cup vegan cream

Directions:
1. Gently sauté the onion and garlic in some olive oil. Add the flour, whisking constantly, and then add the hot vegetable broth slowly, while still whisking. Cook for about 5 minutes.
2. Blend the artichoke, lemon juice, salt, and pepper until smooth. Add the puree to the broth mix, stir well, and then stir in the cream. Cook until heated through. Garnish with a swirl of vegan cream or a sliver of artichoke.

Nutrition: Calories: 1622 kcal Protein: 4.45 g Fat: 181.08 g Carbohydrates: 10.99 g

Tomato Artichoke Soup

Preparation Time: 5 minutes
Cooking Time: 35 minutes
Servings: 4
Ingredients:

- 1 can artichoke hearts, drained
- 1 can diced tomatoes, undrained
- 3 cups vegetable broth
- 1 small onion, chopped
- 2 cloves garlic, crushed
- 1 tbsp. pesto
- Black pepper, to taste

Directions:
1. Combine all ingredients in the slow cooker.
2. Cover and cook on low for 8-10 hours or on high for 4-5 hours.
3. Blend the soup in batches then put it back to the slow cooker. Season with pepper and salt, then serve.

Nutrition: Calories: 1487 kcal Protein: 3.98 g Fat: 167.42 g Carbohydrates: 8.2 g

Super Radish Avocado Salad

Preparation Time: 10 minutes
Cooking Time: 25 minutes
Servings: 2
Ingredients:
- 6 shredded carrots
- 6 ounces diced radishes
- 1 diced avocado
- 1/3 cup ponzu

Directions:
1. Place all together the ingredients in a serving bowl and toss. Enjoy!

Nutrition: Calories: 292 kcal Protein: 7.42 g Fat: 18.29 g Carbohydrates: 29.59 g

Beauty School Ginger Cucumbers

Preparation Time: 10 minutes
Cooking Time: 45 minutes
Servings: 14
Ingredients:
- 1 sliced cucumber
- 3 tsp. rice wine vinegar
- 1 ½ tbsp. sugar
- 1 tsp. minced ginger

Directions:
1. Place all together the ingredients in a mixing bowl, and toss the ingredients well. Enjoy!

Nutrition: Calories: 10 kcal Protein: 0.46 g Fat: 0.43 g Carbohydrates: 0.89 g

Exotic Butternut Squash and Chickpea Curry

Preparation Time: 20 minutes
Cooking Time: 6 hours
Servings: 8
Ingredients:
- 1 1/2 cups of shelled peas
- 1 1/2 cups of chickpeas, uncooked and rinsed
- 2 1/2 cups of diced butternut squash
- 12 ounce of chopped spinach
- 2 large tomatoes, diced
- 1 small white onion, peeled and chopped
- 1 teaspoon of minced garlic
- 1 teaspoon of salt

- 3 tablespoons of curry powder
- 14-ounce of coconut milk
- 3 cups of vegetable broth
- 1/4 cup of chopped cilantro

Directions:
1. Using a 6-quarts slow cooker, place all the ingredients into it except for the spinach and peas.
2. Cover the top, plug in the slow cooker; adjust the cooking time to 6 hours, and cook on the high heat setting or until the chickpeas get tender.
3. 30 minutes to ending your cooking, add the peas and spinach to the slow cooker and cook for the remaining 30 minutes.
4. Stir to check the sauce; if the sauce is runny, stir in a mixture of a 1 tbsp. Cornstarch mixed with 2 tbsp. Water.
5. Serve with boiled rice.

Nutrition: Calories: 774 kcal Protein: 3.71 g Fat: 83.25 g Carbohydrates: 12.64 g

Sage Walnuts and Radishes

Preparation Time: 10 minutes
Cooking Time: 10 minutes
Servings: 6
Ingredients:
- 2 tablespoons olive oil
- 5 celery ribs, chopped
- 3 spring onions, chopped
- ½ pound radishes, halved
- juice of 1 lime
- Zest of 1 lime, grated
- 8 ounces walnuts, chopped
- A pinch of black pepper
- 3 tablespoons sage, chopped

Directions:
1. Heat up a pan with the oil over medium heat, add celery and spring onion, stir and cook for 5 minutes.
2. Add the rest of the ingredients, toss, cook for another 5 minutes, divide into bowls and serve.

Nutrition: calories 200 fat 7 fiber 5 carbs 9.3 protein 4

Garlic Zucchini and Cauliflower

Preparation Time: 10 minutes
Cooking Time: 20 minutes
Servings: 4
Ingredients:
- 4 zucchinis, cut into medium fries
- 1 cup cauliflower florets
- 1 tablespoon capers, drained
- Juice of ½ lemon
- A pinch of salt and black pepper
- ½ teaspoon chili powder
- 1 tablespoon olive oil
- ¼ teaspoon garlic powder

Directions:
1. Spread the zucchini fries on a lined baking sheet, add the rest of the ingredients, toss, introduce in the oven, bake at 400 degrees F for 20 minutes, divide between plates and serve.

Nutrition: calories 185 fat 3 fiber 2 carbs 6.5 protein 8

Garlic Beans

Preparation Time: 10 minutes
Cooking Time: 10 minutes
Servings: 4
Ingredients:
- Juice of 1 lemon
- Zest of 1 lemon, grated
- 2 tablespoons avocado oil
- 4 garlic cloves, minced
- ½ teaspoon turmeric powder
- 1 teaspoon garam masala
- 1 red onion, sliced
- 1 yellow bell pepper, sliced
- 10 ounces green beans, halved
- A pinch of black pepper

Directions:
1. Heat up a pan with the oil over medium-high heat, add the garlic and onion and cook for 2 minutes.
2. Add green beans and the other ingredients, toss, cook for 8 minutes, divide between plates and serve.

Nutrition: calories 180 fat 10 fiber 6 carbs 13 protein 8

Mustard Beets

Preparation Time: 10 minutes
Cooking Time: 0 minutes
Servings: 4
Ingredients:
- 1 tablespoon Dijon mustard
- 1 and ½ tablespoon olive oil
- 8 ounces beets, cooked and sliced
- 1 teaspoon garam masala
- 1 teaspoon coriander, ground
- 1 teaspoon basil, dried
- A pinch of black pepper

Directions:
1. In a bowl, mix the beets with the oil, mustard and the other ingredients, toss and serve.

Nutrition: calories 170 fat 5 fiber 7 carbs 8 proteins 5.5

Parsley Green Beans

Preparation Time: 10 minutes
Cooking Time: 20 minutes
Servings: 6
Ingredients:
- 3 tablespoons olive oil
- 3 pounds green beans, halved
- A pinch of salt and black pepper
- 2 tablespoons balsamic vinegar
- 2 yellow onions, chopped
- 2 and ½ tablespoons parsley, chopped

Directions:
1. Heat up a pan with the oil over medium heat, add the green beans and the other ingredients, toss, cook for 20 minutes, divide between plates and serve.

Nutrition: calories 130 fat 1 fiber 2 carbs 7.4 protein 6

Squash and Tomatoes

Preparation Time: 15 minutes
Cooking Time: 12 minutes
Servings: 2
Ingredients:
- 8 oz yellow squash, peeled and roughly cubed
- 1 cup cherry tomatoes, halved
- 3 tablespoons tomato sauce
- 1 teaspoon sweet paprika
- 1 teaspoon coriander, ground
- 1 teaspoon oregano, dried
- 1 teaspoon olive oil
- 1 teaspoon white pepper

Directions:
1. Heat up a pan with the oil over medium heat, add the squash, tomatoes and the other ingredients, toss, cook for 12 minutes, divide between plates and serve.

Nutrition: calories 41 fat 2.6 fiber 1.5 carbs 4.5 protein 1.5

Bok Choy Salad

Preparation Time: 10 minutes
Cooking Time: 10 minutes
Servings: 5
Ingredients:
- 10 oz bok choy, chopped
- 1 cup cherry tomatoes, halved
- 1 tablespoon black olives, pitted and sliced
- 1 mango, peeled and cubed
- Juice of ½ orange
- 1 teaspoon curry powder
- 1 teaspoon sesame oil
- 1 tablespoon lemon juice

Directions:
1. Heat up a pan with the oil over medium-high heat, add the bok choy, tomatoes and the other ingredients, toss and cook for 10 minutes.
2. Divide into bowls and serve cold.

Nutrition: calories 142 fat 6.8 fiber 0.7 carbs 1.8 protein 9.4

Balsamic Arugula and Beets

Preparation Time: 10 minutes
Cooking Time: 0 minutes
Servings: 4
Ingredients:
- 2 cups baby arugula
- 1 tablespoon balsamic vinegar
- 1 teaspoon olive oil
- 2 red beets, baked, peeled and cubed
- 1 avocado, peeled, pitted and cubed
- 1 teaspoon garam masala
- ½ teaspoon salt
- ½ teaspoon cayenne pepper

Directions:
1. In a bowl, mix the arugula with the beets and the other ingredients, toss and serve.

Nutrition: calories 151 fat 1.4 fiber 2.2 carbs 4.1 protein 5.9

Herbed Beets

Preparation Time: 10 minutes
Cooking Time: 40 minutes
Servings: 3
Ingredients:
- 2 big red beets, peeled and roughly cubed
- 1 tablespoon chives, chopped
- 1 tablespoon cilantro, chopped
- 1 tablespoon basil, chopped
- Juice of 1 lime
- A pinch of salt and black pepper
- ¼ teaspoon dried oregano
- ¼ teaspoon ground nutmeg
- ¼ teaspoon ground cumin
- 1 tablespoon olive oil

Directions:
1. Spread the beets on a lined baking sheet, add the chives, cilantro and the other ingredients, toss and bake at 400 degrees F for 40 minutes.
2. Divide between plates and serve.

Nutrition: calories 188 fat 5.2 fiber 5.9 carbs 8.3 protein 1.6

Marinara Broccoli

Preparation Time: 10 minutes
Cooking Time: 15 minutes
Servings: 4
Ingredients:
- 2 cups broccoli florets
- 1 teaspoon sweet paprika
- 1 teaspoon coriander, ground
- ¼ cup marinara sauce
- ½ teaspoon ground black pepper
- ½ teaspoon salt
- ½ teaspoon garlic powder
- 1 teaspoon olive oil
- Juice of 1 lime

Directions:
1. In a roasting pan, mix the broccoli with the marinara and the other ingredients, toss and bake at 400 degrees F for 15 minutes.
2. Divide between plates and serve.

Nutrition: calories206 fat 4.7 fiber 3.7 carbs 10.6 protein 6.1

Spinach and Pear Salad

Preparation Time: 10 minutes
Cooking Time: 0 minutes
Servings: 2
Ingredients:
- 1 bell pepper, chopped
- ½ cup radishes, halved
- ½ cup cherry tomatoes, halved
- 2 cups baby spinach
- 2 pears, cored and cut into wedges
- 1 tablespoon walnuts, chopped
- 1 teaspoon chives, chopped
- A pinch of salt and black pepper
- Juice of 1 lime

Directions:
1. In a bowl, mix the radishes with the pepper, tomatoes and the other ingredients, toss and serve.

Nutrition: calories 143 fat 2.9 fiber 2.1 carbs 4.9 protein 3.2

Olives and Mango Mix

Preparation Time: 10 minutes
Cooking Time: 0 minutes
Servings: 2
Ingredients:
- 1 cup black olives, pitted and halved
- 1 cup kalamata olives, pitted and halved
- 1 cup mango, peeled and cubed
- A pinch of salt and black pepper
- Juice of 1 lime
- 1 teaspoon sweet paprika
- 1 teaspoon coriander, ground
- 1 tablespoon olive oil

Directions:
1. In a bowl mix the olives with the mango and the other ingredients, toss and serve.

Nutrition: calories 68 fat 4.4 fiber 0 carbs 1.5 protein 3.3

Eggplant and Avocado Mix

Preparation Time: 10 minutes
Cooking Time: 20 minutes
Servings: 4
Ingredients:
- 1 pound eggplant, roughly cubed
- 2 avocados, peeled, pitted and cubed
- 1 red onion, chopped
- 1 teaspoon curry powder
- Juice of 1 lime
- ½ cup crushed tomatoes
- 1 tablespoon olive oil
- 1 teaspoon salt
- 1 teaspoon chili powder

Directions:
1. Heat up a pan with the oil over medium heat, add the onion and cook for 5 minutes.
2. Add the eggplants, avocados and the other ingredients, toss and cook for 15 minutes more.
3. Divide between plates and serve.

Nutrition: calories 231 fat 7.6 fiber 8.5 carbs 9.2 protein 5.4

Red Onion, Avocado and Radishes Mix

Preparation Time: 15 minutes
Cooking Time: 12 minutes
Servings: 2
Ingredients:
- 2 red onions, peeled and sliced
- 2 avocados, peeled, pitted and sliced
- 1 cup radishes, halved
- 1 teaspoon oregano, dried
- 1 teaspoon basil, dried
- 1 tablespoon olive oil
- 1 teaspoon lemon juice
- ¼ teaspoon salt

Directions:
1. Heat up a pan with the oil over medium heat, add the onions, oregano and basil and cook for 5 minutes.

2.   Add the rest of the ingredients, toss, cook for 7 minutes more, divide into bowls and serve.
Nutrition: calories 145 fat 7.1 fiber 2.4 carbs 10.3 protein 6.2

Cajun and Balsamic Okra

Preparation Time: 10 minutes
Cooking Time: 15 minutes
Servings: 2
Ingredients:
- 1 cup okra, sliced
- ½ cup crushed tomatoes
- 1 teaspoon Cajun seasoning
- 2 tablespoons balsamic vinegar
- 1 teaspoon salt
- 1 teaspoon ground black pepper
- 1 tablespoon fresh parsley, chopped
- 1 teaspoon olive oil

Directions:
1.   Heat up a pan with the oil over medium heat, add the okra, seasoning and the remaining ingredients, toss and cook for 15 minutes.
2.   Divide into bowls and serve.
Nutrition: calories 162 fat 4.5 fiber 4.6 carbs 12.6 protein 3

Cashew Zucchinis

Preparation Time: 10 minutes
Cooking Time: 40 minutes
Servings: 4
Ingredients:
- 1 pound zucchinis, sliced
- ½ cup cashews, soaked for a couple of hours and drained
- 1 cup coconut milk
- ¼ teaspoon nutmeg, ground
- 1 teaspoon chili powder
- A pinch of salt and black pepper

Directions:
1.   In a roasting pan, mix the zucchinis with the cashews and the other ingredients, toss gently and cook at 380 degrees F for 40 minutes.
2.   Divide into bowls and serve.
Nutrition: calories 200 fat 5 fiber 3 carbs 7.1 protein 6.5

Chili Fennel

Preparation Time: 10 minutes
Cooking Time: 8 minutes
Servings: 4
Ingredients:
- 2 fennel bulbs, cut into quarters
- 3 tablespoons olive oil
- Salt and black pepper to the taste
- 1 garlic clove, minced
- 1 red chili pepper, chopped
- ¾ cup veggie stock
- Juice of ½ lemon

Directions:
1.   Heat a pan that fits your Air Fryer with the oil over medium-high heat, add garlic and chili pepper, stir and cook for 2 minutes.

2.   Add fennel, salt, pepper, stock, and lemon juice, toss to coat, introduce in your Air Fryer and cook at 350 ° F for at least 6 minutes.
3.   Divide into plates and serve as a side dish.
Nutrition: Calories: 158 kcal Protein: 3.57 g Fat: 11.94 g Carbohydrates: 11.33 g

Collard Greens and Tomatoes

Preparation Time: 10 minutes
Cooking Time: 10 minutes
Servings: 9
Ingredients:
- 1 pound collard greens
- ¼ cup cherry tomatoes, halved
- 1 tablespoon apple cider vinegar
- 2 tablespoons veggie stock
- Salt and black pepper to the taste

Directions:
1.   In a pan that fits the Air Fryer, combine tomatoes, collard greens, vinegar, stock, salt, and pepper, stir, introduce in your Air Fryer and cook at 320 ° F for 10 minutes.
2.   Divide between plates and serve as a side dish.
Nutrition: Calories: 28 kcal Protein: 2.34 g Fat: 0.99 g Carbohydrates: 3.26 g

Bean and Carrot Spirals

Preparation Time: 10 minutes
Cooking Time: 40 minutes
Servings: 24
Ingredients:
- 4 8-inch flour tortillas
- 1 ½ cups of Easy Mean White Bean dip
- 10 ounces spinach leaves
- ½ cup diced carrots
- ½ cup diced red peppers

Directions:
1.   Starts by preparing the bean dip, seen above. Next, spread out the bean dip on each tortilla, making sure to leave about a ¾ inch white border on the tortillas' surface. Next, place spinach in the center of the tortilla, followed by carrots and red peppers.
2.   Roll the tortillas into tight rolls, and cover every rolls with plastic wrap or aluminum foil.
3.   Let them chill in the fridge for twenty-four hours.
4.   Afterward, remove the wrap from the spirals and remove the very ends of the rolls. Slice the rolls into six individual spiral pieces, and arrange them on a platter for serving. Enjoy!
Nutrition: Calories: 205 kcal Protein: 6.41 g Fat: 4.16 g Carbohydrates: 35.13 g

Tofu Nuggets with Barbecue Glaze

Preparation Time: 10 minutes
Cooking Time: 25 minutes
Servings: 9
Ingredients:
- 32 ounces tofu
- 1 cup quick vegan barbecue sauce

Directions:
1.   Set the oven to 425F.

2.	Next, slice the tofu and blot the tofu with clean towels. Next, slice and dice the tofu and completely eliminate the water from the tofu material.
3.	Stir the tofu with the vegan barbecue sauce, and place the tofu on a baking sheet.
4.	Bake the tofu for fifteen minutes. Afterward, stir the tofu and bake the tofu for an additional ten minutes.
5.	Enjoy!
Nutrition: Calories: 311 kcal Protein: 19.94 g Fat: 21.02 g Carbohydrates: 15.55 g

Peppered Pinto Beans

Preparation Time: 10 minutes
Cooking Time: 15 minutes
Servings: 6
Ingredients:
- 1 tsp. Chili powder
- 1 tsp. ground cumin
- .5 cup Vegetable
- 2 cans Pinto beans
- 1 Minced jalapeno
- 1 Diced red bell pepper
- 1 tsp. Olive oil

Directions:
1.	Take out a pot and heat the oil. Cook the jalapeno and pepper for a bit before adding in the pepper, salt, cumin, broth, and beans.
2.	Place to a boil and then reduce the heat to cook for a bit. After 10 minutes, let it cool and serve.
Nutrition: Calories: 183 Carbs: 32g Fat: 2g Protein: 11g

Black Bean Pizza

Preparation Time: 30 minutes
Cooking Time: 20 minutes
Servings: 2
Ingredients:
- 1 Sliced avocado
- 1 Sliced red onion
- 1 Grated carrot
- 1 Sliced tomato
- .5 cup Spicy black bean dip
- 2 Pizza crusts

Directions:
1.	Turn on the oven and let heat to 400 degrees. Layout two crusts on a baking sheet and add the dip onto each one.
2.	Top with the tomato slices and sprinkle the carrots and the onion on a well.
3.	Add to the oven and let it bake for about 20 minutes or so until done. Top with the avocado before serving.
Nutrition: Calories: 379 Carbs: 59g Fat: 13g Protein: 13g

Vegetable and Chickpea Loaf

Preparation Time: 10 minutes
Cooking Time: 15 minutes
Servings: 4
Ingredients:
- 1 tsp. Salt
- .5 tsp. Dried sage
- 1 tsp. Dried savory
- 1 tbsp. Soy sauce
- .25 cup Parsley
- .5 cup Breadcrumbs
- .75 cup Oats
- .75 cup Chickpea flour
- 1.5 cup cooked chickpeas
- 2 Minced garlic cloves
- 1 Chopped yellow onion
- 1 Shredded carrot
- 1 Shredded white potato

Directions:
1.	Set the oven to 350F. Take out a loaf pan and then grease it up.
2.	Squeeze out the liquid from the potato and add to the food processor with the garlic, onion, and carrot.
3.	Add the chickpeas and pulse to blend well. Add in the rest of the ingredients here, and when it is done, use your hands to form this into a loaf and add to the pan.
4.	Place into the oven to bake for a bit until it is nice and firm. Let it cool down and then slice.
Nutrition: Calories: 351 kcal Protein: 16.86 g Fat: 6.51 g Carbohydrates: 64 g

Thyme and Lemon Couscous

Preparation Time: 5 minutes
Cooking Time: 10 minutes
Servings: 6
Ingredients:
- .25 cup Chopped parsley
- 1.5 cup Couscous
- 2 tbsp. Chopped thyme
- Juice and zest of a lemon
- 2.75 cup Vegetable stock

Directions:
1.	Take out a pot and add in the thyme, lemon juice, and vegetable stock. Stir in the couscous after it has gotten to a boil and then take off the heat.
2.	Allow sitting covered until it can take in all of the liquid. Then fluff up with a form.
3.	Stir in the parsley and lemon zest, then serve warm.
Nutrition: Calories: 922 kcal Protein: 2.7 g Fat: 101.04 g Carbohydrates: 10.02 g

Pesto and White Bean Pasta

Preparation Time: 10 minutes
Cooking Time: 10 minutes
Servings: 4
Ingredients:
- .5 cup Chopped black olives
- .25 Diced red onion
- 1 cup Chopped tomato
- .5 cup Spinach pesto
- 1.5 cup Cannellini beans
- 8 oz. Rotini pasta, cooked

Directions:
1.	Bring out a bowl and toss together the pesto, beans, and pasta.

2.	Add in the olives, red onion, and tomato and toss around a bit more before serving.
Nutrition: Calories 544 Carbs 83g Fat 17g Protein 23g

Baked Okra and Tomato

Preparation Time: 10 minutes
Cooking Time: 75 minutes
Servings: 6
Ingredients:
- ½ cup lima beans, frozen
- 4 tomatoes, chopped
- 8 ounces okra, fresh and washed, stemmed, sliced into ½ inch thick slices
- 1 onion, sliced into rings
- ½ sweet pepper, seeded and sliced thin
- Pinch of crushed red pepper
- Salt to taste

Directions:
1.	Preheat your oven to 350 degrees Fahrenheit
2.	Cook lima beans in water accordingly and drain them, take a 2quart casserole tin
3.	Add all listed ingredients to the dish and cover with foil, bake for 45 minutes
4.	Uncover the dish, stir well and bake for 35 minutes more
5.	Stir then serve, and enjoy!
Nutrition: Calories: 55 Fat: 0g Carbohydrates: 12g Protein: 3g

Curried Apple

Preparation Time: 10 minutes
Cooking Time: 90 minutes
Servings: 4
Ingredients:
- 1 tablespoon fresh lemon juice
- ½ cup of water
- 2 apples, Fuji or Honeycrisp, cored and thinly sliced into rings
- 1 teaspoon curry powder

Directions:
1.	Set the oven to 200F, take a rimmed baking sheet and line with parchment paper
2.	Take a bowl and mix in lemon juice and water, add apples and soak for 2 minutes
3.	Pat them dry and arrange in a single layer on your baking sheet, dust curry powder on top of apple slices
4.	Bake for 45 minutes. After 45 minutes, turn the apples and bake for 45 minutes more
5.	Let them cool for extra crispiness, serve and enjoy!
Nutrition: Calories: 240 Fat: 13g Carbohydrates: 20g Protein: 6g

Wild Rice and Millet Croquettes

Preparation Time: 5 minutes
Cooking Time: 20 minutes
Servings: 4
Ingredients:
- ¾ cooked millet
- ½ cup cooked wild rice
- 3 tablespoons extra virgin olive oil
- ¼ cup onion, minced
- 1 celery rib, finely minced
- ¼ cup carrot, shredded
- 1/3 cup all-purpose flour
- ¼ cup fresh parsley, chopped
- 2 teaspoons dried dill weed
- Salt and pepper to taste

Directions:
1.	Add cooked millet and wild rice to a large-sized bowl, keep it to one side
2.	Take a medium skillet and add 1 tablespoon of oil, place it over medium heat
3.	Put onion, celery, and carrot and cook for at least 5 minutes
4.	Add veggies and stir in flour, parsley, salt, pepper, and dill weed
5.	Mix well and transfer to the fridge, let it sit for 20 minutes
6.	Use hands to shape mixture into small patties, take a large skillet and place it over medium heat
7.	Add 2 tablespoons of oil and let it heat up
8.	Add croquettes and cook for 8 minutes in total until golden brown
9.	Serve and enjoy!
Nutrition: Calories: 250 Fat: 9g Carbohydrates: 33g Protein: 9g

Grilled Eggplant Steaks

Preparation Time: 10 minutes
Cooking Time: 10 minutes
Servings: 4
Ingredients:
- 4 Roma tomatoes, diced
- 8 ounces cashew cream
- 2 eggplants
- 1 tablespoon olive oil
- 1 cup parsley, chopped
- 1 cucumber, diced
- Salt and pepper to taste

Directions:
1.	Slice eggplants into three thick steaks, drizzle with oil, and season with salt and pepper
2.	Grill in a pan for 4 minutes per side
3.	Top with remaining ingredients
4.	Serve and enjoy!
Nutrition: Calories: 86 Fat: 7g Carbohydrates: 12g Protein: 8g

Glazed Avocado

Preparation Time: 10 minutes
Cooking Time: 12 minutes
Servings: 4
Ingredients:
- 1 tablespoon stevia
- 1 teaspoon olive oil
- 1 teaspoon water
- 1 teaspoon lemon juice
- ½ teaspoon rosemary, dried
- ½ teaspoon ground black pepper
- 2 avocados, peeled, pitted and cut into large pieces

Directions:
1.   Heat up a pan with the oil over medium heat, add the avocados, stevia and the other ingredients, toss, cook for 12 minutes, divide into bowls and serve.
Nutrition: calories 262 fat 9.6 fiber 0.1 carbs 6.5 protein 7.9

Mango and Leeks Meatballs

Preparation Time: 20 minutes
Cooking Time: 10 minutes
Servings: 4
Ingredients:
- 1 tablespoon mango puree
- 1 cup leeks, chopped
- ½ cup tofu, crumbled
- 1 teaspoon dried oregano
- 1 tablespoon almond flour
- 1 teaspoon olive oil
- 1 tablespoon flax meal
- ½ teaspoon chili flakes

Directions:
1.   In the mixing bowl, mix up mango puree with leeks, tofu and the other ingredients except the oil and stir well.
2.   Make the small meatballs.
3.   After this, pour the olive oil in the skillet and heat it up.
4.   Add the meatballs in the skillet and cook them for 4 minutes from each side.
Nutrition: calories 147 fat 8.6 fiber 4.5 carbs 5.6 protein 5.3

Spicy Carrots and Olives

Preparation Time: 15 minutes
Cooking Time: 10 minutes
Servings: 4
Ingredients:
- ½ teaspoon hot paprika
- 1 red chili pepper, minced
- ¼ teaspoon ground cumin
- ¼ teaspoon dried oregano
- ¼ teaspoon dried basil
- ½ teaspoon salt
- 1 tablespoon olive oil
- 1 pound baby carrots, peeled
- 1 cup kalamata olives, pitted and halved
- juice of 1 lime

Directions:
1.   Heat up a pan with the oil over medium heat, add the carrots, olives and the other ingredients, toss, cook for 10 minutes, divide between plates and serve.
Nutrition: calories 141 fat 5.8 fiber 4.3 carbs 7.5 protein 9.6

Harissa Mushrooms

Preparation Time: 15 minutes
Cooking Time: 30 minutes
Servings: 4
Ingredients:
- 1-pound mushroom caps
- 1 teaspoon harissa
- 1 teaspoon rosemary, dried
- 2 spring onions, chopped
- 1 leek, sliced
- 1 teaspoon thyme, dried
- 1 cup crushed tomatoes
- 1 teaspoon sweet paprika
- A pinch of salt and black pepper
- 1 tablespoon olive oil
- ½ teaspoon lemon juice

Directions:
1.   In a roasting pan, mix the mushrooms with the harissa, rosemary and the other ingredients and toss.
2.   Preheat the oven to 360F and put the pan inside.
3.   Cook the mix for 30 minutes, divide between plates and serve.
Nutrition: calories 250 fat 12.1 fiber 5.3 carbs 14.5 protein 12.9

Leeks and Artichokes Mix

Preparation Time: 10 minutes
Cooking Time: 30 minutes
Servings: 4
Ingredients:
- 2 cups canned artichoke hearts, drained and quartered
- 3 leeks, sliced
- 1 cup cherry tomatoes, halved
- ¼ cup coconut cream
- 1 tablespoon almond flakes
- 1 teaspoon olive oil
- 1 teaspoon oregano, dried
- 1 teaspoon salt
- 1 teaspoon ground black pepper
- ¼ cup of chives, chopped

Directions:
1.   Heat up a pan with the oil over medium heat, add the leeks, oregano, salt and pepper, stir and cook for 10 minutes.
2.   Add artichokes and the other ingredients, toss, cook for 20 minutes, divide into bowls and serve.
Nutrition: calories 234 fat 9.7 fiber 4.2 carbs 9.6 protein 12.3

Coconut Avocado

Preparation Time: 10 minutes
Cooking Time: 0 minutes
Servings: 2
Ingredients:
- 2 avocados, halved, pitted and roughly cubed
- 1 teaspoon dried thyme
- 2 tablespoons coconut cream
- 1 cup spring onions, chopped
- 1 teaspoon turmeric powder
- Salt and black pepper to the taste
- ¼ teaspoon cayenne pepper
- ½ teaspoon onion powder
- ½ teaspoon garlic powder
- 1 teaspoon paprika

- Salt and black pepper to the taste
- 2 tablespoons lemon juice

Directions:
1. In a bowl, mix the avocados with the thyme, coconut cream and the other ingredients, toss, divide between plates and serve.
Nutrition: calories 160 fat 6.9 fiber 7 carbs 12 protein 7

Avocado Cream

Preparation Time: 10 minutes
Cooking Time: 0 minutes
Servings: 4
Ingredients:
- 2 avocados, pitted, peeled and chopped
- 3 cups veggie stock
- 1 teaspoon curry powder
- 1 teaspoon cumin, ground
- 1 teaspoon basil, dried
- 2 scallions, chopped
- Salt and black pepper to the taste
- 2 tablespoons coconut oil
- 2/3 cup coconut cream, unsweetened

Directions:
1. In a blender, mix the avocados with the stock, curry powder and the other ingredients, blend and serve.
Nutrition: calories 212 fat 8 fiber 4 carbs 6.1 protein 4.1

Tamarind Avocado Bowls

Preparation Time: 10 minutes
Cooking Time: 0 minutes
Servings: 2
Ingredients:
- 1 teaspoon cumin seeds
- 1 tablespoon olive oil
- ½ teaspoon garam masala
- 1 teaspoon ground ginger
- 2 avocados, peeled, pitted and roughly cubed
- 1 mango, peeled, and cubed
- 1 cup cherry tomatoes, halved
- ½ teaspoon cayenne pepper
- 1 teaspoon turmeric powder
- 3 tablespoons tamarind paste

Directions:
1. In a bowl, mix the avocados with the mango and the other ingredients, toss and serve.
Nutrition: calories 170 fat 4.5 fiber 3 carbs 5 protein 6

Onion and Tomato Bowls

Preparation Time: 10 minutes
Cooking Time: 0 minutes
Servings: 4
Ingredients:
- 1 tablespoon olive oil
- 2 red bell peppers, cut into thin strips
- 2 red onions, cut into thin strips
- Salt and black pepper to the taste
- 1 teaspoon dried basil

- 1 pound tomatoes, cut into wedges
- 1 teaspoon balsamic vinegar
- 1 teaspoon sweet paprika

Directions:
1. In a bowl, mix the peppers with the onions and the other ingredients, toss and serve.
Nutrition: calories 107 fat 4.5 fiber 2 carbs 7.1 protein 6

Avocado and Leeks Mix

Preparation Time: 10 minutes
Cooking Time: 0 minutes
Servings: 4
Ingredients:
- 1 small red onion, chopped
- 2 avocados, pitted, peeled and chopped
- 1 teaspoon chili powder
- 2 leeks, sliced
- 1 cup cucumber, cubed
- 1 cup cherry tomatoes, halved
- Salt and black pepper to the taste
- 2 tablespoons cumin powder
- 2 tablespoons lime juice
- 1 tablespoon parsley, chopped

Directions:
1. In a bowl, mix the onion with the avocados, chili powder and the other ingredients, toss and serve.
Nutrition: calories 120 fat 2 fiber 2 carbs 7 protein 4

Lemon Lentils and Carrots

Preparation Time: 10 minutes
Cooking Time: 20 minutes
Servings: 6
Ingredients:
- 1 cup brown lentils, soaked overnight and drained
- 1 cup carrots, shredded
- 1 cup spring onions, chopped
- 1 teaspoon curry powder
- 1 teaspoon turmeric powder
- 1 teaspoon garam masala
- 2 tablespoons lemon juice
- ¼ cup parsley, chopped
- 2 garlic cloves, minced
- A pinch of salt and black pepper
- ½ teaspoon thyme, dried
- 2 tablespoons olive oil

Directions:
1. Heat up a pan with the oil over medium heat, add the garlic, carrots and spring onions and cook for 5 minutes.
2. Add the lentils and the other ingredients, toss and simmer over medium heat for 15 minutes.
3. Divide between plates and serve.
Nutrition: calories 240 fat 7 fiber 3.4 carbs 12 protein 6

Cabbage Bowls

Preparation Time: 10 minutes
Cooking Time: 10 minutes
Servings: 4

Ingredients:
- 1 green cabbage head, shredded
- 1 red cabbage head, shredded
- 1 teaspoon garam masala
- 1 teaspoon basil, dried
- 1 teaspoon coriander, ground
- 1 teaspoon mustard seeds
- 1 tablespoon balsamic vinegar
- ¼ cup tomatoes, crushed
- A pinch of salt and black pepper
- 3 carrots, shredded
- 1 yellow bell pepper, chopped
- 1 orange bell pepper, chopped
- 1 red bell pepper, chopped
- 2 tablespoons dill, chopped
- 2 tablespoons olive oil

Directions:
1.   Heat up a pan with the oil over medium heat, add the peppers and carrots and cook for 2 minutes.
2.   Add the cabbage and the other ingredients, toss, cook for 10 minutes, divide between plates and serve.
Nutrition: calories 150 fat 9 fiber 4 carbs 3.3 protein 4.4

Pomegranate and Pears Salad

Preparation Time: 10 minutes
Cooking Time: 0 minutes
Servings: 3
Ingredients:
- 3 big pears, cored and cut with a spiralizer
- ¾ cup pomegranate seeds
- 2 cups baby spinach
- ½ cup black olives, pitted and cubed
- ¾ cup walnuts, chopped1 tablespoon olive oil
- 1 tablespoon coconut sugar
- 1 teaspoon white sesame seeds
- 2 tablespoons chives, chopped
- 1 tablespoon balsamic vinegar
- 1 garlic clove, minced
- A pinch of sea salt and black pepper

Directions:
1.   In a bowl, mix the pears with the pomegranate seeds, spinach and the other ingredients, toss and serve.
Nutrition: calories 200 fat 3.9 fiber 4 carbs 6 protein 3.3

Bulgur and Tomato Mix

Preparation Time: 15 minutes
Cooking Time: 0 minutes
Servings: 4
Ingredients:
- 1 ½ cups hot water
- 1 cup bulgur
- Juice of 1 lime
- 1 cup cherry tomatoes, halved
- 4 tablespoons cilantro, chopped
- ½ cup cranberries, dried
- juice of ½ lemon

- 1 teaspoon oregano, dried
- 1/3 cup almonds, sliced
- ¼ cup green onions, chopped
- ½ cup red bell peppers, chopped
- ½ cup carrots, grated
- 1 tablespoon avocado oil
- A pinch of sea salt and black pepper

Directions:
1.   Place bulgur into a bowl, add boiling water to it, stir, cover and set aside for 15 minutes.
2.   Fluff bulgur with a fork and transfer to a bowl.
3.   Add the rest of the ingredients, toss and serve.
Nutrition: calories 260 fat 4.4 fiber 3 carbs 7 protein 10

Beans Mix

Preparation Time: 10 minutes
Cooking Time: 15 minutes
Servings: 4
Ingredients:
- 1 ½ cups cooked black beans
- 1 cup cooked red kidney beans
- ½ teaspoon garlic powder
- ½ teaspoon smoked paprika
- 2 teaspoons chili powder
- 1 tablespoon olive oil
- 1 ½ cups chickpeas, cooked
- 1 teaspoon garam masala
- 1 red bell pepper, chopped
- 2 tomatoes, chopped
- 1 cup cashews, chopped
- ½ cup veggie stock
- 1 tablespoon balsamic vinegar
- 1 tablespoon oregano, chopped
- 1 tablespoon dill, chopped
- 1 cup corn kernels, chopped

Directions:
1.   Heat up a pan with the oil over medium heat, add the beans, garlic powder, chili powder and the other ingredients, toss and cook for 15 minutes.
2.   Divide between plates and serve.
Nutrition: calories 300 fat 8.3 fiber 3.3 carbs 6 protein 13

Sweet Potato Patties

Total time: 35 minutes
Ingredients
- 1 cup cooked short-grain brown rice, fully cooled
- 1 cup grated sweet potato
- ½ cup diced onion
- Pinch sea salt
- ¼ cup fresh parsley, finely chopped
- 1 tablespoon dried dill, or 2 tablespoons fresh
- 1 to 2 tablespoons nutritional yeast (optional)
- ½ cup whole-grain flour, or breadcrumbs, or gluten-free flour
- 1 teaspoon olive oil

Directions

1. Stir together the rice, sweet potato, onion, and salt in a large bowl. Allow it to sit for a few minutes, so that the salt can draw the moisture out of the potato and onion. Stir in the parsley, dill, and nutritional yeast (if using), then add enough flour to make the batter sticky, adding a spoonful or two of water if necessary.

2. Form the mixture into tight balls, and squish slightly into patties.

3. Heat a large skillet on medium, then add the oil. Cook for 7 to 10 minutes, then flip. Cook another 5 to 7 minutes and serve.

4. Make ahead: Be sure your rice is thoroughly cooled before you begin, or it will not be sticky enough to make into a patty. This is a great way to use up leftover rice.

Simple Sesame Stir-Fry

Total time: 30 minutes

Ingredients

- 1 cup quinoa
- 2 cups water
- Pinch sea salt
- 1 head broccoli
- 1 to 2 teaspoons untoasted sesame oil, or olive oil
- 1 cup snow peas, or snap peas, ends trimmed and cut in half
- 1 cup frozen shelled edamame beans, or peas
- 2 cups chopped Swiss chard, or other large-leafed green
- 2 scallions, chopped
- 2 tablespoons water
- 1 teaspoon toasted sesame oil
- 1 tablespoon tamari, or soy sauce
- 2 tablespoons sesame seeds

Directions

1. Put the quinoa, water, and sea salt in a medium pot, bring it to a boil for a minute, then turn to low and simmer, covered, for 20 minutes. The quinoa is fully cooked when you see the swirl of the grains with a translucent center, and it is fluffy. Do not stir the quinoa while it is cooking.

2. Meanwhile, cut the broccoli into bite-size florets, cutting and pulling apart from the stem. Also chop the stem into bite-size pieces.

3. Heat a large skillet to high, and sauté the broccoli in the untoasted sesame oil, with a pinch of salt to help it soften. Keep this moving continuously, so that it doesn't burn, and add an extra drizzle of oil if needed as you add the rest of the vegetables. Add the snow peas next, continuing to stir. Add the edamame until they thaw. Add the Swiss chard and scallions at the same time, tossing for only a minute to wilt. Then add 2 tablespoons of water to the hot skillet so that it sizzles and finishes the vegetables with a quick steam.

4. Dress with the toasted sesame oil and tamari and toss one last time. Remove from the heat immediately.

5. Serve a scoop of cooked quinoa, topped with stir-fry and sprinkled with some sesame seeds, and an extra drizzle of tamari and/or toasted sesame oil if you like.

Options: I went for a green theme here, but make this with pretty much any vegetables you like (or have left in the fridge): bell peppers, carrots, mushrooms, eggplant, zucchini, cherry tomatoes. Just think through which take the longest to cook, and add them first, finishing with whatever takes the least time to cook.

Spaghetti and Buckwheat Meatballs

Total time: 65 minutes

Ingredients

For the Buckwheat Meatballs
- ½ cup toasted buckwheat
- 2¼ cups water, divided
- Pinch sea salt
- 2 tablespoons ground flaxseed, or chia seeds
- 2 tablespoons tomato paste, or ketchup
- 1 tablespoon stone-ground mustard
- 2 tablespoons tamari, or soy sauce
- 1 tablespoon mixed dried herbs (basil, oregano, marjoram)
- 1 teaspoon onion powder
- 1 teaspoon garlic powder
- ½ teaspoon ground cumin
- ½ teaspoon smoked paprika, or regular paprika

For the Spaghetti
- 7 ounces whole-grain spaghetti, or ½ spaghetti squash
- 2 cups Marinara Sauce
- 2 to 3 tablespoons Cheesy Sprinkle

Directions

1. Preheat the oven to 350°F. Lightly grease a large rectangular baking sheet with olive oil, or line it with parchment paper.

2. Put the buckwheat in a small pot with 2 cups of the water and the salt and bring to a boil. Turn the heat down and simmer, covered, for about 5 minutes. (If you use untoasted buckwheat, it will take closer to 20 minutes to cook after boiling.)

3. In a small bowl, mix the ground flaxseed with the remaining ¼ cup water and set aside.

4. In a large bowl, mix the tomato paste, mustard, tamari, herbs, onion powder, garlic powder, cumin, and paprika. Add the cooked buckwheat and soaked flax and stir to combine.

5. Shape spoonfuls of the mix into 20 to 24 small balls. Transfer to the baking sheet and put in the oven for 30 minutes.

6. Cook the spaghetti (or spaghetti squash) by putting it in a pot of boiling water and boiling until soft, about 10 minutes (15 to 20 for the squash). Drain the pasta, or scoop the flesh out of the squash's skin.

7. Once the meatballs are done, take them out of the oven and let cool for a few minutes.

8.	Serve a plate of spaghetti (or squash) topped with Marinara Sauce, a few buckwheat meatballs, and Cheesy Sprinkle.

Orange Walnut Pasta

Total time: 40 minutes
Ingredients
*	½ spaghetti squash, or 7 ounces whole-grain pasta, or 14 ounces mixed vegetables
*	Zest and juice of 1 orange
*	2 tablespoons olive oil
*	1 garlic clove, pressed
*	Pinch sea salt
*	2 to 3 tablespoons fresh parsley, finely chopped
*	10 olives, pitted and chopped
*	¼ cup walnuts, chopped
*	2 to 3 tablespoons nutritional yeast (optional)
*	1.Cook your noodle of choice:
Directions
1.	Spaghetti squash: Boil until soft, about 15 to 20 minutes. Scoop the flesh out of the skin. Drain for a few minutes.
2.	Whole-grain pasta: Put it in a pot of boiling water with a pinch salt and cook until just soft, about 10 to 15 minutes. Drain.
3.	Mixed vegetables: Peel, and cut the ends flat to each other. Run through a spiralizer, or use a vegetable peeler to make long noodles. Either have them raw (in which case, you can toss with a sprinkle of salt and leave to soften and drain for 20 to 30 minutes), or cook lightly by steaming or boiling for just a few minutes.
4.	In a large bowl, add the orange zest and juice. Whisk in an amount of olive oil that's about half the volume of the orange juice, along with the pressed garlic, and the salt; stir to blend. Add the noodles to the dressing, and toss.
5.	Serve topped with a sprinkling of fresh parsley, chopped olives, walnuts, and a dusting of nutritional yeast (if using).

Roasted Cauliflower Tacos

Total time: 40 minutes
Ingredients
For the Roasted Cauliflower
*	1 head cauliflower, cut into bite-size pieces
*	1 tablespoon olive oil (optional)
*	2 tablespoons whole-grain flour
*	2 tablespoons nutritional yeast
*	1 to 2 teaspoons smoked paprika
*	½ to 1 teaspoon chili powder
*	Pinch sea salt
For the Tacos
*	2 cups shredded lettuce
*	2 cups cherry tomatoes, quartered
*	2 carrots, scrubbed or peeled, and grated
*	½ cup <u>Fresh Mango Salsa</u>
*	½ cup <u>Guacamole</u>
*	8 small whole-grain or corn tortillas
*	1 lime, cut into 8 wedges

Directions
To Make the Roasted Cauliflower
1.	Preheat the oven to 350°F. Lightly grease a large rectangular baking sheet with olive oil, or line it with parchment paper.
2.	In a large bowl, toss the cauliflower pieces with oil (if using), or just rinse them so they're wet. The idea is to get the seasonings to stick.
3.	In a smaller bowl, mix together the flour, nutritional yeast, paprika, chili powder, and salt. Add the seasonings to the cauliflower, and mix it around with your hands to thoroughly coat.
4.	Spread the cauliflower on the baking sheet, and roast for 20 to 30 minutes, or until softened.
To Make the Tacos
1.	Prep the veggies, salsa, and guacamole while the cauliflower is roasting.
2.	Once the cauliflower is cooked, heat the tortillas for just a few minutes in the oven or in a small skillet.
3.	Set everything out on the table, and assemble your tacos as you go. Give a squeeze of fresh lime just before eating.
4.	Leftovers: Double the batch of roasted cauliflower and add it to salads, bowls, and wraps, or serve as a side dish with Avo-nnaise.

Build Your Own Mushroom Fajitas

Total time: 40 minutes
Ingredients
For the Spicy Glazed Mushrooms
*	1 (10- to 12-ounce) package cremini mushrooms
*	1 teaspoon olive oil
*	½ to 1 teaspoon chili powder
*	Pinch freshly ground black pepper
*	Pinch sea salt
*	1 teaspoon maple syrup
For the Fajitas
*	1 onion
*	1 to 2 teaspoons olive oil, or 1 tablespoon vegetable broth or water
*	Pinch sea salt
*	1 zucchini, cut into large matchsticks
*	1 bell pepper, any color, seeded and sliced into long strips
*	½ cup fresh cilantro, finely chopped
*	3 to 4 scallions, sliced
*	2 carrots, grated
*	6 whole-grain or corn tortilla wraps
*	<u>Guacamole</u>
*	<u>Fresh Mango Salsa</u>
*	<u>Cashew Sour Cream</u>
*	Your favorite hot sauce (optional)

Directions
To Make the Spicy Glazed Mushrooms
1.	To glaze the mushrooms, wipe them clean with a paper towel, then cut them into thin slices.
2.	Heat the oil in a large skillet over medium heat, then sauté the mushrooms until soft, about 10 minutes. Add the chili powder, pepper, and salt and stir to coat the mushrooms. Add the maple syrup to

the skillet, stir to coat, and allow to cook for a few minutes to create a glaze.

3. Transfer the mushrooms to a heatproof dish, and keep them warm in the oven on very low, or allow them to cool if you aren't particular.

To Make the Fajitas

1. Cut the onion in half from stem to tip. Then slice the strips perpendicular to that cut, so they make half moons. Separate the layers into arclike shapes.

2. Rinse the mushroom skillet if you want to clear the flavors, or leave it as is, and put the skillet back on the heat. Sauté the onion in the olive oil and salt. Once the onion is translucent, about 5 minutes, add the zucchini and bell pepper, and sauté until they're soft, 7 to 8 minutes.

3. While the zucchini is cooking, prepare the cilantro, scallions, and carrots.

4. Heat your tortilla wraps for a few minutes in a toaster oven, oven, or dry skillet. Place everything on the table so each person can assemble their own fajita.

Sun-dried Tomato and Pesto Quinoa

Total time: 25 minutes

Ingredients
- 1 teaspoon olive oil, or 1 tablespoon vegetable broth or water
- 1 cup chopped onion
- 1 garlic clove, minced
- 1 cup chopped zucchini
- Pinch sea salt
- 1 tomato, chopped
- 2 tablespoons chopped sun-dried tomatoes
- 2 to 3 tablespoons Basil Pesto
- 1 cup chopped spinach
- 2 cups cooked quinoa
- 1 tablespoon Cheesy Sprinkle, optional

Directions

1. Heat the oil in a large skillet on medium-high, then sauté the onion, about 5 minutes. Add the garlic when the onion has softened, then add the zucchini and salt.

2. Once the zucchini is somewhat soft, about 5 minutes, turn off the heat and add the fresh and sun-dried tomatoes. Mix to combine, then toss in the pesto. Toss the vegetables to coat them.

3. Layer the spinach, then quinoa, then the zucchini mixture on a plate, topped with a bit of Cheesy Sprinkle (if using).

Options: This is a great way to use leftover cooked quinoa, but this dish is also nice with whole-grain pasta.

Olive and White Bean Pasta

Total time: 30 minutes

Ingredients
- ½ cup whole-grain pasta
- Pinch sea salt
- 1 teaspoon olive oil, or 1 tablespoon vegetable broth
- ¼ cup thinly sliced red bell pepper
- ¼ cup thinly sliced zucchini
- ½ cup cooked cannellini beans
- ½ cup spinach
- 1 tablespoon balsamic vinegar
- 2 or 3 black olives, pitted and chopped
- 1 tablespoon nutritional yeast

Directions

1. Bring a pot of water to a boil, then add the pasta with the salt to cook until just tender (per the package directions).

2. Meanwhile, in a large skillet, heat the oil and lightly sauté the bell pepper and zucchini, 7 to 8 minutes. Add the beans to warm for 2 minutes, then add the spinach last, just until it wilts. Drizzle with the vinegar at the end.

3. Serve the pasta topped or tossed with the bean mixture, and sprinkled with the olives and nutritional yeast.

Options: Use brown rice, quinoa, or corn pasta to easily make this dish gluten-free. It would also be nice with cooked basmati rice instead of pasta.

Vietnamese Summer Rolls

Total time: 60 minutes

Ingredients
- 10 round rice roll wraps
- ¼ cup fresh basil, mint, cilantro, or parsley leaves (or a combination)
- 10 palm-size lettuce leaves (either small leaves, or tear larger leaves into smaller pieces)
- 2 carrots, grated or julienned
- ½ cucumber, julienned
- 1 mango, peeled and sliced into long, thin pieces
- 3 scallions, sliced lengthwise into quarters
- 1 cup bean sprouts
- ½ cup Peanut Sauce

Directions

1. Fill a deep plate with room-temperature water, and put a rice roll wrap in to soften. It will take a couple of minutes to get very soft. Pull it out of the water and allow it to drip for a few seconds, then place it on a dry plate.

2. Down the center of the wrap, lay 2 fresh basil leaves and a lettuce leaf, then cover with the carrots, cucumber, mango, scallions, and bean sprouts. Don't overfill, or it will be difficult to roll.

3. Fold over the top and bottom of the rice wrap, then fold one side over the filling and tuck it under the filling a bit. Squeeze slightly with your hands and then roll to the end of the other side. Allow the wraps to sit and stick together before serving.

4. Slice each wrap in half, and serve with Peanut Sauce for dipping.

Technique: Put the next wrap in the water to soften while you roll the current one, so that you don't have to wait for them to soften each time.

Potato Skin Samosas

Total time: 50 minutes

Ingredients
- 4 small baking potatoes
- 1 teaspoon coconut oil

- 1 small onion, finely chopped
- 2 garlic cloves, minced
- 1 small piece ginger, minced or grated
- 2 to 3 teaspoons curry powder
- Pinch sea salt
- Pinch freshly ground black pepper
- 2 carrots, grated
- ¼ cup frozen peas, thawed
- ¼ cup fresh cilantro, or parsley, chopped

Directions

1. Preheat the oven to 350°F.
2. Pierce the potatoes with a fork, wrap them in aluminum foil, and bake 30 minutes, or until soft.
3. While the potatoes are cooking, heat the oil in a medium skillet and sauté the onion until it's soft, about 5 minutes. Add the garlic and ginger and sauté until they're soft as well, about 3 minutes. Add the curry powder, salt, and pepper, and stir to fully coat the onion. Turn off the heat.
4. When the potatoes are cooked, take them out of the foil and slice them in half.
5. If you like, you can prepare these in advance and then heat them up in the oven at 350°F for 10 minutes when you're ready to serve.

Toppings: Cashew Sour Cream is lovely with these, as is a drizzle of Peanut Sauce. Or you could try Fresh Mango Salsa.

Spicy Chickpea Sushi Rolls

Total time: 75 minutes

Ingredients

For the Sushi Rice
- 1 cup short-grain brown rice
- 2 cups water
- Pinch sea salt
- 1 to 2 tablespoons brown rice vinegar

For the Spicy Chickpea Filling
- ½ cup cooked chickpeas
- 2 to 3 scallions, finely chopped
- ⅛ teaspoon cayenne pepper (more or less, to your taste)
- 1 to 2 tablespoons Avo-nnaise

For the Sushi Rolls
- 3 cups cooked sushi rice
- 4 nori sheets
- ¼ cucumber, julienned

To Serve
- Tamari or soy sauce
- 1 tablespoon pickled ginger
- 1 teaspoon wasabi

Directions

To Make the Sushi Rice

1. Put the rice and water in a large pot. Add a bit of sea salt, bring to a boil for a couple of minutes, then turn to low and simmer, covered, for 45 minutes. The rice is fully cooked when it is dry and fluffy. Do not stir the rice while it is cooking. This will yield about 3 to 3½ cups sushi rice, which is the perfect amount for 4 rolls.
2. Transfer the rice to a large bowl so that it can fully cool. Stir in the vinegar, just enough to make the rice stick to itself, along with another sprinkle of salt. Stir the rice occasionally to speed up the cooling. You can also put it in the fridge to cool it more quickly.

To Make the Spicy Chickpea Filling

Mash the chickpeas with a potato masher, fork, or your hands. Mix in the scallions, cayenne, and just enough Avo-nnaise to make it stick together. You don't want this to be too creamy, or it will make your sushi soggy.

To Make the Sushi Rolls

1. Set out a small dish of water, then lay out a sheet of nori on your rolling mat. It has a smooth side and a rough side; lay it rough side up, with the long side parallel to you.
2. Lightly wet your hands and put a small handful of rice onto the nori. Gently spread the rice out to cover the sheet. Leave about 1 inch along the top edge free of rice.
3. Spoon about 2 tablespoons spicy chickpea filling along the bottom edge, side to side, along with a few cucumber sticks. All the veggies should only cover about one-third of the nori sheet.
4. Dry your hands, and pick up the bottom of the rolling mat. Roll it over the row of vegetables. Press tightly back toward you as you roll, and press down on the roll a bit. Do not squish, but make sure you are getting a tight roll.
5. Pick up the back end of the rolling mat. Dip a finger in the water, and run it along the top edge of the nori, where there is no rice. Then finish rolling, so the bare edge seals against the outside of the roll. Cover it back over with the mat, and gently compress the roll, just to help it seal.
6. Let your sushi roll sit for a few minutes for the nori to be softened by the rice, then cut into 6 to 8 slices and serve. Repeat to make 4 rolls.
7. Serve with a dipping bowl of tamari, some pickled ginger, and some wasabi.
8. Make ahead: Make double the rice if you want to make 4 of both this roll and the Avocado Red Pepper Sushi Rolls for a sushi party, or make one batch of rice and then 2 of each roll. Enjoy a piece of pickled ginger between as a palate cleanser.

Exquisite Banana, Apple, and Coconut Curry

Total time: 6 hours 10 minutes

Ingredients

- 1/2 cup of amaranth seeds
- 1 apple, cored and sliced
- 1 banana, sliced
- 1 1/2 cups of diced tomatoes
- 3 teaspoons of chopped parsley
- 1 green pepper, chopped
- 1 large white onion, peeled and diced
- 2 teaspoons of minced garlic
- 1 teaspoon of salt
- 1 teaspoon of ground cumin
- 2 1/2 tablespoons of curry powder
- 2 tablespoons of flour
- 2 bay leaves
- 1/2 cup of white wine
- 8 fluid ounce of coconut milk

- 1/2 cup of water

Directions:

1. Using a food processor place the apple, tomatoes, garlic and pulse it until it gets smooth but a little bit chunky.
2. Add this mixture to a 6-quarts slow cooker and add the remaining ingredients.
3. Stir until it mixes properly and cover the top.
4. Plug in the slow cooker; adjust the cooking time to 6 hours and let it cook on the low heat setting or until it is cooked thoroughly.
5. Add the seasoning and serve right away.

Hearty Vegetarian Lasagna Soup

Total time: 7 hours 20 minutes

Ingredients

- 12 ounces of lasagna noodles
- 4 cups of spinach leaves
- 2 cups of brown mushrooms, sliced
- 2 medium-sized zucchinis, stemmed and sliced
- 28 ounces of crushed tomatoes
- 1 medium-sized white onion, peeled and diced
- 2 teaspoon of minced garlic
- 1 tablespoon of dried basil
- 2 bay leaves
- 2 teaspoons of salt
- 1/8 teaspoon of red pepper flakes
- 2 teaspoons of ground black pepper
- 2 teaspoons of dried oregano
- 15-ounce of tomato sauce
- 6 cups of vegetable broth

Directions:

1. Grease a 6-quarts slow cooker and place all the ingredients in it except for the lasagna and spinach.
2. Cover the top, plug in the slow cooker; adjust the cooking time to 7 hours and let it cook on the low heat setting or until it is properly done.
3. In the meantime, cook the lasagna noodles in the boiling water for 7 to 10 minutes or until it gets soft.
4. Then drain and set it aside until the slow cooker is done cooking.
5. When it is done, add the lasagna noodles into the soup along with the spinach and continue cooking for 10 to 15 minutes or until the spinach leaves wilts.
6. Using a ladle, serving it in a bowl.

Inexpensive Bean and Spinach Enchiladas

Total time: 3 hours 5 minutes

Ingredients

- 2 cups of cooked black beans
- 1 cup of frozen corn
- 10 ounces of chopped spinach
- Half of a medium-sized cucumber, peeled and sliced
- 6 cups of chopped lettuce
- 4 medium-sized radishes, peeled and cut into matchsticks
- 1/2 cup of cherry tomatoes, halved
- 1 teaspoon of salt, divided
- 1/2 teaspoon of ground black pepper, divided
- 1/2 teaspoon of ground cumin
- 3 1/2 cups of tomato salsa
- 2 cups of grated vegetarian cheddar cheese
- 8 corn tortillas, about 6-inch
- 3 tablespoons lime juice
- 2 tablespoons olive oil

Directions:

1. Place 1 cup of beans in a medium-sized bowl then ,using a fork mash them.
2. Then add the remaining beans, corn, spinach, 1/2 teaspoon of salt, 1/4 teaspoon of black pepper, 1 cup of cheddar cheese and stir until it mixes well.
3. Take a 6-quarts slow cooker and spread 2 cups of tomato salsa on the bottom.
4. Place the tortillas on a clean working space and proportionally top it with the prepared bean mixture, at least 1/2 cup.
5. Roll up the tortillas and place it into the slow cooker on top of the salsa, seam-side down.
6. Top it with the remaining tomato salsa, cheese and cover the top.
7. Plug in the slow cooker; adjust the cooking time to 3 hours and let it cook on the low heat setting or until the cheese melts completely.
8. In the meantime, using a bowl, place the cucumber, lettuce, radish and tomatoes in it, sprinkle it with the lime juice, oil, the remaining of each salt and black pepper.
9. Toss to cover and serve this with the cooked enchiladas.

Delightful Coconut Vegetarian Curry

Total time: 4 hours 20 minutes

Ingredients

- 5 medium-sized potatoes, peeled and cut into 1-inch cubes
- 1/4 cup of curry powder
- 2 tablespoons of flour
- 1 tablespoon of chili powder
- 1/2 teaspoon of red pepper flakes
- 1/2 teaspoon of cayenne pepper
- 1 large green bell pepper, cut into strips
- 1 large red bell pepper, cut into strips
- 2 tablespoons of onion soup mix
- 14-ounce of coconut cream, unsweetened
- 3 cups of vegetable broth
- 2 medium-sized carrots, peeled and cut into matchstick
- 1 cup of green peas
- 1/4 cup of chopped cilantro

Directions:

1. Take a 6-quarts slow cooker, grease it with a non-stick cooking spray and place the potatoes pieces in the bottom.
2. Add the remaining ingredients except for the carrots, peas and cilantro.
3. Stir properly and cover the top.

4.	Plug in the slow cooker; adjust the cooking time to 4 hours and let it cook on the low heat setting or until it cooks thoroughly.
5.	When the cooking time is over, add the carrots to the curry and continue cooking for 30 minutes.
6.	Then, add the peas and continue cooking for another 30 minutes or until the peas get tender.
7.	Garnish it with cilantro and serve.

Creamy Sweet Potato & Coconut Curry

Total time: 6 hours 20 minutes
Ingredients
- 2 pounds of sweet potatoes, peeled and chopped
- 1/2 pound of red cabbage, shredded
- 2 red chilies, seeded and sliced
- 2 medium-sized red bell peppers, cored and sliced
- 2 large white onions, peeled and sliced
- 1 1/2 teaspoon of minced garlic
- 1 teaspoon of grated ginger
- 1/2 teaspoon of salt
- 1 teaspoon of paprika
- 1/2 teaspoon of cayenne pepper
- 2 tablespoons of peanut butter
- 4 tablespoons of olive oil
- 12-ounce of tomato puree
- 14 fluid ounce of coconut milk
- 1/2 cup of chopped coriander

Directions:
1.	Place a large non-stick skillet pan over an average heat, add 1 tablespoon of oil and let it heat.
2.	Then add the onion and cook for 10 minutes or until it gets soft.
3.	Add the garlic, ginger, salt, paprika, cayenne pepper and continue cooking for 2 minutes or until it starts producing fragrance.
4.	Transfer this mixture to a 6-quarts slow cooker, and reserve the pan.
5.	In the pan, add 1 tablespoon of oil and let it heat.
6.	Add the cabbage, red chili, bell pepper and cook it for 5 minutes.
7.	Then transfer this mixture to the slow cooker and reserve the pan.
8.	Add the remaining oil to the pan; the sweet potatoes in a single layer and cook it in 3 batches for 5 minutes or until it starts getting brown.
9.	Add the sweet potatoes to the slow cooker, along with tomato puree, coconut milk and stir properly.
10.	Cover the top, plug in the slow cooker; adjust the cooking time to 6 hours and let it cook on the low heat setting or until the sweet potatoes are tender.
11.	When done, add the seasoning and pour it in the peanut butter.
12.	Garnish it with coriander and serve.

Comforting Chickpea Tagine

Total time: 4 hours 15 minutes
Ingredients

- 14 ounce of cooked chickpeas
- 12 dried apricots
- 1 red bell pepper, cored and sliced
- 1 small butternut squash, peeled, cored and chopped
- 2 zucchini, stemmed and chopped
- 1 medium-sized white onion, peeled and chopped
- 1 teaspoon of minced garlic
- 1 teaspoon of ground ginger
- 1 1/2 teaspoon of salt
- 1 teaspoon of ground black pepper
- 1 teaspoon of ground cumin
- 2 teaspoon of paprika
- 1 teaspoon of harissa paste
- 2 teaspoon of honey
- 2 tablespoons of olive oil
- 1 pound of passata
- 1/4 cup of chopped coriander

Directions:
1.	Take a 6-quarts slow cooker, grease it with a non-stick cooking spray and place the chickpeas, apricots, bell pepper, butternut squash, zucchini and onion into it.
2.	Sprinkle it with salt, black pepper and set it aside until it is called for.
3.	Place a large non-stick skillet pan over an average temperature of heat; add the oil, garlic, cumin and paprika.
4.	Stir properly and cook for 1 minutes or until it starts producing fragrance.
5.	Then pour in the harissa paste, honey, passata and boil the mixture.
6.	When the mixture is done boiling, pour this mixture over the vegetables in the slow cooker and cover it with the lid.
7.	Plug in the slow cooker; adjust the cooking time to 4 hours and let it cook on the high heat setting or until the vegetables gets tender.
8.	When done, add the seasoning, garnish it with the coriander and serve right away.

Miso Ramen

Total time: 25 minutes
Ingredients
- 1/3 cup of spinach leaves (fresh)
- 1 cup of bean sprouts (fresh)
- 10 oz of ramen noodles (whole-wheat and dried)
- ½ cup of bamboo shoots (sliced, canned)
- ½ cup of corn kernels (fresh/ frozen)
- 8 cups of vegetable broth
- 2 tsp of instant dashi granules
- 1 tbsp of tamari sauce to taste
- 4 tbsp of miso paste
- 1 green onion (chopped finely)

Directions:
1.	Boil, drain and cut spinach, 1 minute.
2.	Boil, drain and remove the sprouts from the beans.
3.	Over medium heat, boil the ramen noodles and cook as directed on the package.

4. In 4 wide servings bowl, divide the noodles, bamboo shoots, corn kernels, bean sprouts and spinach.
5. Pour the stock, instant dashi granules, and tamari sauce in a medium pot. Boil, cool and stir in the miso paste.
6. Pour the mixture into the ramen bowl, garnish with the green onion and serve immediately.

Noodles with Sticky Tofu

Total time: 25 minutes
Ingredients
- ½ large size cucumber
- 2 tbsp of pure date sugar
- 100ml of wine vinegar (rice)
- 100ml of olive oil
- 200g pack of tofu (fir, cut into cubes)
- 2 tbsp of maple syrup
- 4 tbsp of white miso paste
- 30g of sesame seeds (white)
- 250g soba noodles (dried)
- 2 spring onions, (shredded, garnish)

Directions:
1. Cut thin ribbons off the cucumber using a peeler, leaving behind the seeds. In a tub, place the ribbons and reserve. Heat the date sugar, ¼ tsp salt, 100 ml of water and vinegar gently in a casserole over medium heat for 3 to 5 minutes until the date sugar is dissolved, then pour over the cucumbers and leave to pickle in the fridge while preparing the tofu.
2. In a large, non-stick frying pan, warm all but 1 tbsp of the oil over medium heat until bubbles start to come to the surface. Add the tofu and fry for 7-10 minutes until the tofu is uniformly golden brown, turning halfway. Remove the tofu from the pan and place on paper to drain grease.
3. Whisk together the pure maple syrup and miso in a small bowl. Place the sesame seeds on a plate.
4. Brush the tofu with the sticky pure maple syrup sauce and sprinkle with the sesame seeds.
5. Warm the noodles as instructed by the box, then drain and rinse under cold water.
6. Return the frying pan to heat with a little oil, throw in the noodles, and toss.
7. In 4 medium bowls, divide the noodles, tofu, pickled cucumber, spring onion, and some of the miso sauce.
8. Serve immediately.

Almond Butter Tofu Stir- fry

Total time: 65 minutes
Ingredients
- Tofu
- 2 x 12 oz package of tofu (extra firm and pressed)
- Marinade
- 8 tbsp of tamari sauce
- 4 tbsp of sesame oil (divided)
- 4 tbsp of almond butter
- 4 tbsp of lime (squeezed)
- 4 tsp of chili garlic sauce
- 6 tbsp of maple syrup

Directions:
1. Set the oven to 400 degrees F and use baking paper to line a baking tray.
2. Arrange the tofu on the baking sheet and cook in the oven until golden brown, and cooked through, 10 to 15 minutes.
3. In a medium bowl, mix half of the tamari, sesame oil, almond butter, lime juice, garlic chili sauce and maple syrup to a medium bowl.
4. Add the tofu, toss well, and sit for 5 minutes.
5. Heat a little oil in a medium skillet and fry the tofu on both sides until golden brown, 1 to 2 minutes.
6. Serve the tofu with steamed spinach.

Vegetable Farro Harvest Bowl

Total time: 65 minutes
Ingredients
- 16 oz of Brussels sprouts (halved)
- 1 sweet potato (diced)
- 1 red pepper (cut into cubes)
- 2 tbsp of olive oil
- 1/2 tsp of cinnamon (ground)
- 1 red onion (halved and quartered)
- 3 ½ cups of water
- 1 cup of farro
- ½ cup of basil (fresh)
- 2 tbsp of olive oil
- 1 tsp of salt
- 2 tbsp of wine vinegar (red)
- 1 clove of garlic
- Salt and black pepper to taste
- 2 tsp of mustard (Dijon)

Directions:
1. Set the oven to 400 F.
2. Heat the olive oil in a medium skillet and cook the Brussels sprouts, sweet potatoes, red pepper, salt, cinnamon and red onion until softened, 30 minutes.
3. Meanwhile, place the water and farro in a pan. Boil, cover the lid, and simmer for 30 minutes or until the farro softens and the water is absorbed. Fluff and set aside.
4. In a medium bowl, mix the basil, olive oil, wine vinegar, garlic cover, salt, pepper and Dijon mustard until smooth.
5. Divide the vegetables, farro, and dressing into 4 medium bowls, and serve.

Vegan Garlic Slaw Burger

Total time: 45 minutes
Ingredients
- Veggie Burger/ Patties
- ½ cup of green lentils (uncooked)
- 2 cloves of garlic
- ¼ cup of onion (white)
- 1 medium size carrot (chopped roughly)
- ½ tsp of sea salt
- ½ tsp of chili flakes (crushed)
- 1 tsp of tamari sauce
- 1 tsp of sriracha or hot sauce
- 1/3 cup of panko breadcrumbs

- 2 tbsp flax egg
- 1 tsp sesame oil
- 4 whole-wheat burger buns, halved
- Slaw
- 1 tbsp of plant-based yogurt
- 1 tbsp of tofu mayonnaise
- 1 tsp of sesame oil
- 1 tsp of tamari sauce
- 1 tsp of sambal chili sauce
- 3 tbsp of rice vinegar
- 3 minis of cucumbers (julienned finely)
- 2 medium size carrots (julienned finely)
- 2 green onions (sliced thinly)
- 2 tbsp of sesame seeds (toasted)

Directions:
1. Veggie burger/ patties
2. Add all the burgers ingredients except for the oil and bread into a food processor and blend until smooth. Form 4 to 6 patties from the mixture.
3. Heat 2 tbsp of sesame oil in a medium skillet and fry the patties on both sides until golden brown and compacted, 10 minutes.
4. Slaw
5. In a medium bowl, mix the slaw's ingredients and set aside to combine flavors for 10 minutes.
6. To serve, place the burger patties between the burger buns, top with the slaw and serve immediately.

Easy Vegan Samosa Pot- Pie

Total time: 45 minutes
Ingredients
- 1 tbsp of vegetable oil
- 1 large size onion (diced)
- 3 cloves of garlic (minced)
- 2 medium size potatoes (diced and peeled)
- 150g of frozen green peas (defrosted)
- 2 tbsp of curry powder
- 1 tsp of chili powder
- 1 tbsp of cilantro (dried)
- 400g soy (frozen, mince)
- Salt and pepper to taste
- 1 pack of whole-wheat filo pastry (defrosted)
- 2 tbsp of vegetable oil

Directions:
1. Set the oven to 350 F.
2. Heat the olive oil in a medium pot and sauté the onion, garlic, potatoes, and cook until softened, 10 minutes.
3. Mix in the green peas, curry powder, chili powder, cilantro, soy, salt, and pepper. Cook for 2 to 3 minutes or until the green peas warm through.
4. Spoon the mixture into 4 medium ramekins.
5. Roll out the filo pastry, divide into 4 pieces and spread over the ramekins.
6. Brush with a little oil, place on a baking sheet, and bake in the oven for 20 to 25 minutes or until the pastry is golden brown.
7. Remove the ramekins from the oven, allow cooling, and serve warm.

Potato Tofu Scramble

Total time: 15 minutes
Ingredients
- 6 small size of fingerling potatoes
- 16 pcs of mushrooms
- 2 small size of shallot
- 4 tbsp of oil (divided)
- 10oz tofu (dry)
- ½ tsp of turmeric
- 2 tbsp of nutritional yeast
- 4 cups of spinach
- ½ tsp of salt
- Pinch black pepper

Directions:
1. Split the potatoes into ¼- inch cubes. Cut the mushroom into quarters, and chop the shallot in half moon shape.
2. In a frying pan, heat a tbsp of oil over medium heat. Cook in the potatoes until softened and turned brown, 7 minutes.
3. Mix in the mushrooms, shallots and cook for at least 3 minutes or until the mushrooms shallots soften. Use the spoon to move the mixture to the side of the pan.
4. Add 1 tbsp of oil if desire or needed and crumble in the tofu into the saucepan. Cook until golden brown and season with the turmeric and nutritional yeast, 4 minutes.
5. Mix all the ingredients and work in the spinach. Cook until wilted, 3 minutes.

Nutty Stuffed Squash

Total time: 60 minutes
Ingredients
- 3 tbsp of butter (vegan)
- 3 cloves of garlic (minced)
- ¾ tsp of sea salt
- 2 medium size yellow onions (chopped finely)
- 1 tbsp of fresh sage (chopped)
- 2 tbsp flax egg
- 1/3 cup of plant-based yogurt
- ½ cup of parmesan cheese (freshly shredded)
- 2 squash (halved lengthwise, seeded)
- Mixed toasted nuts for topping

Directions:
1. Set the oven to 350 F.
2. Melt the butter over medium - high heat in a saucepan. Cook in the garlic, onion, and season with salt until softened, 3 minutes. Set aside.
3. In a medium bowl, mix the flax egg, yogurt, onion mixture, and parmesan in a mixing container. Split the filling between the squash halves, spread with more parmesan, and bake until soft and brown, 45 minutes.
4. Remove from the oven, top with some nuts and serve warm.

Smoked Tofu and Watercress Cannelloni

Total time: 45 minutes
Ingredients

- Vegetable oil or olive oil
- 2 red onions (diced and peeled)
- 2 cloves of garlic (chopped finely)
- 2 tsp of thyme (dried)
- Salt and pepper to taste
- 225g of spinach
- 225g of watercress
- 2 packs of tofu (smoked)
- 1 tsp of paprika (smoked)
- 20 tubes of cannelloni pasta (whole-wheat and dried)
- 1 cup of tomatoes sauce

Directions:
1. Set the oven at 350 F and grease a baking sheet with cooking spray.
2. In a large pot, heat the oil and sauté the onion, garlic, thyme, and season with salt and black pepper, 3 minutes.
3. Mix in the spinach and watercress and allow wilting, 3 minutes.
4. Add the tofu, paprika, and cook until the tofu warms through, 3 minutes.
5. Spoon the mixture into a piping bag, tear open a wide hole and press the mixture into the cannelloni.
6. Arrange the pasta in the baking dish and pour the tomato sauce on top. Season with salt, black pepper, and scatter some cashew cheese on top,
7. Bake in the oven until the cheese melts and the pasta cooks, 35 minutes.

Grilled Cauliflower Steak with Hummus and Quinoa

Total time: 25 minutes
Ingredients
- 150g of cauliflower
- 60g of quinoa
- 40g of edamame beans
- 25g of hummus
- 20g of hemp seeds
- Coriander leaves (for garnish)
- ¼ lemon (for garnish)

Directions:
1. Boil the whole cauliflower for 10 to 12 minutes.
2. Allow cooling and cut the cauliflower into steak style pieces.
3. Preheat a grill to medium heat and brown the cauliflower steaks on both sides, 5 minutes.
4. Bring water to the boil in a casserole, add quinoa and cook for 10 minutes. After, fluff and set aside.
5. In a cup, mix the olive oil, salt, and edamame beans.
6. Layer the hummus over a sheet and cover with the mixture of quinoa. Put the grilled cauliflower on top, sprinkle with the seeds of hemp and dust the leaves of coriander and voila!

Chirashi Grain Bowl

Total time: 25 minutes
Ingredients
- 1 tbsp of olive oil (extra virgin)
- 1 small size of carrot (julienned, sliced thinly)
- 1 small size ginger (julienned, peeled)
- 1 tsp of sesame seeds
- ½ tsp of toasted sesame oil
- 2 tbsp of vegetable oil
- 1 cup shiitake mushrooms (finely chopped)
- 2 tsp of tamari sauce
- ½ tsp of pure date sugar (granulated)
- 1 tsp of sake
- 1 plum tomato (sliced in bite size)
- 1 tbsp of white miso paste
- 1 tbsp of olive oil (extra virgin)
- ½ cup of baby spinach (chopped finely)
- 1 cup of brown rice or quinoa
- 3 tbsp of rice vinegar
- 2 stalks of scallions (chopped finely)
- shredded nori (optional)

Directions:
1. In a medium saucepan, heat the olive oil over medium heat and sauté the carrots and ginger until softened, 5 minutes.
2. Season with some salt and mix in the sesame seeds and sesame oil. Transfer to a plate and set aside.
3. Heat the vegetable oil in the skillet and cook in the shiitake mushrooms until softened. Add the tamari sauce, date sugar, sake and cook until all of the liquid has absorbed. Place on a plate and reserve.
4. Place the tomatoes with miso paste and extra virgin olive oil in a small bowl. Blend well.
5. Heat the rice or quinoa and pour over the rice vinegar until completely covered.
6. Divide all the cooked foods and remaining ingredients between 4 serving bowls and serve.

Chickpea Sweetcorn Veggie Burger

Total time: 40 minutes
Ingredients
- Olive oil (extra virgin)
- 1 onion (chopped finely)
- 1 clove of garlic (chopped finely)
- 1 tsp of coriander (ground)
- 200g of sweetcorn (cooked)
- 400g of chickpeas (tinned, drained, rinsed)
- 1 tbsp of parsley (chopped)
- 100g of whole-wheat breadcrumbs
- 60g of flour (spelt)
- 1 tbsp flax egg
- To coat the burgers
- 40g of flour (spelt)
- 1 tsp of cumin (ground)

Directions:
1. Preheat the oven to 350 F.
2. Heat the olive oil in a medium saucepan and sauté the onion until softened, 3 minutes. Add the garlic, coriander and cook for 1 to 2 minutes. Set aside.
3. In a medium bowl, mash and mix the chickpeas, parsley, onion mixture, breadcrumbs, flour, and flax egg.

4.	Blend sweetcorn, chickpeas and parsley and pulse until well mixed.
5.	Bring the mixture of onions, breadcrumbs, flour, flax egg and mix. From 4 to 6 patties from the mixture and place on a baking sheet. Bake in the oven until golden brown and compacted, 10 to 15 minutes.
6.	Remove the sheet from the oven and set aside to cool slightly.
7.	In a shallow plate, mix the flour and cumin powder, and coat the burgers in the mixture.
8.	Heat a little olive oil in a medium skillet and fry the patties on both sides until crusty, 3 to 4 minutes.
9.	Place the patties between the burger buns.
10.	Best served with hummus, garden greens, and tofu mayonnaise.
11.	Serve warm.

Grilled Breaded Tofu Steaks

Total time: 25 minutes
Ingredients
- 350g of tofu (extra-firm)
- 4 cloves of garlic
- 1 tbsp of Dijon mustard
- 1 tbsp of maple syrup
- 2 tbsp of tomato paste
- 1 tbsp of tamari sauce
- ¼ tsp of black pepper
- 1 tbsp of water
- ½ cup of panko breadcrumbs (whole wheat)
- 2 tbsp of olive oil
- A BBQ sauce for dipping (your choice)

Directions:
1.	Press the tofu between two pieces of parchment paper and cut into steaks.
2.	In the medium bowl, mix the garlic powder, Dijon mustard, maple syrup, tomato paste, tamari sauce, and black pepper. Add the tofu, mix well and allow marinating for 10 minutes.
3.	Pour the breadcrumbs into a shallow plate and coat the tofu slightly in the crumbs.
4.	Heat the olive oil in a medium skillet and fry on both sides until golden brown and cooked within.
5.	Serve the tofu with the BBQ sauce.

Nourishing Curried Lentil and Sweet Potato Bowl

Total time: 30 minutes
Ingredients
- Lentils
- 1 cup yellow lentils
- Potatoes
- 2 tbsp of avocado oil
- 1 large size of sweet potato (cut into rounds, skin- on)
- ¼ tsp of sea salt
- Cauliflower Rice
- 1 tbsp of water
- 1 tbsp of olive oil
- A pinch of sea salt
- ½ tsp curry powder
- 1 head of cauliflower (grated)
- Kale
- 1 bundle of organic kale (chopped)

Directions:
1.	Cook the lentils in 1 cup of water in a medium pot over medium heat until softened, 10 minutes.
2.	Set the oven to 375 F and line a baking tray with parchment paper.
3.	In a medium bowl, mix the avocado oil, sweet potatoes, salt, and spread on the baking sheet. Bake in the oven until the sweet potatoes soften, 15 to 20 minutes.
4.	Meanwhile, combine the cauliflower ingredients in a safe microwave bowl and steam in the microwave until softened, 1 minute.
5.	Also, heat 1 tsp of avocado oil in a medium skillet and sauté the kale until wilted.
6.	In a medium bowl, divide the lentils, sweet potatoes, cauliflower rice, kale, and serve warm.

Curried Potato and Lentil Soup Pot

Total time: 40 minutes
Ingredients
- 2 tbsp of olive oil
- ½ cup of carrots (diced)
- 1 cup onion (yellow, diced)
- ½ cup of celery (diced)
- 1 tbsp of garlic (minced)
- 1 tsp of pure date sugar
- 1 tbsp of wine vinegar (red)
- 1 tsp of sea salt
- 3 tbsp of curry powder
- 1 tsp of ginger (fresh, grated)
- 1 lb. of green lentils
- 8 cups of vegetable broth (divided)
- 14.5 oz tomatoes petite (diced)
- 1 lb. red potatoes (cut into an inch/pcs)

Directions:
1.	Heat the olive oil in a medium pot and sauté the carrots, onions and celery until softened, 5 minutes.
2.	Mix in the garlic, date sugar, vinegar, salt, curry powder and ginger. Cook for 1 minute, mix well to blend.
3.	After, add the lentils, 6 cups of broth, tomatoes and potatoes. Mix well.
4.	Cover the lid and cook for 6 to 7 minutes or until the potatoes soften.
5.	Adjust the taste with salt, black pepper, and dish the soup.
6.	Serve immediately.

Vegan Teriyaki Tofu

Total time: 25 minutes
Ingredients
- 3 tsp of olive oil
- 4 tbsp of tamari sauce
- 2 tbsp of pure date sugar
- A pinch of ginger (ground)
- 2 tbsp of mirin
- ½ tbsp of oil (rapeseed)
- 2 medium zucchinis (sliced horizontally/ strips)

- 200g of broccoli (tender stem)
- 350g of tofu (block, very firm, cut into slices)
- Black sesame seeds for garnish

Directions:

1. In a medium bowl, mix 1 tsp olive oil, tamari sauce, pure date sugar, mirin and ginger, and rub it all over tofu slices. Place them in a big dish and pour over any remaining marinade. Leave to settle for an hour.

2. After preheat a grill pan over medium-high heat.

3. In a medium bowl, mix the remaining olive oil and rapeseed oil. Brush both sides of the zucchini and broccoli with the oil and cook on both sides until tender, 5 to 7 minutes.

4. Grill the tofu slices on both sides until brown and crispy on the edges, 5 minutes.

5. Serve the tofu with the vegetables.

Sesame Eggplant & Almond Butter Tofu Bowl

Total time: 20 minutes

Ingredients

Tofu

- 8 oz of tofu (extra firm)
- 2 tbsp of sesame oil
- 3 tbsp of cornstarch

Sauce

- 1 tbsp of sesame oil
- 1 tbsp of tamari sauce
- 1 tbsp of lime (squeezed)
- 2 tbsp of almond butter (salted)
- 1 medium size of Birdseye chili (crushed)
- 2 tbsp of maple syrup

Eggplant

- 1 tbsp of sesame oil (toasted)
- 2 medium size of Japanese eggplants (skin-on, stem removed, cut in 1-inch pieces)
- 1 tbsp of maple syrup
- 1 tbsp of tamari sauce

Directions:

1. Wrap the tofu in a clean towel. Place a heavy lid on top for 10 minutes to press out the excess liquid. Cut into cubes and set aside.

2. For the sauce: in a medium bowl, whisk the sesame oil, tamari, lime juice, almond butter, crushed chili and maple syrup to prepare the tofu sauce in a medium bowl and set aside.

3. For the tofu: heat 2 tbsp of sesame oil in a medium skillet, coat the tofu with some cornstarch and fry in the oil on both sides until golden brown.

4. Mix in the almond butter sauce and cook for 2 to 3 minutes. Transfer to a plate and set aside.

5. For the eggplant: heat 1 tbsp of sesame oil in a medium skillet over medium heat and cook in the eggplant until softened.

6. Top with the maple syrup, tamari sauce, and cook until light brown and softened, 2 to 3 minutes.

7. Serve the eggplant and tofu with cooked white rice.

Summer Pistou

Total time: 25 minutes

Ingredients

- 1 tbsp of oil (rapeseed)
- 2 leeks (sliced finely)
- 1 large size of zucchini (diced finely)
- 2 cups of vegetable stock (boiling)
- 3 tomatoes (chopped)
- 200g of beans (green, chopped)
- 400g of haricot beans (drained)
- 3 cloves of garlic (chopped finely)
- 40g of vegan Parmesan cheese
- small pack of basil

Directions:

1. In a medium saucepan, heat olive oil for 5 minutes and sauté the leeks and zucchini. Pour in the stock, add half tomatoes, green beans, three-quarters of haricot beans, and cook for 5 to 8 minutes until vegetables are soft.

2. In a food processor, blend the remaining tomatoes, beans; garlic and basil until fluffy, and then add the vegan Parmesan.

3. Pour the sauce into the soup, simmer for 2 minutes, and serve afterwards.

Lentil Lasagna

Total time: 75 minutes

Ingredients

- 1 tbsp of olive oil
- 1 onion (chopped)
- 1 celery (chopped, stick)
- 1 carrot (chopped)
- 1 clove of garlic (crushed)
- 1 tbsp of corn flour
- 2 cans of 400g lentils (drained, rinsed)
- 400g of tomato (chopped)
- 1 tsp of ketchup (mushroom)
- 1 tsp of vegetable stock (powder)
- 1 tsp of oregano (chopped)
- 2 cauliflower (heads, cut into florets and steamed)
- 2 tbsp of soya milk (unsweetened)
- A pinch of grated nutmeg (freshly)
- 9 egg-free lasagna sheets (dried)

Directions:

1. In a medium saucepan, heat the olive oil and sauté the onion, celery and carrot until softened, 5 minutes. Add the garlic, cook for 2 more minutes, and stir in the corn flour and lentils.

2. Pour tomatoes, mushroom ketchup, stock powder, oregano and some seasoning. Bring to a boil for 15 minutes.

3. In a blender, process the cauliflower, soya milk, and nutmeg until smooth.

4. Preheat the oven to 350 F.

5. Lay over the base, a ceramic casserole dish, a third of the lentil mixture then, fill with a single layer of lasagna sheet. Top with another third of the lentil mixture, then spread over a third of the cauliflower purée, followed by a pasta layer. Finish with the last third of lentils and lasagna, then the remainder of the purée.

6.	Cover with foil and bake for 35 to 45 minutes.
7.	Remove the dish, foil, and allow cooling for 2 minutes.
8.	Serve warm.

Super tasty Vegetarian Chili

Total time: 2 hours 10 minutes
Ingredients
- 16-ounce of vegetarian baked beans
- 16 ounce of cooked chickpeas
- 16 ounce of cooked kidney beans
- 15 ounce of cooked corn
- 1 medium-sized green bell pepper, cored and chopped
- 2 stalks of celery, peeled and chopped
- 12 ounce of chopped tomatoes
- 1 medium-sized white onion, peeled and chopped
- 1 teaspoon of minced garlic
- 1 teaspoon of salt
- 1 tablespoon of red chili powder
- 1 tablespoon of dried oregano
- 1 tablespoon of dried basil
- 1 tablespoon of dried parsley
- 18-ounce of black bean soup
- 4-ounce of tomato puree

Directions:
1.	Take a 6-quarts slow cooker, grease it with a non-stick cooking spray and place all the ingredients into it.
2.	Stir properly and cover the top.
3.	Plug in the slow cooker; adjust the cooking time to 2 hours and let it cook on the high heat setting or until it is cooked thoroughly.
4.	Serve right away.

Vegetable Soup

Total time: 6 hours 30 minutes
Ingredients
- 1/4 cup of vegetable shortening
- 2 cups of all-purpose flour, leveled
- 1/2 cup of barley, uncooked
- 16 ounce of diced tomatoes
- 2 medium-sized potatoes, peeled and cubed
- 16 ounce of frozen mixed vegetables
- 1 large white onion, peeled and diced
- 1 1/2 teaspoon of minced garlic
- 6 cups of vegetable broth
- 1/2 teaspoon of salt
- 1/2 teaspoon of dried basil
- 1/2 teaspoon of ground black pepper
- 1 teaspoon of dried oregano
- 1 teaspoon of dried parsley
- 1 bay leaf
- 6 1/4 cup of vegetable broth

Directions:
1.	Take a 6 quarts slow cooker, grease it with a non-stick cooking spray and add all the ingredients except for flour, vegetable shortening and reserve 1/4 cup of vegetable broth.
2.	Stir properly and cover the top.

3.	Plug in the slow cooker; adjust the cooking time to 6 hours and let it cook on the low heat setting or until it is cooked thoroughly.
4.	In the meantime, place the flour, shortening in a food processor and pulse it until the mixture resembles crumbs.
5.	Then gradually mix the reserved 1/4 cup of vegetable broth until the smooth dough comes together.
6.	Transfer the dough to a clean space filled with flour and roll it into the 1/8 thick dough.
7.	Using a sharp knife cut the dough into small squares and put them in the slow cooker when 6 hours of cooking time is over.
8.	Continue cooking for 1 hour at the high heat setting or until the dumplings are soft.
9.	Scoop it into the serving bowls and serve.

Tastiest Barbecued Tofu and Vegetables

Total time: 4 hours 15 minutes
Ingredients
- 14-ounce of extra-firm tofu, pressed and drained
- 2 medium-sized zucchini, stemmed and diced
- 1/2 large green bell pepper, cored and cubed
- 3 stalks of broccoli stalks
- 8 ounce of sliced water chestnuts
- 1 small white onion, peeled and minced
- 1 1/2 teaspoon of minced garlic
- 2 teaspoons of minced ginger
- 1 1/2 teaspoon of salt
- 1/8 teaspoon of ground black pepper
- 1/4 teaspoon of crushed red pepper
- 1/4 teaspoon of five spice powder
- 2 teaspoons of molasses
- 1 tablespoon of whole-grain mustard
- 1/4 teaspoon of vegan Worcestershire sauce
- 8 ounces of tomato sauce
- 1/4 cup of hoisin sauce
- 1 tablespoon of soy sauce
- 2 tablespoons of apple cider vinegar
- 2 tablespoons of water

Directions:
1.	Take a 6-quarts slow cooker, grease it with a non-stick cooking spray and set it aside until it is required.
2.	Place a medium-sized non-stick skillet pan over an average heat, add the oil and let it heat.
3.	Cut the tofu into 1/2 inch pieces and add it to the skillet pan in a single layer.
4.	Cook for 3 minutes per sides and then transfer it to the prepared slow cooker.
5.	When the tofu turns brown, place it into the pan, add the onion, garlic, ginger and cook for 3 to 5 minutes or until the onions are softened.
6.	Add the remaining ingredients into the pan except for the vegetables which are the broccoli stalks, zucchini, bell pepper and water chestnuts.
7.	Stir until it mixes properly and cook for 2 minutes or until the mixture starts bubbling.

8.	Transfer this mixture into the slow cooker and stir properly.
9.	Cover the top, plug in the slow cooker; adjust the cooking time to 3 hours and let it cook on the high heat setting or until it is cooked thoroughly.
10.	In the meantime, trim the broccoli stalks and cut it into 1/4 inch pieces.
11.	When the tofu is cooked thoroughly, put it into the slow cooker; add the broccoli stalks and the remaining vegetables.
12.	Stir until it mixes properly and then return the top to cover it.
13.	Continue cooking for 1 hour at the high heat setting or until the vegetables are tender.
14.	Serve right away with rice.

Savory Spanish Rice

Total time: 3 hours 10 minutes

Ingredients

- 1 cup of long grain rice, uncooked
- 1/2 cup of chopped green bell pepper
- 14 ounce of diced tomatoes
- 1/2 cup of chopped white onion
- 1 teaspoon of minced garlic
- 1/2 teaspoon of salt
- 1 teaspoon of red chili powder
- 1 teaspoon of ground cumin
- 4-ounce of tomato puree
- 8 fluid ounce of water

Directions:

1.	Grease a 6-quarts slow cooker with a non-stick cooking spray and add all the ingredients into it.
2.	Stir properly and cover the top.
3.	Plug in the slow cooker; adjust the cooking time to 5 hours and let it cook on the high heat setting or until the rice absorbs all the liquid.
4.	Serve right away.

VEGETABLES RECIPES

Steamed Cauliflower

Preparation Time: 5 minutes
Cooking Time: 10 minutes
Servings: 6
Ingredients:
- 1 large head cauliflower
- 1 cup water
- ½ teaspoon salt
- 1 teaspoon red pepper flakes (optional)

Directions:
1. Remove any leaves from the cauliflower, and cut it into florets.
2. In a large saucepan, bring the water to a boil. Place a steamer basket over the water, and add the florets and salt. Cover and steam for 5 to 7 minutes, until tender.
3. In a large bowl, toss the cauliflower with the red pepper flakes (if using). Transfer the florets to a large airtight container or 6 single-serving containers. Let cool before sealing the lids.

Nutrition: Calories: 35 Fat: 0g Protein: 3g Carbohydrates: 7g Fiber: 4g Sugar: 4g Sodium: 236mg

Cajun Sweet Potatoes

Preparation Time: 5 minutes
Cooking Time: 30 minutes
Servings: 4
Ingredients:
- 2 pounds sweet potatoes
- 2 teaspoons extra-virgin olive oil
- ½ teaspoon ground cayenne pepper
- ½ teaspoon smoked paprika
- ½ teaspoon dried oregano
- ½ teaspoon dried thyme
- ½ teaspoon garlic powder
- ½ teaspoon salt (optional)

Directions:
1. Preheat the oven to 400ºF. Line a baking sheet with parchment paper.
2. Wash the potatoes, pat dry, and cut into ¾-inch cubes. Transfer to a large bowl, and pour the olive oil over the potatoes.
3. In a small bowl, combine the cayenne, paprika, oregano, thyme, and garlic powder. Sprinkle the spices over the potatoes and combine until the potatoes are well coated. Spread the potatoes on the prepared baking sheet in a single layer. Season with the salt (if using). Roast for 30 minutes, stirring the potatoes after 15 minutes.
4. Divide the potatoes evenly among 4 single-serving containers. Let cool completely before sealing.

Nutrition: Calories: 219 Fat: 3g Protein: 4g Carbohydrates: 46g Fiber: 7g Sugar: 9g Sodium: 125mg

Smoky Coleslaw

Preparation Time: 10 minutes
Cooking Time: 0 minute
Servings: 6
Ingredients:
- 1-pound shredded cabbage
- 1/3 cup vegan mayonnaise
- ¼ cup unseasoned rice vinegar
- 3 tablespoons plain vegan yogurt or plain soymilk
- 1 tablespoon vegan sugar
- ½ teaspoon salt
- ¼ teaspoon freshly ground black pepper
- ¼ teaspoon smoked paprika
- ¼ teaspoon chipotle powder

Directions:
1. Put the shredded cabbage in a large bowl. In a medium bowl, whisk the mayonnaise, vinegar, yogurt, sugar, salt, pepper, paprika, and chipotle powder.
2. Pour over the cabbage, and mix with a spoon or spatula and until the cabbage shreds are coated. Divide the coleslaw evenly among 6 single-serving containers. Seal the lids.

Nutrition: Calories: 73 Fat: 4g Protein: 1g Carbohydrates: 8g Fiber: 2g Sugar: 5g Sodium: 283mg

Mediterranean Hummus Pizza

Preparation Time: 10 minutes
Cooking Time: 30 minutes
Servings: 2 pizzas
Ingredients:
- ½ zucchini, thinly sliced
- ½ red onion, thinly sliced
- 1 cup cherry tomatoes, halved
- 2 to 4 tablespoons pitted and chopped black olives
- Pinch sea salt
- Drizzle olive oil (optional)
- 2 prebaked pizza crusts
- ½ cup Classic Hummus
- 2 to 4 tablespoons Cheesy Sprinkle

Directions:
1. Preheat the oven to 400°F. Place the zucchini, onion, cherry tomatoes, and olives in a large bowl, sprinkle them with the sea salt, and toss them a bit. Drizzle with a bit of olive oil (if using), to seal in the flavor and keep them from drying out in the oven.
2. Lay the two crusts out on a large baking sheet. Spread half the hummus on each crust, and top with the veggie mixture and some Cheesy Sprinkle. Pop the pizzas in the oven for 20 to 30 minutes, or until the veggies are soft.

Nutrition: Calories: 500; Total fat: 25g Carbs: 58g Fiber: 12g Protein:

Baked Brussels Sprouts

Preparation Time: 10 minutes
Cooking Time: 40 minutes
Servings: 4
Ingredients:
- 1-pound Brussels sprouts
- 2 teaspoons extra-virgin olive or canola oil

- 4 teaspoons minced garlic (about 4 cloves)
- 1 teaspoon dried oregano
- ½ teaspoon dried rosemary
- ½ teaspoon salt
- ¼ teaspoon freshly ground black pepper
- 1 tablespoon balsamic vinegar

Directions:
1. Preheat the oven to 400ºF. Line a rimmed baking sheet with parchment paper. Trim and halve the Brussels sprouts. Transfer to a large bowl. Toss with the olive oil, garlic, oregano, rosemary, salt, and pepper to coat well.
2. Transfer to the prepared baking sheet. Bake for 35 to 40 minutes, shaking the pan occasionally to help with even browning, until crisp on the outside and tender on the inside. Remove from the oven and transfer to a large bowl. Stir in the balsamic vinegar, coating well.
3. Divide the Brussels sprouts evenly among 4 single-serving containers. Let cool before sealing the lids.

Nutrition: Calories: 77 Fat: 3g Protein: 4g Carbohydrates: 12g Fiber: 5g Sugar: 3g Sodium: 320mg

Minted Peas

Preparation Time: 5 minutes
Cooking Time: 5 minutes
Servings: 4
Ingredients:
- 1 tablespoon olive oil
- 4 cups peas, fresh or frozen (not canned)
- ½ teaspoon sea salt
- freshly ground black pepper
- 3 tablespoons chopped fresh mint

Directions:
1. In a large sauté pan, heat the olive oil over medium-high heat until hot. Add the peas and cook, about 5 minutes.
2. Remove the pan from heat. Stir in the salt, season with pepper, and stir in the mint.
3. Serve hot.

Nutrition: Calories: 77 Fat: 3g Protein: 4g Carbohydrates: 12g Fiber: 5g Sugar: 3g Sodium: 320mg

Basic Baked Potatoes

Preparation Time: 5 minutes
Cooking Time: 60 minutes
Servings: 5
Ingredients:
- 5 medium Russet potatoes or a variety of potatoes, washed and patted dry
- 1 to 2 tablespoons extra-virgin olive oil
- ¼ teaspoon salt
- ¼ teaspoon freshly ground black pepper

Directions:
1. Preheat the oven to 400ºF. Pierce each potato several times with a fork or a knife. Brush the olive oil over the potatoes, then rub each with a pinch of the salt and a pinch of the pepper.
2. Place the potatoes on a baking sheet and bake for 50 to 60 minutes, until tender. Place the

potatoes on a baking rack and cool completely. Transfer to an airtight container or 5 single-serving containers. Let cool before sealing the lids.

Nutrition: Calories: 171 Fat: 3g Protein: 4g Carbohydrates: 34g Fiber: 5g Sugar: 3g Sodium: 129mg

Glazed Curried Carrots

Preparation Time: 5 minutes
Cooking Time: 15 minutes
Servings: 6
Ingredients:
- 1-pound carrots, peeled and thinly sliced
- 2 tablespoons olive oil
- 2 tablespoons curry powder
- 2 tablespoons pure maple syrup
- juice of ½ lemon
- sea salt
- freshly ground black pepper

Directions:
1. Place the carrots in a large pot and cover with water. Cook on medium-high heat until tender, about 10 minutes. Drain the carrots and return them to the pan over medium-low heat.
2. Stir in the olive oil, curry powder, maple syrup, and lemon juice. Cook, stirring constantly, until the liquid reduces, about 5 minutes. Season with salt and pepper and serve immediately.

Nutrition: Calories: 171 Fat: 3g Protein: 4g Carbohydrates: 34g Fiber: 5g Sugar: 3g Sodium: 129mg

Miso Spaghetti Squash

Preparation Time: 5 minutes
Cooking Time: 40 minutes
Servings: 4
Ingredients:
- 1 (3-pound) spaghetti squash
- 1 tablespoon hot water
- 1 tablespoon unseasoned rice vinegar
- 1 tablespoon white miso

Directions:
1. Preheat the oven to 400ºF. Line a rimmed baking sheet with parchment paper. Halve the squash lengthwise and place, cut-side down, on the prepared baking sheet.
2. Bake for 35 to 40 minutes, until tender. Cool until the squash is easy to handle. With a fork, scrape out the flesh, which will be stringy, like spaghetti. Transfer to a large bowl. In a small bowl, combine the hot water, vinegar, and miso with a whisk or fork. Pour over the squash. Gently toss with tongs to coat the squash.
3. Divide the squash evenly among 4 single-serving containers. Let cool before sealing the lids.

Nutrition: Calories: 117 Fat: 2g Protein: 3g Carbohydrates: 25g Fiber: 0g Sugar: 0g Sodium: 218mg

Garlic and Herb Noodles

Preparation Time: 10 minutes
Cooking Time: 2 minutes
Servings: 4

Ingredients:
- 1 teaspoon extra-virgin olive oil or 2 tablespoons vegetable broth
- 1 teaspoon minced garlic (about 1 clove)
- 4 medium zucchinis, spiral
- ½ teaspoon dried basil
- ½ teaspoon dried oregano
- ¼ to ½ teaspoon red pepper flakes, to taste
- ¼ teaspoon salt (optional)
- ¼ teaspoon freshly ground black pepper

Directions:
1. In a large skillet over medium-high heat, heat the olive oil.
2. Add the garlic, zucchini, basil, oregano, red pepper flakes, salt (if using), and black pepper. Sauté for 1 to 2 minutes, until barely tender. Divide the noodles evenly among 4 storage containers. Let cool before sealing the lids.

Nutrition: Calories: 44 Fat: 2g Protein: 3g Carbohydrates: 7g Fiber: 2g Sugar: 3g Sodium: 20mg

Thai Roasted Broccoli

Preparation Time: 5 minutes
Cooking Time: 15 minutes
Servings: 4
Ingredients:
- 1 head broccoli, cut into florets
- 2 tablespoons olive oil
- 1 tablespoon soy sauce or gluten-free tamari

Directions:
1. Preheat the oven to 425°F. Line a baking sheet with parchment paper. In a large bowl, combine the broccoli, oil, and soy sauce. Toss well to combine.
2. Spread the broccoli on the prepared baking sheet. Roast for 10 minutes.
3. Toss the broccoli with a spatula and roast for an additional 5 minutes, or until the edges of the florets begin to brown.

Nutrition: Calories: 44 Fat: 2g Protein: 3g Carbohydrates: 7g Fiber: 2g Sugar: 3g Sodium: 20mg

Coconut Curry Noodle

Preparation Time: 10 minutes
Cooking Time: 30 minutes
Servings: 4
Ingredients:
- ½ tablespoon oil
- 3 garlic cloves, minced
- 2 tablespoons lemongrass, minced
- 1 tablespoon fresh ginger, grated
- 2 tablespoons red curry paste
- 1 (14 oz) can coconut milk
- 1 tablespoon brown sugar
- 2 tablespoons soy sauce
- 2 tablespoons fresh lime juice
- 1 tablespoon hot chili paste
- 12 oz linguine
- 2 cups broccoli florets
- 1 cup carrots, shredded
- 1 cup edamame, shelled
- 1 red bell pepper, sliced

Directions:
1. Fill a suitably-sized pot with salted water and boil it on high heat.
2. Add pasta to the boiling water and cook until it is al dente then rinse under cold water.
3. Now place a medium-sized saucepan over medium heat and add oil.
4. Stir in ginger, garlic, and lemongrass, then sauté for 30 seconds.
5. Add coconut milk, soy sauce, curry paste, brown sugar, chili paste, and lime juice.
6. Stir this curry mixture for 10 minutes, or until it thickens.
7. Toss in carrots, broccoli, edamame, bell pepper, and cooked pasta.
8. Mix well, then serve warm.

Nutrition: Calories: 44 Fat: 2g Protein: 3g Carbohydrates: 7g Fiber: 2g Sugar: 3g Sodium: 20mg

Collard Green Pasta

Preparation Time: 10 minutes
Cooking Time: 20 minutes
Servings: 4
Ingredients
- 2 tablespoons olive oil
- 4 garlic cloves, minced
- 8 oz whole wheat pasta
- ½ cup panko bread crumbs
- 1 tablespoon nutritional yeast
- 1 teaspoon red pepper flakes
- 1 large bunch collard greens
- 1 large lemon, zest and juiced

Directions:
1. Fill a suitable pot with salted water and boil it on high heat.
2. Add pasta to the boiling water and cook until it is al dente, then rinse under cold water.
3. Reserve ½ cup of the cooking liquid from the pasta.
4. Place a non-stick pan over medium heat and add 1 tablespoon olive oil.
5. Stir in half of the garlic, then sauté for 30 seconds.
6. Add breadcrumbs and sauté for approximately 5 minutes.
7. Toss in red pepper flakes and nutritional yeast then mix well.
8. Transfer the breadcrumbs mixture to a plate and clean the pan.
9. Add the remaining tablespoon oil to the nonstick pan.
10. Stir in the garlic clove, salt, black pepper, and chard leaves.
11. Cook for 5 minutes until the leaves are wilted.
12. Add pasta along with the reserved pasta liquid.
13. Mix well, then add garlic crumbs, lemon juice, and zest.
14. Toss well, then serve warm.

Nutrition: Calories: 45 Fat: 2.5g Protein: 4g Carbohydrates: 9g Fiber: 4g Sugar: 3g Sodium: 20mg

Jalapeno Rice Noodles

Preparation Time: 10 minutes
Cooking Time: 25 minutes
Servings: 4
Ingredients
- ¼ cup soy sauce
- 1 tablespoon brown sugar
- 2 teaspoons sriracha
- 3 tablespoons lime juice
- 8 oz rice noodles
- 3 teaspoons toasted sesame oil
- 1 package extra-firm tofu, pressed
- 1 onion, sliced
- 2 cups green cabbage, shredded
- 1 small jalapeno, minced
- 1 red bell pepper, sliced
- 1 yellow bell pepper, sliced
- 3 garlic cloves, minced
- 3 scallions, sliced
- 1 cup Thai basil leaves, roughly chopped
- Lime wedges for serving

Directions:
1. Fill a suitably-sized pot with salted water and boil it on high heat.
2. Add pasta to the boiling water and cook until it is al dente, then rinse under cold water.
3. Put lime juice, soy sauce, sriracha, and brown sugar in a bowl then mix well.
4. Place a large wok over medium heat then add 1 teaspoon sesame oil.
5. Toss in tofu and stir for 5 minutes until golden-brown.
6. Transfer the golden-brown tofu to a plate and add 2 teaspoons oil to the wok.
7. Stir in scallions, garlic, peppers, cabbage, and onion.
8. Sauté for 2 minutes, then add cooked noodles and prepared sauce.
9. Cook for 2 minutes, then garnish with lime wedges and basil leaves.
10. Serve fresh.
Nutrition: Calories: 45 Fat: 2.5g Protein: 4g Carbohydrates: 9g Fiber: 4g Sugar: 3g Sodium: 20mg

Rainbow Soba Noodles

Preparation Time: 10 minutes
Cooking Time: 20 minutes
Servings: 4
Ingredients
- 8 oz tofu, pressed and crumbled
- 1 teaspoon olive oil
- ½ teaspoon red pepper flakes
- 10 oz package buckwheat soba noodles, cooked
- 1 package broccoli slaw
- 2 cups cabbage, shredded
- ¼ cup very red onion, thinly sliced
- Peanut Sauce
- ¼ cup peanut butter
- ¾ cup hot water
- 2 tablespoons apple cider vinegar
- 1 tablespoon maple syrup

- 1–2 garlic cloves, minced
- 1 lime, zest, and juice
- Salt and crushed red pepper flakes, to taste
- Cilantro, for garnish
- Crushed peanuts, for garnish

Directions:
1. Crumble tofu on a baking sheet and toss in 1 teaspoon oil and 1 teaspoon red pepper flakes.
2. Bake the tofu for 20 minutes at 400ºF in a preheated oven.
3. Meanwhile, whisk peanut butter with hot water, garlic cloves, maple syrup, cider vinegar, lime zest, salt, lime juice, and pepper flakes in a large bowl.
4. Toss in cooked noodles, broccoli slaw, cabbages, and onion.
5. Mix well, then stir in tofu, cilantro, and peanuts.
6. Enjoy.
Nutrition: Calories: 45 Fat: 2.5g Protein: 4g Carbohydrates: 9g Fiber: 4g Sugar: 3g Sodium: 20mg

Spicy Pad Thai Pasta

Preparation Time: 10 minutes
Cooking Time: 10 minutes
Servings: 4
Ingredients
- Spicy Tofu
- 1 lb. extra-firm tofu, sliced
- 1 tablespoon peanut butter
- 3 tablespoons soy sauce
- 2 tablespoons Sriracha
- 2 tablespoons rice vinegar
- 2 teaspoons sesame oil
- 2 teaspoons ginger, grated
- Pad Thai
- 8 oz brown rice noodles
- 2 teaspoons coconut oil
- 1 red pepper, sliced
- ½ white onion, sliced
- 2 carrots, sliced
- 1 Thai chili, chopped
- ½ cup peanuts, chopped
- ½ cup cilantro, chopped
- Spicy Pad Thai Sauce
- 3 tablespoons soy sauce
- 3 tablespoons fresh lime juice
- 1 tablespoon Sriracha
- 3 tablespoons brown sugar
- 3 tablespoons vegetable broth
- 1 teaspoon garlic-chili paste
- 2 garlic cloves, minced

Directions:
1. Fill a suitably-sized pot with water and soak rice noodles in it.
2. Press the tofu to squeeze excess liquid out of it.
3. Place a non-stick pan over medium-high heat and add tofu.
4. Sear the tofu for 2-3 minutes per side until brown.
5. Whisk all the ingredients for tofu crumbles in a large bowl.

6.   Stir in tofu and mix well.
7.   Separately mix the pad Thai sauce in a bowl and add to the tofu.
8.   Place a wok over medium heat and add 1 teaspoon oil.
9.   Toss in chili, carrots, onion, and red pepper, then sauté for 3 minutes.
10.   Transfer the veggies to the tofu bowl.
11.   Add more oil to the same pan and stir in drained noodles, then stir cook for 1 minute.
12.   Transfer the noodles to the tofu and toss it all well.
13.   Add cilantro and peanuts.
14.   Serve fresh.
Nutrition: Calories: 45 Fat: 2.5g Protein: 4g Carbohydrates: 9g Fiber: 4g Sugar: 3g Sodium: 20mg

Linguine with Wine Sauce

Preparation Time: 10 minutes
Cooking Time: 18 minutes
Servings: 4
Ingredients:
- 1 tablespoon olive oil
- 5 garlic cloves, minced
- 16 oz shiitake, chopped
- ¼ teaspoon salt
- ¼ teaspoon ground pepper
- 1 pinch red pepper flakes
- ½ cup dry white wine
- 12 oz linguine
- 2 teaspoons vegan butter
- ¼ cup Italian parsley, finely chopped

Directions:
1.   Fill a suitably-sized pot with salted water and bring it to a boil on high heat.
2.   Add pasta to the boiling water then cook until it is al dente, then rinse under cold water.
3.   Place a non-stick skillet over medium-high heat then add olive oil.
4.   Stir in garlic and sauté for 1 minute.
5.   Stir in mushrooms and cook for 10 minutes.
6.   Add salt, red pepper flakes, and black pepper for seasoning.
7.   Toss in the cooked pasta and mix well.
8.   Garnish with parsley and butter.
9.   Enjoy.
Nutrition: Calories: 40; Fat: 2.0g Protein: 5g Carbohydrates: 7g Fiber: 4g Sugar: 3g

Cheesy Macaroni with Broccoli

Preparation Time: 10 minutes
Cooking Time: 25 minutes
Servings: 6
Ingredients
- 1/3 cup melted coconut oil
- ¼ cup nutritional yeast
- 1 tablespoon tomato paste
- 1 tablespoon dried mustard
- 2 garlic cloves, minced
- 1 ½ teaspoons salt
- ½ teaspoon ground turmeric
- 4 ½ cups almond milk
- 3 cups cauliflower florets, chopped
- 1 cup raw cashews, chopped
- 1 lb. shell pasta
- 1 tablespoon white vinegar
- 3 cups broccoli florets

Directions:
1.   Place a suitably-sized saucepan over medium heat and add coconut oil.
2.   Stir in mustard, yeast, garlic, salt, tomato paste, and turmeric.
3.   Cook for 1 minute then add almond milk, cashews, and cauliflower florets.
4.   Continue cooking for 20 minutes on a simmer.
5.   Transfer the cauliflower mixture to a blender jug then blend until smooth.
6.   Stir in vinegar and blend until creamy.
7.   Fill a suitably-sized pot with salted water and bring it to a boil on high heat.
8.   Add pasta to the boiling water.
9.   Place a steamer basket over the boiling water and add broccoli to the basket.
10.   Cook until the pasta is al dente. Drain and rinse the pasta and transfer the broccoli to a bowl.
11.   Add the cooked pasta to the cauliflower-cashews sauce.
12.   Toss in broccoli florets, salt, and black pepper.
13.   Mix well then serve.
Nutrition: Calories: 40; Fat: 2.0g Protein: 5g Carbohydrates: 7g Fiber: 4g Sugar: 3g Sodium: 18mg

Soba Noodles with Tofu

Preparation Time: 10 minutes
Cooking Time: 38 minutes
Servings: 4
Ingredients
- Marinated Tofu
- 2 tablespoons olive oil
- 8 oz firm tofu, pressed and drained
- ¼ cup cilantro, finely chopped
- ¼ cup mint, finely chopped
- 1-inch fresh ginger, grated
- Soba Noodles
- 8 oz soba noodles
- ¾ cup edamame
- 2 cucumbers, peeled and julienned
- 1 large carrot, peeled and julienned
- 2 tablespoons black sesame seeds
- 2 tablespoons white sesame seeds
- 2 scallions, chopped
- Ginger-Soy Sauce
- 2 tablespoons fresh lime juice
- 2 tablespoons soy sauce
- 1 tablespoon brown sugar
- 1 tablespoon fresh ginger, grated
- 2 tablespoons sesame oil
- ½ tablespoon garlic chili sauce

Directions:
1.   Blend herbs, ginger, salt, black pepper, and olive oil in a blender.
2.   Add the spice mixture to the tofu and toss it well to coat.

3. Allow the tofu to marinate for 30 minutes at room temperature.
4. Fill a suitably-sized pot with salted water and bring it to a boil on high heat.
5. Add pasta to the boiling water then cook until it is al dente, then rinse under cold water.
6. Place a large wok over medium heat and add marinated tofu.
7. Sauté for 5–8 minutes until golden-brown, then transfer to a large bowl.
8. Add veggies to the same wok and stir until veggies are soft.
9. Transfer the veggies to the tofu and add cooked noodles.
10. Toss well, then serve warm.
11. Enjoy.
Nutrition: Calories: 30; Fat: 3.5.0g Protein: 6g Carbohydrates: 6g Fiber: 4g; Sugar: 5g Sodium: 18mg

Plant Based Keto Lo Mein

Preparation Time: 10 minutes
Cooking Time: 10 minutes
Servings: 2
Ingredients:
- 2 tablespoons carrots, shredded
- 1 package kelp noodles, soaked in water
- 1 cup broccoli, frozen
- For the Sauce
- 1 tablespoon sesame oil
- 2 tablespoons tamari
- ½ teaspoon ground ginger
- ¼ teaspoon Sriracha
- ½ teaspoon garlic powder

Directions:
1. Put the broccoli in a saucepan on medium low heat and add the sauce ingredients.
2. Cook for about 5 minutes and add the noodles after draining water.
3. Allow to simmer about 10 minutes, occasionally stirring to avoid burning.
4. When the noodles have softened, mix everything well and dish out to serve.
Nutrition: Calories: 30; Fat: 3.5.0g Protein: 6g Carbohydrates: 6g Fiber: 4g;

Vegetarian Chow Mein

Preparation Time: 20 minutes
Cooking Time: 30 minutes
Servings: 2
Ingredients:
- ½ large onion, chopped
- ½ small leek, chopped
- ½ tablespoon ginger paste
- ½ tablespoon Worcester sauce
- ½ tablespoon Oriental seasoning
- ½ teaspoon parsley
- Salt and black pepper, to taste
- ½ pound noodles
- 2 large carrots, diced
- 2 celery sticks, chopped
- 1 tablespoon olive oil
- ½ teaspoon garlic paste
- 1½ tablespoons soy sauce

- 1 tablespoon Chinese five spice
- ½ teaspoon coriander
- 2 cups water

Directions:
1. Put olive oil, ginger, garlic paste, and onion in a pot on medium heat and sauté for about 5 minutes.
2. Stir in all the vegetables and cook for about5 minutes.
3. Add rest of the ingredients and combine well.
4. Secure the lid and cook on medium heat for about 20 minutes, stirring occasionally.
5. Open the lid and dish out to serve hot.
Nutrition: Calories: 30; Fat: 3.5.0g Protein: 6g Carbohydrates: 6g Fiber: 4g; Sugar: 5g Sodium: 18mg

Veggie Noodles

Preparation Time: 10 minutes
Cooking Time: 5 minutes
Servings: 2
Ingredients:
- 2 tablespoons vegetable oil
- 4 spring onions, divided
- 1 cup snap pea
- 2 tablespoons brown sugar
- 9 oz. dried rice noodles, cooked
- 5 garlic cloves, minced
- 2 carrots, cut into small sticks
- 3 tablespoons soy sauce

Directions:
1. Heat vegetable oil in a skillet over medium heat and add garlic and 3 spring onions.
2. Cook for about 3 minutes and add the carrots, peas, brown sugar and soy sauce.
3. Add rice noodles and cook for about 2 minutes.
4. Season with salt and black pepper and top with remaining spring onion to serve.
Nutrition: Calories: 25; Fat: 2.0g Protein: 5.2g Carbohydrates: 5.3g Fiber: 4g; Sodium: 18mg

Minutes Vegetarian Pasta

Preparation Time: 5 minutes
Cooking Time: 16 minutes
Servings: 4
Ingredients:
- 3 shallots, chopped
- ¼ teaspoon red pepper flakes
- ¼ cup vegan parmesan cheese
- 2 tablespoons olive oil
- 2 garlic cloves, minced
- 8-ounces spinach leaves
- 8-ounces linguine pasta
- 1 pinch salt
- 1 pinch black pepper

Directions:
1. Boil salted water in a large pot and add pasta.
2. Cook for about 6 minutes and drain the pasta in a colander.
3. Heat olive oil over medium heat in a large skillet and add the shallots.

4.	Cook for about 5 minutes until soft and caramelized and stir in the spinach, garlic, red pepper flakes, salt and black pepper.
5.	Cook for about 5 minutes and add pasta and 2 ladles of pasta water.
6.	Stir in the parmesan cheese and dish out in a bowl to serve.
Nutrition: Calories: 25; Fat: 2.0g Protein: 5.2 Carbohydrates: 5.3g Fiber: 4g; Sodium: 18mg

Asian Veggie Noodles

Preparation Time: 10 minutes
Cooking Time: 20 minutes
Servings: 4
Ingredients:
- ½ cup peas
- 1 teaspoon rice vinegar
- 3 carrots, chopped
- 1 small packet vermicelli
- 3 tablespoons sesame oil
- 1 red pepper, chopped in small cubes
- 1 can baby corn
- 1 clove garlic, chopped
- 2 tablespoons soy sauce
- 1 teaspoon ginger powder
- ½ teaspoon curry powder
- Salt and black pepper, to taste

Directions:
1.	Take a bowl and add ginger powder, vinegar, soy sauce, curry powder, and a pinch of salt to it.
2.	Cook the noodles according to the instructions and drain them.
3.	Heat the sesame oil and cook vegetables in it for 10 minutes on medium heat.
4.	Add noodles to it and cook for 3 more minutes.
5.	Remove from heat and serve to enjoy.
Nutrition: Calories: 25; Fat: 2.0g Protein: 5.2g Carbohydrates: 5.3g Fiber: 4g; Sodium: 18mg

PASTA & NOODLES

Stir Fry Noodles

Preparation Time: 10 minutes
Cooking Time: 8 minutes
Servings: 4
Ingredients:
- 1 cup broccoli, chopped
- 1 cup red bell pepper, chopped
- 1 cup mushrooms, chopped
- 1 large onion, chopped
- 1 batch Stir Fry Sauce, prepared
- Salt and black pepper, to taste
- 2 cups spaghetti, cooked
- 4 garlic cloves, minced
- 2 tablespoons sesame oil

Directions:
1. Heat sesame oil in a pan over medium heat and add garlic, onions, bell pepper, broccoli, mushrooms.
2. Sauté for about 5 minutes and add spaghetti noodles and stir fry sauce.
3. Mix well and cook for 3 more minutes.
4. Dish out in plates and serve to enjoy.

Nutrition: Calories: 567 Total fat: 48g Total carbs: 6g Fiber: 4g; Net carbs: 2g Sodium: 373mg Protein: 33g

Spicy Sweet Chili Veggie Noodles

Preparation Time: 10 minutes
Cooking Time: 7 minutes
Servings: 2
Ingredients:
- 1 head of broccoli, cut into bite sized florets
- 1 onion, finely sliced
- 1 tablespoon olive oil
- 1 courgette, halved
- 2 nests of whole-wheat noodles
- 150g mushrooms, sliced
- For Sauce
- 3 tablespoons soy sauce
- ¼ cup sweet chili sauce
- 1 teaspoon Sriracha
- 1 tablespoon peanut butter
- 2 tablespoons boiled water
- For Topping
- 2 teaspoons sesame seeds
- 2 teaspoons dried chili flakes

Directions:
1. Heat olive oil on medium heat in a saucepan and add onions.
2. Sauté for about 2 minutes and add broccoli, courgette and mushrooms.
3. Cook for about 5 minutes, stirring occasionally.
4. Whisk sweet chili sauce, soy sauce, Sriracha, water and peanut butter in a bowl.
5. Cook the noodles according to packet instructions and add to the vegetables.
6. Stir in the sauce and top with dried chili flakes and sesame seeds to serve.

Nutrition: Calories: 351 Total Fat: 27g Protein: 25g Total Carbs: 2g Fiber: 1g Net Carbs: 1g

Creamy Vegan Mushroom Pasta

Preparation Time: 10 minutes
Cooking Time: 30 minutes
Servings: 6
Ingredients:
- 2 cups frozen peas, thawed
- 3 tablespoons flour, unbleached
- 3 cups almond breeze, unsweetened
- 1 tablespoon nutritional yeast
- 1/3 cup fresh parsley, chopped, plus extra for garnish
- ¼ cup olive oil
- 1 pound pasta of choice
- 4 cloves garlic, minced
- 2/3 cup shallots, chopped
- 8 cups mixed mushrooms, sliced
- Salt and black pepper, to taste

Directions:
1. Take a bowl and boil pasta in salted water.
2. Heat olive oil in a pan over medium heat.
3. Add mushrooms, garlic, shallots and ½ tsp salt and cook for 15 minutes.
4. Sprinkle flour on the vegetables and stir for a minute while cooking.
5. Add almond beverage, stir constantly.
6. Let it simmer for 5 minutes and add pepper to it.
7. Cook for 3 more minutes and remove from heat.
8. Stir in nutritional yeast.
9. Add peas, salt, and pepper.
10. Cook for another minute and add
11. Add pasta to this sauce.
12. Garnish and serve!

Nutrition: Calories: 364 Total Fat: 28g Protein: 24g Total Carbs: 4g Fiber: 2g Net Carbs: 2g

Vegan Chinese Noodles

Preparation Time: 15 minutes
Cooking Time: 8 minutes
Servings: 4
Ingredients:
- 300 g mixed oriental mushrooms, such as oyster, shiitake and enoki, cleaned and sliced
- 200 g thin rice noodles, cooked according to packet instructions and drained
- 2 garlic cloves, minced
- 1 fresh red chili
- 200 g courgettes, sliced
- 6 spring onions, reserving the green part
- 1 teaspoon corn flour
- 1 tablespoon agave syrup
- 1 teaspoon sesame oil
- 100 g baby spinach, chopped
- Hot chili sauce, to serve
- 2(1-inch) pieces of ginger
- ½ bunch fresh coriander, chopped
- 4 tablespoons vegetable oil
- 2 tablespoons low-salt soy sauce
- ½ tablespoon rice wine
- 2 limes, to serve

Directions:

1.   Heat sesame oil over high heat in a large wok and add the mushrooms.
2.   Sauté for about 4 minutes and add garlic, chili, ginger, courgette, coriander stalks and the white part of the spring onions.
3.   Sauté for about 3 minutes until softened and lightly golden.
4.   Meanwhile, combine the corn flour and 2 tablespoons of water in a bowl.
5.   Add soy sauce, agave syrup, sesame oil and rice wine to the corn flour mixture.
6.   Put this mixture in the pan to the veggie mixture and cook for about 3 minutes until thickened.
7.   Add the spinach and noodles and mix well.
8.   Stir in the coriander leaves and top with lime wedges, hot chili sauce and reserved spring onions to serve.
Nutrition: Calories: 314 Total Fat: 22g Protein: 26g Total Carbs: 3g Fiber: 0.3g Net Carbs: 2.7g

Vegetable Penne Pasta

Preparation Time: 15 minutes
Cooking Time: 20 minutes
Servings: 6
Ingredients:
- ½ large onion, chopped
- 2 celery sticks, chopped
- ½ tablespoon ginger paste
- ½ cup green bell pepper
- 1½ tablespoons soy sauce
- ½ teaspoon parsley
- Salt and black pepper, to taste
- ½ pound penne pasta, cooked
- 2 large carrots, diced
- ½ small leek, chopped
- 1 tablespoon olive oil
- ½ teaspoon garlic paste
- ½ tablespoon Worcester sauce
- ½ teaspoon coriander
- 1 cup water

Directions:
1.   Heat olive oil in a wok on medium heat and add onions, garlic and ginger paste.
2.   Sauté for about 3 minutes and stir in all bell pepper, celery sticks, carrots and leek.
3.   Sauté for about 5 minutes and add remaining ingredients except for pasta.
4.   Cover the lid and cook for about 12 minutes.
5.   Stir in the cooked pasta and dish out to serve warm.
Nutrition: Calories: 385 Total Fat: 29g Protein: 26g Total Carbs: 5g Fiber: 1g Net Carbs: 4g

Spaghetti in Spicy Tomato Sauce

Preparation Time: 15 minutes
Cooking Time: 40 minutes
Servings: 4
Ingredients:
- 1 pound dried spaghetti
- 1 red bell pepper, diced
- 4 garlic cloves, minced
- 1 teaspoon red pepper flakes, crushed
- 2 (14-ounce) cans diced tomatoes
- 1 (6-ounce) can tomato paste

- 2 teaspoons vegan sugar, granulated
- 2 tablespoons olive oil
- 1 medium onion, diced
- 1 cup dry red wine
- 1 teaspoon dried thyme
- ½ teaspoon fennel seed, crushed
- 1½ cups coconut milk, full-fat
- Salt and black pepper, to taste

Directions:
1.   Boil water in a large pot and add pasta.
2.   Cook according to the package directions and drain the pasta into a colander.
3.   Dish out the pasta in a large serving bowl and add a dash of olive oil to prevent sticking.
4.   Heat 2 tablespoons of olive oil over medium heat in a large pot and add garlic, onion and bell pepper.
5.   Sauté for about 5 minutes and stir in the wine, thyme, fennel and red pepper flakes.
6.   Allow to simmer on high heat for about 5 minutes until the liquid is reduced by about half.
7.   Add diced tomatoes and tomato paste and allow to simmer for about 20 minutes, stirring occasionally.
8.   Stir in the coconut milk and sugar and simmer for about 10 more minutes.
9.   Season with salt and black pepper and pour the sauce over the pasta.
10.   Toss to coat well and dish out in plates to serve.
Nutrition: Calories: 313 Total Fat: 25g Protein: 21g Total Carbs: 1g Fiber: 0g Net Carbs: 1g

Minutes Vegetarian Pasta

Preparation Time: 5 minutes
Cooking Time: 16 minutes
Servings: 4
Ingredients:
- 3 shallots, chopped
- ¼ teaspoon red pepper flakes
- ¼ cup vegan parmesan cheese
- 2 tablespoons olive oil
- 2 garlic cloves, minced
- 8-ounces spinach leaves
- 8-ounces linguine pasta
- 1 pinch salt
- 1 pinch black pepper

Directions:
1.   Boil salted water in a large pot and add pasta.
2.   Cook for about 6 minutes and drain the pasta in a colander.
3.   Heat olive oil over medium heat in a large skillet and add the shallots.
4.   Cook for about 5 minutes until soft and caramelized and stir in the spinach, garlic, red pepper flakes, salt and black pepper.
5.   Cook for about 5 minutes and add pasta and 2 ladles of pasta water.
6.   Stir in the parmesan cheese and dish out in a bowl to serve.
Nutrition: Calories: 284 Total Fat: 18g Protein: 29g Total Carbs: 1.5g Fiber: 0g Net Carbs: 1.5g

Creamy Vegan Pumpkin Pasta

Preparation Time: 15 minutes
Cooking Time: 5 minutes
Servings: 6
Ingredients:
- 1 tablespoon olive oil
- 1 cup raw cashews, soaked in water 4-8 hours, drained and rinsed
- 12 ounces dried penne pasta
- 1 cup pumpkin puree, canned
- 1 cup almond milk, plus more as needed
- 3 garlic cloves
- ¼ teaspoon ground nutmeg
- Fresh parsley, for garnish
- 1 tablespoon lemon juice
- ¾ teaspoon salt
- 1 tablespoon fresh sage, chopped

Directions:
1. Boil salted water in a large pot and add pasta.
2. Cook according to the package directions and drain the pasta into a colander.
3. Dish out the pasta in a large serving bowl and add a dash of olive oil to prevent sticking.
4. Put the pumpkin, cashews, milk, lemon juice, garlic, salt and nutmeg into the food processor and blend until smooth.
5. Stir in the sauce and sage over the pasta and toss to coat well.
6. Garnish with fresh parsley and dish out to serve hot.

NUTRITION: Calories: 431 Total Fat: 31g Protein: 35g Total Carbs: 3g Fiber: 0.5g Net Carbs: 2.5g

Loaded Creamy Vegan Pesto Pasta

Preparation Time: 15 minutes
Cooking Time: 10 minutes
Servings: 6
Ingredients:
- ¼ onion, finely chopped
- 8 romaine lettuce leaves
- 1 celery stalk, thinly sliced
- ½ cup blue cheese, crumbled
- 1 tablespoon olive oil, plus a dash
- 1 cup almond milk, unflavored and unsweetened
- ½ cup vegan pesto
- 1 cup chickpeas, cooked
- 1 cup fresh arugula, packed
- 2 tablespoons lemon juice
- Salt and black pepper, to taste
- 6-ounces orecchiette pasta, dried
- 1 cup full-fat coconut milk
- 2 tablespoons whole wheat flour
- 1½ cups cherry tomatoes, halved
- ½ cup Kalamata olives, halved
- Red pepper flakes, to taste

Directions:
1. Boil salted water in a large pot and add pasta.
2. Cook according to the package directions and drain the pasta into a colander.
3. Dish out the pasta in a large serving bowl and add a dash of olive oil to prevent sticking.

4. Put olive oil over medium heat in a large pot and whisk in the flour.
5. Cook for about 4 minutes, until the mixture begins to smell nutty and stir in the coconut milk and almond milk.
6. Let the sauce simmer for about 1 minute and add the chickpeas, olives and arugula.
7. Stir well and season with lemon juice, red pepper flakes, and salt and black pepper.
8. Dish out into plates and serve hot.

Nutrition: Calories: 220 Total Fat: 10g Protein: 31g Total Carbs: 1.5g Fiber: 0.5g Net Carbs: 1g

Creamy Vegan Spinach Pasta

Preparation Time: 20 minutes
Cooking Time: 5 minutes
Servings: 4
Ingredients:
- 1 cup raw cashews, soaked in water for 8 hours
- 2 tablespoons lemon juice
- 1 tablespoon olive oil
- 1½ cups vegetable broth
- 2 tablespoons fresh dill, chopped
- Red pepper flakes, to taste
- 10 ounces dried fusilli
- ½ cup almond milk, unflavored and unsweetened
- 2 tablespoons white miso paste
- 4 garlic cloves, divided
- 8-ounces fresh spinach, finely chopped
- ¼ cup scallions, chopped
- Salt and black pepper, to taste

Directions:
1. Boil salted water in a large pot and add pasta.
2. Cook according to the package directions and drain the pasta into a colander.
3. Dish out the pasta in a large serving bowl and add a dash of olive oil to prevent sticking.
4. Put the cashews, milk, miso, lemon juice, and 1 garlic clove into the food processor and blend until smooth.
5. Put olive oil over medium heat in a large pot and add the remaining 3 cloves of garlic.
6. Sauté for about 1 minute and stir in the spinach and broth.
7. Raise the heat and allow to simmer for about 4 minutes until the spinach is bright green and wilted.
8. Stir in the pasta and cashew mixture and season with salt and black pepper.
9. Top with scallions and dill and dish out into plates to serve.

Nutrition: Calories: 94 Total Fat: 10g Protein: 0g Total Carbs: 1g Fiber: 0.3g Net Carbs: 0.7g

Vegan Bake Pasta with Bolognese Sauce and Cashew Cream

Preparation Time: 1 hour 10 minutes
Cooking Time: 20 minutes
Servings: 8
Ingredients:
For the Pasta:
- 1 packet penne pasta

For the Bolognese Sauce:
- 1 tablespoon soy sauce
- 1 small can lentils
- 1 tablespoon brown sugar
- ½ cup tomato paste
- 1 teaspoon garlic, crushed
- 1 tablespoon olive oil
- 2 tomatoes, chopped
- 1 onion, chopped
- 2 cups mushrooms, sliced
- Salt, to taste
- Pepper, to taste
- For the Cashew Cream:
- 1 cup raw cashews
- ½ lemon, squeezed
- ½ teaspoon salt
- ½ cup water
- For the White Sauce:
- 1 teaspoon black pepper
- 1 teaspoon Dijon mustard
- ¼ cup nutritional yeast
- Sea salt, as required
- 2 cups coconut milk
- 3 tablespoons vegan butter
- 2 tablespoons all-purpose flour
- 1/3 cup vegetable broth

Directions:
1. Take a pot and boil water, add pasta to it, boil for 3 minutes and set aside.
2. Fry onion and garlic, mushroom in olive oil and add soy sauce to it.
3. Add in sugar tomato paste, lentils, and canned tomato to it and let it simmer, Bolognese sauce is prepared.
4. Season it with salt and black pepper.
5. Add the lemon juice, cashews, water and salt to the blender, blend for 2 minutes.
6. Add this to the sauce you have prepared and stir pasta in it.
7. Melt the vegan butter in a saucepan, add in the flour and stir.
8. Add vegetable stock and coconut milk to it and whisk well.
9. Stir continuously and let it boil for about 5 minutes, then remove from heat.
10. Add Dijon mustard, nutritional yeast, black pepper, and sea salt.
11. Preheat the oven to 430 degrees F.
12. Prepare rectangular oven-safe dish by placing pasta and Bolognese sauce to it.
13. Pour the white sauce on it and bake for a time period of 20-25 minutes.

Nutrition: Calories: 314 Total Fat: 20g Protein: 31g Total Carbs: 2.5g Fiber: 0.8g Net Carbs: 1.7g

Asian Veggie Noodles

Preparation Time: 10 minutes
Cooking Time: 20 minutes
Servings: 4

Ingredients:
- ½ cup peas
- 1 teaspoon rice vinegar
- 3 carrots, chopped
- 1 small packet vermicelli
- 3 tablespoons sesame oil
- 1 red pepper, chopped in small cubes
- 1 can baby corn
- 1 clove garlic, chopped
- 2 tablespoons soy sauce
- 1 teaspoon ginger powder
- ½ teaspoon curry powder
- Salt and black pepper, to taste

Directions:
1. Take a bowl and add ginger powder, vinegar, soy sauce, curry powder, and a pinch of salt to it.
2. Cook the noodles according to the instructions and drain them.
3. Heat the sesame oil and cook vegetables in it for 10 minutes on medium heat.
4. Add noodles to it and cook for 3 more minutes.
5. Remove from heat and serve to enjoy.

Nutrition: Calories: 329 Total Fat: 25g Protein: 20g Total Carbs: 6g Fiber: 1g Net Carbs: 5g

Ingredients Pasta

Preparation Time: 15 minutes
Cooking Time: 25 minutes
Servings: 5

Ingredients:
- 1 (25 oz.) jar marinara sauce
- Olive oil, as needed
- 1 pound dry vegan pasta
- 1 pound assorted vegetables, like red onion, zucchini and tomatoes
- ¼ cup prepared hummus
- Salt, to taste

Directions:
1. Preheat the oven to 400 degrees F and grease a large baking sheet.
2. Arrange the vegetables in a single layer on the baking sheet and sprinkle with olive oil and salt.
3. Transfer into the oven and roast the vegetables for about 15 minutes.
4. Boil salted water in a large pot and cook the pasta according to the package directions.
5. Drain the water when the pasta is tender and put the pasta in a colander.
6. Mix together the marinara sauce and hummus in a large pot to make a creamy sauce.
7. Stir in the cooked vegetables and pasta to the sauce and toss to coat well.
8. Dish out in a bowl and serve warm.

NUTRITION: Calories: 415 Total Fat: 29g Protein: 33g Total Carbs: 5.5g Fiber: 2g Net Carbs: 3.5g

DIP AND SPREAD RECIPES

Asparagus Spanakopita

Preparation Time: 25 minutes
Cooking Time: 25 minutes
Servings: 12
Ingredients:
- 2 cups cut fresh asparagus (1-inch pieces)
- 20 sheets phyllo dough, (14 inches x 9 inches)
- Nonstick cooking spray
- Refrigerated butter-flavored spray
- 2 cups torn fresh spinach
- 3 oz. crumbled feta cheese
- 2 tablespoon butter
- 1/4 cup all-purpose flour
- 1-1/2 cups fat-free milk
- 3 tablespoon lemon juice
- 1 teaspoon dill weed
- 1 teaspoon dried thyme
- 1/4 teaspoon salt

Directions:
1. In a steamer basket, put the asparagus and place it on top of a saucepan with 1-inch of water, then boil. Put the cover and let it steam for 5 minutes or until it becomes crisp-tender.
2. Put 1 sheet of phyllo dough in a cooking spray-coated 13x9-inch baking dish, then cut if needed. Use the butter-flavored spray to spritz the dough. Redo the layers 9 times. Lay the asparagus, feta cheese, and spinach on top. Cover it using a sheet of phyllo dough, then spritz it using the butter-flavored spray. Redo the process using the leftover phyllo. Slice it into 12 pieces. Let it bake for 15 minutes at 350 degrees F without cover, or until it turns golden brown.
3. To make the sauce, in a small saucepan, melt the butter. Mix in the flour until it becomes smooth, then slowly add the milk. Stir in salt, thyme, dill, and lemon juice, then boil. Let it cook and stir for 5 minutes until it becomes thick. Serve the spanakopita with the sauce.
Nutrition: calories 112 fat 4 carbs 14 protein 5

Black Bean and Corn Salsa from Red Gold

Preparation Time: 15 minutes
Cooking Time: 15 minutes
Servings: 25
Ingredients:
- 2 cans black beans, drained and rinsed
- 1 can whole kernel corn, drained
- 2 cans RED GOLD® Petite Diced Tomatoes & Green Chilies
- 1 can RED GOLD® Diced Tomatoes, drained
- 1/2 cup chopped green onions
- 2 tablespoon chopped fresh cilantro
- Salt and black pepper to taste

Directions:
1. Mix all ingredients to combine in a big bowl. Refrigerate to blend flavors for a few hours to overnight. Serve with chips or crackers.
Nutrition: calories 65 fat 3 carbs 8 protein 9

Avocado Bean Dip

Preparation Time: 15 minutes
Cooking Time: 15 minutes
Servings: 2
Ingredients:
- 1 medium ripe avocado, peeled and cubed
- 1/2 cup fresh cilantro leaves
- 3 tablespoon lime juice
- 1/2 teaspoon onion powder
- 1/2 teaspoon garlic powder
- 1/2 teaspoon chipotle hot pepper sauce
- 1/4 teaspoon salt
- 1/4 teaspoon ground cumin
- Baked tortilla chips

Directions:
1. Mix the first 9 ingredients in a food processor, then cover and blend until smooth. Serve along with chips.
Nutrition: calories 85 fat 4 carbs 13 protein 6

Crunchy Peanut Butter Apple Dip

Preparation Time: 10 minutes
Cooking Time: 10 minutes
Servings: 2
Ingredients:
- 1 carton (8 oz.) reduced-fat spreadable cream cheese
- 1 cup creamy peanut butter
- 1/4 cup fat-free milk
- 1 tablespoon brown sugar
- 1 teaspoon vanilla extract
- 1/2 cup chopped unsalted peanuts
- Apple slices

Directions:
1. Beat the initial 5 ingredients in a small bowl until combined. Mix in peanuts. Serve with slices of apple, then put the leftovers in the fridge.
Nutrition: calories 125 fat 5 carbs 23 protein 9

Herb Pockets

Preparation Time: 25 minutes
Cooking Time: 25 minutes
Servings: 3
Ingredients:
- 2/3 cup reduced-fat garlic-herb spreadable cheese
- 4 oz. reduced-fat cream cheese
- 2 tablespoon half-and-half cream
- 1 garlic clove, minced
- 1 tablespoon dried basil
- 1 teaspoon dried thyme
- 1/2 teaspoon celery salt
- 1/4 teaspoon dill weed
- 1/4 teaspoon salt
- 1/4 teaspoon pepper
- 3 to 4 drops hot pepper sauce
- 1/2 cup chopped canned water-packed artichoke hearts, rinsed and drained
- 1/4 cup chopped roasted red peppers

- 2 tubes (8 oz. each) refrigerated reduced-fat crescent rolls

Directions:

1. Beat garlic, cream, cream cheese, and spreadable cheese until blended in a small bowl. Beat in hot pepper sauce, pepper, salt, and herbs. Fold in red peppers and artichokes. Refrigerate, covered, for at least an hour.

2. Unroll both crescent roll dough tubes. Form every dough tube to a long rectangle on a lightly floured surface. Seal perforations and seams. Roll each to a 16x12-in. rectangle. Cut to 4 strips, lengthwise and 3 strips, width wise. Separate squares.

3. In the middle of each square, put 1 rounded tablespoon filling. Fold into half, making triangles. Seal by crimping edges. Trim if needed. Put onto ungreased baking sheets. Bake for 10-15 minutes or until golden brown at 375 degrees F. Serve warm.

Nutrition: calories 245 fat 5 carbs 10 protein 7

Creamy Cucumber Yogurt Dip

Preparation Time: 15 minutes
Cooking Time: 15 minutes
Servings: 4
Ingredients:

- 1 cup (8 oz.) reduced-fat plain yogurt
- 4 oz. reduced-fat cream cheese
- 1/2 cup chopped seeded peeled cucumber
- 1-1/2 teaspoon. finely chopped onion
- 1-1/2 teaspoon. snipped fresh dill or 1/2 teaspoon dill weed
- 1 teaspoon lemon juice
- 1 teaspoon grated lemon peel
- 1 garlic clove, minced
- 1/4 teaspoon salt
- 1/4 teaspoon pepper
- Assorted fresh vegetables

Directions:

1. Mix the cream cheese and yogurt in a small bowl. Stir in pepper, salt, garlic, peel, lemon juice, dill, onion, and cucumber. Put on the cover and let it chill in the fridge. Serve it with the veggies.

Nutrition: calories 55 fat 4 carbs 12 protein 6

Chunky Cucumber Salsa

Preparation Time: 20 minutes
Cooking Time: 20 minutes
Servings: 4
Ingredients:

- 3 medium cucumbers, peeled and coarsely chopped
- 1 medium mango, coarsely chopped
- 1 cup frozen corn, thawed
- 1 medium sweet red pepper, coarsely chopped
- 1 small red onion, coarsely chopped
- 1 jalapeno pepper, finely chopped
- 3 garlic cloves, minced
- 2 tablespoon white wine vinegar
- 1 tablespoon minced fresh cilantro
- 1 teaspoon salt
- 1/2 teaspoon sugar

- 1/4 to 1/2 teaspoon cayenne pepper

Directions:

1. Mix all ingredients in a big bowl, then chill, covered, about 2 to 3 hours before serving.

Nutrition: calories 215 fat 5 carbs 23 protein 10

Healthier Guacamole

Preparation Time: 10 minutes
Cooking Time: 10 minutes
Servings: 4
Ingredients:

- 3/4 cup crumbled tofu
- 2 avocados - peeled and pitted, divided
- 1 teaspoon salt
- 1 teaspoon minced garlic
- 1 pinch cayenne pepper (optional)

Directions:

1. Prepare a food processor then put one avocado and tofu in it then blend well until it becomes smooth. Combine salt, lime juice, and the left avocado in a bowl.

2. Add in the garlic, tomatoes, cilantro, onion, and tofu-avocado mixture. Put in cayenne pepper.

3. Let it chill in the refrigerator for 1 hour to enhance the flavor or you can serve it right away.

Nutrition: calories 534 fat 5 carbs 23 protein 11

Garlic White Bean Dip

Preparation Time: 15 minutes
Cooking Time: 15 minutes
Servings: 2
Ingredients:

- 1/4 cup soft bread crumbs
- 2 tablespoon dry white wine or water
- 2 tablespoon olive oil
- 2 tablespoon lemon juice
- 4-1/2 teaspoon. minced fresh parsley
- 3 garlic cloves, peeled and halved
- 1/2 teaspoon salt
- 1/2 teaspoon snipped fresh dill or 1/4 teaspoon dill weed
- 1/8 teaspoon cayenne pepper
- Assorted fresh vegetables

Directions:

1. Mix wine and bread crumbs in a small bowl. Mix cayenne, dill, salt, garlic, parsley, beans, lemon juice, and oil in a food processor, then cover and blend until smooth.

2. Put in bread crumb mixture and process until well combined. Serve together with vegetables.

Nutrition: calories 105 fat 5 carbs 12 protein 6

Fruit Skewers

Preparation Time: 20 minutes
Cooking Time: 20 minutes
Servings: 2
Ingredients:

- cream cheese
- fat sour cream
- lime juice
- honey
- 1/2 teaspoon ground ginger
- 2 cups green grapes

- 2 cups fresh or canned unsweetened pineapple chunks
- 2 large red apples, cut into 1-inch pieces

Directions:
1. To make the dip, beat the sour cream and cream cheese in a small bowl until it becomes smooth. Beat in the ginger, honey, and lime juice until it becomes smooth.
2. Put the cover and let it chill in the fridge for a minimum of 1 hour.
3. Alternately thread the apples, pineapple, and grapes on 8 12-inch skewers. Serve it right away with the dip.

Nutrition: calories 180 fat 5 carbs 28 protein 4

Low-fat Stuffed Mushrooms

Preparation Time: 20 minutes
Cooking Time: 25 minutes
Servings: 6
Ingredients:
- 1 lb. large fresh mushrooms
- 3 tablespoons seasoned bread crumbs
- 3 tablespoons fat-free sour cream
- 2 tablespoons grated Parmesan cheese
- 2 tablespoons minced chives
- 2 tablespoons reduced-fat mayonnaise
- 2 teaspoons balsamic vinegar
- 2 to 3 drops hot pepper sauce, optional

Directions:
1. Take out the stems from the mushrooms, then put the cups aside. Chop the stems and set aside 1/3 cup (get rid of the leftover stems or reserve for later use).
2. Mix the reserved mushroom stems, hot pepper sauce if preferred, vinegar, mayonnaise, chives, Parmesan cheese, sour cream, and breadcrumbs in a bowl, then stir well.
3. Put the mushroom caps on a cooking spray-coated baking tray and stuff it with the crumb mixture.
4. Let it boil for 5 to 7 minutes, placed 4-6 inches from the heat source, or until it turns light brown.

Nutrition: calories 435 fat 4 carbs 23 protein 9

Marinated Mushrooms

Preparation Time: 15 minutes
Cooking Time: 25 minutes
Servings: 8
Ingredients:
- 1 cup red wine
- 1/2 cup red wine vinegar
- 1/3 cup olive oil
- 2 tablespoon brown sugar
- 2 cloves garlic, minced
- 1 teaspoon crushed red pepper flakes
- 1/4 cup red bell pepper, diced
- 1 lb. small fresh mushrooms, washed and trimmed
- 1/4 cup chopped green onions
- 1/4 teaspoon dried oregano
- 1/2 teaspoon salt
- 1/4 teaspoon ground black pepper

Directions:
1. Mix the mushrooms, red pepper flakes, bell pepper, garlic, sugar, oil, vinegar, and wine in a saucepan on medium heat, then boil.
2. Put the cover and put it aside to let it cool.
3. Mix in pepper, salt, oregano, and green onions once cooled. Serve it at room temperature or chilled.

Nutrition: calories 135 fat 5 carbs 13 protein 8

Pumpkin Spice Spread

Preparation Time: 10 minutes
Cooking Time: 10 minutes
Servings: 4
Ingredients:
- 1 package (8 oz.) fat-free cream cheese
- 1/2 cup canned pumpkin
- Sugar substitute equivalent to 1/2 cup sugar
- 1 teaspoon ground cinnamon
- 1 teaspoon vanilla extract
- 1 teaspoon maple flavoring
- 1/2 teaspoon pumpkin pie spice
- 1/2 teaspoon ground nutmeg
- 1 carton (8 oz.) frozen reduced-fat whipped topping, thawed

Directions:
1. Mix well together sugar substitute, pumpkin, and cream cheese in a big bowl. Beat in nutmeg, pumpkin pie spice, maple flavoring, vanilla, and cinnamon.
2. Fold in whipped topping and chill until serving.

Nutrition: calories 177 fat 6 carbs 21 protein 11

Maple Bagel Spread

Preparation Time: 10 minutes
Cooking Time: 10 minutes
Servings: 1
Ingredients:
- cream cheese
- maple syrup
- cinnamon
- walnuts

Directions:
1. Beat the cinnamon, syrup, and cream cheese in a big bowl until it becomes smooth, then mix in walnuts.
2. Let it chill until ready to serve. Serve it with bagels.

Nutrition: calories 586 fat 7 carbs 23 protein 4

Italian Stuffed Artichokes

Preparation Time: 20 minutes
Cooking Time: 25 minutes
Servings: 4
Ingredients:
- 4 large artichokes
- 2 teaspoon lemon juice
- 2 cups soft Italian bread crumbs, toasted
- 1/2 cup grated Parmigiano-Reggiano cheese
- 1/2 cup minced fresh parsley

- 2 teaspoon Italian seasoning
- 1 teaspoon grated lemon peel
- 1/2 teaspoon pepper
- 1/4 teaspoon salt
- 1 tablespoon olive oil

Directions:

1. Level the bottom of each artichoke using a sharp knife and trim off 1-inch from the tops. Snip off tips of outer leaves using kitchen scissors, then brush lemon juice on cut edges. In a Dutch oven, stand the artichokes and pour 1-inch of water, then boil. Lower the heat, put the cover, and let it simmer for 5 minutes or until the leaves near the middle pull out effortlessly.

2. Turn the artichokes upside down to drain. Allow it to stand for 10 minutes. Carefully scrape out the fuzzy middle part of the artichokes using a spoon and get rid of it.

3. Mix the salt, pepper, lemon peel, Italian seasoning, garlic, parsley, cheese, and breadcrumbs in a small bowl, then add olive oil and stir well. Gently spread the artichoke leaves apart, then fill it with breadcrumb mixture.

4. Put it in a cooking spray-coated 11x7-inch baking dish. Let it bake for 10 minutes at 350 degrees F without cover, or until the filling turns light brown.

Nutrition: calories 543 fat 5 carbs 44 protein 6

Enchilada sauce

Preparation Time: 10 minutes
Cooking Time: 10 minutes
Servings: 13

Ingredients:

- 1½ tablespoon MCT oil
- ½ tablespoon chili powder
- ½ tablespoon whole wheat flour
- ½ teaspoon ground cumin
- ¼ teaspoon oregano (dried or fresh)
- ¼ teaspoon salt (or to taste)
- 1 garlic clove (minced)
- 1 tablespoon tomato paste
- 1 cup vegetable broth
- ½ teaspoon apple vinegar
- ½ teaspoon ground black pepper

Directions:

1. Heat a small saucepan over medium heat.

2. Add the MCT oil and minced garlic to the pan and sauté for about 1 minute.

3. Mix the dry spices and flour in a medium bowl and pour the dry mixture into the saucepan.

4. Stir in the tomato paste immediately, and slowly pour in the vegetable broth, making sure that everything combines well.

5. When everything is mixed thoroughly, bring up the heat to medium-high until it gets to a simmer and cook for about 3 minutes or until the sauce becomes a bit thicker.

6. Remove the pan from the heat and add the vinegar with the black pepper, adding more salt and pepper to taste.

Nutrition: calories 225 fat 4 carbs 33 protein 5

SMOOTHIES AND BEVERAGES

Kale Smoothie

Preparation Time: 5 minutes
Cooking Time: 0 minutes
Servings: 2
Ingredients:
- 2 cups chopped kale leaves
- 1 banana, peeled
- 1 cup frozen strawberries
- 1 cup unsweetened almond milk
- 4 Medjool dates, pitted and chopped

Directions:
1. Put all the ingredients in a food processor, then blitz until glossy and smooth.
2. Serve immediately or chill in the refrigerator for an hour before serving.
Nutrition: calories: 663 fat: 10.0g carbs: 142.5g fiber: 19.0g protein: 17.4g

Hot Tropical Smoothie

Preparation Time: 5 minutes
Cooking Time: 0 minutes
Servings: 4
Ingredients:
- 1 cup frozen mango chunks
- 1 cup frozen pineapple chunks
- 1 small tangerine, peeled and pitted
- 2 cups spinach leaves
- 1 cup coconut water
- ¼ teaspoon cayenne pepper, optional

Directions:
1. Add all the ingredients in a food processor, then blitz until the mixture is smooth and combine well.
2. Serve immediately or chill in the refrigerator for an hour before serving.
Nutrition: calories: 283 fat: 1.9g carbs: 67.9g fiber: 10.4g protein: 6.4g

Berry Smoothie

Preparation Time: 5 minutes
Cooking Time: 0 minutes
Servings: 4
Ingredients:
- 1 cup berry mix (strawberries, blueberries, and cranberries)
- 4 Medjool dates, pitted and chopped
- 1½ cups unsweetened almond milk, plus more as needed

Directions:
1. Add all the ingredients in a blender, then process until the mixture is smooth and well mixed.
2. Serve immediately or chill in the refrigerator for an hour before serving.
Nutrition: calories: 473 fat: 4.0g carbs: 103.7g fiber: 9.7g protein: 14.8g

Cranberry and Banana Smoothie

Preparation Time: 5 minutes
Cooking Time: 0 minutes
Servings: 4
- 1 cup frozen cranberries
- 1 large banana, peeled
- 4 Medjool dates, pitted and chopped
- 1½ cups unsweetened almond milk

Directions:
1. Add all the ingredients in a food processor, then process until the mixture is glossy and well mixed.
2. Serve immediately or chill in the refrigerator for an hour before serving.
Nutrition: calories: 616 fat: 8.0g carbs: 132.8g fiber: 14.6g protein: 15.7g

Pumpkin Smoothie

Preparation Time: 5 minutes
Cooking Time: 0 minutes
Servings: 5
Ingredients:
- ½ cup pumpkin purée
- 4 Medjool dates, pitted and chopped
- 1 cup unsweetened almond milk
- ¼ teaspoon vanilla extract
- ¼ teaspoon ground cinnamon
- ½ cup ice
- Pinch ground nutmeg

Directions:
1. Add all the ingredients in a blender, then process until the mixture is glossy and well mixed.
2. Serve immediately.
Nutrition: calories: 417 fat: 3.0g carbs: 94.9g fiber: 10.4g protein: 11.4g

Super Smoothie

Preparation Time: 5 minutes
Cooking Time: 0 minutes
Servings: 4
Ingredients:
- 1 banana, peeled
- 1 cup chopped mango
- 1 cup raspberries
- ¼ cup rolled oats
- 1 carrot, peeled
- 1 cup chopped fresh kale
- 2 tablespoons chopped fresh parsley
- 1 tablespoon flaxseeds
- 1 tablespoon grated fresh ginger
- ½ cup unsweetened soy milk
- 1 cup water

Directions:
1. Put all the ingredients in a food processor, then blitz until glossy and smooth.
2. Serve immediately or chill in the refrigerator for an hour before serving.
Nutrition: calories: 550 fat: 39.0g carbs: 31.0g fiber: 15.0g protein: 13.0g

Kiwi and Strawberry Smoothie

Preparation Time: 5 minutes
Cooking Time: 0 minutes
Servings: 3

Ingredients:
- 1 kiwi, peeled
- 5 medium strawberries
- ½ frozen banana
- 1 cup unsweetened almond milk
- 2 tablespoons hemp seeds
- 2 tablespoons peanut butter
- 1 to 2 teaspoons maple syrup
- ½ cup spinach leaves
- Handful broccoli sprouts

Directions:
1. Put all the ingredients in a food processor, then blitz until creamy and smooth.
2. Serve immediately or chill in the refrigerator for an hour before serving.

Nutrition: calories: 562 fat: 28.6g carbs: 63.6g fiber: 15.1g protein: 23.3g

Banana and Chai Chia Smoothie

Preparation Time: 5 minutes
Cooking Time: 0 minutes
Servings: 3
Ingredients:
- 1 banana
- 1 cup alfalfa sprouts
- 1 tablespoon chia seeds
- ½ cup unsweetened coconut milk
- 1 to 2 soft Medjool dates, pitted
- ¼ teaspoon ground cinnamon
- 1 tablespoon grated fresh ginger
- 1 cup water
- Pinch ground cardamom

Directions:
1. Add all the ingredients in a blender, then process until the mixture is smooth and creamy. Add water or coconut milk if necessary.
2. Serve immediately.

Nutrition: calories: 477 fat: 41.0g carbs: 31.0g fiber: 14.0g protein: 8.0g

Chocolate and Peanut Butter Smoothie

Preparation Time: 5 minutes
Cooking Time: 0 minutes
Servings: 4
Ingredients:
- 1 tablespoon unsweetened cocoa powder
- 1 tablespoon peanut butter
- 1 banana
- 1 teaspoon maca powder
- ½ cup unsweetened soy milk
- ¼ cup rolled oats
- 1 tablespoon flaxseeds
- 1 tablespoon maple syrup
- 1 cup water

Directions:
1. Add all the ingredients in a blender, then process until the mixture is smooth and creamy. Add water or soy milk if necessary.
2. Serve immediately.

Nutrition: calories: 474 fat: 16.0g carbs: 27.0g fiber: 18.0g protein: 13.0g

Golden Milk

Preparation Time: 5 minutes
Cooking Time: 0 minutes
Servings: 4
Ingredients:
- ¼ teaspoon ground cinnamon
- ½ teaspoon ground turmeric
- ½ teaspoon grated fresh ginger
- 1 teaspoon maple syrup
- 1 cup unsweetened coconut milk
- Ground black pepper, to taste
- 2 tablespoon water

Directions:
1. Combine all the ingredients in a saucepan. Stir to mix well.
2. Heat over medium heat for 5 minutes. Keep stirring during the heating.
3. Allow to cool for 5 minutes, then pour the mixture in a blender. Pulse until creamy and smooth. Serve immediately.

Nutrition: calories: 577 fat: 57.3g carbs: 19.7g fiber: 6.1g protein: 5.7g

Mango Agua Fresca

Preparation Time: 5 minutes
Cooking Time: 0 minutes
Servings: 2
Ingredients:
- 2 fresh mangoes, diced
- 1½ cups water
- 1 teaspoon fresh lime juice
- Maple syrup, to taste
- 2 cups ice
- 2 slices fresh lime, for garnish
- 2 fresh mint sprigs, for garnish

Directions:
1. Put the mangoes, lime juice, maple syrup, and water in a blender. Process until creamy and smooth.
2. Divide the beverage into two glasses, then garnish each glass with ice, lime slice, and mint sprig before serving.

Nutrition: calories: 230 fat: 1.3g carbs: 57.7g fiber: 5.4g protein: 2.8g

Light Ginger Tea

Preparation Time: 5 minutes
Cooking Time: 10 to 15 minutes
Servings: 2
Ingredients:
- 1 small ginger knob, sliced into four 1-inch chunks
- 4 cups water
- Juice of 1 large lemon
- Maple syrup, to taste

Directions:
1. Add the ginger knob and water in a saucepan, then simmer over medium heat for 10 to 15 minutes.
2. Turn off the heat, then mix in the lemon juice. Strain the liquid to remove the ginger, then fold in the maple syrup and serve.

Nutrition: calories: 32 fat: 0.1g carbs: 8.6g fiber: 0.1g protein: 0.1g

Classic Switchel

Preparation Time: 5 minutes
Cooking Time: 0 minutes
Servings: 4
Ingredients:
- 1-inch piece ginger, minced
- 2 tablespoons apple cider vinegar
- 2 tablespoons maple syrup
- 4 cups water
- ¼ teaspoon sea salt, optional

Directions:
1. Combine all the ingredients in a glass. Stir to mix well.
2. Serve immediately or chill in the refrigerator for an hour before serving.
Nutrition: calories: 110 fat: 0g carbs: 28.0g fiber: 0g protein: 0g

Lime and Cucumber Electrolyte Drink

Preparation Time: 5 minutes
Cooking Time: 0 minutes
Servings: 4
Ingredients:
- ¼ cup chopped cucumber
- 1 tablespoon fresh lime juice
- 1 tablespoon apple cider vinegar
- 2 tablespoons maple syrup
- ¼ teaspoon sea salt, optional
- 4 cups water

Directions:
1. Combine all the ingredients in a glass. Stir to mix well.
2. Refrigerate overnight before serving.
Nutrition: calories: 114 fat: 0.1g carbs: 28.9g fiber: 0.3g protein: 0.3g

Easy and Fresh Mango Madness

Preparation Time: 5 minutes
Cooking Time: 0 minutes
Servings: 4
Ingredients:
- 1 cup chopped mango
- 1 cup chopped peach
- 1 banana
- 1 cup strawberries
- 1 carrot, peeled and chopped
- 1 cup water

Directions:
1. Put all the ingredients in a food processor, then blitz until glossy and smooth.
2. Serve immediately or chill in the refrigerator for an hour before serving.
Nutrition: calories: 376 fat: 22.0g carbs: 19.0g fiber: 14.0g protein: 5.0g

Simple Date Shake

Preparation Time: 10 minutes
Cooking Time: 0 minutes
Servings: 2
Ingredients:
- 5 Medjool dates, pitted, soaked in boiling water for 5 minutes
- ¾ cup unsweetened coconut milk
- 1 teaspoon vanilla extract
- ½ teaspoon fresh lemon juice
- ¼ teaspoon sea salt, optional
- 1½ cups ice

Directions:
1. Put all the ingredients in a food processor, then blitz until it has a milkshake and smooth texture.
2. Serve immediately.
Nutrition: calories: 380 fat: 21.6g carbs: 50.3g fiber: 6.0g protein: 3.2g

Beet and Clementine Protein Smoothie

Preparation Time: 10 minutes
Cooking Time: 0 minutes
Servings: 3
Ingredients:
- 1 small beet, peeled and chopped
- 1 clementine, peeled and broken into segments
- ½ ripe banana
- ½ cup raspberries
- 1 tablespoon chia seeds
- 2 tablespoons almond butter
- ¼ teaspoon vanilla extract
- 1 cup unsweetened almond milk
- 1/8 teaspoon fine sea salt, optional

Directions:
1. Combine all the ingredients in a food processor, then pulse on high for 2 minutes or until glossy and creamy.
2. Refrigerate for an hour and serve chilled.
Nutrition: calories: 526 fat: 25.4g carbs: 61.9g fiber: 17.3g protein: 20.6g

Matcha Limeade

Preparation Time: 10 minutes
Cooking Time: 0 minutes
Servings: 4
Ingredients:
- 2 tablespoons matcha powder
- ¼ cup raw agave syrup
- 3 cups water, divided
- 1 cup fresh lime juice
- 3 tablespoons chia seeds

Directions:
1. Lightly simmer the matcha, agave syrup, and 1 cup of water in a saucepan over medium heat. Keep stirring until no matcha lumps.
2. Pour the matcha mixture in a large glass, then add the remaining ingredients and stir to mix well.
3. Refrigerate for at least an hour before serving.
Nutrition: calories: 152 fat: 4.5g carbs: 26.8g fiber: 5.3g protein: 3.7g

Stir-Fried, Grilled Vegetables Crusty Grilled Corn

Preparation Time: 10 minutes
Cooking Time: 15 minutes

Servings: 4
Ingredients:
- 2 corn cobs
- 1/3 cup Vegenaise
- 1 small handful cilantro
- ½ cup breadcrumbs
- 1 teaspoon lemon juice

Directions:
1. Preheat the gas grill on high heat.
2. Add corn grill to the grill and continue grilling until it turns golden-brown on all sides.
3. Mix the Vegenaise, cilantro, breadcrumbs, and lemon juice in a bowl.
4. Add grilled corn cobs to the crumbs mixture.
5. Toss well then serve.

Nutrition: Calories: 253 Total Fat: 13g Protein: 31g Total Carbs: 3g Fiber: 0g Net Carbs: 3g

Grilled Carrots with Chickpea Salad

Preparation Time: 10 minutes
Cooking Time: 10 minutes
Servings: 8
Ingredients:
- Carrots
- 8 large carrots
- 1 tablespoon oil
- 1 ½ teaspoon salt
- 1 teaspoon dried oregano
- 1 teaspoon dried thyme
- 2 teaspoon paprika powder
- 1 ½ tablespoon soy sauce
- ½ cup of water
- Chickpea Salad
- 14 oz canned chickpeas
- 3 medium pickles
- 1 small onion
- A big handful of lettuce
- 1 teaspoon apple cider vinegar
- ½ teaspoon dried oregano
- ½ teaspoon salt
- Ground black pepper, to taste
- ½ cup vegan cream

Directions:
1. Toss the carrots with all of its ingredients in a bowl.
2. Thread one carrot on a stick and place it on a plate.
3. Preheat the grill over high heat.
4. Grill the carrots for 2 minutes per side on the grill.
5. Toss the ingredients for the salad in a large salad bowl.
6. Slice grilled carrots and add them on top of the salad.
7. Serve fresh.

Nutrition: Calories: 661 Total Fat: 68g Carbs: 17g Net Carbs: 7g Fiber: 2g Protein: 4g

Grilled Avocado Guacamole

Preparation Time: 10 minutes
Cooking Time: 20 minutes
Servings: 4

Ingredients:
- ½ teaspoon olive oil
- 1 lime, halved
- ½ onion, halved
- 1 serrano chile, halved, stemmed, and seeded
- 3 Haas avocados, skin on
- 2–3 tablespoons fresh cilantro, chopped
- ½ teaspoon smoked salt

Directions:
1. Preheat the grill over medium heat.
2. Brush the grilling grates with olive oil and place chile, onion, and lime on it.
3. Grill the onion for 10 minutes, chile for 5 minutes, and lime for 2 minutes.
4. Transfer the veggies to a large bowl.
5. Now cut the avocados in half and grill them for 5 minutes.
6. Mash the flesh of the grilled avocado in a bowl.
7. Chop the other grilled veggies and add them to the avocado mash.
8. Stir in remaining ingredients and mix well.
9. Serve.

Nutrition: Calories: 165 Total Fat: 17g Carbs: 4g Net Carbs: 2g Fiber: 1g Protein: 1g

Grilled Fajitas with Jalapeño Sauce

Preparation Time: 10 minutes
Cooking Time: 25 minutes
Servings: 4
Ingredients:
- Marinade
- ¼ cup olive oil
- ¼ cup lime juice
- 2 garlic cloves, minced
- 1 teaspoon chili powder
- 1 teaspoon ground cumin
- 1 teaspoon dried oregano
- ½ teaspoon salt
- ½ teaspoon black pepper
- Jalapeño Sauce
- 6 jalapeno peppers stemmed, halved, and seeded
- 1–2 teaspoons olive oil
- 1 cup raw cashews, soaked and drained
- ½ cup almond milk
- ¼ cup water
- ¼ cup lime juice
- 2 teaspoons agaves
- ½ cup fresh cilantro
- Salt, to taste
- Grilled Vegetables
- ½ lb. asparagus spears, trimmed
- 2 large portobello mushrooms, sliced
- 1 large zucchini, sliced
- 1 red bell pepper, sliced
- 1 red onion, sliced

Directions:
1. Dump all the ingredients for the marinade in a large bowl.

2.		Toss in all the veggies and mix well to marinate for 1 hour.
3.		Meanwhile, prepare the sauce and brush the jalapenos with oil.
4.		Grill the jalapenos for 5 minutes per side until slightly charred.
5.		Blend the grilled jalapenos with other ingredients for the sauce in a blender.
6.		Transfer this sauce to a separate bowl and keep it aside.
7.		Now grill the marinated veggies in the grill until soft and slightly charred on all sides.
8.		Pour the prepared sauce over the grilled veggies.
9.		Serve.
Nutrition: Calories: 663 Total Fat: 68g Carbs: 20g Net Carbs: 10g Fiber: 2g Protein: 4g

Grilled Ratatouille Kebabs

Preparation Time: 10 minutes
Cooking Time: 20 minutes
Servings: 6
Ingredients:
- 3 tablespoons soy sauce
- 3 tablespoons balsamic vinegar
- 1 teaspoon dried thyme leaves
- 2 tablespoons extra virgin olive oil
- Veggies
- 1 zucchini, diced
- ½ red onion, diced
- ½ red capsicum, diced
- 2 tomatoes, diced
- 1 small eggplant, diced
- 8 button mushrooms, diced

Directions:
1.		Toss the veggies with soy sauce, olive oil, thyme, and balsamic vinegar in a large bowl.
2.		Thread the veggies alternately on the wooden skewers and reserve the remaining marinade.
3.		Marinate these skewers for 1 hour in the refrigerator.
4.		Preheat the grill over medium heat.
5.		Grill the marinated skewers for 5 minutes per side while basting with the reserved marinade.
6.		Serve fresh.
Nutrition: Calories: 166 Total Fat: 17g Carbs: 5g Net Carbs: 3g Fiber: 1g Protein: 1g

Tofu Hoagie Rolls

Preparation Time: 10 minutes
Cooking Time: 20 minutes
Servings: 6
Ingredients:
- ½ cup vegetable broth
- ¼ cup hot sauce
- 1 tablespoon vegan butter
- 1 (16 ounce) package tofu, pressed and diced
- 4 cups cabbage, shredded
- 2 medium apples, grated
- 1 medium shallot, grated
- 6 tablespoons vegan mayonnaise

- 1 tablespoon apple cider vinegar
- Salt and black pepper
- 4 6-inch hoagie rolls, toasted

Directions:
1.		In a saucepan, combine broth with butter and hot sauce and bring to a boil.
2.		Add tofu and reduce the heat to a simmer.
3.		Cook for 10 minutes then remove from heat and let sit for 10 minutes to marinate.
4.		Toss cabbage and rest of the ingredients in a salad bowl.
5.		Prepare and set up a grill on medium heat.
6.		Drain the tofu and grill for 5 minutes per side.
7.		Lay out the toasted hoagie rolls and add grilled tofu to each hoagie
8.		Add the cabbage mixture evenly between them then close it.
9.		Serve.
Nutrition: Calories: 111 Total Fat: 11g Carbs: 5g Net Carbs: 1g Fiber: 0g Protein: 1g

Grilled Avocado with Tomatoes

Preparation Time: 10 minutes
Cooking Time: 15 minutes
Servings: 6
Ingredients:
- 3 avocados, halved and pitted
- 3 limes, wedged
- 1½ cup grape tomatoes
- 1 cup fresh corn
- 1 cup onion, chopped
- 3 serrano peppers
- 2 garlic cloves, peeled
- ¼ cup cilantro leaves, chopped
- 1 tablespoon olive oil
- Salt and black pepper to taste

Directions:
1.		Prepare and set a grill over medium heat.
2.		Brush the avocado with oil and grill it for 5 minutes per side.
3.		Meanwhile, toss the garlic, onion, corn, tomatoes, and pepper in a baking sheet.
4.		At 550 degrees F, roast the vegetables for 5 minutes.
5.		Toss the veggie mix and stir in salt, cilantro, and black pepper.
6.		Mix well then fill the grilled avocadoes with the mixture.
7.		Garnish with lime.
8.		Serve.
Nutrition: Calories: 56 Total Fat: 6g Carbs: 3g Net Carbs: 1g Fiber: 0g Protein: 1g

Grilled Tofu with Chimichurri Sauce

Preparation Time: 10 minutes
Cooking Time: 12 minutes
Servings: 4
Ingredients:
- 2 tablespoons plus 1 teaspoon olive oil
- 1 teaspoon dried oregano
- 1 cup parsley leaves
- ½ cup cilantro leaves

- 2 Fresno peppers, seeded and chopped
- 2 tablespoons white wine vinegar
- 2 tablespoons water
- 1 tablespoon fresh lime juice
- Salt and black pepper
- 1 cup couscous, cooked
- 1 teaspoon lime zest
- ¼ cup toasted pumpkin seeds
- 1 cup fresh spinach, chopped
- 1 (15.5 ounce) can kidney beans, rinsed and drained
- 1 (14 to 16 ounce) block tofu, diced
- 2 summer squashes, diced
- 3 spring onions, quartered

Directions:
1. In a saucepan, heat 2 tablespoons oil and add oregano over medium heat.
2. After 30 seconds add parsley, chili pepper, cilantro, lime juice, 2 tablespoons water, vinegar, salt and black pepper.
3. Mix well then blend in a blender.
4. Add the remining oil, pumpkin seeds, beans and spinach and cook for 3 minutes.
5. Stir in couscous and adjust seasoning with salt and black pepper.
6. Prepare and set up a grill on medium heat.
7. Thread the tofu, squash, and onions on the skewer in an alternating pattern.
8. Grill these skewers for 4 minutes per side while basting with the green sauce.
9. Serve the skewers on top of the couscous with green sauce.
10. Enjoy.
Nutrition: Calories: 813 Total Fat: 83g Carbs: 25g Net Carbs: 11g Fiber: 1g Protein: 7g

Grilled Seitan with Creole Sauce

Preparation Time: 10 minutes
Cooking Time: 14 minutes
Servings: 4
Ingredients:
Grilled Seitan Kebabs:
- 4 cups seitan, diced
- 2 medium onions, diced into squares
- 8 bamboo skewers
- 1 can coconut milk
- 2½ tablespoons creole spice
- 2 tablespoons tomato paste
- 2 cloves of garlic

Creole Spice Mix:
- 2 tablespoons paprika
- 12 dried peri peri chili peppers
- 1 tablespoon salt
- 1 tablespoon freshly ground pepper
- 2 teaspoons dried thyme
- 2 teaspoons dried oregano

Directions:
1. Prepare the creole seasoning by blending all its ingredients and preserve in a sealable jar.
2. Thread seitan and onion on the bamboo skewers in an alternating pattern.

3. On a baking sheet, mix coconut milk with creole seasoning, tomato paste and garlic.
4. Soak the skewers in the milk marinade for 2 hours.
5. Prepare and set up a grill over medium heat.
6. Grill the skewers for 7 minutes per side.
7. Serve.
Nutrition: Calories: 407 Total Fat: 42g Carbs: 13g Net Carbs: 6g Fiber: 1g Protein: 4g

Mushroom Steaks

Preparation Time: 10 minutes
Cooking Time: 24 minutes
Servings: 4
Ingredients:
- 1 tablespoon vegan butter
- ½ cup vegetable broth
- ½ small yellow onion, diced
- 1 large garlic clove, minced
- 3 tablespoons balsamic vinegar
- 1 tablespoon mirin
- ½ tablespoon soy sauce
- ½ tablespoon tomato paste
- 1 teaspoon dried thyme
- ½ teaspoon dried basil
- A dash of ground black pepper
- 2 large, whole portobello mushrooms

Directions:
1. Melt butter in a saucepan over medium heat and stir in half of the broth.
2. Bring to a simmer then add garlic and onion. Cook for 8 minutes.
3. Whisk the rest of the ingredients except the mushrooms in a bowl.
4. Add this mixture to the onion in the pan and mix well.
5. Bring this filling to a simmer then remove from the heat.
6. Clean the mushroom caps inside and out and divide the filling between the mushrooms.
7. Place the mushrooms on a baking sheet and top them with remaining sauce and broth.
8. Cover with foil then place it on a grill to smoke.
9. Cover the grill and broil for 16 minutes over indirect heat.
10. Serve warm.
Nutrition: Calories: 887 Total Fat: 93g Carbs: 29g Net Carbs: 13g Fiber: 4g Protein: 8g

Zucchini Boats with Garlic Sauce

Preparation Time: 10 minutes
Cooking Time: 10 minutes
Servings: 2
Ingredients:
- 1 zucchini
- 1 tbsp olive oil
- Salt, to taste
- Black pepper, to taste
- Filling:
- 1 cup organic walnuts
- 2 tablespoons olive oil
- ½ teaspoon smoked paprika

- ½ teaspoon ground cumin
- 1 pinch salt

Sauce:
- ½ cup cashews
- ½ cup water
- 2 teaspoons olive oil
- 2 teaspoons lemon juice
- 1 clove garlic
- 1/8 teaspoon salt

Directions:
- Cut the zucchini squash in half and scoop out some flesh from the center to make boats.
- Rub the zucchini boats with oil, salt, and black pepper.
- Prepare and set up a grill over medium heat.
- Grill the boats for 5 minutes per side.
- In a blender, add all the filling ingredients and blend them well.
- Divide the filling between the zucchini boats.
- Blend all of the sauce ingredients until it is lump free.
- Pour the sauce over the zucchini boats.
- Serve.

Nutrition: Calories: 444 Total Fat: 47g Carbs: 15g Net Carbs: 7g Fiber: 2g Protein: 4g

Grilled Eggplant with Pecan Butter Sauce

Preparation Time: 10 minutes
Cooking Time: 31 minutes
Servings: 02
Ingredients:
- Marinated Eggplant:
- 1 eggplant, sliced
- Salt to taste
- 4 tablespoons olive oil
- ¼ teaspoon smoked paprika
- ¼ teaspoon ground turmeric
- Black Bean and Pecan Sauce:
- 1/3 cup vegetable broth
- 1/3 cup red wine
- 1/3 cup red wine vinegar
- 1 large shallot, chopped
- 1 teaspoon ground coriander
- 2 teaspoons minced cilantro
- ½ cup pecan pieces, toasted
- 2 roasted garlic cloves
- 4 small banana peppers, seeded, and diced
- 8 tablespoons butter
- 1 tablespoon chives, chopped
- 1 (15.5 ounce) can black beans, rinsed and drained
- Salt and black pepper to taste
- 1 teaspoon fresh lime juice

Directions:
1. In a saucepan, add broth, wine, vinegar, shallots, coriander, cilantro and garlic.
2. Cook while stirring for 20 minutes on a simmer.
3. Meanwhile blend butter with chives, pepper, and pecans in a blender.
4. Add this mixture to the broth along with salt, lime juice, black pepper, and beans.
5. Mix well and cook for 5 minutes.
6. Rub the eggplant with salt and spices.
7. Prepare and set up the grill over medium heat.
8. Grill the eggplant slices for 6 minutes per side.
9. Serve the eggplant with prepared sauce.
10. Enjoy.

Nutrition: Calories: 441 Total Fat: 42g Carbs: 21g Net Carbs: 8g Fiber: 1g Protein: 7g

Sweet Potato Grilled Sandwich

Preparation Time: 10 minutes
Cooking Time: 12 minutes
Servings: 2
Ingredients:
- 1 small sweet potato, sliced
- ½ cup sweet bell peppers, sliced
- 1 cup canned black beans, roughly mashed
- ½ cup salsa
- 1 avocado, peeled and sliced
- 4 slices bread
- 1-2 tablespoons vegan butter

Directions:
1. Prepare and set up the grill over medium heat.
1. Grill the sweet potato slices for 5 minutes and the bell pepper slices for 3 minutes.
2. Spread each slice of bread liberally with butter.
3. On two of the bread slices, layer sweet potato slices, bell peppers, beans, salsa and avocado slices.
4. Place the other two slices of bread on top to make two sandwiches.
5. Cut them in half diagonally then grill the sandwiches for 1 minute per side.
6. Serve.

Nutrition: Calories: 221 Total Fat: 21g Carbs: 11g Net Carbs: 4g Fiber: 1g Protein: 4g

Grilled Eggplant

Preparation Time: 10 minutes
Cooking Time: 10 minutes
Servings: 04
Ingredients:
- 2 tablespoons salt
- 1 cup water
- 3 medium eggplants, sliced
- 1/3 cup olive oil

Directions:
1. Mix water with salt in a bowl and soak eggplants for 10 minutes.
2. Drain the eggplant and leave them in a colander.
3. Pat them dry with a paper towel.
4. Prepare and set up the grill at medium heat.
5. Toss the eggplant slices in olive oil.
6. Grill them for 5 minutes per side.
7. Serve.

Nutrition: Calories: 807 Total Fat: 85g Carbs: 15g Net Carbs: 7g Fiber: 1g Protein: 8g

Grilled Portobello

Preparation Time: 10 minutes
Cooking Time: 8 minutes
Servings: 04
Ingredients:

- 4 portobello mushrooms
- ¼ cup soy sauce
- ¼ cup tomato sauce
- 2 tablespoons maple syrup
- 1 tablespoon molasses
- 2 tablespoons minced garlic
- 1 tablespoon onion powder
- 1 pinch salt and pepper

Directions:
1. Mix all the ingredients except mushrooms in a bowl.
2. Add mushrooms to this marinade and mix well to coat.
3. Cover and marinate for 1 hour.
4. Prepare and set up the grill at medium heat. Grease it with cooking spray.
5. Grill the mushroom for 4 minutes per side.
6. Serve

Nutrition: Calories: 404 Total Fat: 43g Carbs: 8g Net Carbs: 4g Fiber: 1g Protein: 4g

Ginger Sweet Tofu

Preparation Time: 10 minutes
Cooking Time: 15 minutes
Servings: 04
Ingredients:

- ½ pound firm tofu, drained and diced
- 2 tablespoons peanut oil
- 1-inch piece ginger, sliced
- 1/3 pound bok choy, leaves separated
- 1 tablespoon shao sing rice wine
- 1 tablespoon rice vinegar
- ½ teaspoon dried chili flakes

Marinade:

- 1 tablespoon grated ginger
- 1 teaspoon dark soy sauce
- 2 tablespoons light soy sauce
- 1 tablespoon brown sugar

Directions:
1. Toss the tofu cubes with the marinade ingredients and marinate for 15 minutes.
2. In a wok, add half of the oil and ginger, then sauté for 30 secs.
3. Toss in bok choy and cook for 2 minutes.
4. Add a splash of water and steam for 2 minutes.
5. Transfer the bok choy to a bowl.
6. Add remaining oil and tofu to the pan then sauté for 10 minutes.
7. Add the tofu to the bok choy.
8. Serve.

Nutrition: Calories: 827 Total Fat: 85g Carbs: 17g Net Carbs: 7g Fiber: 2g Protein: 8g

Singapore Tofu

Preparation Time: 10 minutes
Cooking Time: 8 minutes
Servings: 04
Ingredients:

- ounces fine rice noodles, boiled
- 4 ounces firm tofu, boiled
- 2 tablespoons sunflower oil
- 3 spring onions, shredded
- 1 small piece of ginger, chopped
- 1 red pepper, thinly sliced
- ounces snap peas
- ounces beansprouts
- 1 teaspoon tikka masala paste
- 2 teaspoons reduced-salt soy sauce
- 1 tablespoon sweet chili sauce
- Chopped coriander and lime
- Lime wedges, to serve

Directions:
1. In a wok, add 1 tablespoon oil and the tofu then sauté for 5 minutes.
2. Transfer the sautéed tofu to a bowl.
3. Add more oil and the rest of the ingredients except noodles to the wok.
4. Stir fry for 3 minutes then add the tofu.
5. Toss well and then add noodles.
6. Mix and serve with lime wedges.

Nutrition: Calories: 414 Total Fat: 43g Carbs: 9g Net Carbs: 4g Fiber: 1g Protein: 4g

Wok Fried Broccoli

Preparation Time: 10 minutes
Cooking Time: 16 minutes
Servings: 02
Ingredients:

- 3 ounces whole, blanched peanuts
- 2 tablespoons olive oil
- 1 banana shallot, sliced
- 10 ounces broccoli, trimmed and cut into florets
- ¼ red pepper, julienned
- ½ yellow pepper, julienned
- 1 teaspoon soy sauce

Directions:
1. Toast peanuts on a baking sheet for 15 minutes at 350 degrees F.
2. In a wok, add oil and shallots and sauté for 10 minutes.
3. Toss in broccoli and peppers.
4. Stir fry for 3 minutes then add the rest of the ingredients.
5. Cook for 3 additional minutes and serve.

Nutrition:
Calories: 391
Total Fat: 39g
Carbs: 15g
Net Carbs: 5g
Fiber: 2g
Protein: 6g

Broccoli & Brown Rice Satay

Preparation Time: 10 minutes
Cooking Time: 10 minutes
Servings: 4

Ingredients:
- 6 trimmed broccoli florets, halved
- 1-inch piece of ginger, shredded
- 2 garlic cloves, shredded
- 1 red onion, sliced
- 1 roasted red pepper, cut into cubes
- 2 teaspoons olive oil
- 1 teaspoon mild chili powder
- 1 tablespoon reduced salt soy sauce
- 1 tablespoon maple syrup
- 1 cup cooked brown rice

Directions:
1. Boil broccoli in water for 4 minutes then drain immediately.
2. In a pan add olive oil, ginger, onion, and garlic.
3. Stir fry for 2 minutes then add the rest of the ingredients.
4. Cook for 3 minutes then serve.

Nutrition: Calories: 196 Total Fat: 20g Carbs: 8g Net Carbs: 3g Fiber: 1g Protein: 3g

Sautéed Sesame Spinach

Preparation Time: 1 hr. 10 minutes
Cooking Time: 3 minutes
Servings: 04
Ingredients:
- 1 tablespoon toasted sesame oil
- ½ tablespoon soy sauce
- ½ teaspoon toasted sesame seeds, crushed
- ½ teaspoon rice vinegar
- ½ teaspoon golden caster sugar
- 1 garlic clove, grated
- 8 ounces spinach, stem ends trimmed

Directions:
1. Sauté spinach in a pan until it is wilted.
2. Whisk the sesame oil, garlic, sugar, vinegar, sesame seeds, soy sauce and black pepper together in a bowl.
3. Stir in spinach and mix well.
4. Cover and refrigerate for 1 hour.
5. Serve.

Nutrition: Calories: 677 Total Fat: 60g Carbs: 71g Net Carbs: 7g Fiber: 0g; Protein: 20g

SIDE DISHES

Glazed Carrots

Preparation Time: 15 minutes
Cooking Time: 8 minutes
Servings: 4
Ingredients:

- 1-pound baby carrots, peeled
- 1 tablespoon Maple syrup
- 1 tablespoon olive oil
- 1 teaspoon coriander, ground
- 1/2 teaspoon minced garlic
- 1 teaspoon turmeric powder
- 1 tablespoon apple cider vinegar
- 1 tablespoon sesame seeds
- 1/2 cup of water

Directions:

1. In a bowl, mix the carrots with the maple syrup and the other Ingredients, toss and leave aside for 10 minutes.
2. Transfer the mix in the instant pot. Add water and cook on Manual mode (High pressure) for 8 minutes.
3. Then make quick pressure release.
4. Transfer the mix in the serving bowls and serve.

Nutrition: Calories: 172, Fat: 4.9, Fiber: 1.5, Carbs: 6.1, Protein: 4.3

Broccoli Puree

Preparation Time: 15 minutes
Cooking Time: 15 minutes
Servings: 6
Ingredients:

- 1 pound broccoli florets
- 1/3 cup almond milk
- 1 cup of water
- 1 teaspoon dried oregano
- 1/2 teaspoon coriander, ground

Directions:

1. Put the broccoli and the water in the instant pot and close the lid.
2. Cook on Manual mode (High pressure) for 15 minutes. Use natural pressure release for 10 minutes.
3. Strain, transfer to the food processor, add the rest of the Ingredients and pulse.
4. Divide between plates and serve.

Nutrition: Calories: 182, Fat: 3.8, Fiber: 4.8, Carbs: 11.1, Protein: 2

Lemon Cauliflower

Preparation Time: 7 minutes
Cooking Time: 8 minutes
Servings: 4
Ingredients:

- 1 pound cauliflower florets
- 1 teaspoon lemon zest
- 1 tablespoon lemon juice
- 1 teaspoon turmeric powder
- 1 teaspoon black pepper
- 1 teaspoon Pink salt
- 1 tablespoon fresh dill, chopped
- 1/4 cup vegetable broth
- 1 tablespoon olive oil

Directions:

1. In the instant pot, mix the cauliflower with the lemon juice, zest and the other Ingredients, close the lid and cook on Manual mode for 8 minutes.
2. Allow natural pressure release.

Nutrition: Calories: 205, Fat: 4.5, Fiber: 3.3, Carbs: 14.5, Protein: 4.2

Lemongrass Rice

Preparation Time: 15 minutes
Cooking Time: 15 minutes
Servings: .3
Ingredients:

- 1 cup wild rice
- 1 cup vegetable broth
- 1 tablespoon lemongrass, chopped
- 1 teaspoon turmeric powder
- 1 teaspoon oregano, dried
- 1 tablespoon almond butter
- 3/4 teaspoon ground nutmeg
- 1/3 teaspoon Pink salt

Directions:

1. Put quinoa in an instant pot.
2. Add the rest of the Ingredients and toss. Close the lid, seal it, and set Manual mode (high pressure).
3. Cook for 15 minutes and allow natural pressure release for 10 minutes.
4. Divide between plates and serve.

Nutrition: Calories: 225, Fat: 7.1, Fiber: 4.6, Carbs: 22.3, Protein: 10.8

Chives Couscous

Preparation Time: 15 minutes
Cooking Time: 5 minutes
Servings: 4
Ingredients:

- 1 1/2 cup yellow couscous
- 2 cups of water
- 1 tablespoon chives, chopped
- 1 teaspoon cumin, ground
- 1 teaspoon coriander, ground
- 1 teaspoon cayenne pepper
- 1 tablespoon olive oil
- 1 teaspoon salt

Directions:

1. Preheat instant pot on Saute mode for 3 minutes.
2. Pour olive oil inside it and add couscous.
3. Stir it gently and saute for 2 minutes.
4. Add the rest of the Ingredients and toss. Close the lid. Set manual mode (High pressure).
5. Cook the side dish for 2 minutes.
6. Release the pressure manually for 10 minutes.

Nutrition: Calories: 96, Fat: 3.6, Fiber: 0.8, Carbs: 11.5, Protein: 4.5

Coconut Cauliflower Mix

Preparation Time: 10 minutes
Cooking Time: 10 minutes
Servings: 6
Ingredients:
- 1 pound cauliflower florets
- 1 cup of water
- 1/4 cup of coconut milk
- 1 tablespoon coconut yogurt
- 1 teaspoon salt
- 1 teaspoon hot paprika
- 1 teaspoon Italian seasoning
- 1 tablespoon chives, chopped

Directions:
1. Place cauliflower and water in the instant pot. Add salt and close the lid.
2. Cook the vegetables on Manual mode for 10 minutes.
3. Then use quick pressure release.
4. Open the lid, drain water and mash the cauliflower.
5. Add the rest of the Ingredients, stir well and serve.

Nutrition: Calories: 211, Fat: 4.6, Fiber: 5.3, Carbs: 24.2, Protein: 3.9

Peppers Bowl

Preparation Time: 10 minutes
Cooking Time: 10 minutes
Servings: 2
Ingredients:
- 1 pound red bell peppers, roughly sliced
- 1/2 red onion, chopped
- 1 teaspoon salt
- 1 teaspoon black pepper
- 1 teaspoon chili powder
- 1/2 jalapeno pepper, chopped
- 1/2 cup vegetable stock
- 1/4 teaspoon ground coriander
- 1 teaspoon dried rosemary
- 1 teaspoon olive oil

Directions:
1. In the instant pot, mix the peppers with the onion, salt and the other Ingredients except the stock, set the pot on Saute mode and saute for 3 minutes.
2. Then the stock. Close the lid and set manual mode (High pressure) for 7 minutes.
3. Make a quick pressure release.
4. Transfer into the bowls.

Nutrition: Calories: 201, Fat: 4.3, Fiber: 3.8, Carbs: 14.3, Protein: 5.3

Chili Cauliflower Rice

Preparation Time: 10 minutes
Cooking Time: 6 minutes
Servings: 4
Ingredients:
- 2 1/2 cup cauliflower florets, grated
- 1 teaspoon black pepper
- 1 teaspoon oregano, dried
- 1 teaspoon turmeric powder
- 1 teaspoon salt
- 1/2 cup of water
- 1 teaspoon olive oil
- 1 tablespoon chives, chopped

Directions:
1. In the instant pot, mix the cauliflower rice with black pepper and the other Ingredients and close the lid.
2. Set manual mode and cook on High for 6 minute. Make a quick pressure release.
3. Chill the cauliflower rice for 2-5 minutes before serving.

Nutrition: Calories: 32, Fat: 1.4, Fiber: 1.6, Carbs: 3.5, Protein: 1.7

Potato Mash

Preparation Time: 10 minutes
Cooking Time: 9 minutes
Servings: 6
Ingredients:
- 1 and 1/2 pounds white potatoes, peeled, chopped
- 1 teaspoon salt
- 1/2 teaspoon hot paprika
- 1 teaspoon dill, dried
- 1 tablespoon coconut butter
- 1 teaspoon ground black pepper
- 1 cup vegetable broth
- 1 tablespoon fresh parsley, chopped

Directions:
1. Put potatoes, salt, and vegetable broth in the instant pot.
2. Close the lid and set manual mode. Cook on High for 9 minutes.
3. Then make quick pressure release, strain the sweet potatoes and mash until smooth.
4. Add the rest of the Ingredients, stir well and serve.

Nutrition: Calories: 123, Fat: 4.3, Fiber: 2.2, Carbs: 11.4, Protein: 4.3

Red Cabbage and Carrots

Preparation Time: 10 minutes
Cooking Time: 7 minutes
Servings: 3
Ingredients:
- 1-pound red cabbage, shredded
- 2 carrots, peeled and grated
- 1 teaspoon turmeric powder
- 1 teaspoon coriander, ground
- 1 teaspoon black pepper
- 1 teaspoon salt
- 1/4 cup of coconut milk
- 3/4 cup almond milk
- 1/2 tablespoon chives, chopped

Directions:
1. In the instant pot, mix the cabbage with the carrots and the other Ingredients, toss and set manual mode (High pressure).
2. Cook the cabbage for 7 minutes. Then allow natural pressure release.
3. Transfer the meal into the serving bowls and cool down before serving.

Nutrition: Calories: 182, Fat: 5.1, Fiber: 3.4, Carbs: 12.3, Protein: 2.6

Spaghetti Squash and Leeks

Preparation Time: 15 minutes
Cooking Time: 10 minutes
Servings: 4
Ingredients:
- 2 leeks, sliced
- 1 teaspoon chili powder
- 1 teaspoon cumin, ground
- 1 teaspoon onion powder
- 1 teaspoon apple cider vinegar
- 1-pound spaghetti squash, halved, seeds removed
- 1 tablespoon Italian seasoning
- 1 cup water, for cooking

Directions:
1. Pour water in the instant pot and insert steamer rack.
2. Arrange spaghetti squash on the rack and close the lid.
3. Cook it on High for 10 minutes. Then allow natural pressure release for 5 minutes.
4. Check if the spaghetti squash is soft, shred the flesh with the help of a fork and transfer to a bowl.
5. Add the rest of the Ingredients, toss and serve.

Nutrition: Calories: 110, Fat: 1.7, Fiber: 0, Carbs: 4.3, Protein: 0.8

Paprika Sweet Potato

Preparation Time: 10 minutes
Cooking Time: 11 minutes
Servings: 2
Ingredients:
- 2 sweet potatoes
- 2 teaspoons sweet paprika
- 1/2 teaspoon oregano, dried
- 1 teaspoon chili powder
- 1 teaspoon chives, chopped
- 1/2 cup of water

Directions:
1. Pour water in the instant pot and insert steamer rack.
2. Put potatoes on the rack and close the lid.
3. Set Manual mode (High pressure) and cook for 11 minutes. Then use quick pressure release.
4. Transfer the potatoes on the plate, cut into halves, sprinkle the rest of the Ingredients on top and serve.

Nutrition: Calories: 159, Fat: 3.4, Fiber: 2.8, Carbs: 33.8, Protein: 3.6

Cinnamon Carrots

Preparation Time: 10 minutes
Cooking Time: 15 minutes
Servings: 4
Ingredients:
- 1 pound baby carrots, scrubbed
- 1/3 cup water
- 1 teaspoon ground cinnamon
- 1/4 teaspoon chili powder
- 1 teaspoon black pepper

Directions:
1. In the instant pot, mix the carrots with the water and the other Ingredients, close the lid and Manual mode (High pressure) for 15 minutes.
2. After this, use quick pressure release.
3. Divide between plates and serve.

Nutrition: Calories: 147, Fat: 0.5, Fiber: 7.1, Carbs: 9.9, Protein: 4.3

Wild Rice and Corn

Preparation Time: 10 minutes
Cooking Time: 8 minutes
Servings: 4
Ingredients:
- 1 cup wild rice
- 1 tablespoon Italian seasoning
- 1/4 cup corn kernels, canned
- 1 teaspoon chili powder
- 1 teaspoon salt
- 2 cups vegetable broth
- 1 tablespoon chives, chopped
- 2 tablespoons olive oil

Directions:
1. Pour olive oil in the instant pot and set Saute mode.
2. Add rice and seasoning and cook for 2 minutes.
3. Add the rest of the Ingredients and toss.
4. Set Manual mode (High pressure) and close the lid. Seal it.
5. Cook rice for 6 minutes. Use quick pressure release.

Nutrition: Calories: 254 Fat: 4.3 Fiber: 1.5 Carbs: 25.4 Protein: 5.4

Kale Polenta

Preparation Time: 5 minutes
Cooking Time: 8 minutes
Servings: 5
Ingredients:
- 1 cup polenta
- 1/2 cup kale, chopped
- 1 teaspoon turmeric powder
- 1 teaspoon smoked paprika
- 4 cups vegetable broth
- 2 tablespoons coconut milk
- 1/2 teaspoon ground black pepper
- 1 teaspoon salt

Directions:
1. Whisk together polenta and vegetable broth.
2. Pour mixture in the instant pot, add the rest of the Ingredients and toss.
3. Close the lid and cook it on Manual mode (High pressure) for 8 minutes. Use quick pressure release/
4. Transfer cooked polenta in the bowl, stir and serve.

Nutrition: Calories: 182, Fat: 2.8, Fiber: 1, Carbs: 20.5, Protein: 6.3

SOUObS AND STEWS

Tomato Gazpacho

Preparation Time: 30 minutes
Cooking Time: 55 minutes
Servings: 6
Ingredients:
- 2 Tablespoons + 1 Teaspoon Red Wine Vinegar, Divided
- ½ Teaspoon Pepper
- 1 Teaspoon Sea Salt
- 1 Avocado,
- ¼ Cup Basil, Fresh & Chopped
- 3 Tablespoons + 2 Teaspoons Olive Oil, Divided
- 1 Clove Garlic, crushed
- 1 Red Bell Pepper, Sliced & Seeded
- 1 Cucumber, Chunked
- 2 ½ lbs. Large Tomatoes, Cored & Chopped

Directions:
1. Place half of your cucumber, bell pepper, and ¼ cup of each tomato in a bowl, covering. Set it in the fried.
2. Puree your remaining tomatoes, cucumber and bell pepper with garlic, three tablespoons oil, two tablespoons of vinegar, sea salt and black pepper into a blender, blending until smooth. Transfer it to a bowl, and chill for two hours.
3. Chop the avocado, adding it to your chopped vegetables, adding your remaining oil, vinegar, salt, pepper and basil.
4. Ladle your tomato puree mixture into bowls, and serve with chopped vegetables as a salad.
5. Interesting Facts:
6. Avocados themselves are ranked within the top five of the healthiest foods on the planet, so you know that the oil that is produced from them is too. It is loaded with healthy fats and essential fatty acids. Like race bran oil it is perfect to cook with as well! Bonus: Helps in the prevention of diabetes and lowers cholesterol levels.
Nutrition: Calories 201 Protein 23g Fat 4 Carbs 2

Tomato Pumpkin Soup

Preparation Time: 25 minutes
Cooking Time: 25 minutes
Servings: 4
Ingredients:
- 2 cups pumpkin, diced
- 1/2 cup tomato, chopped
- 1/2 cup onion, chopped
- 1 1/2 tsp curry powder
- 1/2 tsp paprika
- 2 cups vegetable stock
- 1 tsp olive oil
- 1/2 tsp garlic, minced

Directions:
1. In a saucepan, add oil, garlic, and onion and sauté for 3 minutes over medium heat.
2. Add remaining ingredients into the saucepan and bring to boil.
3. Reduce heat and cover and simmer for 10 minutes.
4. Puree the soup using a blender until smooth.
5. Stir well and serve warm.
Nutrition: Calories: 340 Protein: 50 g Carbohydrate: 14 g Fat: 10g

Cauliflower Spinach Soup

Preparation Time: 45 minutes
Cooking Time: 45 minutes
Servings: 5
Ingredients:
- 1/2 cup unsweetened coconut milk
- 5 oz fresh spinach, chopped
- 5 watercress, chopped
- 8 cups vegetable stock
- 1 lb. cauliflower, chopped
- Salt

Directions:
1. Add stock and cauliflower in a large saucepan and bring to boil over medium heat for 15 minutes.
2. Add spinach and watercress and cook for another 10 minutes.
3. Remove from heat and puree the soup using a blender until smooth.
4. Add coconut milk and stir well. Season with salt.
5. Stir well and serve hot.
Nutrition: Calories: 300 Protein: 43 g Carbohydrate: 12 g Fat: 10 g

Avocado Mint Soup

Preparation Time: 10 minutes
Cooking Time: 10 minutes
Servings: 2
Ingredients:
- 1 medium avocado, peeled, pitted, and cut into pieces
- 1 cup coconut milk
- 2 romaine lettuce leaves
- 20 fresh mint leaves
- 1 tbsp fresh lime juice
- 1/8 tsp salt

Directions:
1. Add all ingredients into the blender and blend until smooth. Soup should be thick not as a puree.
2. Pour into the serving bowls and place in the refrigerator for 10 minutes.
3. Stir well and serve chilled.
Nutrition: Calories 234 Protein 20g Fat 3 Carbs 12

Creamy Squash Soup

Preparation Time: 35 minutes
Cooking Time: 35 minutes
Servings: 8
Ingredients:
- 3 cups butternut squash, chopped
- 1 ½ cups unsweetened coconut milk

- 1 tbsp coconut oil
- 1 tsp dried onion flakes
- 1 tbsp curry powder
- 4 cups water
- 1 garlic clove
- 1 tsp kosher salt

Directions:
1. Add squash, coconut oil, onion flakes, curry powder, water, garlic, and salt into a large saucepan. Bring to boil over high heat.
2. Turn heat to medium and simmer for 20 minutes.
3. Puree the soup using a blender until smooth. Return soup to the saucepan and stir in coconut milk and cook for 2 minutes.
4. Stir well and serve hot.

Nutrition: Calories: 270 Protein: 23 g Carbohydrate: 10 g Fat: 23 g

Zucchini Soup

Preparation Time: 20 minutes
Cooking Time: 20 minutes
Servings: 8
Ingredients:
- 2 ½ lbs. zucchini, peeled and sliced
- 1/3 cup basil leaves
- 4 cups vegetable stock
- 4 garlic cloves, chopped
- 2 tbsp olive oil
- 1 medium onion, diced
- Pepper
- Salt

Directions:
1. Heat olive oil in a pan over medium-low heat.
2. Add zucchini and onion and sauté until softened. Add garlic and sauté for a minute.
3. Add vegetable stock and simmer for 15 minutes.
4. Remove from heat. Stir in basil and puree the soup using a blender until smooth and creamy. Season with pepper and salt.
5. Stir well and serve.

Nutrition: Calories: 350 Fat: 13 g Carbohydrate: 10 g Protein: 51 g

Creamy Celery Soup

Preparation Time: 40 minutes
Cooking Time: 40 minutes
Servings: 4
Ingredients:
- 6 cups celery
- ½ tsp dill
- 2 cups water
- 1 cup coconut milk
- 1 onion, chopped
- Pinch of salt

Directions:
1. Add all ingredients into the electric pot and stir well.
2. Cover electric pot with the lid and select soup setting.

3. Release pressure using a quick release method than open the lid.
4. Puree the soup using an immersion blender until smooth and creamy.
5. Stir well and serve warm.

Nutrition: Calories 301 Protein 13g Fat 8 Carbs 7

Avocado Cucumber Soup

Preparation Time: 40 minutes
Cooking Time: 40 minutes
Servings: 3
Ingredients:
- 1 large cucumber, peeled and sliced
- ¾ cup water
- ¼ cup lemon juice
- 2 garlic cloves
- 6 green onion
- 2 avocados, pitted
- ½ tsp black pepper
- ½ tsp pink salt

Directions:
1. Add all ingredients into the blender and blend until smooth and creamy.
2. Place in refrigerator for 30 minutes.
3. Stir well and serve chilled.

Nutrition: Calories 181 Protein 43g Fat 11 Carbs 9

Creamy Garlic Onion Soup

Preparation Time: 45 minutes
Cooking Time: 25 minutes
Servings: 4
Ingredients:
- 1 onion, sliced
- 4 cups vegetable stock
- 1 1/2 tbsp olive oil
- 1 shallot, sliced
- 2 garlic clove, chopped
- 1 leek, sliced
- Salt

Directions:
1. Add stock and olive oil in a saucepan and bring to boil.
2. Add remaining ingredients and stir well.
3. Cover and simmer for 25 minutes.
4. Puree the soup using an immersion blender until smooth.
5. Stir well and serve warm.

Nutrition: Calories 115 Protein 30g Fat 0 Carbs 3

Avocado Broccoli Soup

Preparation Time: 20 minutes
Cooking Time: 5 minutes
Servings: 4
Ingredients:
- 2 cups broccoli florets, chopped
- 5 cups vegetable broth
- 2 avocados, chopped
- Pepper
- Salt

Directions:
1. Cook broccoli in boiling water for 5 minutes. Drain well.

2.	Add broccoli, vegetable broth, avocados, pepper, and salt to the blender and blend until smooth.
3.	Stir well and serve warm.
Nutrition: Calories 265 Protein 35g Fat 13 Carbs 5

Green Spinach Kale Soup

Preparation Time: 10 minutes
Cooking Time: 5 minutes
Servings: 6
Ingredients:
- 2 avocados
- 8 oz spinach
- 8 oz kale
- 1 fresh lime juice
- 1 cup water
- 3 1/3 cup coconut milk
- 3 oz olive oil
- 1/4 tsp pepper
- 1 tsp salt

Directions:
1.	Heat olive oil in a saucepan over medium heat.
2.	Add kale and spinach to the saucepan and sauté for 2-3 minutes. Remove saucepan from heat. Add coconut milk, spices, avocado, and water. Stir well.
3.	Puree the soup using an immersion blender until smooth and creamy. Add fresh lime juice and stir well.
4.	Serve and enjoy.
Nutrition: Calories: 312 Protein: 9g Fat: 10 Carbs: 22

Cauliflower Asparagus Soup

Preparation Time: 10 minutes
Cooking Time: 30 minutes
Servings: 4
Ingredients:
- 20 asparagus spears, chopped
- 4 cups vegetable stock
- ½ cauliflower head, chopped
- 2 garlic cloves, chopped
- 1 tbsp coconut oil
- Pepper
- Salt

Directions:
1.	Heat coconut oil in a large saucepan over medium heat.
2.	Add garlic and sauté until softened.
3.	Add cauliflower, vegetable stock, pepper, and salt. Stir well and bring to boil.
4.	Reduce heat to low and simmer for 20 minutes.
5.	Add chopped asparagus and cook until softened.
6.	Puree the soup using an immersion blender until smooth and creamy.
7.	Stir well and serve warm.
Nutrition: kcal: 298 Carbohydrates: 26 g Protein: 21 g Fat: 9 g

African Pineapple Peanut Stew

Preparation Time: 10 minutes

Cooking Time: 20 minutes
Servings: 4
Ingredients:
- 4 cups sliced kale
- 1 cup chopped onion
- 1/2 cup peanut butter
- 1 tbsp. hot pepper sauce or 1 tbsp. Tabasco sauce
- 2 minced garlic cloves
- 1/2 cup chopped cilantro
- 2 cups pineapple, undrained, canned & crushed
- 1 tbsp. vegetable oil

Directions:
1.	In a saucepan (preferably covered), sauté the garlic and onions in the oil until the onions are lightly browned, approximately 10 minutes, stirring often.
2.	Wash the kale, till the time the onions are sauté.
3.	Get rid of the stems. Mound the leaves on a cutting surface & slice crosswise into slices (preferably 1" thick).
4.	Now put the pineapple and juice to the onions & bring to a simmer. Stir the kale in, cover and simmer until just tender, stirring frequently, approximately 5 minutes.
5.	Mix in the hot pepper sauce, peanut butter & simmer for more 5 minutes.
6.	Add salt according to your taste.
Nutrition: kcal: 402 Carbohydrates: 7 g Protein: 21 g Fat: 34 g

Cabbage & Beet Stew

Preparation Time: 20 minutes
Cooking Time: 10 minutes
Servings: 4
Ingredients:
- 2 Tablespoons Olive Oil
- 3 Cups Vegetable Broth
- 2 Tablespoons Lemon Juice, Fresh
- ½ Teaspoon Garlic Powder
- ½ Cup Carrots, Shredded
- 2 Cups Cabbage, Shredded
- 1 Cup Beets, Shredded
- Dill for Garnish
- ½ Teaspoon Onion Powder
- Sea Salt & Black Pepper to Taste

Directions:
1.	Heat oil in a pot, and then sauté your vegetables.
2.	Pour your broth in, mixing in your seasoning. Simmer until it's cooked through, and then top with dill.
Nutrition: kcal: 263 Carbohydrates: 8 g Protein: 20.3 g Fat: 24 g

Basil Tomato Soup

Preparation Time: 10 minutes
Cooking Time: 10 minutes
Servings: 6
Ingredients:
- 28 oz can tomatoes

- ¼ cup basil pesto
- ¼ tsp dried basil leaves
- 1 tsp apple cider vinegar
- 2 tbsp erythritol
- ¼ tsp garlic powder
- ½ tsp onion powder
- 2 cups water
- 1 ½ tsp kosher salt

Directions:
1. Add tomatoes, garlic powder, onion powder, water, and salt in a saucepan.
2. Bring to boil over medium heat. Reduce heat and simmer for 2 minutes.
3. Remove saucepan from heat and puree the soup using a blender until smooth.
4. Stir in pesto, dried basil, vinegar, and erythritol.
5. Stir well and serve warm.

Nutrition: kcal: 662 Carbohydrates: 18 g Protein: 8 g Fat: 55 g

Mushroom & Broccoli Soup

Preparation Time: 20 minutes
Cooking Time: 45 minutes
Servings: 8
Ingredients:
- 1 bundle broccoli (around 1-1/2 pounds)
- 1 tablespoon canola oil
- 1/2 pound cut crisp mushrooms
- 1 tablespoon diminished sodium soy sauce
- 2 medium carrots, finely slashed
- 2 celery ribs, finely slashed
- 1/4 cup finely slashed onion
- 1 garlic clove, minced
- 1 container (32 ounces) vegetable juices
- 2 cups of water
- 2 tablespoons lemon juice

Directions:
1. Cut broccoli florets into reduced down pieces. Strip and hack stalks.
2. In an enormous pot, heat oil over medium-high warmth; saute mushrooms until delicate, 4-6 minutes. Mix in soy sauce; expel from skillet.
3. In the same container, join broccoli stalks, carrots, celery, onion, garlic, soup, and water; heat to the point of boiling. Diminish heat; stew, revealed, until vegetables are relaxed, 25-30 minutes.
4. Puree soup utilizing a drenching blender. Or then again, cool marginally and puree the soup in a blender; come back to the dish.
5. Mix in florets and mushrooms; heat to the point of boiling. Lessen warmth to medium; cook until broccoli is delicate, 8-10 minutes, blending infrequently. Mix in lemon juice.

Nutrition: kcal: 830 Carbohydrates: 8 g Protein: 45 g Fat: 64 g

Creamy Cauliflower Pakora Soup

Preparation Time: 20 minutes
Cooking Time: 20 minutes
Servings: 8
Ingredients:

- 1 huge head cauliflower, cut into little florets
- 5 medium potatoes, stripped and diced
- 1 huge onion, diced
- 4 medium carrots, stripped and diced
- 2 celery ribs, diced
- 1 container (32 ounces) vegetable stock
- 1 teaspoon garam masala
- 1 teaspoon garlic powder
- 1 teaspoon ground coriander
- 1 teaspoon ground turmeric
- 1 teaspoon ground cumin
- 1 teaspoon pepper
- 1 teaspoon salt
- 1/2 teaspoon squashed red pepper chips
- Water or extra vegetable stock
- New cilantro leaves
- Lime wedges, discretionary

Directions:
1. In a Dutch stove over medium-high warmth, heat initial 14 fixings to the point of boiling. Cook and mix until vegetables are delicate, around 20 minutes. Expel from heat; cool marginally. Procedure in groups in a blender or nourishment processor until smooth. Modify consistency as wanted with water (or extra stock). Sprinkle with new cilantro. Serve hot, with lime wedges whenever wanted.
2. Stop alternative: Before including cilantro, solidify cooled soup in cooler compartments. To utilize, in part defrost in cooler medium-term.
3. Warmth through in a pan, blending every so often and including a little water if fundamental. Sprinkle with cilantro. Whenever wanted, present with lime wedges.

Nutrition: kcal: 248 Carbohydrates: 7 g Protein: 1 g Fat: 19 g

Garden Vegetable and Herb Soup

Preparation Time: 20 minutes
Cooking Time: 30 minutes
Servings: 8
Ingredients:
- 2 tablespoons olive oil
- 2 medium onions, hacked
- 2 huge carrots, cut
- 1 pound red potatoes (around 3 medium), cubed
- 2 cups of water
- 1 can (14-1/2 ounces) diced tomatoes in sauce
- 1-1/2 cups vegetable soup
- 1-1/2 teaspoons garlic powder
- 1 teaspoon dried basil
- 1/2 teaspoon salt
- 1/2 teaspoon paprika
- 1/4 teaspoon dill weed
- 1/4 teaspoon pepper
- 1 medium yellow summer squash, split and cut
- 1 medium zucchini, split and cut

Directions:

1. In a huge pan, heat oil over medium warmth. Include onions and carrots; cook and mix until onions are delicate, 4-6 minutes. Include potatoes and cook 2 minutes. Mix in water, tomatoes, juices, and seasonings.
2. Heat to the point of boiling. Diminish heat; stew, revealed, until potatoes and carrots are delicate, 9 minutes.
3. Include yellow squash and zucchini; cook until vegetables are delicate, 9 minutes longer. Serve or, whenever wanted, puree blend in clusters, including extra stock until desired consistency is accomplished.
Nutrition: kcal: 252 Carbohydrates: 12 g Protein: 1 g Fat: 11 g

The Mediterranean Delight with Fresh Vinaigrette

Preparation Time: 5 minutes
Cooking Time: 10 minutes
Servings: 2
Ingredients:
- Herbed citrus vinaigrette:
- 1 tablespoon of lemon juice
- 2 tablespoons of orange juice
- ½ teaspoon of lemon zest
- ½ teaspoon of orange zest
- 2 tablespoons of olive oil
- 1 tablespoon of finely chopped fresh oregano leaves
- Salt to taste
- Black pepper to taste
- 2-3 tablespoons of freshly julienned mint leaves
- Salad:
- 1 freshly diced medium-sized cucumber
- 2 cups of cooked and rinsed chickpeas
- ½ cup of freshly diced red onion
- 2 freshly diced medium-sized tomatoes
- 1 freshly diced red bell pepper
- ¼ cup of green olives
- ½ cup of pomegranates

Directions:
1. In a large salad bowl, add the juice and zest of both the lemon and the orange along with oregano and olive oil. Whisk together so that they are mixed well. Season the vinaigrette with salt and pepper to taste.
2. After draining the chickpeas, add them to the dressing. Then, add the onions. Give them a thorough mix, so that the onion and chickpeas absorb the flavors.
3. Now, chop the rest of the veggies and start adding them to the salad bowl. Give them a good toss.
4. Lastly, add the olives and fresh mint. Adjust the salt and pepper as required.
5. Serve this Mediterranean delight chilled — a cool summer salad that is good for the tummy and the soul.
Nutrition: kcal: 286 Carbohydrates: 29 g Protein:1 g Fat: 11 g

Vegetable Broth Sans Sodium

Preparation Time: 5 minutes
Cooking Time: 60 minutes
Servings: 1 cup
Ingredients:
- 5 sprigs of dill
- 2 freshly sliced yellow onions
- 4 chives
- 6 freshly peeled and sliced carrots
- 10 cups of water
- 4 freshly sliced celery stalks
- 3 cloves of freshly minced garlic
- 4 sprigs of parsley

Directions:
1. Put a large pot on medium heat and stir the onions. Fry the onions for 1 minute until they become fragrant. Add the garlic, celery, carrots, and dill along with the chives and parsley and cook everything. You will know that the mix is ready when it becomes fragrant.
2. Add the water and allow the mixture to boil. Reduce the heat and allow everything to cook for 45 minutes.
3. Turn off the heat. The broth will cool in about 15 minutes.
4. Strain the broth with the help of a sieve so that you have a clear vegetable broth.
5. If you are not using the broth right away, store it as ice cubes. You can store the ice cubes for a week.
Nutrition: kcal: 362 Carbohydrates: 21 g Protein: 12 g Fat: 21 g

Amazing Chickpea and Noodle Soup

Preparation Time: 10 minutes
Cooking Time: 20 minutes
Servings: 1 cup
Ingredients:
- 1 freshly diced celery stalk
- ¼ cup of 'chicken' seasoning
- 1 cup of freshly diced onion
- 3 cloves of freshly crushed garlic
- 2 cups of cooked chickpeas
- 4 cups of vegetable broth
- Freshly chopped cilantro
- 2 freshly cubed medium-size potatoes
- Salt
- 2 freshly sliced carrots
- ½ teaspoon of dried thyme
- Pepper
- 2 cups of water
- 6 ounces of gluten-free spaghetti
- 'Chicken' seasoning
- 1 tablespoon of garlic powder
- 2 teaspoons of sea salt
- 1 1/3 cup of nutritional yeast
- 3 tablespoons of onion powder
- 1 teaspoon of oregano
- ½ teaspoon of turmeric
- 1 ½ tablespoons of dried basil

Directions:
1. Put a pot on medium heat and sauté the onion. It will soften within 3 minutes.

2.   Add celery, potato, and carrots and sauté for another 3 minutes
3.   Add the 'chicken' seasoning to the garlic, thyme, water, and vegetable broth.
4.   Simmer the mix on medium-high heat. Cook the veggies for about 20 minutes until they soften.
5.   Add the cooked pasta and chickpeas.
6.   Add salt and pepper to taste.
7.   Put the fresh cilantro on top and enjoy the fresh soup!
Nutrition: kcal: 405 Carbohydrates: 1 g Protein: 19 g Fat: 38 g

Lentil Soup the Vegan Way

Preparation Time: 5 minutes
Cooking Time: 20 minutes
Servings: 1 cup
Ingredients:
- 2 tablespoons of water
- 4 stalks of thinly sliced celery
- 2 cloves of freshly minced garlic
- 4 thinly sliced large carrots
- Sea salt
- 2 freshly diced small shallots
- Pepper
- 3 cups of red/yellow baby potatoes
- 2 cups of chopped sturdy greens
- 4 cups of vegetable broth
- 1 cup of uncooked brown or green lentils
- Fresh rosemary/thyme

Directions:
1.   Put a large pot over medium heat. Once the pot is hot enough, add the shallots, garlic, celery, and carrots in water. Season the veggies with a little bit of pepper and salt.
2.   Sauté the veggies for 5 minutes until they are tender. You will know that the veggies are ready when they have turned golden brown. Be careful with the garlic, because it can easily burn.
3.   Add the potatoes and some more seasoning. Cook for 2 minutes.
4.   Mix the vegetable broth with the rosemary. Now Increase the heat to medium-high. Allow the veggies to be in a rolling simmer. Add the lentils and give everything a thorough stir.
5.   Once it starts to simmer again, decrease the heat and simmer for about 20 minutes without a cover. You will know that the veggies are ready when both the lentils and potatoes are soft
6.   Add the greens. Cook for 4 minutes until they wilt. You can adjust the flavor with seasonings.
7.   Enjoy this with rice or flatbread. The leftovers are equally tasty, so store them well to enjoy on a day when you are not in the mood to cook.
Nutrition: kcal: 284 Carbohydrates: 21 g Protein: 11 g Fat: 19 g

Beet and Kale Salad

Preparation Time: 5 minutes
Cooking Time: 5 minutes
Servings: 1
Ingredients:
- 8 ounces of beet and kale blend

- 1 tablespoon of olive oil
- 1 cucumber
- ounce of chickpeas
- Salt
- 2 tablespoons of red wine vinegar
- Pepper
- ¼ cup of walnuts
- 2 ounces of dried cranberries
- Cashew cheese

Directions:
1.   Cut the veggies and combine everything in a big salad bowl.
2.   Serve the fresh salad and enjoy a hearty meal.
Nutrition: kcal: 490 Carbohydrates: 31 g Protein: 19 g Fat: 21 g

Kale and Cauliflower Salad

Preparation Time: 10 minutes
Cooking Time: 15 minutes
Servings: 1 portion
Ingredients:
- 6 ounces of Lacinato kale
- 8 ounces of cauliflower florets
- 1 lemon
- 1 tablespoon of Italian spice
- 2 radishes
- ounce of butter beans
- Olive oil
- ¼ cup of walnuts
- ¼ cup of vegan Caesar dressing
- Pepper
- Salt

Directions:
1.   Preheat the oven to 400°F. Put the cauliflower florets on a baking sheet, toss them with olive oil and spices, and add salt. Roast the cauliflower until it is brown. It will be done within 15-20 minutes.
2.   De-stem the kale and slice the leaves. Slice the radishes. Both kale and radish should be sliced thinly. Cut the lemon in half.
3.   Put the kale in a large bowl and add the lemon juice and salt along with the pepper. Massage the kale so that it is properly covered with seasoning. The leaves will soon turn dark green. Mix the radishes.
4.   Rinse the butter beans and pat them dry with a towel. On medium-high heat, put a large skillet, add some olive oil, and sauté the butter beans in a layer. Sprinkle some salt on top and shake the pan. The butter beans will be brown in places within 7 minutes.
5.   Take two large plates and divide both the kale and beans equally. Put the walnuts and roasted cauliflower on top. Add the Caesar dressing on top and enjoy the amazing salad.
Nutrition: kcal: 378 Carbohydrates: 11 g Protein: 18 g Fat: 27 g

Asian Delight with Crunchy Dressing

Preparation Time: 20 minutes

Cooking Time: 10 minutes
Servings: 1 bowl
Ingredients:
Salad Dressing:
- ½ teaspoon of powdered ginger or 1 teaspoon of freshly chopped ginger
- 1 tablespoon of honey
- ¼ cup of rice wine vinegar
- 2 tablespoons of soy sauce
- 3 tablespoons of sesame oil
- 3 tablespoons of creamy peanut butter
- ¼ cup of vegetable oil
- 2 tablespoons of toasted sesame seeds

Salad:
- 1 finely shredded carrot
- 1 thinly sliced red bell pepper
- 6 cups of washed and dried spinach
- ¼ thinly sliced red onion
- 1 thinly sliced cucumber
- ½ pound of snap peas
- ½ cup of roasted peanuts
- 1 tablespoon of toasted sesame seeds

Directions:
1. In a medium bowl, mix the dressing ingredients and whisk them well. Do not put the sesame seeds in this dressing mixture.
2. Put some water in the pot and bring it to a boil. Add the sugar snap peas and cook them for about 5 minutes until they are crisp and tender. Drain and rinse them repeatedly in cold water so that the peas retain their crispy nature.
3. In a large bowl, add all the other ingredients for the salad. Put the salad dressing on top so that the veggies are well-coated. Add the toasted sesame seeds. Enjoy this salad when you are not in the mood for anything heavy.
Nutrition: kcal: 378 Carbohydrates: 11 g Protein: 18 g Fat: 27 g

Broccoli Salad the Thai Way

Preparation Time: 10 minutes
Cooking Time: 25 minutes
Servings: 1 portion
Ingredients
- 1 tablespoon of tamari
- ¾ cup of mung beans
- 1 lime
- 2 garlic cloves
- 3 tablespoons of cashew butter
- 1 cucumber
- ¼ ounce of fresh mint
- 1 tablespoon of chili-garlic sauce
- 1 head of artisan lettuce
- 3 Thai chilis
- 6 ounces of broccoli florets
- 2 tablespoons of olive oil
- Salt
- Pepper

Directions:
1. On high heat, add the mung beans to 3 cups of cold water. After they start boiling, reduce the heat to medium. Allow the beans to simmer, but stir them from time to time. The mung beans will be tender within 20 minutes. Drain the excess water and add some salt.
2. Mince the garlic and cut the lime in half. In a medium bowl, mix the lime juice, minced garlic, tamari, and cashew butter with chili-garlic sauce. Add 3 tablespoons of warm water. Whisk the mixture well.
3. Slice the cucumber, cut the broccoli into bite-size pieces, and chop the lettuce. Pick the mint leaves as well. Lastly, slice the Thai chilis.
4. On a non-stick skillet, put 2 tablespoons of olive oil. Turn the heat to medium-high. Once the oil is hot, add the broccoli florets and cook until they are brown. They will be crisp-tender. Add some pepper and salt to the broccoli and add the lime juice and Thai chilis.
5. In a shallow bowl, spread some cashew sauce. Add some chopped lettuce, mung beans, broccoli, and cucumber. Add mint leaves and mix the Thai chilies. Add some more cashew sauce and enjoy the salad!
Nutrition: Calories: 203 kcal Fat: 1.4g Carbs: 41.6g Proteins: 4.8g

Sweet Potato, Corn and Jalapeno Bisque

Preparation Time: 10 minutes
Cooking Time: 15 minutes
Servings: 4
Ingredients:
- 4 ears corn
- 1 seeded and chopped jalapeno
- 4 cups vegetable broth
- 1 tablespoon olive oil
- 3 peeled and cubed sweet potatoes
- 1 chopped onion
- ½ tablespoon salt
- ¼ teaspoon black pepper
- 1 minced garlic clove

Directions:
1. In a pan, heat the oil over medium flame and sauté onion and garlic in it and cook for around 3 minutes. Put broth and sweet potatoes in it and bring it to boil. Reduce the flame and cook it for an additional 10 minutes.
2. Remove it from the stove and blend it with a blender. Again, put it on the stove and add corn, jalapeno, salt, and black pepper and serve it.
Nutrition: Carbohydrates 31g protein 6g fats 4g sugar 11g.

Creamy Pea Soup with Olive Pesto

Preparation Time: 20 minutes
Cooking Time: 20 minutes
Servings: 4
Ingredients:
- 1 grated carrot
- 1 rinsed chopped leek
- 1 minced garlic clove
- 2 tablespoons olive oil
- 1 stem fresh thyme leaves
- 15 ounces rinsed and drained peas
- ½ tablespoon salt

- ¼ teaspoon ground black pepper
- 2 ½ cups vegetable broth
- ¼ cup parsley leaves
- 1 ¼ cups pitted green olives
- 1 teaspoon drained capers
- 1 garlic clove

Directions:
1. Take a pan with oil and put it over medium flame and whisk garlic, leek, thyme, and carrot in it. Cook it for around 4 minutes.
2. Add broth, peas, salt, and pepper and increase the heat. When it starts boiling, lower down the heat and cook it with a lid on for around 15 minutes and remove from heat and blend it.
3. For making pesto whisk parsley, olives, capers, and garlic and blend it in a way that it has little chunks. Top the soup with the scoop of olive pesto.

Nutrition: Carbohydrates 23g protein 6g fats 15g sugar 4g calories 230.

Spinach Soup with Dill and Basil

Preparation Time: 10 minutes
Cooking Time: 25 minutes
Servings: 8
Ingredients:
- 1 pound peeled and diced potatoes
- 1 tablespoon minced garlic
- 1 teaspoon dry mustard
- 6 cups vegetable broth
- 20 ounces chopped frozen spinach
- 2 cups chopped onion
- 1 ½ tablespoons salt
- ½ cup minced dill
- 1 cup basil
- ½ teaspoon ground black pepper

Directions:
1. Whisk onion, garlic, potatoes, broth, mustard, and salt in a pan and cook it over medium flame. When it starts boiling, low down the heat and cover it with the lid and cook for 20 minutes.
2. Add the remaining ingredients in it and blend it and cook it for few more minutes and serve it.

Nutrition: Carbohydrates 12g protein 13g fats 1g calories 165.

Coconut Watercress Soup

Preparation Time: 10 minutes
Cooking Time: 20 minutes
Servings: 4
Ingredients:
- 1 teaspoon coconut oil
- 1 onion, diced
- ¾ cup coconut milk

Directions:
Preparing the ingredients.
1. Melt the coconut oil in a large pot over medium-high heat. Add the onion and cook until soft, about 5 minutes, then add the peas and the water. Bring to a boil, then lower the heat and add the watercress, mint, salt, and pepper.

2. Cover and simmer for 5 minutes. Stir in the coconut milk, and purée the soup until smooth in a blender or with an immersion blender.
3. Try this soup with any other fresh, leafy green—anything from spinach to collard greens to arugula to swiss chard.

Nutrition: Calories: 160 kcal Fat: 5g Carbs: 25g Proteins: 2g

Roasted Red Pepper and Butternut Squash Soup

Preparation Time: 10 minutes
Cooking Time: 45 minutes
Servings: 6
Ingredients:
- 1 small butternut squash
- 1 tablespoon olive oil
- 1 teaspoon sea salt
- 2 red bell peppers
- 1 yellow onion
- 1 head garlic
- 2 cups water, or vegetable broth
- Zest and juice of 1 lime
- 1 to 2 tablespoons tahini
- Pinch cayenne pepper
- ½ teaspoon ground coriander
- ½ teaspoon ground cumin
- Toasted squash seeds (optional)

Directions:
1. Preparing the ingredients.
2. Preheat the oven to 350°f.
3. Prepare the squash for roasting by cutting it in half lengthwise, scooping out the seeds, and poking some holes in the flesh with a fork. Reserve the seeds if desired.
4. Rub a small amount of oil over the flesh and skin, then rub with a bit of sea salt and put the halves skin-side down in a large baking dish. Put it in the oven while you prepare the rest of the vegetables.
5. Prepare the peppers the exact same way, except they do not need to be poked.
6. Slice the onion in half and rub oil on the exposed faces. Slice the top off the head of garlic and rub oil on the exposed flesh.
7. After the squash has cooked for 20 minutes, add the peppers, onion, and garlic, and roast for another 20 minutes. Optionally, you can toast the squash seeds by putting them in the oven in a separate baking dish 10 to 15 minutes before the vegetables are finished.
8. Keep a close eye on them. When the vegetables are cooked, take them out and let them cool before handling them. The squash will be very soft when poked with a fork.
9. Scoop the flesh out of the squash skin into a large pot (if you have an immersion blender) or into a blender.
10. Chop the pepper roughly, remove the onion skin and chop the onion roughly, and squeeze the garlic cloves out of the head, all into the pot or blender. Add the water, the lime zest and juice, and the tahini. Purée the soup, adding more water if you like, to your desired consistency. Season with the salt,

cayenne, coriander, and cumin. Serve garnished with toasted squash seeds (if using).
Nutrition: calories: 156 protein: 4g total fat: 7g saturated fat: 11g carbohydrates: 22g fiber: 5g

Cauliflower Spinach Soup

Preparation Time: 30 minutes
Cooking Time: 25 minutes
Servings: 5
Ingredients:
- 1/2 cup unsweetened coconut milk
- 5 oz fresh spinach, chopped
- 5 watercress, chopped
- 8 cups vegetable stock
- 1 lb. cauliflower, chopped
- Salt

Directions:
1. Add stock and cauliflower in a large saucepan and bring to boil over medium heat for 15 minutes.
2. Add spinach and watercress and cook for another 10 minutes.
3. Remove from heat and puree the soup using a blender until smooth.
4. Add coconut milk and stir well. Season with salt.
5. Stir well and serve hot.
Nutrition: Calories: 271 kcal Fat: 3.7g Carbs: 54g Proteins: 6.5g

Avocado Mint Soup

Preparation Time: 10 minutes
Cooking Time: 10 minutes
Servings: 2
Ingredients:
- 1 medium avocado, peeled, pitted, and cut into pieces
- 1 cup coconut milk
- 2 romaine lettuce leaves
- 20 fresh mint leaves
- 1 tbsp fresh lime juice
- 1/8 tsp salt

Directions:
1. Add all ingredients into the blender and blend until smooth. Soup should be thick not as a puree.
2. Pour into the serving bowls and place in the refrigerator for 10 minutes.
3. Stir well and serve chilled.
Nutrition: Calories: 377 kcal Fat: 14.9g Carbs: 60.7g Protein: 6.4g

Creamy Squash Soup

Preparation Time: 10 minutes
Cooking Time: 25 minutes
Servings: 8
Ingredients:
- 3 cups butternut squash, chopped
- 1 ½ cups unsweetened coconut milk
- 1 tbsp coconut oil
- 1 tsp dried onion flakes
- 1 tbsp curry powder
- 4 cups water

- 1 garlic clove
- 1 tsp kosher salt

Directions:
1. Add squash, coconut oil, onion flakes, curry powder, water, garlic, and salt into a large saucepan. Bring to boil over high heat.
2. Turn heat to medium and simmer for 20 minutes.
3. Puree the soup using a blender until smooth. Return soup to the saucepan and stir in coconut milk and cook for 2 minutes.
4. Stir well and serve hot.
Nutrition: Calories: 271 kcal Fat: 3.7g Carbs: 54g Protein:6.5g

Zucchini Soup

Preparation Time: 10 minutes
Cooking Time: 15 minutes
Servings: 8
Ingredients:
- 2 ½ lbs. zucchini, peeled and sliced
- 1/3 cup basil leaves
- 4 cups vegetable stock
- 4 garlic cloves, chopped
- 2 tbsp olive oil
- 1 medium onion, diced
- Pepper
- Salt

Directions:
1. Heat olive oil in a pan over medium-low heat.
2. Add zucchini and onion and sauté until softened. Add garlic and sauté for a minute.
3. Add vegetable stock and simmer for 15 minutes.
4. Remove from heat. Stir in basil and puree the soup using a blender until smooth and creamy. Season with pepper and salt.
5. Stir well and serve.
Nutrition: Calories: 434 kcal Fat: 35g Carbs: 27g Protein: 6.7g

Creamy Celery Soup

Preparation Time: 20 minutes
Cooking Time: 20 minutes
Servings: 4
Ingredients:
- 6 cups celery
- ½ tsp dill
- 2 cups water
- 1 cup coconut milk
- 1 onion, chopped
- Pinch of salt

Directions:
1. Add all ingredients into the electric pot and stir well.
2. Cover electric pot with the lid and select soup setting.
3. Release pressure using a quick release method than open the lid.
4. Puree the soup using an immersion blender until smooth and creamy.
5. Stir well and serve warm.

Nutrition: Calories: 159kcal Fat: 8.4g Carbs: 19.8g Proteins: 4.6g

Avocado Cucumber Soup

Preparation Time: 20 minutes
Cooking Time: 0 minutes
Servings: 3
Ingredients:
- 1 large cucumber, peeled and sliced
- ¾ cup water
- ¼ cup lemon juice
- 2 garlic cloves
- 6 green onion
- 2 avocados, pitted
- ½ tsp black pepper
- ½ tsp pink salt

Directions:
1. Add all ingredients into the blender and blend until smooth and creamy.
2. Place in refrigerator for 30 minutes.
3. Stir well and serve chilled.

Nutrition: Calories: 127 kcal Fat: 6.6g Carbs: 13g Protein: 0.7g

Garden Vegetable Stew

Preparation Time: 5 minutes
Cooking Time: 60 minutes
Servings: 4
Ingredients:
- 2 tablespoons olive oil
- 1 medium red onion, chopped
- 1 medium carrot, cut into 1/4-inch slices
- 1/2 cup dry white wine
- 3 medium new potatoes, unpeeled and cut into 1-inch pieces
- 1 medium red bell pepper, cut into 1/2-inch dice
- 11/2 cups vegetable broth
- 1 tablespoon minced fresh savory or 1 teaspoon dried

Directions:
1. In a large saucepan, heat the oil over medium heat. Add the onion and carrot, cover, and cook until softened, 7 minutes. Add the wine and cook, uncovered, for 5 minutes. Stir in the potatoes, bell pepper, and broth and bring to a boil. Reduce the heat to medium and simmer for 15 minutes.
2. Add the zucchini, yellow squash, and tomatoes. Season with salt and black pepper to taste, cover, and simmer until the vegetables are tender, 20 to 30 minutes. Stir in the corn, peas, basil, parsley, and savory. Taste, adjusting seasonings if necessary. Simmer to blend flavors, about 10 minutes more. Serve immediately.

Nutrition: Calories: 219 kcal Fat: 4.5g Carbs: 38.2g Protein: 6.4g

Moroccan Vermicelli Vegetable Soup

Preparation Time: 5 minutes
Cooking Time: 35 minutes
Servings: 4 to 6
Ingredients:
- 1 tablespoon olive oil
- 1 small onion, chopped
- 1 large carrot, chopped
- 1 celery rib, chopped
- 3 small zucchini, cut into 1/4-inch dice
- 1 (28-ounce) can diced tomatoes, drained
- 2 tablespoons tomato paste
- 11/2 cups cooked or 1 (15.5-ounce) can chickpeas, drained and rinsed
- 2 teaspoons smoked paprika
- 1 teaspoon ground cumin
- 1 teaspoon za'atar spice (optional)
- 1/4 teaspoon ground cayenne
- 6 cups vegetable broth, homemade (see light vegetable broth) or store-bought, or water
- Salt
- 4 ounces vermicelli
- 2 tablespoons minced fresh cilantro, for garnish

Directions:
1. In a large soup pot, heat the oil over medium heat. Add the onion, carrot, and celery. Cover and cook until softened, about 5 minutes. Stir in the zucchini, tomatoes, tomato paste, chickpeas, paprika, cumin, za'atar, and cayenne.
2. Add the broth and salt to taste. Bring to a boil, then reduce heat to low and simmer, uncovered, until the vegetables are tender, about 30 minutes.
3. Shortly before serving, stir in the vermicelli and cook until the noodles are tender, about 5 minutes. Ladle the soup into bowls, garnish with cilantro, and serve.

Nutrition: Calories: 236 kcal Fat: 1.8g Carbs: 48.3g Protein: 7g

Moroccan Vegetable Stew

Preparation Time: 5 minutes
Cooking Time: 35 minutes
Servings: 4
Ingredients:
- 1 tablespoon olive oil
- 2 medium yellow onions, chopped
- 2 medium carrots, cut into 1/2-inch dice
- 1/2 teaspoon ground cumin
- 1/2 teaspoon ground cinnamon or allspice
- 1/2 teaspoon ground ginger
- 1/2 teaspoon sweet or smoked paprika
- 1/2 teaspoon saffron or turmeric
- 1 (14.5-ounce) can diced tomatoes, undrained
- 8 ounces green beans, trimmed and cut into 1-inch pieces
- 2 cups peeled, seeded, and diced winter squash
- 1 large russet or other baking potato, peeled and cut into 1/2-inch dice
- 11/2 cups vegetable broth
- 11/2 cups cooked or 1 (15.5-ounce) can chickpeas, drained and rinsed
- ¾ cup frozen peas
- 1/2 cup pitted dried plums (prunes)
- 1 teaspoon lemon zest
- Salt and freshly ground black pepper

- 1/2 cup pitted green olives
- 1 tablespoon minced fresh cilantro or parsley, for garnish
- 1/2 cup toasted slivered almonds, for garnish

Directions:
1. In a large saucepan, heat the oil over medium heat. Add the onions and carrots, cover, and cook for 5 minutes. Stir in the cumin, cinnamon, ginger, paprika, and saffron. Cook, uncovered, stirring, for 30 seconds.
2. Add the tomatoes, green beans, squash, potato, and broth and bring to a boil. Reduce heat to low, cover, and simmer until the vegetables are tender, about 20 minutes.
3. Add the chickpeas, peas, dried plums, and lemon zest. Season with salt and pepper to taste. Stir in the olives and simmer, uncovered, until the flavors are blended, about 10 minutes. Sprinkle with cilantro and almonds and serve immediately.

Nutrition: Calories: 71 kcal Fat: 2.8g Carbs: 9.8g Protein: 3.7g

Basic Recipe for Vegetable Broth

Preparation Time: 10 Minutes
Cooking Time: 60 Minutes
Servings: Makes 2 Quarts
Ingredients:
- 8 cups Water
- 1 Onion, chopped
- 4 Garlic cloves, crushed
- 2 Celery Stalks, chopped
- Pinch of Salt
- 1 Carrot, chopped
- Dash of Pepper
- 1 Potato, medium & chopped
- 1 tbsp. Soy Sauce
- 3 Bay Leaves

Directions:
1. To make the vegetable broth, you need to place all of the ingredients in a deep saucepan.
2. Heat the pan over a medium-high heat. Bring the vegetable mixture to a boil.
3. Once it starts boiling, lower the heat to medium-low and allow it to simmer for at least an hour or so. Cover it with a lid.
4. When the time is up, pass it through a filter and strain the vegetables, garlic, and bay leaves.
5. Allow the stock to cool completely and store in an air-tight container.

Nutrition: Calories: 44 kcal Fat: 0.6g Carbs: 9.7g Protein: 0.9g

Cucumber Dill Gazpacho

Preparation Time: 10 Minutes
Cooking Time: 2 hours
Serving Size: 4
Ingredients:
- 4 large cucumbers, peeled, deseeded, and chopped
- 1/8 tsp salt
- 1 tsp chopped fresh dill + more for garnishing
- 2 tbsp freshly squeezed lemon juice
- 1 ½ cups green grape, seeds removed
- 3 tbsp extra virgin olive oil
- 1 garlic clove, minced

Directions:
1. Add all the ingredients to a food processor and blend until smooth.
2. Pour the soup into serving bowls and chill for 1 to 2 hours.
3. Garnish with dill and serve chilled.

Nutrition: Calories: 236 kcal Fat: 1.8g Carbs: 48.3g Protein: 7g

Red Lentil Soup

Preparation Time: 5 Minutes
Cooking Time: 25 Minutes
Servings: Makes 6 cups
Ingredients:
- 2 tbsp. Nutritional Yeast
- 1 cup Red Lentil, washed
- ½ tbsp. Garlic, minced
- 4 cups Vegetable Stock
- 1 tsp. Salt
- 2 cups Kale, shredded
- 3 cups Mixed Vegetables

Directions:
1. To start with, place all ingredients needed to make the soup in a large pot.
2. Heat the pot over medium-high heat and bring the mixture to a boil.
3. Once it starts boiling, lower the heat to low. Allow the soup to simmer.
4. Simmer it for 1o to 15 minutes or until cooked.
5. Serve and enjoy.

Nutrition: Calories: 212 kcal Fat: 11.9g Carbs: 31.7g Protein: 7.3g

Spinach and Kale Soup

Preparation Time: 5 Minutes
Cooking Time: 5 Minutes
Servings: 2
Ingredients:
- 3 oz. vegan butter
- 1 cup fresh spinach, chopped coarsely
- 1 cup fresh kale, chopped coarsely
- 1 large avocado
- 3 tbsp chopped fresh mint leaves
- 3 ½ cups coconut cream
- 1 cup vegetable broth
- Salt and black pepper to taste
- 1 lime, juiced

Directions:
1. Melt the vegan butter in a medium pot over medium heat and sauté the kale and spinach until wilted, 3 minutes. Turn the heat off.
2. Stir in the remaining ingredients and using an immersion blender, puree the soup until smooth.
3. Dish the soup and serve warm.

Nutrition: Calories 380 Fat 10 g Protein 20 g Carbohydrates 30 g

Coconut and Grilled Vegetable Soup

Preparation Time: 10 Minutes
Cooking Time: 45 Minutes
Servings: 4
Ingredients:
- 2 small red onions cut into wedges
- 2 garlic cloves
- 10 oz. butternut squash, peeled and chopped
- 10 oz. pumpkins, peeled and chopped
- 4 tbsp melted vegan butter
- Salt and black pepper to taste
- 1 cup of water
- 1 cup unsweetened coconut milk
- 1 lime juiced
- ¾ cup vegan mayonnaise
- Toasted pumpkin seeds for garnishing

Directions:
1. Preheat the oven to 400 F.
2. On a baking sheet, spread the onions, garlic, butternut squash, and pumpkins and drizzle half of the butter on top. Season with salt, black pepper, and rub the seasoning well onto the vegetables. Roast in the oven for 45 minutes or until the vegetables are golden brown and softened.
3. Transfer the vegetables to a pot; add the remaining ingredients except for the pumpkin seeds and using an immersion blender puree the ingredients until smooth.
4. Dish the soup, garnish with the pumpkin seeds and serve warm.

Nutrition: Calories 290 Fat 10 g Protein 30 g Carbohydrates 0 g

Celery Dill Soup

Preparation Time: 5 Minutes
Cooking Time: 25 Minutes
Servings: 4
Ingredients:
- 2 tbsp coconut oil
- ½ lb. celery root, trimmed
- 1 garlic clove
- 1 medium white onion
- ¼ cup fresh dill, roughly chopped
- 1 tsp cumin powder
- ¼ tsp nutmeg powder
- 1 small head cauliflower, cut into florets
- 3½ cups seasoned vegetable stock
- 5 oz. vegan butter
- Juice from 1 lemon
- ¼ cup coconut cream
- Salt and black pepper to taste

Directions:
1. Melt the coconut oil in a large pot and sauté the celery root, garlic, and onion until softened and fragrant, 5 minutes.
2. Stir in the dill, cumin, and nutmeg, and stir-fry for 1 minute. Mix in the cauliflower and vegetable stock. Allow the soup to boil for 15 minutes and turn the heat off.
3. Add the vegan butter and lemon juice, and puree the soup using an immersion blender.

4. Stir in the coconut cream, salt, black pepper, and dish the soup.
5. Serve warm.

Nutrition: Calories 320 Fat 10 g Protein 20 g Carbohydrates 30 g

Broccoli Fennel Soup

Preparation Time: 15 Minutes
Cooking Time: 10 Minutes
Servings: 4
Ingredients:
- 1 fennel bulb, white and green parts coarsely chopped
- 10 oz. broccoli, cut into florets
- 3 cups vegetable stock
- Salt and freshly ground black pepper
- 1 garlic clove
- 1 cup dairy-free cream cheese
- 3 oz. vegan butter
- ½ cup chopped fresh oregano

Directions:
1. In a medium pot, combine the fennel, broccoli, vegetable stock, salt, and black pepper. Bring to a boil until the vegetables soften, 10 to 15 minutes.
2. Stir in the remaining ingredients and simmer the soup for 3 to 5 minutes.
3. Adjust the taste with salt and black pepper, and dish the soup.
4. Serve warm.

Nutrition: Calories 240 Fat 0 g Protein 0 g Carbohydrates 20 g

Tofu Goulash Soup

Preparation Time: 35 Minutes
Cooking Time: 20 Minutes
Servings: 4
Ingredients:
- 4¼ oz. vegan butter
- 1 white onion, chopped
- 2 garlic cloves, minced
- 1 ½ cups butternut squash
- 1 red bell pepper, deseeded and chopped
- 1 tbsp paprika powder
- ¼ tsp red chili flakes
- 1 tbsp dried basil
- ½ tbsp crushed cardamom seeds
- Salt and black pepper to taste
- 1 ½ cups crushed tomatoes
- 3 cups vegetable broth
- 1½ tsp red wine vinegar
- Chopped parsley to serve

Directions:
1. Place the tofu between two paper towels and allow draining of water for 30 minutes. After, crumble the tofu and set aside.
2. Melt the vegan butter in a large pot over medium heat and sauté the onion and garlic until the veggies are fragrant and soft, 3 minutes.
3. Stir in the tofu and cook until golden brown, 3 minutes.
4. Add the butternut squash, bell pepper, paprika, red chili flakes, basil, cardamom seeds, salt,

and black pepper. Cook for 2 minutes to release some flavor and mix in the tomatoes and 2 cups of vegetable broth.
5.	Close the lid, bring the soup to a boil, and then simmer for 10 minutes.
6.	Stir in the remaining vegetable broth, the red wine vinegar, and adjust the taste with salt and black pepper.
7.	Dish the soup, garnish with the parsley and serve warm.
Nutrition: Calories 320 Fat 10 g Protein 10 g Carbohydrates 20 g

Pesto Pea Soup

Preparation Time: 10 Minutes
Cooking Time: 20 Minutes
Servings: 4
Ingredients:
- 2 cups Water
- 8 oz. Tortellini
- ¼ cup Pesto
- 1 Onion, small & finely chopped
- 1 lb. Peas, frozen
- 1 Carrot, medium & finely chopped
- 1 ¾ cup Vegetable Broth, less sodium
- 1 Celery Rib, medium & finely chopped

Directions:
1.	To start with, boil the water in a large pot over a medium-high heat.
2.	Next, stir in the tortellini to the pot and cook it following the instructions given in the packet.
3.	In the meantime, cook the onion, celery, and carrot in a deep saucepan along with the water and broth.
4.	Cook the celery-onion mixture for 6 minutes or until softened.
5.	Now, spoon in the peas and allow it to simmer while keeping it uncovered.
6.	Cook the peas for few minutes or until they are bright green and soft.
7.	Then, spoon in the pesto to the peas mixture. Combine well.
8.	Pour the mixture into a high-speed blender and blend for 2 to 3 minutes or until you get a rich, smooth soup.
9.	Return the soup to the pan. Spoon in the cooked tortellini.
10.	Finally, pour into a serving bowl and top with more cooked peas if desired.
11.	Tip: If desired, you can season it with Maldon salt at the end.
Nutrition: Calories 100 Fat 0 g Protein 0 g Carbohydrates 0 g

Tofu and Mushroom Soup

Preparation Time: 15 Minutes
Cooking Time: 10 Minutes
Servings: 4
Ingredients:
- 2 tbsp olive oil
- 1 garlic clove, minced
- 1 large yellow onion, finely chopped
- 1 tsp freshly grated ginger
- 1 cup vegetable stock
- 2 small potatoes, peeled and chopped
- ¼ tsp salt
- ¼ tsp black pepper
- 2 (14 oz) silken tofu, drained and rinsed
- 2/3 cup baby Bella mushrooms, sliced
- 1 tbsp chopped fresh oregano
- 2 tbsp chopped fresh parsley to garnish

Directions:
1.	Heat the olive oil in a medium pot over medium heat and sauté the garlic, onion, and ginger until soft and fragrant.
2.	Pour in the vegetable stock, potatoes, salt, and black pepper. Cook until the potatoes soften, 12 minutes.
3.	Stir in the tofu and using an immersion blender, puree the ingredients until smooth.
4.	Mix in the mushrooms and simmer with the pot covered until the mushrooms warm up while occasionally stirring to ensure that the tofu doesn't curdle, 7 minutes.
5.	Stir oregano, and dish the soup.
6.	Garnish with the parsley and serve warm.
Nutrition: Calories 310 Fat 10 g Protein 40.0 g Carbohydrates 0 g

Avocado Green Soup

Preparation Time: 5 Minutes
Cooking Time: 5 Minutes
Servings: 4
Ingredients:
- 2 tbsp olive oil
- 1 ½ cup fresh kale, chopped coarsely
- 1 ½ cup fresh spinach, chopped coarsely
- 3 large avocados, halved, pitted and pulp extracted
- 2 cups of soy milk
- 2 cups no-sodium vegetable broth
- 3 tbsp chopped fresh mint leaves
- ¼ tsp salt
- ¼ tsp black pepper
- 2 limes, juiced

Directions:
1.	Heat the olive oil in a medium saucepan over medium heat and mix in the kale and spinach. Cook until wilted, 3 minutes and turn off the heat.
2.	Add the remaining ingredients and using an immersion blender, puree the soup until smooth.
3.	Dish the soup and serve immediately.
Nutrition: Calories 400 Fat 10 g Protein 20 g Carbohydrates 30 g

Black Bean Nacho Soup

Preparation Time: 5 Minutes
Cooking Time: 30 Minutes
Servings: 4
Ingredients:
- 30 oz. Black Bean
- 1 tbsp. Olive Oil
- 2 cups Vegetable Stock
- ½ of 1 Onion, large & chopped
- 2 ½ cups Water

- 3 Garlic cloves, minced
- 14 oz. Mild Green Chillies, diced
- 1 tsp. Cumin
- 1 cup Salsa
- ½ tsp. Salt
- 16 oz. Tomato Paste
- ½ tsp. Black Pepper

Directions:
1. For making this delicious fare, heat oil in a large pot over medium-high heat.
2. Once the oil becomes hot, stir in onion and garlic to it.
3. Sauté for 4 minutes or until the onion is softened.
4. Next, spoon in chilli powder, salt, cumin, and pepper to the pot. Mix well.
5. Then, stir in tomato paste, salsa, water, green chillies, and vegetable stock to onion mixture. Combine.
6. Bing the mixture to a boil. Allow the veggies to simmer.
7. When the mixture starts simmering, add the beans.
8. Bring the veggie mixture to a simmer again and lower the heat to low.
9. Finally, cook for 15 to 20 minutes and check for seasoning. Add more salt and pepper if needed.
10. Garnish with the topping of your choice. Serve it hot.

Nutrition: Calories 270 Fat 10 g Protein 10 g Carbohydrates 10 g

Potato Leek Soup

Preparation Time: 5 Minutes
Cooking Time: 5 Minutes
Servings: 4
Ingredients:
- 1 cup fresh cilantro leaves
- 6 garlic cloves, peeled
- 3 tbsp vegetable oil
- 3 leeks, white and green parts chopped
- 2 lb. russet potatoes, peeled and chopped
- 1 tsp cumin powder
- ¼ tsp salt
- ¼ tsp black pepper
- 2 bay leaves
- 6 cups no-sodium vegetable broth

Directions:
1. In a spice blender, process the cilantro and garlic until smooth paste forms.
2. Heat the vegetable oil in a large pot and sauté the garlic mixture and leeks until the leeks are tender, 5 minutes.
3. Mix in the remaining ingredients and allow boiling until the potatoes soften, 15 minutes.
4. Turn the heat off, open the lid, remove and discard the bay leaves.
5. Using an immersion blender, puree the soup until smooth.
6. Dish the food and serve warm.

Nutrition: Calories 215 Fat 0 g Protein 10 g Carbohydrates 20.0 g

Lentil Soup

Preparation Time: 15 Minutes

Cooking Time: 25 Minutes
Servings: 4
Ingredients:
- 1 tbsp. Olive Oil
- 4 cups Vegetable Stock
- 1 Onion, finely chopped
- 2 Carrots, medium
- 1 cup Lentils, dried
- 1 tsp. Cumin

Directions:
1. To make this healthy soup, first, you need to heat the oil in a medium-sized skillet over medium heat.
2. Once the oil becomes hot, stir in the cumin and then the onions.
3. Sauté them for 3 minutes or until the onion is slightly transparent and cooked.
4. To this, add the carrots and toss them well.
5. Next, stir in the lentils. Mix well.
6. Now, pour in the vegetable stock and give a good stir until everything comes together.
7. As the soup mixture starts to boil, reduce the heat and allow it to simmer for 10 minutes while keeping the pan covered.
8. Turn off the heat and then transfer the mixture to a bowl.
9. Finally, blend it with an immersion blender or in a high-speed blender for 1 minute or until you get a rich, smooth mixture.
10. Serve it hot and enjoy.

Nutrition: Calories: 266 Fat: 13 Fiber: 8 Carbs: 10 Protein: 11

Kale White Bean Soup

Preparation Time: 10 Minutes
Cooking Time: 45 Minutes
Servings: 4
Ingredients:
- 1 Onion, medium & finely sliced
- 3 cups Kale, coarsely chopped
- 2 tsp. Olive Oil
- 15 oz. White Beans
- 4 cups Vegetable Broth
- 4 Garlic Cloves, minced
- Sea Salt & Pepper, as needed
- 2 tsp. Rosemary, fresh & chopped
- 1 lb. White Potatoes, cubed

Directions:
1. Begin by taking a large saucepan and heat it over a medium-high heat.
2. Once the pan becomes hot, spoon in the oil.
3. Next, stir in the onion and sauté for 8 to 9 minutes or until the onions are cooked and lightly browned.
4. Then, add the garlic and rosemary to the pan.
5. Sauté for a further minute or until aromatic.
6. Now, pour in the broth along with the potatoes, black pepper, and salt. Mix well.
7. Bring the mixture to a boil, and when it starts boiling, lower the heat.
8. Allow it to simmer for 32 to 35 minutes or until the potatoes are cooked and tender.
9. After that, mash the potatoes slightly by using the back of the spoon.

10. Finally, add the kale and beans to the soup and cook for 8 minutes or until the kale is wilted.
11. Check the seasoning. Add more salt and pepper if needed.
12. Serve hot.
Nutrition: Calories: 198 Fat: 11 Fiber: 1 Carbs: 12 Protein: 12

Black Bean Mushroom Soup

Preparation Time: 10 Minutes
Cooking Time: 40 Minutes
Servings: 2
Ingredients:
- 2 tbsp. Olive Oil
- 1 clove of Garlic, peeled & minced
- ½ cup Vegetable Stock
- 1 tsp. Thyme, dried
- 15 oz. Black Beans
- 1 2/3 cup Water, hot
- oz. Mushrooms
- 1 Onion, finely chopped
- 4 Sourdough Bread Slices
- Vegan Butter, to serve

Directions:
1. To begin with, spoon the oil into a medium-sized deep saucepan over a medium heat.
2. Once the oil becomes hot, stir in the onion and garlic.
3. Sauté for 5 minutes or until the onion is translucent.
4. Next, spoon in the mushrooms and thyme. Mix well.
5. Cook for another 5 minutes or until dark brown.
6. Then, pour the water into the mixture along with the stock and beans.
7. Allow it to simmer for 20 minutes or until the mushroom is soft.
8. Pour the mixture to a high-speed blender and pulse for 1 to 2 minutes until it is smooth yet grainy.
9. Serve and enjoy.
Nutrition: Calories: 400 Fat: 32 Fiber: 6 Carbs: 4 Protein: 25

Broccoli Soup

Preparation Time: 5 Minutes
Cooking Time: 15 Minutes
Servings: 2
Ingredients:
- 3 cup Vegetable Broth
- 2 Green Chili
- 2 cups Broccoli Florets
- 1 tbsp. Chia Seeds
- 1 cup Spinach
- 1 tsp. Oil
- 4 Celery Stalk
- 1 Potato, medium & cubed
- 4 Garlic cloves
- Salt, as needed
- Juice of ½ of 1 Lemon

Directions:
1. First, heat the oil in a large sauté pan over a medium-high heat.
2. Once the oil becomes hot, add the potatoes to it.

3. When the potatoes become soft, stir all the remaining ingredients into the pan, excluding the spinach, chia seeds, and lemon.
4. Cook until the broccoli is soft, and then add the spinach and chia seed to the pan.
5. Turn off the heat after cooking for 2 minutes.
6. Allow the spinach mixture to cool slightly. Pour the mixture into a high-speed blender and blend for two minutes or until smooth.
7. Pour the lemon juice over the soup. Stir and serve immediately.
8. Enjoy.
Nutrition: Calories: 200 Fat: 3 Fiber: 2 Carbs: 5 Protein: 4

Squash Lentil Soup

Preparation Time: 10 Minutes
Cooking Time: 35 Minutes
Servings: 4
Ingredients:
- 7 cups Vegetable Broth
- 2 tbsp. Olive Oil
- 2 tsp, Sage dried
- 1 Yellow Onion, medium & diced.
- Salt & Pepper t0 taste
- 1 Butternut Squash
- 1 ½ cup Red Lentils

Directions:
1. Start by heating the oil in a large saucepan, and stir in the onions.
2. Sauté the onions for to 2 to 3 minutes or until softened.
3. Once cooked, stir in squash and sage while stirring continuously.
4. Then, spoon in the lentils, salt, and pepper.
5. Bring the lentil mixture to a boil for about 30 minutes. Lower the heat.
6. Then, allow the soup to cool down until the lentils are soft.
7. Finally, transfer the mixture to a high-speed blender and blend for 3 to 4 minutes or until smooth.
8. Serve hot.
Nutrition: Calories: 200 Fat: 7 Fiber: 4 Carbs: 7 Protein: 5

Mexican Soup

Preparation Time: 10 Minutes
Cooking Time: 45 Minutes
Servings: 6
Ingredients:
- 2 tbsp. Extra Virgin Olive Oil
- 8 oz. can of Diced Tomatoes & Chilies
- 1 Yellow Onion, diced
- 2 cups Green Lentils
- ½ tsp. Salt
- 2 Celery Stalks, diced
- 8 cups Vegetable Broth
- 2 Carrots, peeled & diced
- 2 cups Diced Tomatoes & Juices
- 3 Garlic cloves, minced
- 1 Red Bell Pepper, diced
- 1 tsp. Oregano
- 1 tbsp. Cumin

- ¼ tsp. Smoked Paprika
- 1 Avocado, pitted & diced

Directions:
1. Heat oil in a large-sized pot over a medium heat.
2. Once the oil becomes hot, stir in the onion, bell pepper, carrot, and celery into the pot.
3. Cook the onion mixture for 5 minutes or until the veggies are soft.
4. Then, spoon in garlic, oregano, cumin, and paprika into it and sauté for one minute or until aromatic.
5. Next, add the tomatoes, salt, chilies, broth, and lentils to the mixture.
6. Now, bring the tomato-chili mixture to a boil and allow it to simmer for 32 to 40 minutes or until the lentils become soft.
7. Check the seasoning and add more if needed.
8. Serve along with avocado and hot sauce.
Nutrition: Calories: 344 Fat: 23 Fiber: 12 Carbs: 3 Protein: 16

Celery Dill Soup

Preparation Time: 10 Minutes
Cooking Time: 20 Minutes
Servings: 4
Ingredients:
- 2 tbsp coconut oil
- ½ lb. celery root, trimmed
- 1 garlic clove
- 1 medium white onion
- ¼ cup fresh dill, roughly chopped
- 1 tsp cumin powder
- ¼ tsp nutmeg powder
- 1 small head cauliflower, cut into florets
- 3½ cups seasoned vegetable stock
- 5 oz. vegan butter
- Juice from 1 lemon
- ¼ cup coconut cream
- Salt and black pepper to taste

Directions:
1. Melt the coconut oil in a large pot and sauté the celery root, garlic, and onion until softened and fragrant, 5 minutes.

2. Stir in the dill, cumin, and nutmeg, and stir-fry for 1 minute. Mix in the cauliflower and vegetable stock. Allow the soup to boil for 15 minutes and turn the heat off.
3. Add the vegan butter and lemon juice, and puree the soup using an immersion blender.
4. Stir in the coconut cream, salt, black pepper, and dish the soup.
5. Serve warm.
Nutrition: Calories: 180 Fat: 12 Fiber: 4 Carbs: 5 Protein: 17

Medley of Mushroom Soup

Preparation Time: 10 Minutes
Cooking Time: 20 Minutes
Servings: 4
Ingredients:
- 4 oz. unsalted vegan butter
- 1 small onion, finely chopped
- 1 garlic clove, minced
- 2 cups sliced mixed mushrooms
- ½ lb. celery root, chopped
- ½ tsp dried rosemary
- 3 cups of water
- 1 vegan stock cube, crushed
- 1 tbsp plain vinegar
- 1 cup coconut cream
- 6 leaves basil, chopped

Directions:
1. Melt the vegan butter in a medium pot and sauté the onion, garlic, mushrooms, celery, and rosemary until the vegetables soften, 5 minutes.
2. Stir in the water, stock cube, and vinegar. Cover the pot, allow boiling, and then, simmer for 10 minutes.
3. Mix in the coconut cream and puree the ingredients using an immersion blender until smooth. Simmer for 2 minutes.
4. Dish the soup and serve warm.
Nutrition: Calories: 140 Fat: 3 Fiber: 2 Carbs: 1. 5 Protein: 7

BREAD RECIPES

Delicious Cheese Bread

Preparation Time: 10 Minutes
Cooking Time: 35 Minutes
Servings: 12
Ingredients:
- All-purpose flour – 2 cups
- Butter – 1/2 cup, melted
- Buttermilk – 1 cup
- Baking soda – 1/2 teaspoon.
- Baking powder – 1/2 teaspoon.
- Sugar – 1 teaspoon.
- Cheddar cheese – 1 cup, shredded
- Salt– 1/2 teaspoon.

Directions:
1. Preheat the oven for 350 F. In a large mixing bowl, mix flour, baking soda, baking powder, sugar, cheese, pepper, and salt.
2. In a small bowl, beat eggs with buttermilk, and butter.
3. Transfer mixture into the greased 9*5-inch loaf pan and bake in preheated oven for 35-40 minutes.
4. Allow to cool for 15 minutes. Slice and serve.

Nutrition: Calories 202, Carbs 17.6g, Fat 11.9g, Protein 6.2g

Strawberry Bread

Preparation Time: 15 Minutes
Cooking Time: 60 Minutes
Servings: 10
Ingredients:
- All-purpose flour – 2 cups
- Vanilla – 1 teaspoon.
- Vegetable oil – 1/2 cup
- Baking soda – 1 teaspoon.
- Cinnamon – 1/2 teaspoon.
- Brown sugar – 1/2 cup
- White sugar – 1/2 cup
- Fresh strawberries – 2 1/4 cups, chopped
- Salt – 1/2 teaspoon.

Directions:
1. Preheat the oven to 350 F. Grease 9.5-inch loaf pan and set aside.
2. In a mixing bowl, mix together flour, baking soda, cinnamon, brown sugar, white sugar, and salt.
3. In a separate bowl, vanilla, and oil. Stir in strawberries.
4. Add flour mixture to the strawberries mixture and stir until well combined.
5. Pour batter into the prepared loaf pan and bake in preheated oven for 50-60 minutes.
6. Allow to cool for 10-15 minutes. Slice and serve.

Nutrition: Calories 364, Carbs 40.1g, Fat 21.g, Protein 4.2g

Moist Banana Bread

Preparation Time: 10 Minutes
Cooking Time: 60 Minutes
Servings: 6
Ingredients:
- Baking powder – 1 teaspoon.
- Sugar – 1/2 cup
- Vanilla – 1 teaspoon.
- Butter – 1/2 cup, melted
- Ripe bananas – 3
- All-purpose flour – 1 1/2 cups
- Pinch of salt

Directions:
1. Preheat the oven to 350 F. In a large bowl, add bananas and mash until smooth. Add vanilla, butter, and mix well.
2. Add flour, baking powder, sugar, and salt and mix until well combined.
3. Pour batter into the greased loaf pan and bake in a preheated oven for 60 minutes. Slice and serve.

Nutrition: Calories 388, Carbs 54.6g, Fat 17.3g, Protein 5.9g

Sweet Rolls

Preparation Time: 2 hours
Cooking Time: 30 Minutes
Servings: 8
Ingredients:
- 2 tablespoons cane sugar
- 1 teaspoon rapid dry yeast
- 2 1/2 tablespoons warm water
- 1/2 cup pineapple juice, plus more for brushing tops of rolls
- 2 tablespoons coconut oil, melted
- 1 3/4 cups unbleached all-purpose flour, plus more for rolling out the dough

Directions:
1. In a small bowl, combine the sugar, yeast, and warm water. Stir gently and set aside for 10 minutes.
2. In another small bowl, combine 1/2 cup of pineapple juice and the coconut oil and stir.
3. Add the yeast mixture to the pineapple mixture and stir gently.
4. Add 1 3/4 cups of flour, and mix with your hands until well combined. The dough should not be too sticky. Knead in the bowl for 10 minutes, or until the dough is soft and smooth.
5. Place the dough in an oiled bowl, cover with a clean, damp towel, and place in a warm area for 1 hour to allow it to rise.
6. On a lightly floured surface, knead the dough, incorporating the flour from the surface. Break the dough into 8 equal pieces and form rolls.
7. Place the rolls on an oiled baking pan and allow to rise again for 30 to 40 minutes. Twenty minutes into this second rise, preheat the oven to 375 degree F.
8. Use a pastry brush to brush the tops of the rolls with pineapple juice.
9. Bake for 25 to 30 minutes or until golden brown.

Nutrition: Calories 115, Carbs 2.5g, Fat 11.5g, Protein 6.7g

Cornbread Waffles

Preparation Time: 6 Minutes
Cooking Time: 10 Minutes
Servings: 5
Ingredients:
- 1/3cup unsweetened plant-based milk
- 1 teaspoon apple cider vinegar
- 1/2 teaspoon baking powder
- 1/2 teaspoon baking soda
- 1 cup fine cornmeal
- 1/2 cup masa
- 1 cup unbleached all-purpose flour
- 1/3 cup unsweetened applesauce
- 1/4 cup sunflower oil
- Coconut oil cooking spray

Directions:
1.   In a small bowl, whisk together the milk and vinegar and set aside.
2.   In another small bowl, whisk the baking powder, baking soda, cornmeal, masa, and flour together.
3.   Add the applesauce and oil to the bowl containing the milk and stir to mix.
4.   Pour the wet Ingredients into the dry Ingredients and whisk until well combined.
5.   Turn a waffle iron on and coat with cooking spray.
6.   When the iron is hot, pour in enough batter to fill the waffle iron and cook for 4 to 5 minutes, or until lightly golden brown.
7.   Take the waffle out of the waffle iron and cut it in half. Repeat with the remaining batter

Nutrition: Calories 175, Carbs 2.5g, Fat 9.5g, Protein 5.7g

Buttermilk Biscuits

Preparation Time: 15 Minutes
Cooking Time: 15 Minutes

Servings: 8
Ingredients:
- 1 cup plant-based milk
- 1 tablespoon apple cider vinegar
- 2 cups unbleached all-purpose flour, plus more for cutting out the biscuits
- 1 tablespoon baking powder
- 1/2 teaspoon baking soda
- 1/2 teaspoon salt
- 1 tablespoon cane sugar
- 4 tablespoons (1/2 stick) Earth Balance vegan butter, cold

Directions:
1.   Preheat the oven to 450 degree F and line a baking pan with parchment paper.
2.   In a small bowl, mix the milk and vinegar and allow to curdle, usually no more than 5 minutes.
3.   In a medium mixing bowl, whisk together the flour, baking powder, baking soda, salt, and sugar.
4.   Add the cold butter and use your fingers or a pastry cutter to combine until only small pieces remain and the mixture looks grainy, like sand. Work fast so the butter doesn't get too soft.
5.   Make a well in the dry Ingredients, and use a wooden spoon to stir gently while pouring in the milk mixture 1/4 cup at a time. Stir until well combined.
6.   Sprinkle flour on a clean surface and dump the dough onto it. Dust the top of the dough with flour. Gently flatten the dough with your hands until it is about 1 inch thick, then dip a coffee mug rim into the flour to coat it and use it to cut out the biscuits.
7.   Place the cut biscuits on the lined baking pan, and bake for 6 minutes, then turn and bake another 6 minutes or until the tops and edges turn golden brown.

Nutrition: Calories 115, Carbs 2.5g, Fat 10.5g, Protein 4.7g

INSTANT POT

Oatmeal with Berries

Preparation Time: 25 minutes
Cooking Time: 0 minutes
Servings: 1
Ingredients:
- 1 2/3 cups water
- 1 cup quick oats
- 1 cup frozen berries
- 1 banana, chopped
- 1-2 tablespoon brown sugar
- 1/4 cup soy milk or almond milk
- 1-2 tablespoon brown sugar

For Garnishing (Optional):
- Almonds, chopped
- Coconut flakes

Directions:
1. Add water and oats directly to Instant Pot and cover it.
2. Switch on manual button for 6 minutes over high pressure. When the timer goes off allow the pressure to release naturally for about 10 minutes.
3. After 10 minutes, change the steam handle to 'venting'.
4. Open the lid and transfer the oats to a bowl and top it with mixed berries, banana, non-dairy milk and brown sugar.
Nutrition: Calories: 200 Fat: 10 Fiber: 2 Carbs: 11 Protein: 15

Pumpkin and Oats Recipe

Preparation Time: 30 Minutes
Cooking Time: 0
Servings: 1
Ingredients:
- 1 cup steel cut oats
- 1 2/3 cups water
- 1 frozen banana
- 1/2 cup pumpkin purée
- 3 medjool dates, chopped
- 1 tablespoon of buckwheat groats
- 1 tablespoon of coconut flakes

Directions:
1. Add 1 cup steel cut oats to Instant Pot, along with water, pumpkin purée, banana, and chopped dates.
2. Stir it once and set steam release handle to 'sealing'. Switch on manual button for 10 minutes.
3. Once time is up, allow it for natural release for 10 minutes. Switch on 'Keep Warm/Cancel' button and change steam release handle to 'venting'.
4. Using a spoon, mix it around. Make sure to mash banana and dates together with oatmeal.
5. Serve it topped with some buckwheat groats and coconut flakes.
Nutrition: Calories: 181 Fat: 15.2 Fiber: 4 Carbs: 10.8 Protein: 3.7

Strawberries and Cream Oatmeal

Preparation Time: 15 minutes
Cooking Time: 0 minutes
Servings: 4
Ingredients:
- 1 cup steel-cut oats
- 3 cups water
- 1 teaspoon strawberry extract
- Vanilla-flavored nondairy milk
- 1 cup fresh strawberries, chopped

Directions:
1. Spray the instant pot with nonstick spray. Stir in the oats and water, then seal the lid and cook on high 3 minutes.
2. Let the pressure release naturally, then stir in the vanilla milk and fresh strawberries.
Nutrition: Calories: 695 Fat: 66.7 Fiber: 11.1 Carbs: 22 Protein: 14.3

Pecan Pumpkin Spice Oatmeal

Preparation Time: 15 minutes
Cooking Time: 0 minutes
Servings: 2
Ingredients:
- 1/2 cup steel-cut oats
- 1/2 cup pumpkin purée
- 1 1/2 cups unsweetened almond milk
- 1/2 teaspoon cinnamon
- 1/8 teaspoon nutmeg
- 1 teaspoon vanilla extract
- 1/8 teaspoon of ground cloves
- 1/8 teaspoon ginger
- 1/4 cup brown sugar
- Chopped pecans, for serving

Directions:
1. Spray the instant pot with nonstick spray. Combine everything except for the brown sugar and pecans.
2. Seal the lid and cook on high 3 minutes, then let the pressure release naturally.
3. Stir in the brown sugar and top with chopped pecans.
Nutrition: Calories 251 carbs 16 fat 6 fiber 8 protein 7

Carrot Cake Oatmeal with Cream Cheese Frosting

Preparation Time: 20 minutes
Cooking Time: 0 minutes
Servings: 2
Ingredients:
- 1 small white sweet potato, peeled and steamed
- 1 small carrot, grated
- 1/4 small zucchini, grated
- 1/2 cup steel-cut oats
- 1 1/2 cups nondairy milk
- 1/2 teaspoon lemon juice
- 1/2 teaspoon apple cider vinegar
- 1/8 teaspoon of salt
- 1/8 teaspoon ground cloves
- 1/8 teaspoon nutmeg
- 1/2 teaspoon cinnamon

- 2 tablespoons brown sugar
- 2 tablespoons maple syrup
- 1 1/2 tablespoons coconut oil
- 1 tablespoon water

Directions:
1. To make the cream cheese frosting, puree half of the steamed sweet potato in a food processor.
2. Add the maple syrup, water, coconut oil, lemon juice, and apple cider vinegar and puree until smooth.
3. Add more sweet potato if the mixture is not thick enough.
4. Spray the instant pot with nonstick spray. Combine the rest of the **Ingredients:**, then seal the lid and cook on high 3 minutes.
5. Let the pressure release naturally. Add additional milk to the oatmeal if needed, and top each serving with a dollop of the cream cheese frosting.

Nutrition: Calories: 300 Fat: 15 Fiber: 5 Carbs: 8 Protein: 16

Chocolate Walnut Oatmeal

Preparation Time: 15 minutes
Cooking Time: 5 minutes
Servings: 2
Ingredients:
- 1/2 cup steel-cut oats
- 2 tablespoons cocoa powder
- 1 teaspoon brown sugar
- 1 tablespoon agave nectar
- 1 teaspoon vanilla extract
- 1/2 cup unsweetened almond milk
- 1 1/2 cups water
- Semi-sweet chocolate chips, for topping
- Walnuts for topping

Directions:
1. Spray the instant pot with nonstick spray. Combine the oats, cocoa powder, water, vanilla, brown sugar, and agave nectar.
2. Cook on high 3 minutes, then let the pressure release naturally. Stir in the almond milk.
3. Top with chocolate chips and walnuts.

Nutrition: Calories: 275 Fat: 16.5 Fiber: 4.3 Carbs: 17.2 Protein: 17.4

Breakfast Burrito Filling

Preparation Time: 15 minutes
Cooking Time: 5 minutes
Servings: 4
Ingredients:
- 15 ounces tofu, drained and crumbled
- 1/2 cup water
- 1 clove garlic, minced
- 1/2 bell pepper, chopped
- 1/2 teaspoon chili powder
- 1/4 teaspoon chipotle chili powder
- 1/4 teaspoon sriracha sauce
- 1 teaspoon lime juice
- Salt and pepper, to taste
- 1/4 cup shredded vegan cheddar cheese, for serving
- Warm tortillas, for serving
- Salsa, for serving

Directions:
1. Combine all the **Ingredients:** in the instant pot. Seal the lid and cook on high 4 minutes, then let the pressure release naturally.
2. If the mixture is too wet, drain off some of the water. Stir in the cheese to melt it. Serve wrapped warm tortillas with salsa.

Nutrition: Calories: 186 Fat: 17.1 Fiber: 0.8 Carbs: 1.8 Protein: 7.4

Tofu Breakfast Custard and Potatoes

Preparation Time: 25 minutes
Cooking Time: 2 minutes
Servings: 4
Ingredients:
- 12 ounces frozen hash browns
- 1 shallot, chopped
- 2 tablespoons vegan chicken-flavored bouillon
- 10 ounces silken tofu
- 1/2 cup shredded vegan cheddar cheese
- 1/2 cup nondairy milk
- 1/4 teaspoon onion powder
- 1/8 teaspoon garlic powder
- 1/2 teaspoon seasoned salt
- 1/4 teaspoon freshly ground pepper
- 1 tablespoon olive oil
- Hot sauce, for serving

Directions:
1. Puree the tofu, milk, bouillon, garlic powder, onion powder and seasoned salt in a food processor.
2. Heat the oil in the instant pot on the sauté setting and cook the shallot for 3 minutes.
3. Spread the hash browns on top of the cooked shallots, and top with the cheese.
4. Pour the tofu puree over the top, then sprinkle with fresh ground pepper.
5. Cook on high 5 minutes, then quick release the pressure.
6. The tofu mixture should be a jiggly custard texture. If it is too moist, return the instant pot to the sauté setting and cook longer with the lid on but vented.
7. Serve with hot sauce!

Nutrition: Calories: 224 Fat: 19g Protein: 18g Carbohydrates: 0g

Apple and Sausage French Toast Casserole

Preparation Time: 25 minutes
Cooking Time: 5 minutes
Servings: 4
Ingredients:
- 4 links vegan breakfast sausages, chopped into coins
- 2 apples, peeled and chopped
- Juice of 1/2 lemon
- Zest of 1/2 lemon
- 1/2 loaf whole wheat bread, chopped into cubes
- 1 1/2 cups water
- 1 teaspoon vanilla extract

- 3 tablespoons unsweetened applesauce
- 1/2 teaspoon cinnamon
- 1 tablespoon olive oil
- Maple syrup, for serving

Directions:
1. Heat olive oil in the instant pot using the sauté setting. Add the sausage and cook for 10 minutes.
2. Add the water, applesauce, vanilla extract, lemon juice, and cinnamon to the instant pot.
3. Add the apples, then the bread cubes. Push the bread down to make sure it is all coated with the mixture.
4. Seal the lid and cook on high 4 minutes, then let the pressure release naturally. Dust with powdered sugar and lemon zest and serve.

Nutrition: Calories: 327 Fat: 25g Protein: 36g Carbohydrates: 0.3g

Spiced Apple Oats

Preparation Time: 10 minutes
Cooking Time: 40 minutes
Servings: 4
Ingredients:
- 3 cups water
- 2 cups apple juice
- 2 apples, peeled, cored, and chopped
- 1 1/4 cups steel-cut oats
- 1/2 cup golden raisins or dried cranberries
- 1/4 cup packed light brown sugar or granulated natural sugar, or more to taste
- 1 tablespoon ground flaxseed
- 1 teaspoon ground cinnamon
- 1/2 teaspoon salt

Directions:
1. Lightly oil your Instant Pot insert with cooking spray.
2. Combine the Ingredients.
3. Seal and cook on Stew for 40 minutes.

Nutrition: Calories: 200 Fat: 9g Protein: 4g Carbohydrates: 28g

PB&J Oats

Preparation Time: 10 minutes
Cooking Time: 40 minutes
Servings: 6
Ingredients:
- 5 1/2 cups water
- 1 1/2 cups steel-cut oats
- 1/2 cup strawberry jam
- 1/2 cup creamy peanut butter, at room temperature
- 1 teaspoon ground cinnamon
- 3/4 teaspoon salt

Directions:
1. Lightly oil your Instant Pot insert with cooking spray.
2. Combine the oats, water, cinnamon, and salt.
3. Seal and cook on Stew for 40 minutes.
4. Release the pressure naturally and stir in the peanut butter and jam.

Nutrition: Calories: 359 Fat: 18g Protein: 15g Carbohydrates: 21g

Amish Oats

Preparation Time: 5 minutes
Cooking Time: 10 minutes
Servings: 4
Ingredients:
- 3 cups unsweetened almond milk or other non-dairy milk
- 2 1/2 cups old-fashioned rolled oats
- 2/3 cup sweetened dried cranberries
- 1/2 cup packed light brown sugar or maple syrup
- 1/2 cup toasted slivered blanched almonds or chopped walnuts
- 2 tablespoons vegan butter, melted
- 2 teaspoons pure vanilla extract
- 1 1/2 teaspoons ground cinnamon
- 1 1/2 teaspoons baking powder
- 1/2 teaspoon salt

Directions:
1. Lightly oil your Instant Pot insert with cooking spray.
2. In a bowl mix the almond milk, butter, vanilla, sugar, baking powder, salt, and cinnamon.
3. Stir in the oats, cranberries, and nuts.
4. Seal and cook on Beans for 12 minutes.

Nutrition: Calories: 328 Fat: 13g Protein: 38g Carbohydrates: 8g

Sweet Pumpkin Quinoa

Preparation Time: 5 minutes
Cooking Time: 40 minutes
Servings: 2
Ingredients:
- 4 cups unsweetened almond milk
- 1 cup quinoa, rinsed and drained
- 1/2 cup canned solid-pack pumpkin
- 1/4 cup pure maple syrup
- 1 teaspoon pure vanilla extract
- 1 teaspoon ground cinnamon
- 1/2 teaspoon salt
- 1/4 teaspoon ground ginger
- 1/4 teaspoon ground allspice
- 1/4 teaspoon ground nutmeg

Directions:
1. Spray the insert of your Instant Pot with cooking oil.
2. Add the **Ingredients:**.
3. Seal and cook on Stew for 38 minutes.
4. Depressurize naturally and serve.

Nutrition: Calories: 299 Fat: 3g Protein: 64g Carbohydrates: 2g

SAUCES, DRESSINGS, AND DIPS

Satay Sauce

Preparation Time: 5 minutes
Cooking Time: 8 minutes
Servings: 2
Ingredients:
- ½ yellow onion, diced
- 3 garlic cloves, minced
- 1 fresh red chile, thinly sliced (optional)
- 1-inch (2.5-cm) piece fresh ginger, peeled and minced
- ¼ cup smooth peanut butter
- 2 tablespoons coconut aminos
- 1 (13.5-ounce / 383-g) can unsweetened coconut milk
- ¼ teaspoon freshly ground black pepper
- ¼ teaspoon salt (optional)

Directions:
1. Heat a large nonstick skillet over medium-high heat until hot.
2. Add the onion, garlic cloves, chile (if desired), and ginger to the skillet, and sauté for 2 minutes.
3. Pour in the peanut butter and coconut aminos and stir well. Add the coconut milk, black pepper, and salt (if desired) and continue whisking, or until the sauce is just beginning to bubble and thicken.
4. Remove the sauce from the heat to a bowl. Taste and adjust the seasoning if necessary.

Nutrition: calories: 322 fat: 28.8g carbs: 9.4gprotein: 6.3g fiber: 1.8g

Tahini BBQ Sauce

Preparation Time: 10 minutes
Cooking Time: 0 minutes
Servings: 4
ingredients:
- ½ cup water
- ¼ cup red miso
- 3 cloves garlic, minced
- 1-inch (2.5 cm) piece ginger, peeled and minced
- 2 tablespoons rice vinegar
- 2 tablespoons tahini
- 2 tablespoons chili paste or chili sauce
- 1 tablespoon date sugar
- ½ teaspoon crushed red pepper (optional)

Directions:
1. Place all the ingredients in a food processor, and purée until thoroughly mixed and smooth. You can thin the sauce out by stirring in ½ cup of water, or keep it thick.
2. Transfer to the refrigerator to chill until ready to serve.

Nutrition: calories: 206 fat: 10.2g carbs: 21.3g protein: 7.2g fiber: 4.4g

Tamari Vinegar Sauce

Preparation Time: 10 minutes
Cooking Time: 0 minutes
Servings: 1
Ingredients:
- ¼ cup tamari
- ½ cup nutritional yeast
- 2 tablespoons balsamic vinegar
- 2 tablespoons apple cider vinegar
- 2 tablespoons Worcestershire sauce
- 2 teaspoons Dijon mustard
- 1 tablespoon plus 1 teaspoon maple syrup
- ½ teaspoon ground turmeric
- ¼ teaspoon black pepper

Directions:
1. Place all the ingredients in an airtight container, and whisk until everything is well incorporated. Store in the refrigerator for up to 3 weeks.

Nutrition: calories: 216 fat: 9.9g carbs: 18.0g protein: 13.7g fiber: 7.7g

Sweet and Tangy Ketchup

Preparation Time: 5 minutes
Cooking Time: 15 minutes
Servings: 2
Ingredients:
- 1 cup water
- ¼ cup maple syrup
- 1 cup tomato paste
- 3 tablespoons apple cider vinegar
- 1 teaspoon onion powder
- 1 teaspoon garlic powder

Directions:
1. Add the water to a medium saucepan and bring to a rolling boil over high heat.
2. Reduce the heat to low, stir in the maple syrup, tomato paste, vinegar, onion powder, and garlic powder. Cover and bring to a gently simmer for about 10 minutes, stirring frequently, or until the sauce begins to thicken and bubble.
3. Let the sauce rest for 30 minutes until cooled completely. Transfer to an airtight container and refrigerate for up to 1 month.

Nutrition: calories: 46 fat: 5.2g carbs: 1.0g protein: 1.1g fiber: 1.0g

Homemade Tzatziki Sauce

Preparation Time: 20 minutes
Cooking Time: 0 minutes
Servings: 1
Ingredients:
- 2 ounces (57 g) raw, unsalted cashews (about ½ cup)
- 2 tablespoons lemon juice
- 1/3 cup water
- 1 small clove garlic
- 1 cup chopped cucumber, peeled
- 2 tablespoons fresh dill

Directions:
1. In a blender, add the cashews, lemon juice, water, and garlic. Keep it aside for at least 15 minutes to soften the cashews.

2.   Blend the ingredients until smooth. Stir in the chopped cucumber and dill, and continue to blend until it reaches your desired consistency. It doesn't need to be totally smooth. Feel free to add more water if you like a thinner consistency.
3.   Transfer to an airtight container and chill for at least 30 minutes for best flavors.
4.   Bring the sauce to room temperature and shake well before serving.
Nutrition: calories: 208 fat: 13.5g carbs:15.0 g protein: 6.7g fiber: 2.8g

Tangy Cashew Mustard Dressing

Preparation Time: 20 minutes
Cooking Time: 0 minutes
Servings: 1
Ingredients:
- 2 ounces (57 g) raw, unsalted cashews (about ½ cup)
- ½ cup water
- 3 tablespoons lemon juice
- 2 teaspoons apple cider vinegar
- 2 tablespoons Dijon mustard
- 1 medium clove garlic

Directions:
1.   Put all the ingredients in a food processor and keep it aside for at least 15 minutes.
2.   Purée until the ingredients are combined to a smooth and creamy mixture. Thin the dressing with a little extra water as needed to achieve your preferred consistency.
3.   Store in an airtight container in the refrigerator for up to 5 days.
Nutrition: calories: 187 fat: 13.0g carbs: 11.5g protein: 5.9g fiber: 1.7g

Avocado-dill Dressing

Preparation Time: 20 minutes
Cooking Time: 0 minutes
Servings: 1
Ingredients:
- 2 ounces (57 g) raw, unsalted cashews (about ½ cup)
- ½ cup water
- 3 tablespoons lemon juice
- ½ medium, ripe avocado, chopped
- 1 medium clove garlic
- 2 tablespoons chopped fresh dill
- 2 green onions, white and green parts, chopped

Directions:
1.   Put the cashews, water, lemon juice, avocado, and garlic into a blender. Keep it aside for at least 15 minutes to soften the cashews.
2.   Blend until everything is fully mixed. Fold in the dill and green onions, and blend briefly to retain some texture.
3.   Store in an airtight container in the fridge for up to 3 days and stir well before serving.
Nutrition: calories: 312 fat: 21.1g carbs: 22.6gprotein: 8.0g fiber: 7.1g

Easy Lemon Tahini Dressing

Preparation Time: 5 minutes
Cooking Time: 0 minutes
Servings: 1
Ingredients:
- ½ cup tahini
- ¼ cup fresh lemon juice (about 2 lemons)
- 1 teaspoon maple syrup
- 1 small garlic clove, chopped
- 1/8 teaspoon black pepper
- ¼ teaspoon salt (optional)
- ¼ to ½ cup water

Directions:
1.   Process the tahini, lemon juice, maple syrup, garlic, black pepper, and salt (if desired) in a blender (high-speed blenders work best for this). Gradually add the water until the mixture is completely smooth.
2.   Store in an airtight container in the fridge for up to 5 days.
Nutrition: calories: 128 fat: 9.6g carbs: 6.8g protein: 3.6g fiber: 1.9g

Sweet Mango and Orange Dressing

Preparation Time: 5 minutes
Cooking Time: 0 minutes
Servings: 1
Ingredients:
- 1 cup (165 g) diced mango, thawed if frozen
- ½ cup orange juice
- 2 tablespoons rice vinegar
- 2 tablespoons fresh lime juice
- ¼ teaspoon salt (optional)
- 1 teaspoon date sugar (optional)
- 2 tablespoons chopped cilantro

Directions:
1.   Pulse all the ingredients except for the cilantro in a food processor until it reaches the consistency you like. Add the cilantro and whisk well.
2.   Store in an airtight container in the fridge for up to 2 days.
Nutrition: calories: 32 fat: 0.1g carbs: 7.4g protein: 0.3g fiber: 0.5g

Creamy Avocado Cilantro Lime Dressing

Preparation Time: 5 minutes
Cooking Time: 0 minutes
Servings: 2
Ingredients:
- 1 avocado, diced
- ½ cup water
- ¼ cup cilantro leaves
- ¼ cup fresh lime or lemon juice (about 2 limes or lemons)
- ½ teaspoon ground cumin
- ¼ teaspoon salt (optional)

Directions:
1.   Put all the ingredients in a blender (high-speed blenders work best for this), and pulse until well combined. Taste and adjust the seasoning as needed. It is best served within 1 day.
Nutrition: calories: 94 fat: 7.4g carbs: 5.7g protein: 1.1g fiber: 3.5g

Maple Dijon Dressing

Preparation Time: 5 minutes
Cooking Time: 0 minutes
Servings: 1
Ingredients:
- ¼ cup apple cider vinegar
- 2 teaspoons Dijon mustard
- 2 tablespoons maple syrup
- 2 tablespoons low-sodium vegetable broth
- ¼ teaspoon black pepper
- Salt, to taste (optional)

Directions:
1. Mix together the apple cider vinegar, Dijon mustard, maple syrup, vegetable broth, and black pepper in a resealable container until well incorporated. Season with salt to taste, if desired.
2. The dressing can be refrigerated for up to 5 days.

Nutrition: calories: 82 fat: 0.3g carbs: 19.3g protein: 0.6g fiber: 0.7g

Avocado-chickpea Dip

Preparation Time: 15 minutes
Cooking Time: 0 minutes
Servings: 2
Ingredients:
- 1 (15-ounce / 425-g) can cooked chickpeas, drained and rinsed
- 2 large, ripe avocados, chopped
- ¼ cup red onion, finely chopped
- 1 tablespoon Dijon mustard
- 1 to 2 tablespoons lemon juice
- 2 teaspoons chopped fresh oregano
- 1/2 teaspoon garlic clove, finely chopped

Directions:
1. In a medium bowl, mash the cooked chickpeas with a potato masher or the back of a fork, or until the chickpeas pop open (a food processor works best for this).
2. Stir in the remaining ingredients and continue to mash until completely smooth.
3. Place in the refrigerator to chill until ready to serve.

Nutrition: calories: 101 fat: 1.9g carbs: 16.2g protein: 4.7g fiber: 4.6g

Beer "Cheese" Dip

Preparation Time: 10 minutes
Cooking Time: 7 minutes
Servings: 3
Ingredients:
- ¾ cup water
- ¾ cup brown ale
- ½ cup raw walnuts, soaked in hot water for at least 15 minutes, then drained
- ½ cup raw cashews, soaked in hot water for at least 15 minutes, then drained
- 2 tablespoons tomato paste
- 2 tablespoons fresh lemon juice
- 1 tablespoon apple cider vinegar
- ½ cup nutritional yeast
- ½ teaspoon sweet or smoked paprika
- 1 tablespoon arrowroot powder

- 1 tablespoon red miso

Directions:
1. Place the water, brown ale, walnuts, cashews, tomato paste, lemon juice, and apple cider vinegar into a high-speed blender, and purée until thoroughly mixed and smooth.
2. Transfer the mixture to a saucepan over medium heat. Add the nutritional yeast, paprika, and arrowroot powder, and whisk well. Bring to a simmer for about 7 minutes, stirring frequently, or until the mixture begins to thicken and bubble.
3. Remove from the heat and whisk in the red miso. Let the dip cool for 10 minutes and refrigerate in an airtight container for up to 5 days.

Nutrition: calories: 113 fat: 5.1g carbs: 10.4g protein: 6.3g fiber: 3.8g

Creamy Black Bean Dip

Preparation Time: 10 minutes
Cooking Time: 0 minutes
Servings: 3
Ingredients:
- 4 cups cooked black beans, rinsed and drained
- 2 tablespoons Italian seasoning
- 2 tablespoons minced garlic
- 2 tablespoon low-sodium vegetable broth
- 2 tablespoons onion powder
- 1 tablespoon lemon juice, or more to taste
- ¼ teaspoon salt (optional)

Directions:
1. In a large bowl, mash the black beans with a potato masher or the back of a fork until mostly smooth.
2. Add the remaining ingredients to the bowl and whisk to combine.
3. Taste and add more lemon juice or salt, if needed. Serve immediately, or refrigerate for at least 30 minutes to better incorporate the flavors.

Nutrition: calories: 387 fat: 6.5gcarbs: 63.0gprotein: 21.2gfiber: 16.0g

Spicy and Tangy Black Bean Salsa

Preparation Time: 15 minutes
Cooking Time: 0 minutes
Servings: 3
Ingredients:
- 1 (15-ounce / 425-g) can cooked black beans, drained and rinsed
- 1 cup chopped tomatoes
- 1 cup corn kernels, thaw if frozen
- ½ cup cilantro or parsley, chopped
- ¼ cup finely chopped red onion
- 1 tablespoon lemon juice
- 1 tablespoon lime juice
- 1 teaspoon chili powder
- ½ teaspoon ground cumin
- ½ teaspoon regular or smoked paprika
- 1 medium clove garlic, finely chopped

Directions:
1. Put all the ingredients in a large bowl and stir with a fork until well incorporated.

2. Serve immediately, or chill for 2 hours in the refrigerator to let the flavors blend.
Nutrition: calories: 83 fat: 0.5g carbs: 15.4g protein: 4.3g fiber: 4.6g

Homemade Chimichurri

Preparation Time: 5 minutes
Cooking Time: 0 minutes
Servings: 1
Ingredients:
- 1 cup finely chopped flat-leaf parsley leaves
- Zest and juice of 2 lemons
- ¼ cup low-sodium vegetable broth
- 4 garlic cloves
- 1 teaspoon dried oregano

Directions:
1. Place all the ingredients into a food processor, and pulse until it reaches the consistency you like.
2. Refrigerate the chimichurri in an airtight container for up to 5 days. It's best served within 1 day.
Nutrition: calories: 19 fat: 0.2g carbs: 3.7g protein: 0.7g fiber: 0.7g

Cilantro Coconut Pesto

Preparation Time: 5 minutes
Cooking Time: 0 minutes
Servings: 2
Ingredients:
- 1 (13.5-ounce / 383-g) can unsweetened coconut milk
- 2 jalapeños, seeds and ribs removed
- 1 bunch cilantro, leaves only
- 1 tablespoon white miso
- 1-inch (2.5 cm) piece ginger, peeled and minced
- Water, as needed

Directions:
1. Pulse all the ingredients in a blender until creamy and smooth.
2. Thin with a little extra water as needed to reach your preferred consistency.
3. Store in an airtight container in the fridge for up t0 2 days or in the freezer for up to 6 months.
Nutrition: calories: 141 fat: 13.7g carbs: 2.8g protein: 1.6g fiber: 0.3g

Fresh Mango Salsa

Preparation Time: 10 minutes
Cooking Time: 0 minutes
Servings: 6
Ingredients:
- 2 small mangoes, diced
- 1 red bell pepper, finely diced
- ½ red onion, finely diced
- Juice of ½ lime, or more to taste
- 2 tablespoon low-sodium vegetable broth
- Handful cilantro, chopped
- Freshly ground black pepper, to taste
- Salt, to taste (optional)

Directions:

1. Stir together all the ingredients in a large bowl until well incorporated.
2. Taste and add more lime juice or salt, if needed.
3. Store in an airtight container in the fridge for up to 5 days.
Nutrition: calories: 86 fat: 1.9g carbs: 13.3g protein: 1.2g fiber: 0.9g

Pineapple Mint Salsa

Preparation Time: 10 minutes
Cooking Time: 0 minutes
Servings: 3
Ingredients:
- 1 pound (454 g) fresh pineapple, finely diced and juices reserved
- 1 bunch mint, leaves only, chopped
- 1 minced jalapeño, (optional)
- 1 white or red onion, finely diced
- Salt, to taste (optional)

Directions:
1. In a medium bowl, mix the pineapple with its juice, mint, jalapeño (if desired), and onion, and whisk well. Season with salt to taste, if desired.
2. Refrigerate in an airtight container for at least 2 hours to better incorporate the flavors.
Nutrition: calories: 58 fat: 0.1g carbs: 13.7g protein: 0.5g fiber: 1.0g

Cashew Yogurt

Total time: 12 hours 5 minutes
Ingredients
- 3 probiotic supplements
- 2 2/3 cups cashews, unsalted , soaked in warm water for 15 minutes
- 1/4 teaspoon sea salt
- 4 tablespoon lemon juice
- 1 1/2 cup water

Directions:
1. Drain the cashews, add them into the food processor, then add remaining ingredients, except for probiotic supplements, and pulse for 2 minutes until smooth.
2. Tip the mixture in a bowl, add probiotic supplements, stir until mixed, then cover the bowl with a cheesecloth and let it stand for 12 hours in a dark and cool room.
3. Serve straight away.

Nacho Cheese Sauce

Total time: 20 minutes
Ingredients
- 2 cups cashews, unsalted , soaked in warm water for 15 minutes
- 2 teaspoons salt
- 1/2 cup nutritional yeast
- 1 teaspoon garlic powder
- 1/2 teaspoon smoked paprika
- 1/2 teaspoon red chili powder
- 1 teaspoon onion powder
- 2 teaspoons Sriracha
- 3 tablespoons lemon juice
- 4 cups water, divided

Directions:
1.   Drain the cashews, transfer them to a food processor, then add remaining ingredients, reserving 3 cups water, and , and pulse for 3 minutes until smooth.
2.   Tip the mixture in a saucepan, place it over medium heat and cook for 3 to 5 minutes until the sauce has thickened and bubbling, whisking constantly.
3.   When done, taste the sauce to adjust seasoning and then serve.

Spicy Red Wine Tomato Sauce

Total time: 1 hour 5 minutes
Ingredients
- 28 ounces puree of whole tomatoes, peeled
- 4 cloves of garlic, peeled
- 1 tablespoon dried basil
- ¼ teaspoon ground black pepper
- 1 tablespoon dried oregano
- ¼ teaspoon red pepper flakes
- 1 tablespoon dried sage
- 1 tablespoon dried thyme
- 3 teaspoon coconut sugar
- 1/2 of lemon, juice
- 1/4 cup red wine

Directions
1.   Take a large saucepan, place it over medium heat, add tomatoes and remaining ingredients, stir and simmer for 1 hour or more until thickened and cooked.
2.   Serve sauce over pasta.

Vodka Cream Sauce

Total time: 10 minutes
Ingredients
- 1/4 cup cashews, unsalted , soaked in warm water for 15 minutes
- 24-ounce marinara sauce
- 2 tablespoons vodka
- 1/4 cup water

Directions:
1.   Drain the cashews, transfer them in a food processor, pour in water, and blend for 2 minutes until smooth.
2.   Tip the mixture in a pot, stir in pasta sauce and vodka and simmer for 3 minutes over medium heat until done, stirring constantly.
3.   Serve sauce over pasta.

Barbecue Sauce

Total time: 5 minutes
Ingredients
- 8 ounces tomato sauce
- 1 teaspoon garlic powder
- ¼ teaspoon ground black pepper
- 1/2 teaspoon. sea salt
- 2 Tablespoons Dijon mustard
- 3 packets stevia
- 1 teaspoon molasses
- 1 Tablespoon apple cider vinegar
- 2 Tablespoons tamari

- 1 teaspoon liquid aminos

Directions:
1.   Take a medium bowl, place all the ingredients in it, and stir until combined.
2.   Serve straight away

Bolognese Sauce

Total time: 55 minutes
Ingredients
- ½ of small green bell pepper, chopped
- 1 stalk of celery, chopped
- 1 small carrot, chopped
- 1 medium white onion, peeled, chopped
- 2 teaspoons minced garlic
- 1/2 teaspoon crushed red pepper flakes
- 3 tablespoons olive oil
- 8-ounce tempeh, crumbled
- 8 ounces white mushrooms, chopped
- 1/2 cup dried red lentils
- 28-ounce crushed tomatoes
- 28-ounce whole tomatoes, chopped
- 1 teaspoon dried oregano
- 1/2 teaspoon fennel seed
- 1/2 teaspoon ground black pepper
- 1/2 teaspoon salt
- 1 teaspoon dried basil
- 1/4 cup chopped parsley
- 1 bay leaf
- 6-ounce tomato paste
- 1 cup dry red wine

Directions:
1.   Take a Dutch oven, place it over medium heat, add oil, and when hot, add the first six ingredients, stir and cook for 5 minutes until sauté.
2.   Then switch heat to medium-high level, add two ingredients after olive oil, stir and cook for 3 minutes.
3.   Switch heat to medium-low level, stir in tomato paste, and continue cooking for 2 minutes.
4.   Add remaining ingredients except for lentils, stir and bring the mixture to boil.
5.   Switch heat to the low level, simmer sauce for 10 minutes, covering the pan partially, then add lentils and continue cooking for 20 minutes until tender.
6.   Serve sauce with cooked pasta.

Cilantro and Parsley Hot Sauce

Total time: 5 minutes
Ingredients
- 2 cups of parsley and cilantro leaves with stems
- 4 Thai bird chilies, destemmed, deseeded, torn
- 2 teaspoons minced garlic
- 1 teaspoon salt
- 1/4 teaspoon coriander seed, ground
- 1/4 teaspoon ground black pepper
- 1/2 teaspoon cumin seeds, ground
- 3 green cardamom pods, toasted, ground
- 1/2 cup olive oil

Directions:

1.   Take a spice blender or a food processor, place all the ingredients in it, and process for 5 minutes until the smooth paste comes together.
2.   Serve straight away.

Sweet Mustard Salad Dressing

Total time: 5 minutes
Ingredients
- 2 tbsp maple syrup
- 2 tbsp spicy brown mustard
- 2 tsp rice vinegar
- 1 cup roasted vidalia onion, pureed* (optional)

Directions:
Vidalia Onion Option: Gently roast a large vidalia onion and then add it, along with a trip batch of this recipe, to a blender. Sweet onion flavor!

Alfredo Sauce

Total time: 5 minutes
Ingredients
- 1 cup cashews, unsalted, soaked in warm water for 15 minutes
- 1 teaspoon minced garlic
- 1/4 teaspoon ground black pepper
- 1/3 teaspoon salt
- 1/4 cup nutritional yeast
- 2 tablespoons tamari
- 2 tablespoons olive oil
- 4 tablespoons water

Directions:
1.   Drain the cashews, transfer them into a food processor, add remaining ingredients in it, and pulse for 3 minutes until thick sauce comes together.
2.   Serve straight away.

Garden Pesto

Total time: 5 minutes
Ingredients
- 1/4 cup pistachios, shelled
- 3/4 cup parsley leaves
- 1 cup cilantro leaves
- ½ teaspoon minced garlic
- 1/4 cup mint leaves
- 1 cup basil leaves
- ¼ teaspoon ground black pepper
- 1/3 teaspoon salt
- 1/2 cup olive oil
- 1 1/2 teaspoons miso
- 2 teaspoons lemon juice

Directions:
1.   Place all the ingredients in the order in a food processor or blender and then pulse for 3 to 5 minutes at high speed until smooth.
2.   Tip the pesto in a bowl and then serve.

Hot Sauce

Total time: 25 minutes
Ingredients
- 4 Serrano peppers, destemmed
- 1/2 of medium white onion, chopped
- 1 medium carrot, chopped
- 10 habanero chilies, destemmed
- 6 cloves of garlic, unpeeled
- 2 teaspoons sea salt
- 1 cup apple cider vinegar
- 1/2 teaspoon brown rice syrup
- 1 cup of water

Directions:
1.   Take a skillet pan, place it medium heat, add garlic, and cook for 15 minutes until roasted, frequently turning garlic, set aside to cool.
2.   Meanwhile, take a saucepan, place it over medium-low heat, add remaining ingredients in it, except for salt and syrup, stir and cook for 12 minutes until vegetables are tender.
3.   When the garlic has roasted and cooled, peel them and add them to a food processor.
4.   Then add cooked saucepan along with remaining ingredients, and pulse for 3 minutes until smooth.
5.   Let sauce cool and then serve straight away

Hot Sauce

Total time: 5 minutes
Ingredients
- 4 cloves of garlic, peeled
- 15 Hot peppers, de-stemmed, chopped
- 1/2 teaspoon. coriander
- 1/2 teaspoon. sea salt
- 1/2 teaspoon. red chili powder
- 1/2 of lime, zested
- 1/4 teaspoon. cumin
- 1/2 lime, juiced
- 1 cup apple cider vinegar

Directions:
1.   Place all the ingredients in the order in a food processor or blender and then pulse for 3 to 5 minutes at high speed until smooth.
2.   Tip the sauce in a bowl and then serve.

Thai Peanut Sauce

Total time: 20 minutes
Ingredients
- 2 tablespoons ground peanut, and more for topping
- 2 tablespoons Thai red curry paste
- ½ teaspoon salt
- 1 tablespoon sugar
- 1/2 cup creamy peanut butter
- 2 tablespoons apple cider vinegar
- 3/4 cup coconut milk, unsweetened

Directions:
1.   Take a saucepan, place it over low heat, add all the ingredients, whisk well until combined, and then bring the sauce to simmer.
2.   Then remove the pan from heat, top with ground peanuts, and serve.

Garlic Alfredo Sauce

Total time: 15 minutes
Ingredients
- 1 1/2 cups cashews, unsalted , soaked in warm water for 15 minutes
- 6 cloves of garlic, peeled, minced

- 1/2 medium sweet onion, peeled, chopped
- 1 teaspoon salt
- 1/4 cup nutritional yeast
- 1 tablespoon lemon juice
- 2 tablespoons olive oil
- 2 cups almond milk, unsweetened
- 12 ounces fettuccine pasta, cooked, for serving

Directions:
1. Take a small saucepan, place it over medium heat, add oil and when hot, add onion and garlic, and cook for 5 minutes until sauté.
2. Meanwhile, drain the cashews, transfer them into a food processor, add remaining ingredients including onion mixture, except for pasta, and pulse for 3 minutes until very smooth.
3. Pour the prepared sauce over pasta, toss until coated and serve.

Barbecue Tahini Sauce

Total time: 5 minutes
Ingredients
- 6 tablespoons tahini
- 3/4 teaspoon garlic powder
- 1/8 teaspoon red chili powder
- 2 teaspoons maple syrup
- 1/4 teaspoon salt
- 3 teaspoons molasses
- 3 teaspoons apple cider vinegar
- 1/4 teaspoon liquid smoke
- 10 teaspoons tomato paste
- 1/2 cup water

Directions:
1. Place all the ingredients in the order in a food processor or blender and then pulse for 3 to 5 minutes at high speed until smooth.
2. Tip the sauce in a bowl and then serve.

Vegan Ranch Dressing

Total time: 5 minutes
Ingredients
- 1/4 teaspoon. ground black pepper
- 2 teaspoon. chopped parsley
- 1/2 teaspoon. garlic powder
- 1 tablespoon chopped dill
- 1/2 teaspoon. onion powder
- 1 cup vegan mayonnaise
- 1/2 cup soy milk, unsweetened

Directions:
1. Take a medium bowl, add all the ingredients in it and then whisk until combined.
2. Serve straight away

Sweet Mustard Salad Dressing

Total time: 10 minutes
Ingredients
- 2 tbsp maple syrup
- 2 tbsp spicy brown mustard
- 2 tsp rice vinegar
- 1 cup roasted vidalia onion, pureed* (optional)

Directions:

1. Vidalia Onion Option: Gently roast a large vidalia onion and then add it, along with a trip batch of this recipe, to a blender. Sweet onion flavor!

Spiced Peach Compote

Total time: 17 minutes
Ingredients
- 1 ½ cups fresh or frozen peaches, peeled and pitted, chopped small
- 2 tbsp water
- ½ tsp pumpkin pie spice blend
- ¼ tsp vanilla

Directions:
1. 1 tbsp cornstarch mixed into 2 tbsp water (cornstarch slurry)
2. In a small saucepan over medium heat, add first four ingredients and mix together. Allow to come to a simmer and cook for 7 minutes.
3. Mash lightly and add the cornstarch slurry.
4. Bring back to a simmer and then remove from heat.
5. Allow to cool slightly and thicken before serving.

Tzatziki Sauce

Total time: 40 minutes
Ingredients.
- ¼ cup raw cashews, soaked in boiling water for 15 min
- ¼ cup white potatoes, peeled, boiled, and diced small
- 1 tsp dry dill (fresh if available)
- ½ tsp powdered garlic (or 1 clove finely minced)
- ½ med. cucumber, unpeeled (about ⅓ cup grated)
- ½ cup plant milk, unsweetened OR liquid from cucumber
- 1 lemon, juice & zest
- ½ tsp apple cider vinegar

Directions:
1. Finely grate the cucumber into a thin tea towel, then squeeze the liquid out into a bowl until mostly dry. Save the liquid.
2. Into a wide mouth quart jar, add: juice & zest of one lemon, vinegar, dill, garlic, soaked cashews, potatoes and almond milk or equivalent cucumber liquid.
3. Using an immersion blender, blend until creamy.
4. Add cucumber and blend some more. Add a bit more almond milk or cucumber liquid to thin if necessary.
5. Allow to rest in the refrigerator for 30 minutes before using.

BBQ Sauce

Total time: 10 minutes
Ingredients
- ½ cup diced bell pepper, sauteed
- ½ cup diced sweet onion, sauteed
- 1 cup ketchup OR 3 tbsp tomato paste and ½ cup water

- 3 tbsp brown mustard
- 1/4 cup maple syrup
- 1/2 cup water
- 1 tsp liquid smoke

Directions:
1. Process all of the ingredients in a blender, store in an airtight container in the refrigerator.

Creamy Corn Sauce

Total time: 15 minutes

Ingredients
- 1 tablespoon vegan butter
- 2 garlic cloves, minced
- 1 tablespoon all-purpose flour
- 1 ¾ cups full-fat coconut milk
- 2 tablespoons nutritional yeast
- ½ teaspoon salt
- ½ teaspoon black pepper
- 3 cups corn kernels

Directions:
1. Place a medium-sized skillet over medium heat and add vegan butter.
2. Stir in garlic and sauté for 30 seconds, then stir in flour.
3. Whisk well and cook for another 30 seconds, then stir in salt, coconut milk, yeast, and black pepper.
4. Stir for 1 minute then add corn kernels.
5. Cook for 2 minutes then serve.

Cranberry Sauce

Total time: 25 minutes

Ingredients
- 12 oz fresh cranberries
- 1 cup of sugar
- 1 cup of water
- 1 lemon, zested

Directions:
1. Dump all the ingredients into a medium-sized saucepan.
2. Let it simmer for 15 minutes until the sauce thickens.
3. Serve.

Soy Ranch Dressing

Total time: 10 minutes

Ingredients
- 1 cup mayonnaise
- 1½ teaspoon garlic finely powdered
- ½ teaspoon onion finely powdered
- ¼ teaspoon pepper powder
- 2 teaspoons parsley, chopped
- 1 tablespoon dill, chopped
- ½ cup soy milk

Directions:
1. Dump all the ranch dressing ingredients into a blender jug.
2. Blend the dressing mixture for 1 minute.
3. Serve.

Chili Marinara Sauce

Total time: 60 minutes

Ingredients
- 4 tbsp olive oil
- 1 small white onion, chopped
- 5 garlic cloves, minced
- 10 cups fresh tomatoes, crushed
- 4 tbsp tomato paste
- Salt and black pepper to taste
- ½ cup red wine
- ½ cup water
- 2 tsp dried basil
- 2 tsp dried oregano
- 2 tbsp dried parsley
- 2 tbsp Italian seasoning
- 1 tsp pure maple syrup
- 1 tsp red chili powder

Directions:
1. Heat the olive oil in a pot over medium heat and sauté the onion to make it soft, 3 minutes. Mix in the garlic and cook until fragrant, 30 seconds.
2. Pour in the remaining ingredients, stir, and close the lid.
3. Bring the ingredients to a boil, then reduce the heat to low, and simmer until the tomatoes are very soft, 30 to 40 minutes.
4. Open the lid and using an immersion blender, puree the ingredients until smooth.
5. Spoon the sauce into jars.
6. Use for stews, pasta, and rice dishes.

Onion Gravy with Red Onion

Total time: 15 minutes

Ingredients
- 2 tbsp plant butter
- 1 shallot, finely chopped
- 1 tsp whole-wheat flour
- 1 tbsp red wine vinegar
- 2 cups red wine
- 1 cup thinly sliced red onion
- 1 cup vegetable stock
- 1 tsp dried oregano
- 1 tbsp Dijon mustard
- 1 tbsp cornstarch
- Salt to taste

Directions:
1. Melt half of the butter in a medium pot and sauté the shallots until softened, 2 minutes. Mix in the flour until breadcrumb-like mixture forms.
2. Mix in the red wine vinegar until thick paste forms and then, stir in the red wine.
3. Add the vegetable stock, oregano, and Dijon mustard. Combine well and allow simmering for 3 to 5 minutes.
4. Whisk in the cornstarch and cook until the sauce thickens, 1 to 2 minutes.
5. Season with a little salt, spoon into serving cups and use over or with grilled vegetables, tofu, seitan, etc.

Velote Sauce

Total time: 10 minutes

Ingredients
- 2 tbsp unsalted plant butter
- 2 tbsp whole-wheat flour

- 1 cup vegetable broth, warmed
- 3 tbsp cashew cream
- ½ lemon, juiced
- Salt and black pepper to taste

Directions:
1. Melt the plant butter in a medium pot over medium heat and whisk in the flour; cook until golden, 1 minute.
2. Mix in the vegetable broth until smooth and cook until the sauce is slightly syrupy, 2 to 3 minutes. Turn the heat off.
3. Vigorously whisk in the cashew cream, lemon juice, salt, and black pepper.
4. Spoon the sauce into serving cups and use over grilled vegetables and plant-protein options.

Tangy Pea Butter Sauce

Total time: 20 minutes

Ingredients
- 1 cup unsalted plant butter
- 1 garlic clove, minced
- ¼ cup chopped fresh cilantro
- 1 cup fresh garden peas
- ½ cup vegetable broth
- 2 limes, juiced
- Salt and black pepper to taste

Directions:
1. Melt the plant butter in a large pot and sauté the garlic until fragrant, 30 seconds.
2. Mix in the remaining ingredients, cover the pot, and simmer until the peas are very soft, 10 to 15 minutes.
3. Open the lid and transfer the food to a blender. Process until smooth.
4. Pour the sauce into serving cups and use immediately with grilled vegetables, tofu, tempeh, etc.

Alfredo Sauce

Total time: 15 minutes

Ingredients
- ½ cup vegetable broth
- 4 garlic cloves, minced
- 4 leaves fresh basil, chopped
- ¼ cup freshly chopped parsley
- 4 tbsp plant butter
- 2 cups coconut cream
- 8 oz cashew cheese, softened
- 1 cup grated plant-based Parmesan cheese

Directions:
1. Combine the vegetable broth, garlic, basil, and parsley in a medium pot and simmer over low heat for 10 minutes.
2. Stir in the plant butter, coconut cream, cashew cheese, and plant-based Parmesan cheese until the cheeses melt.
3. Use the sauce immediately for Alfredo pasta dishes.

Garlic Alfredo Sauce

Total time: 22 minutes

Ingredients
- 1 medium white onion, diced
- 2 cups vegetable broth

- ½ teaspoon salt
- ½ teaspoon ground black pepper
- 4 garlic cloves, minced
- ½ cup raw cashews
- 2 tablespoons lemon juice
- 4 tablespoons nutritional yeast

Directions:
1. Cook onion with 1 cup broth in a large pan for 8 minutes over medium heat.
2. Stir in garlic and cook for another 4 minutes until it is creamy.
3. Puree this veggie mixture in a blender jug.
4. Now add remaining broth, black pepper, salt, cashews, nutritional yeast, and lemon juice.
5. Blend well until smooth.
6. Enjoy.

Molasses Tahini Sauce

Total time: 10 minutes

Ingredients
- 6 tablespoons tahini
- 10 teaspoons tomato paste
- 2 teaspoons maple syrup
- ¾ teaspoon garlic powder
- 3 teaspoons apple cider vinegar
- 3 teaspoons molasses
- ¼ teaspoon liquid smoke
- Sea salt, to taste
- 1/8 teaspoon chili powder
- ½ cup water

Directions:
1. Dump all the tahini sauce ingredients into a blender jug.
2. Blend the tahini mixture for 2 minutes.
3. Serve.

Teriyaki Sauce

Total time: 10 minutes

Ingredients!
- 1 tbsp soy sauce or tamari or coconut aminos
- 1 tsp ginger, powdered
- 1 tsp garlic, powdered
- 1 tbsp maple syrup
- 1 tbsp tahini
- ¼ cup water
- 3 tbsp sesame seeds

Directions:
1. In a small saucepan, whisk together the first 5 ingredients.
2. Over medium heat, bring the mixture to a simmer and allow to cook, covered, for 5 minutes.
3. Immediately remove from the heat and allow to cool slightly.
4. In a dry skillet over medium heat, lightly toast 3 tbsp sesame seeds.
5. Add sesame seeds to the sauce right before serving.

White 'Cream' Sauce

Total time: 10 minutes

Ingredients
- 1 ½ cup plant milk, unsweetened

- ⅓ cup cooked chickpeas
- ½ cup aquafaba or water
- ¼ cup raw cashews, soaked in boiling water for 10 min, then rinsed and drained OR
- 1 cup boiled yukon gold potatoes, cubed
- 1 tbsp lemon juice
- 1 tbsp Dijon mustard
- 1 1/2 tbsp cornstarch dissolved in 3 tbsp water
- 1 tbsp miso paste
- 1 tsp thyme, dried
- 1/2 tsp freshly ground black pepper
- 1 tsp garlic powder
- 1 tsp onion powder

Directions:
1. Blend all ingredients together until smooth.

Blueberry Sauce

Total time: 13 minutes
Ingredients
- 3/4 cup blueberries
- ¼ tsp cinnamon
- Pinch of powdered cloves
- ½ tsp vanilla
- 2 tbsp water

Directions:
1. In a small saucepan, bring all the ingredients to a simmer and mash the berries slightly.
2. Allow to simmer for 3 minutes, then turn off the heat.
3. Allow berries to rest for 5 minutes.

Cranberry Mandarin Sauce

Total time: 17 minutes
Ingredients
- 1 cup cranberries
- 1 cup raisins
- 1 ½ cup water, divided
- 2 peeled mandarin oranges, diced
- ½ tsp cinnamon

Directions:
1. 1/16 tsp (a pinch!) each of ground mace, allspice, cloves
2. In a small saucepan, bring ¾ cup of water to a boil, add the fruit, juice, and spices, and simmer on low for 7 minutes.
3. When raisins are soft and cranberries are splitting, add everything to a blender, add the remaining water, and blend until smooth.
Should be a smooth, spreadable viscosity

SALADS RECIPES

Cashew Siam Salad

Preparation Time: 10 minutes
Cooking Time: 3 minutes
Servings: 4
Ingredients:
Salad:
- 4 cups baby spinach, rinsed, drained
- ½ cup pickled red cabbage

Dressing:
- 1-inch piece ginger, finely chopped
- 1 tsp. chili garlic paste
- 1 tbsp. soy sauce
- ½ tbsp. rice vinegar
- 1 tbsp. sesame oil
- 3 tbsp. avocado oil

Toppings:
- ½ cup raw cashews, unsalted
- ¼ cup fresh cilantro, chopped

Directions:
1. Put the spinach and red cabbage in a large bowl. Toss to combine and set the salad aside.
2. Toast the cashews in a frying pan over medium-high heat, stirring occasionally until the cashews are golden brown. This should take about 3 minutes. Turn off the heat and set the frying pan aside.
3. Mix all the dressing ingredients in medium-sized bowl and use a spoon to mix them into a smooth dressing.
4. Pour the dressing over the spinach salad and top with the toasted cashews.
5. Toss the salad to combine all ingredients and transfer the large bowl to the fridge. Allow the salad to chill for up to one hour – doing so will guarantee a better flavor. Alternatively, the salad can be served right away, topped with the optional cilantro. Enjoy!

Nutrition: Calories 160 Total Fat 12.9g Saturated Fat 2.4g Cholesterol 0mg Sodium 265mg Total Carbohydrate 9.1g Dietary Fiber 2.1g Total Sugars 1.4g Protein 4.1g Vitamin D 0mcg Calcium 45mg Iron 2mg Potassium 344mg

Cucumber Edamame Salad

Preparation Time: 5 minutes
Cooking Time: 8 minutes
Servings: 2
Ingredients:
- 3 tbsp. avocado oil
- 1 cup cucumber, sliced into thin rounds
- ½ cup fresh sugar snap peas, sliced or whole
- ½ cup fresh edamame
- ¼ cup radish, sliced
- 1 large Hass avocado, peeled, pitted, sliced
- 1 nori sheet, crumbled
- 2 tsp. roasted sesame seeds
- 1 tsp. salt

Directions:

1. Bring a medium-sized pot filled half way with water to a boil over medium-high heat.
2. Add the sugar snaps and cook them for about 2 minutes.
3. Take the pot off the heat, drain the excess water, transfer the sugar snaps to a medium-sized bowl and set aside for now.
4. Fill the pot with water again, add the teaspoon of salt and bring to a boil over medium-high heat.
5. Add the edamame to the pot and let them cook for about 6 minutes.
6. Take the pot off the heat, drain the excess water, transfer the soybeans to the bowl with sugar snaps and let them cool down for about 5 minutes.
7. Combine all ingredients, except the nori crumbs and roasted sesame seeds, in a medium-sized bowl.
8. Carefully stir, using a spoon, until all ingredients are evenly coated in oil.
9. Top the salad with the nori crumbs and roasted sesame seeds.
10. Transfer the bowl to the fridge and allow the salad to cool for at least 30 minutes.
11. Serve chilled and enjoy!

Nutrition: Calories 182 Total Fat 10.9g Saturated Fat 1.3g Cholesterol 0mg Sodium 1182mg Total Carbohydrate 14.2g Dietary Fiber 5.4g Total Sugars 1.9g Protein 10.7g Vitamin D 0mcg, Calcium 181mg Iron 4mg Potassium 619mg

Spinach and Mashed Tofu Salad

Preparation Time: 20 minutes
Cooking Time: 0 minutes
Servings: 4
Ingredients:
- 2 8-oz. blocks firm tofu, drained
- 4 cups baby spinach leaves
- 4 tbsp. cashew butter
- 1½ tbsp. soy sauce
- 1tbsp ginger, chopped
- 1 tsp. red miso paste
- 2 tbsp. sesame seeds
- 1 tsp. organic orange zest
- 1 tsp. nori flakes
- 2 tbsp. water

Directions:
1. Use paper towels to absorb any excess water left in the tofu before crumbling both blocks into small pieces.
2. In a large bowl, combine the mashed tofu with the spinach leaves.
3. Mix the remaining ingredients in another small bowl and, if desired, add the optional water for a more smooth dressing.
4. Pour this dressing over the mashed tofu and spinach leaves.
5. Transfer the bowl to the fridge and allow the salad to chill for up to one hour. Doing so will guarantee a better flavor. Or, the salad can be served right away. Enjoy!

Nutrition: Calories 623 Total Fat 30.5g Saturated Fat 5.8g Cholesterol 0mg Sodium 2810mg Total Carbohydrate 48g Dietary Fiber 5.9g Total Sugars 3g Protein 48.4g Vitamin D 0mcg Calcium 797mg Iron 22mg Potassium 2007mg

Super Summer Salad

Preparation Time: 10 minutes
Cooking Time: 0 minutes
Servings: 2
Ingredients:
Dressing:
- 1 tbsp. olive oil
- ¼ cup chopped basil
- 1 tsp. lemon juice
- ¼ tsp Salt
- 1 medium avocado, halved, diced
- ¼ cup water

Salad:
- ¼ cup dry chickpeas
- ¼ cup dry red kidney beans
- 4 cups raw kale, shredded
- 2 cups Brussel sprouts, shredded
- 2 radishes, thinly sliced
- 1 tbsp. walnuts, chopped
- 1 tsp. flax seeds
- Salt and pepper to taste

Directions:
1. Prepare the chickpeas and kidney beans according to the method.
2. Soak the flax seeds according the method, and then drain excess water.
3. Prepare the dressing by adding the olive oil, basil, lemon juice, salt, and half of the avocado to a food processor or blender, and pulse on low speed.
4. Keep adding small amounts of water until the dressing is creamy and smooth.
5. Transfer the dressing to a small bowl and set it aside.
6. Combine the kale, Brussel sprouts, cooked chickpeas, kidney beans, radishes, walnuts, and remaining avocado in a large bowl and mix thoroughly.
7. Store the mixture, or, serve with the dressing and flax seeds, and enjoy!
Nutrition: Calories 266 Total Fat 26.6g Saturated Fat 5.1g Cholesterol 0mg Sodium 298mg Total Carbohydrate 8.8g Dietary Fiber 6.8g Total Sugars 0.6g Protein 2g Vitamin D 0mcg Calcium 19mg Iron 1mg Potassium 500mg

Roasted Almond Protein Salad

Preparation Time: 30 minutes
Cooking Time: 0 minutes
Servings: 4
Ingredients:
- ½ cup dry quinoa
- ½ cup dry navy beans
- ½ cup dry chickpeas
- ½ cup raw whole almonds
- 1 tsp. extra virgin olive oil
- ½ tsp. salt
- ½ tsp. paprika
- ½ tsp. cayenne
- Dash of chili powder
- 4 cups spinach, fresh or frozen
- ¼ cup purple onion, chopped

Directions:
1. Prepare the quinoa according to the recipe. Store in the fridge for now.
2. Prepare the beans according to the method. Store in the fridge for now.
3. Toss the almonds, olive oil, salt, and spices in a large bowl, and stir until the ingredients are evenly coated.
4. Put a skillet over medium-high heat, and transfer the almond mixture to the heated skillet.
5. Roast while stirring until the almonds are browned, around 5 minutes. You may hear the ingredients pop and crackle in the pan as they warm up. Stir frequently to prevent burning.
6. Turn off the heat and toss the cooked and chilled quinoa and beans, onions, and spinach or mixed greens in the skillet. Stir well before transferring the roasted almond salad to a bowl.
7. Enjoy the salad with a dressing of choice, or, store for later!
Nutrition: Calories 347 Total Fat 10.5g Saturated Fat 1g Cholesterol 0mg Sodium 324mg Total Carbohydrate 49.2g Dietary Fiber 14.7g Total Sugars 4.7g Protein 17.2g Vitamin D 0mcg Calcium 139mg Iron 5mg Potassium 924mg

Lentil, Lemon & Mushroom Salad

Preparation Time: 10 minutes
Cooking Time: 0 minutes
Servings: 2
Ingredients:
- ½ cup dry lentils of choice
- 2 cups vegetable broth
- 3 cups mushrooms, thickly sliced
- 1 cup sweet or purple onion, chopped
- 4 tsp. extra virgin olive oil
- 2 tbsp. garlic powder
- ¼ tsp. chili flakes
- 1 tbsp. lemon juice
- 2 tbsp. cilantro, chopped
- ½ cup arugula
- ¼ tsp Salt
- ¼ tsp pepper

Directions:
1. Sprout the lentils according the method. (Don't cook them).
2. Place the vegetable stock in a deep saucepan and bring it to a boil.
3. Add the lentils to the boiling broth, cover the pan, and cook for about 5 minutes over low heat until the lentils are a bit tender.
4. Remove the pan from heat and drain the excess water.
5. Put a frying pan over high heat and add 2 tablespoons of olive oil.
6. Add the onions, garlic, and chili flakes, and cook until the onions are almost translucent, around 5 to 10 minutes while stirring.

7.	Add the mushrooms to the frying pan and mix in thoroughly. Continue cooking until the onions are completely translucent and the mushrooms have softened; remove the pan from the heat.
8.	Mix the lentils, onions, mushrooms, and garlic in a large bowl.
9.	Add the lemon juice and the remaining olive oil. Toss or stir to combine everything thoroughly.
10.	Serve the mushroom/onion mixture over some arugala in bowl, adding salt and pepper to taste, or, store and enjoy later!
Nutrition: Calories 365 Total Fat 11.7g Saturated Fat 1.9g Cholesterol 0mg Sodium 1071mg Total Carbohydrate 45.2g Dietary Fiber 18g Total Sugars 8.2g Protein 22.8g Vitamin D 378mcg Calcium 67mg Iron 8mg Potassium 1212mg

Sweet Potato & Black Bean Protein Salad

Preparation Time: 15 minutes
Cooking Time: 0 minutes
Servings: 2
Ingredients:
- 1 cup dry black beans
- 4 cups of spinach
- 1 medium sweet potato
- 1 cup purple onion, chopped
- 2 tbsp. olive oil
- 2 tbsp. lime juice
- 1 tbsp. minced garlic
- ½ tbsp. chili powder
- ¼ tsp. cayenne
- ¼ cup parsley
- ¼ tsp Salt
- ¼ tsp pepper

Directions:
1.	Prepare the black beans according to the method.
2.	Preheat the oven to 400°F.
3.	Cut the sweet potato into ¼-inch cubes and put these in a medium-sized bowl. Add the onions, 1 tablespoon of olive oil, and salt to taste.
4.	Toss the ingredients until the sweet potatoes and onions are completely coated.
5.	Transfer the ingredients to a baking sheet lined with parchment paper and spread them out in a single layer.
6.	Put the baking sheet in the oven and roast until the sweet potatoes are starting to turn brown and crispy, around 40 minutes.
7.	Meanwhile, combine the remaining olive oil, lime juice, garlic, chili powder, and cayenne thoroughly in a large bowl, until no lumps remain.
8.	Remove the sweet potatoes and onions from the oven and transfer them to the large bowl.
9.	Add the cooked black beans, parsley, and a pinch of salt.
10.	Toss everything until well combined.
11.	Then mix in the spinach, and serve in desired portions with additional salt and pepper.
12.	Store or enjoy!
Nutrition: Calories 558 Total Fat 16.2g Saturated Fat 2.5g Cholesterol 0mg Sodium 390mg Total Carbohydrate 84g Dietary Fiber 20.4g Total Sugars 8.9g Protein 25.3g Vitamin D 0mcg Calcium 220mg Iron 10mg Potassium 2243mg

Lentil Radish Salad

Preparation Time: 15 minutes
Cooking Time: 0 minutes
Servings: 3
Ingredients:
Dressing:
- 1 tbsp. extra virgin olive oil
- 1 tbsp. lemon juice
- 1 tbsp. maple syrup
- 1 tbsp. water
- ½ tbsp. sesame oil
- 1 tbsp. miso paste, yellow or white
- ¼ tsp. salt
- ¼ tsp Pepper

Salad:
- ½ cup dry chickpeas
- ¼ cup dry green or brown lentils
- 1 14-oz. pack of silken tofu
- 5 cups mixed greens, fresh or frozen
- 2 radishes, thinly sliced
- ½ cup cherry tomatoes, halved
- ¼ cup roasted sesame seeds

Directions:
1.	Prepare the chickpeas according to the method.
2.	Prepare the lentils according to the method.
3.	Put all the ingredients for the dressing in a blender or food processor. Mix on low until smooth, while adding water until it reaches the desired consistency.
4.	Add salt, pepper (to taste), and optionally more water to the dressing; set aside.
5.	Cut the tofu into bite-sized cubes.
6.	Combine the mixed greens, tofu, lentils, chickpeas, radishes, and tomatoes in a large bowl.
7.	Add the dressing and mix everything until it is coated evenly.
8.	Top with the optional roasted sesame seeds, if desired.
9.	Refrigerate before serving and enjoy, or, store for later!
Nutrition: Calories 621 Total Fat 19.6g Saturated Fat 2.8g Cholesterol 0mg Sodium 996mg Total Carbohydrate 82.7g Dietary Fiber 26.1g Total Sugars 20.7g Protein 31.3g Vitamin D 0mcg Calcium 289mg Iron 9mg Potassium 1370mg

Southwest Style Salad

Preparation Time: 10 minutes
Cooking Time: 0 minutes
Servings: 3
Ingredients:
- ½ cup dry black beans
- ½ cup dry chickpeas
- 1/3 cup purple onion, diced
- 1 red bell pepper, pitted, sliced
- 4 cups mixed greens, fresh or frozen, chopped
- 1 cup cherry tomatoes, halved or quartered

* 1 medium avocado, peeled, pitted, and cubed
* 1 cup sweet kernel corn, canned, drained
* ½ tsp. chili powder
* ¼ tsp. cumin
* ¼ tsp Salt
* ¼ tsp pepper
* 2 tsp. olive oil
* 1 tbsp. vinegar

Directions:
1. Prepare the black beans and chickpeas according to the method.
2. Put all of the ingredients into a large bowl.
3. Toss the mix of veggies and spices until combined thoroughly.
4. Store, or serve chilled with some olive oil and vinegar on top!

Nutrition: Calories 635 Total Fat 19.9g Saturated Fat 3.6g Cholesterol 0mg Sodium 302mg Total Carbohydrate 95.4g Dietary Fiber 28.1g Total Sugars 18.8g Protein 24.3g Vitamin D 0mcg Calcium 160mg Iron 7mg Potassium 1759mg

Shaved Brussel Sprout Salad

Preparation Time: 25 minutes
Cooking Time: 0 minutes
Servings: 4
Ingredients:
Dressing:
* 1 tbsp. brown mustard
* 1 tbsp. maple syrup
* 2 tbsp. apple cider vinegar
* 2 tbsp. extra virgin olive oil
* ½ tbsp. garlic minced

Salad:
* ½ cup dry red kidney beans
* ¼ cup dry chickpeas
* 2 cups Brussel sprouts
* 1 cup purple onion
* 1 small sour apple
* ½ cup slivered almonds, crushed
* ½ cup walnuts, crushed
* ½ cup cranberries, dried
* ¼ tsp Salt
* ¼ tsp pepper

Directions:
1. Prepare the beans according to the method.
2. Combine all dressing ingredients in a bowl and stir well until combined.
3. Refrigerate the dressing for up to one hour before serving.
4. Using a grater, mandolin, or knife to thinly slice each Brussel sprout. Repeat this with the apple and onion.
5. Take a large bowl to mix the chickpeas, beans, sprouts, apples, onions, cranberries, and nuts.
6. Drizzle the cold dressing over the salad to coat.
7. Serve with salt and pepper to taste, or, store for later!

Nutrition: Calories 432 Total Fat 23.5g Saturated Fat 2.2g Cholesterol 0mg Sodium 197mg Total Carbohydrate 45.3g Dietary Fiber 12.4g Total Sugars 14g Protein 15.9g Vitamin D 0mcg Calcium 104mg Iron 4mg Potassium 908mg

Colorful Protein Power Salad

Preparation Time: 20 minutes
Cooking Time: 0 minutes
Servings: 2
Ingredients:
* ½ cup dry quinoa
* 2 cups dry navy beans
* 1 green onion, chopped
* 2 tsp. garlic, minced
* 3 cups green or purple cabbage, chopped
* 4 cups kale, fresh or frozen, chopped
* 1 cup shredded carrot, chopped
* 2 tbsp. extra virgin olive oil
* 1 tsp. lemon juice
* ¼ tsp Salt
* ¼ tsp pepper

Directions:
1. Prepare the quinoa according to the recipe.
2. Prepare the beans according to the method.
3. Heat up 1 tablespoon of the olive oil in a frying pan over medium heat.
4. Add the chopped green onion, garlic, and cabbage, and sauté for 2-3 minutes.
5. Add the kale, the remaining 1 tablespoon of olive oil, and salt. Lower the heat and cover until the greens have wilted, around 5 minutes. Remove the pan from the stove and set aside.
6. Take a large bowl and mix the remaining ingredients with the kale and cabbage mixture once it has cooled down. Add more salt and pepper to taste.
7. Mix until everything is distributed evenly.
8. Serve topped with a dressing, or, store for later!

Nutrition: Calories 1100 Total Fat 19.9g Saturated Fat 2.7g Cholesterol 0mg Sodium 420mg Total Carbohydrate 180.8g Dietary Fiber 60.1g Total Sugars 14.4g Protein 58.6g Vitamin D 0mcg Calcium 578mg Iron 16mg Potassium 3755mg

Edamame & Ginger Citrus Salad

Preparation Time: 15 minutes
Cooking Time: 0 minutes
Servings: 3
Ingredients:
Dressing:
* ¼ cup orange juice
* 1 tsp. lime juice
* ½ tbsp. maple syrup
* ½ tsp. ginger, finely minced
* ½ tbsp. sesame oil

Salad:
* ½ cup dry green lentils
* 2 cups carrots, shredded
* 4 cups kale, fresh or frozen, chopped
* 1 cup edamame, shelled
* 1 tablespoon roasted sesame seeds
* 2 tsp. mint, chopped
* Salt and pepper to taste

- 1 small avocado, peeled, pitted, diced

Directions:
1. Prepare the lentils according to the method.
2. Combine the orange and lime juices, maple syrup, and ginger in a small bowl. Mix with a whisk while slowly adding the sesame oil.
3. Add the cooked lentils, carrots, kale, edamame, sesame seeds, and mint to a large bowl.
4. Add the dressing and stir well until all the ingredients are coated evenly.
5. Store or serve topped with avocado and an additional sprinkle of mint.

Nutrition: Calories 507 Total Fat 23.1g Saturated Fat 4g Cholesterol 0mg Sodium 303mg Total Carbohydrate 56.8g Dietary Fiber 21.6g Total Sugars 8.4g Protein 24.6g Vitamin D 0mcg Calcium 374mg Iron 8mg Potassium 1911mg

Taco Tempeh Salad

Preparation Time: 25 minutes
Cooking Time: 0 minutes
Servings: 3
Ingredients:
- 1 cup dry black beans
- 1 8-oz. package tempeh
- 1 tbsp. lime or lemon juice
- 2 tbsp. extra virgin olive oil
- 1 tsp. maple syrup
- ½ tsp. chili powder
- ¼ tsp. cumin
- ¼ tsp. paprika
- 1 large bunch of kale, fresh or frozen, chopped
- 1 large avocado, peeled, pitted, diced
- ½ cup salsa
- ¼ tsp Salt
- ¼ tsp pepper

Directions:
1. Prepare the beans according to the method.
2. Cut the tempeh into ¼-inch cubes, place in a bowl, and then add the lime or lemon juice, 1 tablespoon of olive oil, maple syrup, chili powder, cumin, and paprika.
3. Stir well and let the tempeh marinate in the fridge for at least 1 hour, up to 12 hours.
4. Heat the remaining 1 tablespoon of olive oil in a frying pan over medium heat.
5. Add the marinated tempeh mixture and cook until brown and crispy on both sides, around 10 minutes.
6. Put the chopped kale in a bowl with the cooked beans and prepared tempeh.
7. Store, or serve the salad immediately, topped with salsa, avocado, and salt and pepper to taste.

Nutrition: Calories 627 Total Fat 31.7g Saturated Fat 6.1g Cholesterol 0mg Sodium 493mg Total Carbohydrate 62.7g Dietary Fiber 16g Total Sugars 4.5g Protein 31.4g Vitamin D 0mcg Calcium 249mg Iron 7mg Potassium 1972mg

Lebanese Potato Salad

Preparation Time: 5 minutes
Cooking Time: 10 minutes
Servings: 4
Ingredients:
- 1-pound Russet potatoes
- 1 ½ tablespoons extra virgin olive oil
- 2 scallions, thinly sliced
- Freshly ground pepper to taste
- 2 tablespoons lemon juice
- ¼ teaspoon salt or to taste
- 2 tablespoons fresh mint leaves, chopped

Directions:
1. Place a saucepan half filled with water over medium heat. Add salt and potatoes and cook for 10 minutes until tender. Drain the potatoes and place in a bowl of cold water. When cool enough to handle, peel and cube the potatoes. Place in a bowl.
To make dressing:
2. Add oil, lemon juice, salt and pepper in a bowl and whisk well. Drizzle dressing over the potatoes. Toss well.
3. Add scallions and mint and toss well.
4. Divide into 4 plates and serve.

Nutrition: Calories 129 Total Fat 5.5g Saturated Fat 0.9g Cholesterol 0mg Sodium 158mg Total Carbohydrate 18.8g Dietary Fiber 3.2g Total Sugars 1.6g Protein 2.2g Vitamin D 0mcg Calcium 22mg Iron 1mg Potassium 505mg

Chickpea and Spinach Salad

Preparation Time: 5 minutes
Cooking Time: 0 minutes
Servings: 4
Ingredients:
- 2 cans (14.5 ounces each) chickpeas, drained, rinsed
- 7 ounces vegan feta cheese, crumbled or chopped
- 1 tablespoon lemon juice
- 1/3 -½ cup olive oil
- ½ teaspoon salt or to taste
- 4-6 cups spinach, torn
- ½ cup raisins
- 2 tablespoons honey
- 1-2 teaspoons ground cumin
- 1 teaspoon chili flakes

Directions:
1. Add cheese, chickpeas and spinach into a large bowl.
2. To make dressing: Add rest of the ingredients into another bowl and mix well.
3. Pour dressing over the salad. Toss well and serve.

Nutrition: Calories 822 Total Fat 42.5g Saturated Fat 11.7g Cholesterol 44mg Sodium 910mg Total Carbohydrate 89.6g Dietary Fiber 19.7g Total Sugars 32.7g Protein 29g Vitamin D 0mcg Calcium 417mg Iron 9mg Potassium 1347mg

Tempeh "Chicken" Salad

Preparation Time: 10 minutes
Cooking Time: 0 minutes
Servings: 2
Ingredients:

- 4 tablespoons light mayonnaise
- 2 scallions, sliced
- Pepper to taste
- 4 cups mixed salad greens
- 4 teaspoons white miso
- 2 tablespoons chopped fresh dill
- 1 ½ cups crumbled tempeh
- 1 cup sliced grape tomatoes

Directions:

To make dressing:

1. Add mayonnaise, scallions, miso, dill and pepper into a bowl and whisk well.
2. Add tempeh and fold gently.

To serve:

3. Divide the greens into 4 plates. Divide the tempeh among the plates. Top with tomatoes and serve.

Nutrition: Calories 452 Total Fat 24.5g Saturated Fat 4.4g Cholesterol 8mg Sodium 733mg Total Carbohydrate 37.2g Dietary Fiber 2.6g Total Sugars 5.3g Protein 29.9g Vitamin D 0mcg Calcium 261mg Iron 8mg Potassium 1377mg

Spinach & Dill Pasta Salad

Preparation Time: 5 minutes
Cooking Time: 0 minutes
Servings: 4
Ingredients:

For salad:

- 3 cups cooked whole-wheat fusilli
- 2 cups cherry tomatoes, halved
- ½ cup vegan cheese, shredded
- 4 cups spinach, chopped
- 2 cups edamame, thawed
- 1 large red onion, finely chopped

For dressing:

- 2 tablespoons white wine vinegar
- ½ teaspoon dried dill
- 2 tablespoons extra-virgin olive oil
- Salt to taste
- Pepper to taste

Directions:

To make dressing:

1. Add all the ingredients for dressing into a bowl and whisk well. Set aside for a while for the flavors to set in.

To make salad:

2. Add all the ingredients of the salad in a bowl. Toss well.
3. Drizzle dressing on top. Toss well.
4. Divide into 4 plates and serve.

Nutrition: Calories 684 Total Fat 33.6g Saturated Fat 4.6g Cholesterol 4mg Sodium 632mg Total Carbohydrate 69.5g Dietary Fiber 12g Total Sugars 6.4g Protein 31.7g Vitamin D 0mcg Calcium 368mg Iron 8mg Potassium 1241mg

Italian Veggie Salad

Preparation Time: 10 minutes
Cooking Time: 0 minutes
Servings: 8
Ingredients:

For salad:

- 1 cup fresh baby carrots, quartered lengthwise
- 1 celery rib, sliced
- 3 large mushrooms, thinly sliced
- 1 cup cauliflower florets, bite sized, blanched
- 1 cup broccoli florets, blanched
- 1 cup thinly sliced radish
- 4-5 ounces hearts of romaine salad mix to serve

For dressing:

- ½ package Italian salad dressing mix
- 3 tablespoons white vinegar
- 3 tablespoons water
- 3 tablespoons olive oil
- 3-4 pepperoncino, chopped

Directions:

To make salad:

1. Add all the ingredients of the salad except hearts of romaine to a bowl and toss.

To make dressing:

2. Add all the ingredients of the dressing in a small bowl. Whisk well.
3. Pour dressing over salad and toss well. Refrigerate for a couple of hours.
4. Place romaine in a large bowl. Place the chilled salad over it and serve.

Nutrition: Calories 84 Total Fat 6.7g Saturated Fat 1.2g Cholesterol 3mg Sodium 212mg Total Carbohydrate 5g Dietary Fiber 1.4g Total Sugars 1.6g Protein 2g Vitamin D 31mcg Calcium 27mg Iron 1mg Potassium 193mg

SNACK AND SIDES

Black Bean Lime Dip

Preparation Time: 5 minutes
Cooking Time: 6 minutes
Servings: 4
Ingredients:
- 15.5 ounces cooked black beans
- 1 teaspoon minced garlic
- ½ of a lime, juiced
- 1 inch of ginger, grated
- 1/3 teaspoon salt
- 1/3 teaspoon ground black pepper
- 1 tablespoon olive oil

Directions:
1. Take a frying pan, add oil and when hot, add garlic and ginger and cook for 1 minute until fragrant.
2. Then add beans, splash with some water and fry for 3 minutes until hot.
3. Season beans with salt and black pepper, drizzle with lime juice, then remove the pan from heat and mash the beans until smooth pasta comes together.
4. Serve the dip with whole-grain breadsticks or vegetables.

Nutrition: Calories: 374 Cal Fat: 14 g Carbs: 46 g Protein: 15 g Fiber: 17 g

Beetroot Hummus

Preparation Time: 10 minutes
Cooking Time: 60 minutes
Servings: 4
Ingredients:
- 15 ounces cooked chickpeas
- 3 small beets
- 1 teaspoon minced garlic
- 1/2 teaspoon smoked paprika
- 1 teaspoon of sea salt
- 1/4 teaspoon red chili flakes
- 2 tablespoons olive oil
- 1 lemon, juiced
- 2 tablespoon tahini
- 1 tablespoon chopped almonds
- 1 tablespoon chopped cilantro

Directions:
1. Drizzle oil over beets, season with salt, then wrap beets in a foil and bake for 60 minutes at 425 degrees F until tender.
2. When done, let beet cool for 10 minutes, then peel and dice them and place them in a food processor.
3. Add remaining ingredients and pulse for 2 minutes until smooth, tip the hummus in a bowl, drizzle with some more oil, and then serve straight away.

Nutrition: Calories: 50.1 Cal Fat: 2.5 g Carbs: 5 g Protein: 2 g Fiber: 1 g

Zucchini Hummus

Preparation Time: 5 minutes
Cooking Time: 0 minute
Servings: 8
Ingredients:
- 1 cup diced zucchini
- 1/2 teaspoon sea salt
- 1 teaspoon minced garlic
- 2 teaspoons ground cumin
- 3 tablespoons lemon juice
- 1/3 cup tahini

Directions:
1. Place all the ingredients in a food processor and pulse for 2 minutes until smooth.
2. Tip the hummus in a bowl, drizzle with oil and serve.

Nutrition: Calories: 65 Cal Fat: 5 g Carbs: 3 g Protein: 2 g Fiber: 1 g

Chipotle and Lime Tortilla Chips

Preparation Time: 10 minutes
Cooking Time: 15 minutes
Servings: 4
Ingredients:
- 12 ounces whole-wheat tortillas
- 4 tablespoons chipotle seasoning
- 1 tablespoon olive oil
- 4 limes, juiced

Directions:
1. Whisk together oil and lime juice, brush it well on tortillas, then sprinkle with chipotle seasoning and bake for 15 minutes at 350 degrees F until crispy, turning halfway.
2. When done, let the tortilla cool for 10 minutes, then break it into chips and serve.

Nutrition: Calories: 150 Cal Fat: 7 g Carbs: 18 g Protein: 2 g Fiber: 2 g

Carrot and Sweet Potato Fritters

Preparation Time: 10 minutes
Cooking Time: 8 minutes
Servings: 10
Ingredients:
- 1/3 cup quinoa flour
- 1½ cups shredded sweet potato
- 1 cup grated carrot
- 1/3 teaspoon ground black pepper
- 2/3 teaspoon salt
- 2 teaspoons curry powder
- 2 flax eggs
- 2 tablespoons coconut oil

Directions:
1. Place all the ingredients in a bowl, except for oil, stir well until combined and then shape the mixture into ten small patties
2. Take a large pan, place it over medium-high heat, add oil and when it melts, add patties in it and cook for 3 minutes per side until browned.
3. Serve straight away

Nutrition: Calories: 70 Cal Fat: 3 g Carbs: 8 g Protein: 1 g Fiber: 1 g

Buffalo Quinoa Bites

Preparation Time: 15 minutes
Cooking Time: 30 minutes

Servings: 20
Ingredients:
For the Bites:

- 1 cup cooked quinoa
- 15 ounces cooked white beans
- 3 tablespoons chickpea flour
- 1 medium shallot, peeled, chopped
- 3 cloves of garlic, peeled
- ½ teaspoon ground black pepper
- 1/2 teaspoon salt
- 1 teaspoon smoked paprika
- 1/4 cup vegan buffalo sauce

For the Dressing:

- 1/4 cup chives
- 2 tablespoons hemp hearts
- 1 tablespoon nutritional yeast
- 1 teaspoon garlic powder
- 1 teaspoon onion powder
- 1/2 teaspoon salt
- ½ teaspoon ground black pepper
- 2 teaspoons dried dill
- 1 lemon, juiced
- 1/4 cup tahini
- 3/4 cup water

Directions:
1. Prepare the bites, and for this, place half of the beans in a food processor, add garlic and shallots, and pulse for 2 minutes until mixture comes together.
2. Then add all the spices of the bites and buffalo sauce and pulse for 2 minutes until smooth. Add remaining beans along with chickpea flour and quinoa and pulse until just combined.
3. Tip the mixture in a dish, shape it in the dough, shape it into twenty balls, about the golf-ball size, and bake for 30 minutes at 350 degrees F until crispy and browned, turning halfway.
4. Meanwhile, prepare the dressing and for this, place all of its ingredients in a food processor and pulse for 2 minutes until smooth.
5. Serve bites with prepared dressing.
Nutrition: Calories: 78 Cal Fat: 3 g Carbs: 9 g Protein: 4 g Fiber: 2 g

Tomato and Pesto Toast

Preparation Time: 5 minutes
Cooking Time: 0 minute
Servings: 4
Ingredients:

- 1 small tomato, sliced
- ¼ teaspoon ground black pepper
- 1 tablespoon vegan pesto
- 2 tablespoons hummus
- 1 slice of whole-grain bread, toasted
- Hemp seeds as needed for garnishing

Directions:
1. Spread hummus on one side of the toast, top with tomato slices and then drizzle with pesto.
2. Sprinkle black pepper on the toast along with hemp seeds and then serve straight away.
Nutrition: Calories: 214 Cal Fat: 7.2 g Carbs: 32 g Protein: 6.5 g Fiber: 3 g

Avocado and Sprout Toast

Preparation Time: 5 minutes
Cooking Time: 0 minute
Servings: 4
Ingredients:

- 1/2 of a medium avocado, sliced
- 1 slice of whole-grain bread, toasted
- 2 tablespoons sprouts
- 2 tablespoons hummus
- ¼ teaspoon lemon zest
- ½ teaspoon hemp seeds
- ¼ teaspoon red pepper flakes

Directions:
1. Spread hummus on one side of the toast and then top with avocado slices and sprouts.
2. Sprinkle with lemon zest, hemp seeds, and red pepper flakes and then serve straight away.
Nutrition: Calories: 200 Cal Fat: 10.5 g Carbs: 22 g Protein: 7 g Fiber: 7 g

Apple and Honey Toast

Preparation Time: 5 minutes
Cooking Time: 0 minute
Servings: 4
Ingredients:

- ½ of a small apple, cored, sliced
- 1 slice of whole-grain bread, toasted
- 1 tablespoon honey
- 2 tablespoons hummus
- 1/8 teaspoon cinnamon

Directions:
1. Spread hummus on one side of the toast, top with apple slices and then drizzle with honey.
2. Sprinkle cinnamon on it and then serve straight away.
Nutrition: Calories: 212 Cal Fat: 7 g Carbs: 35 g Protein: 4 g Fiber: 5.5 g

Thai Snack Mix

Preparation Time: 15 minutes
Cooking Time: 90 minutes
Servings: 4
Ingredients:

- 5 cups mixed nuts
- 1 cup chopped dried pineapple
- 1 cup pumpkin seed
- 1 teaspoon onion powder
- 1 teaspoon garlic powder
- 2 teaspoons paprika
- 1/2 teaspoon ground black pepper
- 1 teaspoon of sea salt
- 1/4 cup coconut sugar
- 1/2 teaspoon red chili powder
- 1 tablespoon red pepper flakes
- 1/2 tablespoon red curry powder
- 2 tablespoons soy sauce
- 2 tablespoons coconut oil

Directions:
1. Switch on the slow cooker, add all the ingredients in it except for dried pineapple and red pepper flakes, stir until combined and cook for 90

minutes at high heat setting, stirring every 30 minutes.

2.   When done, spread the nut mixture on a baking sheet lined with parchment paper and let it cool.

3.   Then spread dried pineapple on top, sprinkle with red pepper flakes and serve.

Nutrition: Calories: 230 Cal Fat: 17.5 g Carbs: 11.5 g Protein: 6.5 g Fiber: 2 g

Zucchini Fritters

Preparation Time: 10 minutes
Cooking Time: 6 minutes
Servings: 12
Ingredients:
- 1/2 cup quinoa flour
- 3 1/2 cups shredded zucchini
- 1/2 cup chopped scallions
- 1/3 teaspoon ground black pepper
- 1 teaspoon salt
- 2 tablespoons coconut oil
- 2 flax eggs

Directions:
1.   Squeeze moisture from the zucchini by wrapping it in a cheesecloth and then transfer it to a bowl.
2.   Add remaining ingredients, except for oil, stir until combined and then shape the mixture into twelve patties.
3.   Take a skillet pan, place it over medium-high heat, add oil and when hot, add patties and cook for 3 minutes per side until brown.
4.   Serve the patties with favorite vegan sauce.

Nutrition: Calories: 37 Cal Fat: 1 g Carbs: 4 g Protein: 2 g Fiber: 1 g

Zucchini Chips

Preparation Time: 10 minutes
Cooking Time: 120 minutes
Servings: 4
Ingredients:
- 1 large zucchini, thinly sliced
- 1 teaspoon salt
- 2 tablespoons olive oil

Directions:
1.   Pat dry zucchini slices and then spread them in an even layer on a baking sheet lined with parchment sheet.
2.   Whisk together salt and oil, brush this mixture over zucchini slices on both sides and then bake for 2 hours or more until brown and crispy.
3.   When done, let the chips cool for 10 minutes and then serve straight away.

Nutrition: Calories: 54 Cal Fat: 5 g Carbs: 1 g Protein: 0 g Fiber: 0.3 g

Rosemary Beet Chips

Preparation Time: 10 minutes
Cooking Time: 20 minutes
Servings: 3
Ingredients:
- 3 large beets, scrubbed, thinly sliced
- 1/8 teaspoon ground black pepper

- ¼ teaspoon of sea salt
- 3 sprigs of rosemary, leaves chopped
- 4 tablespoons olive oil

Directions:
1.   Spread beet slices in a single layer between two large baking sheets, brush the slices with oil, then season with spices and rosemary, toss until well coated, and bake for 20 minutes at 375 degrees F until crispy, turning halfway.
2.   When done, let the chips cool for 10 minutes and then serve.

Nutrition: Calories: 79 Cal Fat: 4.7 g Carbs: 8.6 g Protein: 1.5 g Fiber: 2.5 g

Quinoa Broccoli Tots

Preparation Time: 10 minutes
Cooking Time: 20 minutes
Servings: 16
Ingredients:
- 2 tablespoons quinoa flour
- 2 cups steamed and chopped broccoli florets
- 1/2 cup nutritional yeast
- 1 teaspoon garlic powder
- 1 teaspoon miso paste
- 2 flax eggs
- 2 tablespoons hummus

Directions:
1.   Place all the ingredients in a bowl, stir until well combined, and then shape the mixture into sixteen small balls.
2.   Arrange the balls on a baking sheet lined with parchment paper, spray with oil and bake at 400 degrees F for 20 minutes until brown, turning halfway.
3.   When done, let the tots cool for 10 minutes and then serve straight away.

Nutrition: Calories: 19 Cal Fat: 0 g Carbs: 2 g Protein: 1 g Fiber: 0.5 g

Spicy Roasted Chickpeas

Preparation Time: 10 minutes
Cooking Time: 20 minutes
Servings: 6
Ingredients:
- 30 ounces cooked chickpeas
- ½ teaspoon salt
- 2 teaspoons mustard powder
- ½ teaspoon cayenne pepper
- 2 tablespoons olive oil

Directions:
1.   Place all the ingredients in a bowl and stir until well coated and then spread the chickpeas in an even layer on a baking sheet greased with oil.
2.   Bake the chickpeas for 20 minutes at 400 degrees F until golden brown and crispy and then serve straight away.

Nutrition: Calories: 187.1 Cal Fat: 7.4 g Carbs: 24.2 g Protein: 7.3 g Fiber: 6.3 g

Beetroot Hummus

Total time: 70 minutes
Ingredients

- 15 ounces cooked chickpeas
- 3 small beets
- 1 teaspoon minced garlic
- 1/2 teaspoon smoked paprika
- 1 teaspoon of sea salt
- 1/4 teaspoon red chili flakes
- 2 tablespoons olive oil
- 1 lemon, juiced
- 2 tablespoon tahini
- 1 tablespoon chopped almonds
- 1 tablespoon chopped cilantro

Directions:

1. Drizzle oil over beets, season with salt, then wrap beets in a foil and bake for 60 minutes at 425 degrees F until tender.
2. When done, let beet cool for 10 minutes, then peel and dice them and place them in a food processor.
3. Add remaining ingredients and pulse for 2 minutes until smooth, tip the hummus in a bowl, drizzle with some more oil, and then serve straight away.

Carrot and Sweet Potato Fritters

Total time: 18 minutes

Ingredients

- 1/3 cup quinoa flour
- 1½ cups shredded sweet potato
- 1 cup grated carrot
- 1/3 teaspoon ground black pepper
- 2/3 teaspoon salt
- 2 teaspoons curry powder
- 2 flax eggs
- 2 tablespoons coconut oil

Directions:

1. Place all the ingredients in a bowl, except for oil, stir well until combined and then shape the mixture into ten small patties
2. Take a large pan, place it over medium-high heat, add oil and when it melts, add patties in it and cook for 3 minutes per side until browned.
3. Serve straight away

Black Bean Lime Dip

Total time: 11 minutes

Ingredients

- 15.5 ounces cooked black beans
- 1 teaspoon minced garlic
- ½ of a lime, juiced
- 1 inch of ginger, grated
- 1/3 teaspoon salt
- 1/3 teaspoon ground black pepper
- 1 tablespoon olive oil

Directions:

1. Take a frying pan, add oil and when hot, add garlic and ginger and cook for 1 minute until fragrant.
2. Then add beans, splash with some water and fry for 3 minutes until hot.
3. Season beans with salt and black pepper, drizzle with lime juice, then remove the pan from heat and mash the beans until smooth pasta comes together.

4. Serve the dip with whole-grain breadsticks or vegetables.

Apple and Honey Toast

Total time: 5 minutes

Ingredients

- ½ of a small apple, cored, sliced
- 1 slice of whole-grain bread, toasted
- 1 tablespoon honey
- 2 tablespoons hummus
- 1/8 teaspoon cinnamon

Directions:

1. Spread hummus on one side of the toast, top with apple slices and then drizzle with honey.
2. Sprinkle cinnamon on it and then serve straight away.

Thai Snack Mix

Total time: 115 minutes

Ingredients

- 5 cups mixed nuts
- 1 teaspoon onion powder
- 1 cup chopped dried pineapple
- 1 cup pumpkin seed
- 2 teaspoons paprika
- 1/2 teaspoon ground black pepper
- 1 teaspoon of sea salt
- 1/4 cup coconut sugar
- 1/2 teaspoon red chili powder
- 1 tablespoon red pepper flakes
- 1 teaspoon garlic powder
- 1/2 tablespoon red curry powder
- 2 tablespoons soy sauce
- 2 tablespoons coconut oil

Directions:

1. Switch on the slow cooker, add all the ingredients in it except for dried pineapple and red pepper flakes, stir until combined and cook for 90 minutes at high heat setting, stirring every 30 minutes.
2. When done, spread the nut mixture on a baking sheet lined with parchment paper and let it cool.
3. Then spread dried pineapple on top, sprinkle with red pepper flakes and serve.

Zucchini Fritters

Total time: 16 minutes

Ingredients

- 1/2 cup quinoa flour
- 3 1/2 cups shredded zucchini
- 1/2 cup chopped scallions
- 1/3 teaspoon ground black pepper
- 1 teaspoon salt
- 2 tablespoons coconut oil
- 2 flax eggs

Directions:

1. Squeeze moisture from the zucchini by wrapping it in a cheesecloth and then transfer it to a bowl.

2.	Add remaining ingredients, except for oil, stir until combined and then shape the mixture into twelve patties.
3.	Take a skillet pan, place it over medium-high heat, add oil and when hot, add patties and cook for 3 minutes per side until brown.
4.	Serve the patties with favorite vegan sauce.

Quinoa Broccoli Tots

Total time: 30 minutes
Ingredients
- 2 tablespoons quinoa flour
- 2 cups steamed and chopped broccoli florets
- 1/2 cup nutritional yeast
- 1 teaspoon garlic powder
- 1 teaspoon miso paste
- 2 flax eggs
- 2 tablespoons hummus

Directions:
1.	Place all the ingredients in a bowl, stir until well combined, and then shape the mixture into sixteen small balls.
2.	Arrange the balls on a baking sheet lined with parchment paper, spray with oil and bake at 400 degrees F for 20 minutes until brown, turning halfway.
3.	When done, let the tots cool for 10 minutes and then serve straight away.

Spicy Roasted Chickpeas

Total time: 30 minutes
Ingredients
- 30 ounces cooked chickpeas
- ½ teaspoon salt
- 2 teaspoons mustard powder
- ½ teaspoon cayenne pepper
- 2 tablespoons olive oil

Directions:
1.	Place all the ingredients in a bowl and stir until well coated and then spread the chickpeas in an even layer on a baking sheet greased with oil.
2.	Bake the chickpeas for 20 minutes at 400 degrees F until golden brown and crispy and then serve straight away.

Nacho Kale Chips

Total time: 14 hours 10 minutes
Ingredients
- 2 bunches of curly kale
- 2 cups cashews, soaked, drained
- 1/2 cup chopped red bell pepper
- 1 teaspoon garlic powder
- 1 teaspoon salt
- 2 tablespoons red chili powder
- 1/2 teaspoon smoked paprika
- 1/2 cup nutritional yeast
- 1 teaspoon cayenne
- 3 tablespoons lemon juice
- 3/4 cup water

Directions:
1.	Place all the ingredients except for kale in a food processor and pulse for 2 minutes until smooth.

2.	Place kale in a large bowl, pour in the blended mixture, mix until coated, and dehydrate for 14 hours at 120 degrees F until crispy.
3.	If dehydrator is not available, spread kale between two baking sheets and bake for 90 minutes at 225 degrees F until crispy, flipping halfway.
4.	When done, let chips cool for 15 minutes and then serve.

Marinated Mushrooms

Total time: 17 minutes
Ingredients
- 1/4 teaspoon dried thyme
- 1/2 teaspoon sea salt
- 1/2 teaspoon dried basil
- 1/2 teaspoon red pepper flakes
- 1/4 teaspoon dried oregano
- 1/2 teaspoon maple syrup
- 1 teaspoon minced garlic
- 1/4 cup apple cider vinegar
- 1/4 cup and 1 teaspoon olive oil
- 2 tablespoons chopped parsley
- 12 ounces small button mushrooms

Directions:
1.	Take a skillet pan, place it over medium-high heat, add 1 teaspoon oil and when hot, add mushrooms and cook for 5 minutes until golden brown.
2.	Meanwhile, prepare the marinade and for this, place remaining ingredients in a bowl and whisk until combined.
3.	When mushrooms have cooked, transfer them into the bowl of marinade and toss until well coated.
4.	Serve straight away

Hummus Quesadillas

Total time: 20 minutes
Ingredients
- 1 tortilla, whole wheat
- 1/4 cup diced roasted red peppers
- 1 cup baby spinach
- 1/3 teaspoon minced garlic
- ¼ teaspoon salt
- ¼ teaspoon ground black pepper
- 1/4 teaspoon olive oil
- 1/4 cup hummus
- Oil as needed

Directions:
1.	Place a large pan over medium heat, add oil and when hot, add red peppers and garlic, season with salt and black pepper and cook for 3 minutes until sauté.
2.	Then stir in spinach, cook for 1 minute, remove the pan from heat and transfer the mixture in a bowl.
3.	Prepare quesadilla and for this, spread hummus on one-half of the tortilla, then spread spinach mixture on it, cover the filling with the other half of the tortilla and cook in a pan for 3 minutes per side until browned.
4.	When done, cut the quesadilla into wedges and serve.

Nacho Cheese Sauce

Total time: 15 minutes
Ingredients
- 3 tablespoons flour
- 1/4 teaspoon garlic salt
- 1/4 teaspoon salt
- 1/2 teaspoon cumin
- 1/4 teaspoon paprika
- 1 teaspoon red chili powder
- 1/8 teaspoon cayenne powder
- 1 cup vegan cashew yogurt
- 1 1/4 cups vegetable broth

Directions
1. Take a small saucepan, place it over medium heat, pour in vegetable broth, and bring it to a boil.
2. Then whisk together flour and yogurt, add to the boiling broth, stir in all the spices, switch heat to medium-low level and cook for 5 minutes until thickened.
3. Serve straight away.

Salted Almonds

Total time: 25 minutes
Ingredients
- 2 cups almonds
- 4 tablespoons salt
- 1 cup boiling water

Directions:
1. Stir the salt into the boiling water in a pan, then add almonds in it and let them soak for 20 minutes.
2. Then drain the almonds, spread them in an even layer on a baking sheet lined with baking paper and sprinkle with salt.
3. Roast the almonds for 20 minutes at 300 degrees F, then cool them for 10 minutes and serve.

Pumpkin Cake Pops

Total time: 20 minutes
Ingredients
- 1 cup coconut flour
- ¼ teaspoon cinnamon
- 1/4 cup coconut sugar
- 1/4 cup chocolate chips, unsweetened
- 3/4 cup pumpkin puree

Directions:
1. Place all the ingredients in a bowl, except for chocolate chips, stir until incorporated, and then fold in chocolate chips until combined.
2. Shape the mixture into small balls, then place them on a cookie sheet greased with oil and bake for 10 minutes at 350 degrees F until done.
3. Let the balls cool completely and then serve.

Watermelon Pizza

Total time: 10 minutes
Ingredients
- 1/2 cup strawberries, halved
- 1/2 cup blueberries
- 1 watermelon
- 1/2 cup raspberries
- 1 cup of coconut yogurt
- 1/2 cup pomegranate seeds
- 1/2 cup cherries
- Maple syrup as needed

Directions:
1. Cut watermelon into 3-inch thick slices, then spread yogurt on one side, leaving some space in the edges and then top evenly with fruits and drizzle with maple syrup.
2. Cut the watermelon into wedges and then serve.

Rosemary Popcorn

Total time: 20 minutes
Ingredients
- 1/2 cup popcorn kernels
- 1/2 teaspoon sea salt
- 1 tablespoon and 1/2 teaspoon minced rosemary
- 3 tablespoons unsalted vegan butter
- 1/4 cup olive oil
- 1/3 teaspoon ground black pepper

Directions:
1. Take a pot, place it over medium-low heat, add oil and when it melts, add four kernels and wait until they sizzle.
2. Then add remaining kernel, toss until coated, add 1 tablespoon minced rosemary, shut the pot with the lid, and shake the kernels until popped completely.
3. Once all the kernels have popped, transfer them in a bowl, cook remaining rosemary into melted butter, then drizzle this mixture over popcorn and toss until well coated.
4. Season popcorn with salt and black pepper, toss until mixed and serve.

Masala Popcorn

Total time: 20 minutes
Ingredients
- 3 cups popped popcorn
- 2 hot chili peppers, sliced
- 1 teaspoon ground cumin
- 6 curry leaves
- 1 teaspoon ground coriander
- 1/3 teaspoon salt
- 1/8 teaspoon chaat masala
- 1/4 teaspoon turmeric powder
- ¼ teaspoon red pepper flakes
- 1/4 teaspoon garam masala
- 1/3 cup olive oil

Directions:
1. Take a large pot, place it over medium heat, add half of the oil and when hot, add chili peppers and curry leaves and cook for 3 minutes until golden.
2. When done, transfer curry leaves and pepper to a plate lined with paper towels and set aside until required.
3. Add remaining oil into the pot, add remaining ingredients except for popcorns, stir until mixed and cook for 1 minute until fragrant.

4.	Then tip in popcorns, remove the pan from heat, stir well until coated, and then sprinkle with bay leaves and red chili.
5.	Toss until mixed and serve straight away.

Applesauce

Total time: 25 minutes
Ingredients
*	4 pounds mixed apples, cored, ½-inch chopped
*	1 strip of orange peel, about 3-inch
*	1/2 cup coconut sugar
*	1/2 teaspoon salt
*	1 cinnamon stick, about 3-inch
*	2 tablespoons apple cider vinegar
*	Apple cider as needed for consistency of the sauce

Directions:
1.	Take a large pot, place apples in it, then add remaining ingredients except for cider, stir until mixed and cook for 15 minutes over medium heat until apples have wilted, stirring every 10 minutes.
2.	When done, remove the cinnamon stick and orange peel and puree the mixture by using an immersion blender until smooth and stir in apple cider until sauce reaches to desired consistency.
3.	Serve straight away.

Black Bean and Corn Quesadillas

Total time: 45 minutes
Ingredients
For the Black Beans and Corn:
*	1/2 of a medium white onion, peeled, chopped
*	1/2 cup cooked black beans
*	1/2 cup cooked corn kernels
*	1 teaspoon minced garlic
*	½ of jalapeno, deseeded, diced
*	1/2 teaspoon salt
*	1 teaspoon red chili powder
*	1 teaspoon cumin
*	1 tablespoon olive oil
For the Quesadillas:
*	4 large corn tortillas
*	4 green onions, chopped
*	½ cup vegan nacho cheese sauce
*	½ cup chopped cilantro
*	1 large tomato, diced
*	Salsa as needed for dipping

Directions:
1.	Prepare beans and for this, take a frying pan, place it over medium-high heat, add oil and when hot, add onion, jalapeno, and garlic and cook for 3 minutes.
2.	Then add remaining ingredients, stir until mixed and cook for 2 minutes until hot.
3.	Take a large skillet pan, place over medium heat, place the tortilla in it and cook for 1 minute until toasted and then flip it.
4.	Spread some of the cheese sauce on one half of the top, spread with beans mixture, top with cilantro, onion, and tomato and then fold the filling with the other side of the tortilla.

5.	Pat down the tortilla, cook it for 2 minutes, then carefully flip it, continue cooking for 2 minutes until hot, and then slide to a plate.
6.	Cook remaining quesadilla in the same manner, then cut them into wedges and serve.

Zaatar Popcorn

Total time: 10 minutes
Ingredients
*	8 cups popped popcorns
*	1/4 cup za'atar spice blend
*	¾ teaspoon salt
*	4 tablespoons olive oil

Directions:
1.	Place all the ingredients except for popcorns in a large bowl and whisk until combined.
2.	Then add popcorns, toss until well coated, and serve straight away.

Chocolate-Covered Almonds

Total time: 1 hour 45 minutes 30 seconds
Ingredients
*	8 ounces almonds
*	1/2 teaspoon sea salt
*	6 ounces chocolate disks, semisweet, melted

Directions:
1.	Microwave chocolate in a heatproof bowl for 30 seconds until it melts, then dip almonds in it, four at a time, and place them on a baking sheet.
2.	Let almonds stand for 1 hour until hardened, then sprinkle with salt, and cool them in the refrigerator for 30 minutes.
3.	Serve straight away.

Beans and Spinach Tacos

Total time: 25 minutes
Ingredients
*	12 ounces spinach
*	4 tablespoons cooked kidney beans
*	½ of medium red onion, peeled, chopped
*	½ teaspoon minced garlic
*	1 medium tomato, chopped
*	3 tablespoons chopped parsley
*	½ of avocado, sliced
*	½ teaspoon ground black pepper
*	1 teaspoon salt
*	2 tablespoons olive oil
*	4 slices of vegan brie cheese
*	4 tortillas, about 6-inches

Directions:
1.	Take a skillet pan, place it over medium heat, add oil and when hot, add onion and cook for 10 minutes until softened.
2.	Then stir in spinach, cook for 4 minutes until its leaves wilts, then drain it and distribute evenly between tortillas.
3.	Top evenly with remaining ingredients, season with black pepper and salt, drizzle with lemon juice and then serve.

Zucchini and Amaranth Patties

Total time: 40 minutes

Ingredients
- 1 1/2 cups shredded zucchini
- ½ of a medium onion, shredded
- 1 1/2 cups cooked white beans
- 1/2 cup amaranth seeds
- 1 teaspoon red chili powder
- 1/2 teaspoon cumin
- 1/2 cup cornmeal
- 1/4 cup flax meal
- 1 tablespoon salsa
- 1 1/2 cups vegetable broth

Directions:
1. Stir together stock and amaranth on a pot, bring it to a boil over medium-high heat, then switch heat to medium-low level and simmer until all the liquid is absorbed.
2. Mash the white beans in a bowl, add remaining ingredients including cooked amaranth and stir until well mixed.
3. Shape the mixture into patties, then place them on a baking sheet lined with parchment sheet and bake for 30 minutes until browned and crispy, turning halfway.
4. Serve straight away.

Rice Pizza

Total time: 45 minutes
Ingredients
For the Crust:
- 1 1/2 cup short-grain rice, cooked
- 1/2 teaspoon garlic powder
- 1 teaspoon coconut sugar
- 1 tablespoon red chili flakes

For the Sauce:
- 1/4 teaspoon onion powder
- 1 tablespoon nutritional yeast
- 1/4 teaspoon garlic powder
- 1/4 teaspoon ginger powder
- 1 tablespoon red chili flakes
- 1 teaspoon soy sauce
- 1/2 cup tomato purée

For the Toppings:
- 2 1/2 cups oyster mushrooms
- 1 chili pepper, deseeded, sliced
- 2 scallions, sliced
- 1 teaspoon coconut sugar
- 1 teaspoon soy sauce
- Baby corn as needed

Directions:
1. Prepare the crust and for this, place all of its ingredients in a bowl and stir until well combined.
2. Then take a pizza pan, line it with parchment sheet, place rice mixture in it, spread it evenly, and then bake for 20 minutes at 350 degrees F.
3. Then spread tomato sauce over the crust, top evenly with remaining ingredients for the topping and continue baking for 15 minutes.
4. When done, slice the pizza into wedges and serve.

Loaded Baked Potatoes

Total time: 42 minutes
Ingredients
- 1/2 cup cooked chickpeas
- 2 medium potatoes, scrubbed
- 1 cup broccoli florets, steamed
- 1/4 cup vegan bacon bits
- 2 tablespoons all-purpose seasoning
- ¼ cup vegan cheese sauce
- 1/2 cup vegan sour cream

Directions:
1. Pierce hole in the potatoes, microwave them for 12 minutes over high heat setting until soft to touch, and then bake them for 20 minutes at 450 degrees F until very tender.
2. Open the potatoes, mash the flesh with a fork, then top evenly with remaining ingredients and serve.

Coconut Rice

Total time: 25 minutes
Ingredients
- 1 1/2 cups white rice
- 1 teaspoon coconut sugar
- 1/8 teaspoon salt
- 14 ounces coconut milk, unsweetened
- 1 1/4 cups water

Directions:
1. Take a saucepan, place it over medium heat, add all the ingredients in it, stir well and bring the mixture to a boil.
2. Switch heat to medium-low level, simmer the rice for 20 minutes until tender, and then serve straight away.

Potato Chips

Total time: 30 minutes
Ingredients
- 3 medium potatoes, scrubbed, thinly sliced, soaked in warm water for 10 min
- ½ teaspoon garlic powder
- ½ teaspoon onion powder
- ½ teaspoon red chili powder
- ½ teaspoon curry powder
- 1 teaspoon of sea salt
- 1 tablespoon apple cider vinegar
- 2 tablespoons olive oil

Directions:
1. Drain the potato slices, pat dry, then place them in a large bowl, add remaining ingredients and toss until well coated.
2. Spread the potatoes in a single layer on a baking sheet and bake for 20 minutes until crispy, turning halfway.
3. Serve straight away.

Spinach and Artichoke Dip

Total time: 35 minutes
Ingredients
- 28 ounces artichokes
- 1 small white onion, peeled, diced
- 1 1/2 cups cashews, soaked, drained
- 4 cups spinach

- 4 cloves of garlic, peeled
- 1 1 1/2 teaspoons salt
- 1/4 cup nutritional yeast
- 1 tablespoon olive oil
- 2 tablespoons lemon juice
- 1 1/2 cups coconut milk, unsweetened

Directions:
1. Cook onion and garlic in hot oil for 3 minutes until saute and then set aside until required.
2. Place cashews in a food processor; add 1 teaspoon salt, yeast, milk, and lemon juice and pulse until smooth.
3. Add spinach, onion mixture, and artichokes and pulse until the chunky mixture comes together.
4. Tip the dip in a heatproof dish and bake for 20 minutes at 425 degrees F until the top is browned and dip bubbles.
5. Serve straight away with vegetable sticks.

Avocado Toast with Herbs and Peas

Total time: 10 minutes
Ingredients
- ½ of a medium avocado, peeled, pitted, mashed
- 6 slices of radish
- 2 tablespoons baby peas
- ¼ teaspoon ground black pepper
- 1 teaspoon chopped basil
- ¼ teaspoon salt
- 1/2 lemon, juiced
- 1 slice of bread, whole-grain, toasted

Directions:
1. Spread mashed avocado on the one side of the toast and then top with peas, pressing them into the avocado.
2. Layer the toast with radish slices, season with salt and black pepper, sprinkle with basil, and drizzle with lemon juice.
3. Serve straight away.

Oven-Dried Grapes

Total time: 4 hours 5 minutes
Ingredients
- 3 large bunches of grapes, seedless
- Olive oil as needed for greasing

Directions:
1. Spread grapes into two greased baking sheets and bake for 4 hours at 225 degrees F until semi-dried.
2. When done, let the grape cool completely and then serve.

Queso Dip

Total time: 5 minutes
Ingredients
- 1 cup cashews
- ½ teaspoon minced garlic
- 1/2 teaspoon salt
- 1/2 teaspoon ground cumin
- 1 teaspoon red chili powder
- 2 tablespoons nutritional yeast
- 1 tablespoon harissa
- 1 cup hot water

Directions:
1. Place all the ingredients in a food processor and pulse for 2 minutes until smooth and well combined.
2. Tip the dip in a bowl, taste to adjust seasoning and then serve.

Nooch Popcorn

Total time: 20 minutes
Ingredients
- 1/3 cup nutritional yeast
- 1 teaspoon of sea salt
- 3 tablespoons coconut oil
- ½ cup popcorn kernels

Directions:
1. Place yeast in a large bowl, stir in salt, and set aside until required.
2. Take a medium saucepan, place it over medium-high heat, add oil and when it melts, add four kernels and wait until they sizzle.
3. Then add remaining kernel, toss until coated, shut the pan with the lid, and shake the kernels until popped completely.
4. When done, transfer popcorns tot eh yeast mixture, shut with lid and shape well until coated.
5. Serve straight away

Honey-Almond Popcorn

Total time: 15 minutes
Ingredients
- 1/2 cup popcorn kernels
- 2 tablespoons honey
- 1/2 teaspoon sea salt
- 2 tablespoons coconut sugar
- 1 cup roasted almonds
- 1/4 cup walnut oil

Directions:
1. Take a pot, place it over medium-low heat, add oil and when it melts, add four kernels and wait until they sizzle.
2. Then add remaining kernel, toss until coated, sprinkle with sugar, drizzle with honey, shut the pot with the lid, and shake the kernels until popped completely, adding almonds halfway.
3. Once all the kernels have popped, season them with salt and serve straight away.

Turmeric Snack Bites

Total time: 35 minutes
Ingredients
- 1 cup Medjool dates, pitted, chopped
- 1/2 cup walnuts
- 1 teaspoon ground turmeric
- 1 tablespoon cocoa powder, unsweetened
- 1/2 teaspoon cinnamon
- 1/2 cup shredded coconut, unsweetened

Directions:
1. Place all the ingredients in a food processor and pulse for 2 minutes until a smooth mixture comes together.
2. Tip the mixture in a bowl and then shape it into ten small balls, 1 tablespoon of the mixture per ball and then refrigerate for 30 minutes.

3.	Serve straight away.

Avocado Tomato Bruschetta

Total time: 10 minutes
Ingredients
- 3 slices of whole-grain bread
- 6 chopped cherry tomatoes
- ½ of sliced avocado
- ½ teaspoon minced garlic
- ½ teaspoon ground black pepper
- 2 tablespoons chopped basil
- ½ teaspoon of sea salt
- 1 teaspoon balsamic vinegar

Directions:
1.	Place tomatoes in a bowl, and then stir in vinegar until mixed.
2.	Top bread slices with avocado slices, then top evenly with tomato mixture, garlic and basil, and season with salt and black pepper.
3.	Serve straight away

Cinnamon Bananas

Total time: 13 minutes
Ingredients
- 2 bananas, peeled, sliced
- 1 teaspoon cinnamon
- 2 tablespoons granulated Splenda
- 1/4 teaspoon nutmeg

Directions
1.	Prepare the cinnamon mixture and for this, place all the ingredients in a bowl, except for banana, and stir until mixed.
2.	Take a large skillet pan, place it over medium heat, spray with oil, add banana slices and sprinkle with half of the prepared cinnamon mixture.
3.	Cook for 3 minutes, then sprinkle with remaining prepared cinnamon mixture and continue cooking for 3 minutes until tender and hot.
4.	Serve straight away.

Red Salsa

Total time: 10 minutes
Ingredients
- 30 ounces diced fire-roasted tomatoes
- 4 tablespoons diced green chilies
- 1 medium jalapeño pepper, deseeded
- 1/2 cup chopped green onion
- 1 cup chopped cilantro
- 1 teaspoon minced garlic
- ½ teaspoon of sea salt
- 1 teaspoon ground cumin
- ¼ teaspoon stevia
- 3 tablespoons lime juice

Directions:
1.	Place all the ingredients in a food processor and process for 2 minutes until smooth.
2.	Tip the salsa in a bowl, taste to adjust seasoning and then serve.

Tomato Hummus

Total time: 5 minutes
Ingredients
- 1/4 cup sun-dried tomatoes, without oil
- 1 ½ cups cooked chickpeas
- 1 teaspoon minced garlic
- 1/2 teaspoon salt
- 2 tablespoons sesame oil
- 1 tablespoon lemon juice
- 1 tablespoon olive oil
- 1/4 cup of water

Directions:
1.	Place all the ingredients in a food processor and process for 2 minutes until smooth.
2.	Tip the hummus in a bowl, drizzle with more oil, and then serve straight away.

Zucchini Chips

Total time: 130 minutes
Ingredients
- 1 large zucchini, thinly sliced
- 1 teaspoon salt
- 2 tablespoons olive oil

Directions:
1.	Pat dry zucchini slices and then spread them in an even layer on a baking sheet lined with parchment sheet.
2.	Whisk together salt and oil, brush this mixture over zucchini slices on both sides and then bake for 2 hours or more until brown and crispy.
3.	When done, let the chips cool for 10 minutes and then serve straight away.

Rosemary Beet Chips

Total time: 30 minutes
Ingredients
- 3 large beets, scrubbed, thinly sliced
- 1/8 teaspoon ground black pepper
- ¼ teaspoon of sea salt
- 3 sprigs of rosemary, leaves chopped
- 4 tablespoons olive oil

Directions:
1.	Spread beet slices in a single layer between two large baking sheets, brush the slices with oil, then season with spices and rosemary, toss until well coated, and bake for 20 minutes at 375 degrees F until crispy, turning halfway.
2.	When done, let the chips cool for 10 minutes and then serve.

Tomato and Pesto Toast

Total time: 5 minutes
Ingredients
- 1 small tomato, sliced
- ¼ teaspoon ground black pepper
- 1 tablespoon vegan pesto
- 2 tablespoons hummus
- 1 slice of whole-grain bread, toasted
- Hemp seeds as needed for garnishing

Directions:
1.	Spread hummus on one side of the toast, top with tomato slices and then drizzle with pesto.
2.	Sprinkle black pepper on the toast along with hemp seeds and then serve straight away.

Avocado and Sprout Toast

Total time: 5 minutes

Ingredients
- 1/2 of a medium avocado, sliced
- 1 slice of whole-grain bread, toasted
- 2 tablespoons sprouts
- 2 tablespoons hummus
- ¼ teaspoon lemon zest
- ½ teaspoon hemp seeds
- ¼ teaspoon red pepper flakes

Directions:
1. Spread hummus on one side of the toast and then top with avocado slices and sprouts.
2. Sprinkle with lemon zest, hemp seeds, and red pepper flakes and then serve straight away.

Zucchini Hummus

Total time: 5 minutes

Ingredients
- 1 cup diced zucchini
- 1/2 teaspoon sea salt
- 1 teaspoon minced garlic
- 2 teaspoons ground cumin
- 3 tablespoons lemon juice
- 1/3 cup tahini

Directions:
1. Place all the ingredients in a food processor and pulse for 2 minutes until smooth.
2. Tip the hummus in a bowl, drizzle with oil and serve.

Chipotle and Lime Tortilla Chips

Total time: 25 minutes

Ingredients
- 12 ounces whole-wheat tortillas
- 4 tablespoons chipotle seasoning
- 1 tablespoon olive oil
- 4 limes, juiced

Directions:
1. Whisk together oil and lime juice, brush it well on tortillas, then sprinkle with chipotle seasoning and bake for 15 minutes at 350 degrees F until crispy, turning halfway.
2. When done, let the tortilla cool for 10 minutes, then break it into chips and serve.

ENTRÉES

BLT Panini with Eggplant "Bacon"

Preparation Time: 10 minutes
Cooking Time: 25 minutes
Servings: 2
Ingredients:

- Eggplant, medium – 1
- Tomato, sliced into rounds – 1
- Cucumber, medium, sliced into rounds - .5
- Arugula lettuce - .5 cup
- Vegan mayonnaise – 2 tablespoons
- Ciabatta buns – 2
- Tamari sauce – 1 tablespoon
- Sea salt - 1.25 teaspoon
- Maple syrup – 1 teaspoon
- Olive oil – 1 tablespoon
- Paprika, smoked – 1 teaspoon
- Black pepper, ground - .25 teaspoon

Directions:

1. Peel the eggplant, slice it into rounds, and soak it in salt water made with one teaspoon of the sea salt. Allow the eggplant to sit in the saltwater for ten minutes. Remove the eggplant from the saltwater once soaked for the ten-minute duration and then pat it dry with a clean kitchen towel.
2. In a small bowl whisk together the tamari sauce, sea salt, maple syrup, olive oil, smoked paprika, and ground black pepper.
3. Place the eggplant slices on a baking sheet. Use the combined sauce and with a pastry brush cover it over the eggplant slices on all sides. Bake the eggplant slices until tender, for about twenty minutes in a large oven preheated to a temperature of three-hundred- and seventy-five-degrees Fahrenheit.
4. Once the eggplant is done cooking prepare your panini. Begin by slicing the ciabatta rolls in half. Spread the inside of the rolls with vegan mayonnaise before topping with the eggplant "bacon," tomato, cucumber, and lastly the arugula. Close the sandwich with the top half of the rolls.
5. Wrap the sandwiches in aluminum foil before placing them in a panini grill. However, if you do not have a panini grill, you can do this in a large skillet by weighing down the sandwich with a heavy pan, such as a small cast iron pan.
6. Allow the sandwiches to grill until warm and crispy, about three to four minutes. Enjoy the sandwich immediately, or leave it in the aluminum foil to take on-the-go.

Nutrition: Number of Calories in Individual **Servings:** 364 Protein Grams: 10 Fat Grams: 14 Total Carbohydrates Grams: 51 Net Carbohydrates Grams: 41

Veggie Hummus Wraps

Preparation Time: 10 minutes
Cooking Time: 6 minutes
Servings: 2
Ingredients:

- Zucchini, peeled, sliced lengthwise into .25-inch-thick strips – 1
- Sea salt - .5 teaspoon
- Tomato, sliced – 1
- Kale, chopped – 1 cup
- Red onion, sliced - .125 cup
- Avocado, sliced – 1
- Olive oil – 1 tablespoon
- Black pepper, ground - .25 teaspoon
- Apple cider vinegar – 2 teaspoons
- Water – 1 tablespoon
- Hummus - .25 cup
- Whole-wheat tortillas, large – 2

Directions:

1. Heat a large non-stick skillet or grill pan on the stove over medium heat. Meanwhile, coat the sliced zucchini with the olive oil, ground black pepper, and sea salt.
2. Place the seasoned zucchini on the preheated pan and let it cook on the first side for three minutes, flip it over, and cook for an additional two minutes. Remove the zucchini from the heat of the stove and set it aside.
3. Set the whole-wheat tortillas in the hot pan and allow them to toast for a minute. You want the tortillas to be lightly toasted, warm, and easy to wrap without tearing.
4. Combine the apple cider vinegar and water, then toss the avocado in the mixture. This will help prevent the avocado from browning. Drain off any excess liquid.
5. Divide the ingredients in half, so that you can fill both tortillas with an even amount of ingredients. To prepare spread the hummus down the center of the warm tortilla, top with the zucchini, tomato, red onion, kale, and avocado.
6. Wrap in the ends of the tortillas and then tightly wrap the sides around the filling. By folding it this way, you will prevent the filling from falling out. Serve immediately or store in the fridge until lunchtime.

Nutrition: Number of Calories in Individual **Servings:** 438 Protein Grams: 9 Fat Grams: 28 Total Carbohydrates Grams: 40 Net Carbohydrates Grams: 36

Quick and Easy Curry

Preparation Time: 10 minutes
Cooking Time: 25 minutes
Servings: 4
Ingredients:

- Bell peppers, red, thinly sliced – 2
- Chickpeas, cooked, liquid drained off – 2.5 cups or a 19 ounce can
- Broccoli florets, roughly chopped – 4 cups
- Onion, diced – 1
- Light coconut milk – 14 ounces
- Maple syrup – 1 teaspoon
- Sea salt – 1 teaspoon
- Tamari sauce – 1 tablespoon
- Garlic, minced – 4 cloves
- Cumin – 1 tablespoon

- Curry powder – 1 tablespoon
- Black pepper, ground - .25 teaspoon
- Water - .25 cup

Directions:

1. Place all of the vegetables and the water into a large non-stick skillet and allow them to cook together over a temperature of medium-high heat for three minutes.

2. Add the remaining ingredients and continue to cook the curry for seven to eight minutes, until the vegetables are tender but still have a little bite. You don't want to overcook the vegetables until they become mush, as they are best with their texture intact.

3. Remove the curry from the heat, give it a good stir, and serve it with your favorite cooked grains or pasta.

Nutrition: Number of Calories in Individual **Servings:** 342 Protein Grams: 15 Fat Grams: 6 Total Carbohydrates Grams: 52 Net Carbohydrates Grams: 39

Chickpea Avocado Salad Sandwiches

Preparation Time: 10 minutes
Cooking Time: 0 minutes
Servings: 4
Ingredients:

- Chickpeas, liquid drained, rinsed – 15 ounce can (1.5 cups)
- Red onion, diced - .5 cup
- Lemon juice – 2 tablespoons
- Cilantro, fresh, chopped - .25 cup
- Thyme, fresh, chopped – 1 tablespoon
- Avocado, diced – 1 cup
- Red grapes, sliced in half - .5 cup
- Celery, finely sliced - .25 cup
- Sea salt – 1 teaspoon
- Whole-wheat bread – 6 slices

Directions:

1. Place the drained and rinse chickpeas and the diced avocado in a medium-sized bowl for the purpose of mixing. Using a fork or potato masher smash the ingredients together until you form a chunky and creamy mixture. You can do this to your preference, either leaving the chickpeas mostly whole or smashing them until they are mostly creamy.

2. Add the red onion, lemon juice, fresh cilantro, fresh thyme, red grapes, celery, and sea salt to the bowl and stir all of the ingredients together until combined.

3. Divide the chickpea salad mixture between three slices of bread, and then top it off with the remaining three slices. Of course, you can always save the mixture in the fridge for another day, and then assemble your sandwiches on the day you plan to consume them. Don't fill your sandwiches with the filling more than a day ahead of time, as you don't want soggy bread.

Nutrition: Number of Calories in Individual **Servings:** 486 Protein Grams: 16 Fat Grams: 13 Total Carbohydrates Grams: 80 Net Carbohydrates Grams: 65

Italian "Meatball" Subs

Preparation Time: 5 minutes
Cooking Time: 55 minutes
Servings: 4
Ingredients:

- Chickpeas, liquid drained, rinsed – 15 ounces (1.5 cups)
- Bread crumbs - .25 cup
- Flaxseed, ground – 1.5 tablespoons
- Water, warm - .25 cup
- Nutritional yeast – 2 tablespoons
- Italian seasoning - .5 teaspoon
- Sea salt - .5 teaspoon
- Garlic powder – 2 teaspoons
- Sub rolls, medium – 3
- Vegan mozzarella cheese, shredded (such as Daiya or homemade) - .75 cup
- Marinara sauce – 1 cup

Directions:

1. Preheat your large oven to a temperature of Fahrenheit four-hundred and twenty-five degrees. Meanwhile, assemble your chickpea "meatballs."

2. In a medium-sized bowl for the purpose of mixing whisk together the warm water and flaxseed until all of the clumps are gone. Allow it to sit for five minutes.

3. Meanwhile, place the chickpeas in the food processor with the standard blade and pulse them until they are finely ground with no whole beans remaining. Place the chickpea meal into the bowl with the flaxseed mixture.

4. Add the sea salt, bread crumbs, Italian seasoning, nutritional yeast, and garlic powder to the chickpea and flaxseed bowl, combining the ingredients together completely with a spoon.

5. Using a mini cookie scoop or tablespoon measure out evenly sized "meatballs" with the mixture, rolling them into balls in the palms of your hands. Place these prepared meatballs on a baking sheet lined with kitchen parchment and allow them to cook in the hot oven for fifteen minutes before turning the pan around and cooking for an additional fifteen minutes.

6. Reduce the oven temperature to that of Fahrenheit four-hundred degrees.

7. Place the cooked meatballs in a large saucepan and add in the marinara sauce, heating it on a stove burner set to medium-low heat until the sauce is hot all the way through. Occasionally stir the chickpea meatballs in the marinara sauce so that they are evenly coated.

8. Fill the sub rolls with the meatballs and sauce, top them with the dairy-free cheese, and place them in the hot often on the baking sheet for fifteen minutes, or until the dairy-free cheese is melted and the bread is warm. Enjoy the subs hot and fresh from the oven.

Nutrition: Number of Calories in Individual **Servings:** 376 Protein Grams: 16 Fat Grams: 9 Total Carbohydrates Grams: 57 Net Carbohydrates Grams: 67

Sundried Tomato and Mushroom Penne Pasta

Preparation Time: 10 minutes
Cooking Time: 20 minutes
Servings: 4
Ingredients:

- Penne pasta, uncooked – 250 grams
- Corn starch – 2.5 tablespoons
- Olive oil – 4 teaspoons
- Garlic, minced – 6 cloves
- Sundried tomatoes, drained from the oil - .75 cup
- Soy milk (or almond), unsweetened – 2 cups
- Onion, diced – 1
- Oregano, dried -.5 teaspoon
- Nutritional yeast – 1 tablespoon
- Sea salt – 1 teaspoon
- Mushrooms, sliced – 1.5 cups
- Chili flakes – 1 teaspoon
- Black pepper, ground - .25 teaspoon

Directions:

1. Place the pasta in a large pot of salted boiling water and cook it according to the individual brand's instructions, but don't cook it quite all the way. Instead, allow the pasta to remain slightly under-cooked, as you will finish cooking it later on. Drain the pasta, reserving the pasta water.
2. Place a large frying pan on the large burner of your stove surface and set it to a medium temperature. Add in three teaspoons of the olive oil and the mushrooms, cooking for two minutes before adding in the garlic. Cook for an additional two minutes, until the mushrooms, are tender, and the garlic is fragrant.
3. Remove the mushrooms and garlic from the skillet and set them aside.
4. Add the corn starch, sea salt, and half of the soy milk into the hot skillet. Use a whisk to make sure that there are no clumps of corn starch and that the sauce is smooth. Once thickened, add the remaining soy milk and whisk again.
5. Into a blender pour the hot sauce mixture, nutritional yeast, half of the sundried tomatoes, and .33 cup of the hot pasta water. Blend the mixture on medium to high speed, being sure that it does not overflow from the heat buildup. Once blended smooth set the sauce aside.
6. Rinse out the previously used skillet and then add in the remaining teaspoon of olive oil. Chop the remaining sundried tomatoes and add them into the skillet along with the diced onion, allowing them to cook for three minutes until the onion becomes translucent. Add in the dried oregano and chili flakes, cooking the skillet for an additional minute until fragrant. If the ingredients begin to stick to the skillet simply add in a small amount of the reserved pasta water.
7. Add the prepared sauce into the skillet with the onion and sundried tomatoes, stirring all of the ingredients together. Add in the pasta, coating it in the sauce and adding any pasta water if you need to loosen the sauce.
8. Continue to cook the ingredients together until the pasta is al dente and then serve.

Nutrition: Number of Calories in Individual **Servings:** 350 Protein Grams: 14 Fat Grams: 8 Total Carbohydrates Grams: 55 Net Carbohydrates Grams: 50

ASIAN RECIPES

Goulash Soup

Preparation Time: 10 Minutes
Cooking Time: 35 Minutes
Servings: 7
Ingredients:
- 1/2 t. black pepper
o oz. tomatoes, diced
- 8 little rutabagas, chopped into 1/2 inch chunks
- 1/4 c. dry red wine 4 tablespoon paprika
- 1 t. salt
- 3 c. vegetable broth
- 6 cloves of garlic, minced
- 2 red bell peppers, chopped 2 c. onion, finely chopped

Directions:
1. Prior to starting, ensure that you have all the vegetables washed and chopped. This recipe moves very quickly.
2. In a pot that is big enough for 7, add the onion, garlic, and bell pepper after it has warmed in a medium heat setting.
3. Add to the pot 1/2 teaspoon of salt and 1 cup of the broth. Wait for it to bubble and then leave it cooking until the broth is gone. This usually just takes about 8 minutes.
4. Lower the temperature, and add the wine when most of the broth has evaporated. Add the paprika. Let the flavor seep in for a couple of minutes or a bit more.
5. Next, add the rest of the salt, pepper, tomatoes, rutabagas, and 1 1/2 cup of broth. If you would like your dish to become saucier, add in the additional broth.
6. Cook for 20 minutes or until the rutabaga is tender.
Nutrition: Calories: 267 Carbohydrates: 51.7 g
Proteins: 11.7 g Fats: 3.1 g

Celery Dill Soup

Preparation Time: 10-15 minutes
Cooking Time: 35 minutes
Servings: 4
Ingredients:
- 3 t. olive oil
- 1/2 c. pickle juice
- 1/2 onion, chopped
- 1/2 t. xanthan gum
- 1/4 c dill pickle, finely chopped 1 stalk celery, chopped
- 1/4 c. vegetable broth 1 t. of the following:
- Parsley
- Garlic, minced
- 1 tablespoon. ghee
- 1/2 c. vegan bacon, crumbled

Directions:
1. Before beginning, ensure you have chopped all vegetables. In a big saucepan, melt ghee and garlic.
2. Add in the chopped pickles, onion, celery, and parsley and sauté for 5 minutes. Next, add vegetable broth and pickle juice and bring to a boil.
3. In a little bowl, whisk together xanthan gum and olive oil then pour into the soup. Continue to stir the soup frequently as it thickens.
4. Once thick, add crumbled bacon and serve.
Nutrition: Calories: 176 Carbohydrates: 30.2 g
Proteins: 5.6 g Fats: 13.6 g

Broccoli Fennel Soup

Preparation Time: 10-15 minutes
Cooking Time: 35 minutes
Servings: 4
Ingredients:
- 2 1/2 c. kale
- 2 tablespoon lemon juice 3 c. water
- 1/2 c. cashews
- 1 medium onion, chopped 5 cloves garlic, minced
- 2 tablespoon olive oil
- 2 c. fennel, chopped 4 c. broccoli florets

Directions:
1. Bring the oven to 400 heat setting.
2. Prepare a cookie sheet by lining it with paper.
3. Spread the florets and fennel on the cookie sheet; be careful not to overlap them and drizzle with 1 tablespoon of olive oil.
4. Place in the oven and roast for 10 minutes then flip and roast for another 10 minutes. While it is roasting, bring a heat a saucepan over medium-low heat.
5. Add in the remaining olive oil, and sauté the garlic for about 3 minutes; add in the onion and sauté for an additional 3 minutes.
6. After broccoli and fennel are finished roasting, add to the pan with the onion and garlic; mix thoroughly.
7. Finally, add the kale, lemon juice, water, and cashews. Simmer this for approximately 5 minutes.
8. Remove it from the stove and then blend using a machine you prefer, as long as it gets smooth.
9. Dust some salt and pepper or not, if you don't like additional salt. Serve.
Nutrition: Calories: 242 Carbohydrates: 23.2 g
Proteins: 7.6 g Fats: 15.4 g

Broccoli and Cauliflower Soup

Preparation Time: 10-15 minutes
Cooking Time: 35 minutes
Servings: 8
Ingredients:
- 1 tablespoon lemon juice 1 1/2 t. salt
- 1/3 c. nutritional yeast
- 1 c. almond milk, unsweetened 4 c. vegetable broth
- 1/4 c. almond flour
- 4 c. cauliflower, finely chopped
- 4 c. broccoli, finely chopped 2 carrots, diced

- 2 cloves garlic, minced 1 onion, chopped
- 2 tablespoon extra virgin olive oil

Directions:

1. Pour some olive oil to a big-enough saucepan that has warmed using the medium heat setting. Sauté for more than a couple of minutes the garlic, onion, and seasonings.
2. Add the chopped veggies (carrots, cauliflower, and broccoli) and sauté for another 5 minutes. Next, add in the flour and stir to combine.
3. Once combined, add in the nutritional yeast, milk, and broth and then wait for it to boil just before turning the heat setting to medium-low.
4. While covered, let it simmer for about a quarter of an hour or less. Stir once in a while as you wait.
5. Remove from the heat and add in lemon juice. Using a hand blender, blend the soup contents until your desired level of chunkiness.
6. Dust with some salt and pepper to your taste and serve.

Nutrition: Calories: 204 Carbohydrates: 14.7 g Proteins: 9.5 g Fats: 13.6 g

Keto-Vegan Chili

Preparation Time: 10-15 minutes
Cooking Time: 41 minutes
Servings: 6
Ingredients:

- 1 tablespoon cocoa powder, unsweetened 1 c. raw walnuts
- 16 oz. tofu, extra firm
- 1/2 c. coconut milk 3 c. water
- 15 oz. diced tomatoes 1 1/2 tablespoon tomato paste
- 8 oz. cremini mushrooms 2 zucchini, diced
- 2 green bell peppers, diced
- 2 chipotle peppers in adobo sauce, minced 1 ½ t. paprika
- 4 t. cumin
- 2 t. chili powder
- 1 1/2 t. cinnamon, ground 2 cloves garlic
- 5 stalks celery, diced
- 2 tablespoon extra-virgin olive oil
- Salt and pepper to taste

Directions:

1. Prepare the tofu by taking it out of the package and blotting with a paper towel until most of the moisture is gone.
2. Bring a skillet to medium heat; crumble the tofu and cook until browned.
3. In a big saucepan, heat the olive oil under medium heat, add celery, and cook for 4 minutes.
4. Add the celery, paprika, cumin, chili powder, cinnamon, and garlic and sauté for 2 minutes.
5. Next, add the mushrooms, zucchini, and bell peppers and cook for approximately 5 minutes.
6. In the big saucepan add cocoa powder, walnuts, tofu, coconut milk, water, tomatoes, tomato paste, and chipotle and simmer for 20-25 minutes or until thick.
7. Dust with some salt and pepper according to preference.

Nutrition: Calories: 294 Carbohydrates: 17.1 g Proteins: 10.6 g Fats: 23.7 g

Creamy Avocado Soup

Preparation Time: 10-15 minutes
Cooking Time: 46 minutes
Servings: 3
Ingredients:

- 1/3 c. cilantro
- 1/8 t. black pepper
- 1/4 t. salt
- 1 lime, juiced
- 1/3 c. coconut milk
- 1/2 c. vegetable stock
- 1/4 c. cucumber 2 cloves garlic
- 2 avocados

Directions:

1. In a blender, add avocado, cucumber, lime juice, cilantro, coconut milk, vegetable stock, and garlic.
2. Blend until completely smooth. If you prefer a thinner soup, add additional vegetable stock.
3. Transfer to a big serving bowl and refrigerate for 30 minutes. Dust some salt and pepper to your taste and serve.

Nutrition: Calories: 226.3 Carbohydrates: 5.8 g Proteins: 3.3 g Fats: 20 g

Red Onion Soup

Preparation Time: 10-15 minutes
Cooking Time: 20 minutes
Servings: 2
Ingredients:

- 2 t. pesto
- 4 tablespoon walnuts
- 5 tablespoon olive oil
- 2 tablespoon lemon juice
- 2 1/2 c. vegetable broth 2 cloves garlic, minced
- 2 red onions
- 1 t. oregano

Directions:

1. Begin by cutting the onion into thin rings and set to the side. In a big pot, add garlic and onions and sauté for 5 minutes.
2. Add in the vegetable broth, oregano, and lemon juice and bring to a simmer for approximately 10 minutes, stirring occasionally.
3. In a skillet, add some olive oil and walnuts; fry for 3 minutes until toasted. Then add to the soup.
4. Finally, add the rest of the seasoning, including the pesto, according to your preference. Serve piping hot.

Nutrition: Calories: 521 Carbohydrates: 15.1 g Proteins: 11.9 g Fats: 48.4 g

Thai Pumpkin Soup

Preparation Time: 10-15 minutes
Cooking Time: 20 minutes
Servings: 4
Ingredients:

- 1 red chili pepper sliced
- oz. coconut milk

- 30 oz. pumpkin puree, can 4 c. vegetable broth
- 2 tablespoon red curry paste

Directions:
1. Sit a big saucepan over medium heat; cook the curry paste for about 60 seconds or until the kitchen smells like curry heaven.
2. Pour in the broth, including the pumpkin, stirring to integrate the flavors.
3. Under the same heat setting, wait for the soup to bubble slightly. That's your cue to add the coconut
4. Milk. When combined, cook for about 3 minutes.
5. Finally, add to individual bowls and garnish with sliced red chili pepper. Enjoy hot.

Nutrition: Calories: 361 Carbohydrates: 24.9 g Proteins: 9.4 g Fats: 27 g

Zucchini Basil Soup

Preparation Time: 10-15 minutes
Cooking Time: 20 minutes
Servings: 4
Ingredients:
- 1 c. basil leaves
- 3/4 t. salt 2 c. water
- 4 cloves garlic
- 1 1/2 pound sliced zucchini
- 1/2 t. apple cider vinegar
- 2 tablespoon olive oil 1 onion, diced

Directions:
1. Place a medium-size saucepan over medium-high heat. Sauté the onions and garlic for 2 minutes.
2. Add zucchini and water to the pan and bring to a simmer, cover, and cook for 15 minutes, stirring occasionally.
3. Remove from the heat, and using a hand blender, carefully add in the basil and blend until smooth. Once smooth, add in vinegar and salt and pepper to taste.
4. Finally, add to individual bowls and enjoy.

Nutrition: Calories: 200 Carbohydrates: 18 g Proteins: 3 g Fats: 14.3 g

Tomato Cream Soup With Dried Tomatoes

Preparation Time: 10-20 Minutes
Cooking Time: 40 Minutes
Servings: 5
Ingredients:
- 185g potatoes
- 50g Celery
- 110g Carrots
- 130g Onion
- 450g Tomatoes
- 85g Dried tomatoes in olive oil
- 650ml Water
- 15g Garlic
- 65ml Olive oil
- Black pepper ground to taste
- Salt to taste

Directions:
1. In a large pot, heat the olive oil, fry the garlic and basil so that they give the juice back.
2. Cut potatoes, celery, carrots and onions into large cubes, put the vegetables into a pot and stew for 10 minutes over medium heat.
3. Cut tomatoes into four parts and add to the vegetables, stew until the tomatoes give away almost all the juice.
4. Then add the dried tomatoes, Napoli sauce, salt, and pepper, and pour water. Stew until the vegetables are fully cooked, then punch everything in the blender.
5. Serve ready, warm soup with olive oil and basil leaves.

Nutrition: Calories: 236kcal Protein: 4.7 grams Total Fat: 14.4 grams Carbohydrates: 23.6 grams

NUTRIENT-PACKED PROTEIN SALAD RECIPES

Quinoa & Chickpea Salad

Preparation Time: 20 Minutes
Cooking Time: 0 Minutes
Servings: 4
Ingredients:
- 2 cups cooked quinoa
- 1½ cups canned red kidney beans, rinsed and drained
- 3 cups fresh baby spinach
- ¼ cup sun-dried tomatoes, chopped
- ¼ cup fresh dill
- ¼ cup fresh parsley
- ½ cup sunflower seeds
- ¼ cup walnuts, chopped
- 3 tablespoons fresh lemon juice
- Salt and ground black pepper, as required

Directions:
1. In a large bowl, add all the Ingredients and toss to coat well.
2. Serve immediately.

Nutrition: Calories 489 Total Fat 13.1 g Cholesterol 0 mg Sodium 84 mg Total Carbs 73.4 g Fiber 15.7 g Sugar 0.9 g Protein 22.7 g

Mixed Grain Salad

Preparation Time: 20 Minutes
Cooking Time: 0 Minutes
Servings: 6
Ingredients:
Dressing
- ¼ cup fresh lime juice
- 2 tablespoons maple syrup
- 1 tablespoon Dijon mustard
- ½ teaspoon ground cumin
- 1 teaspoon garlic powder
- Salt and ground black pepper, to taste
- ½ cup extra-virgin olive oil

Salad
- 2 cups fresh mango, peeled, pitted, and cubed
- 2 tablespoon fresh lime juice, divided
- 2 avocados, peeled, pitted, and cubed
- Pinch of salt
- 1 cup cooked quinoa
- 2 (14-ounce) cans black beans, rinsed and drained
- 1 (15¼-ounce) can corn, rinsed and drained
- 1 small red onion, chopped
- 1 jalapeño, seeded and chopped finely
- ½ cup fresh cilantro, chopped
- 6 cups romaine lettuce, shredded

Directions:
1. For dressing: in a blender, add all the Ingredients (except oil) and pulse until well combined.
2. While the motor is running, gradually add the oil and pulse until smooth.
3. For salad: in a bowl, add the mango and 1 tablespoon of lime juice and toss to coat well.
4. In another bowl, add the avocado, a pinch of salt, and remaining lime juice and toss to coat well.
5. In a large serving bowl, add the mango, avocado, and remaining salad Ingredients and mix.
6. Place the dressing and toss to coat well.
7. Serve immediately.

Nutrition: Calories 631 Total Fat 33.6 g Cholesterol 0 mg Sodium 100 mg Total Carbs 73 g Fiber 16.4 g Sugar 15.2 g Protein 15.9 g

Rice & Tofu Salad

Preparation Time: 15 Minutes
Cooking Time: 0 Minutes
Servings: 4
Ingredients:
Salad:
- 1 (12-ounce) package firm tofu, pressed, drained, and sliced
- 1½ cups cooked brown rice
- 3 large tomatoes, peeled and chopped
- ¼ cup fresh basil leaves

Dressing
- 3 scallions, chopped
- 2 tablespoons black sesame seeds, toasted
- 2 tablespoons low-sodium soy sauce
- ½ teaspoon sesame oil, toasted
- Drop of hot pepper sauce
- 1 tablespoon maple syrup
- ¼ teaspoon red chili powder

Directions:
1. In a large serving bowl, place all the Ingredients and toss to coat well.
2. Serve immediately.

Nutrition: Calories 393 Total Fat 8.6 g Cholesterol 0 mg Sodium 464 mg Total Carbs 66.9 g Fiber 5.7 g Sugar 7.9 g Protein 15.1 g

Kidney Bean & Pomegranate Salad

Preparation Time: 15 Minutes
Cooking Time: 0 Minutes
Servings: 3
Ingredients:
- 2 cups canned white kidney beans, rinsed and drained
- 1 cup fresh pomegranate seeds
- 1/3 cup scallion (green part), chopped finely
- 2 tablespoons fresh parsley, chopped
- 1 tablespoon fresh lime juice
- Salt and ground black pepper, as required

Directions:
1. In a large serving bowl, place all the Ingredients and toss to coat well.
2. Serve immediately.

Nutrition: Calories 180 Total Fat 0 g Cholesterol 0 mg Sodium 74 mg Total Carbs 35 g Fiber 14.1 g Sugar 5.3 g Protein 12 g

Warm Vegetable Salad

Preparation Time: 25 Minutes
Cooking Time: 0 Minutes

Servings: 4
Ingredients:
- Cashew cream (1 c.)
- Pepper
- Dried dill (2 teaspoon.)
- Lime juice (2 Tablespoon.)
- Olive oil (1 Tablespoon.)
- Sliced carrots (1 lb.)
- Quartered red potatoes (
- Salt

Directions:
1. Bring some salted water to a pot and add in the potatoes. After 8 minutes of cooking, add in the carrots and cook until these are done.
2. Drain out the water and return Ingredients to the pot. Add in the oil, dill, salt, and lime juice and stir to combine.
3. Divide these between four containers and then top with the cream before serving.

Nutrition: Calories 393 Carbs 52g Fat 15g Protein 10g

Not-Tuna Salad

Preparation Time: 5 Minutes
Cooking Time: 0 Minutes
Servings: 4
Ingredients:
- Pepper (.25 teaspoon.)
- Salt (.5 teaspoon.)
- Vegan mayo (.25 c.)
- Diced celery (.5 c.)
- Chopped white onion (.5 c.)
- Hearts of palm (1 can)
- Chickpeas (1 can)

Directions:
1. Bring out a bowl and use a potato masher to help mash up the chickpeas to make chunky. Add in the pepper, salt, vegan mayo, celery, onion, and hearts of palm.
2. Combine and add in some more mayo if you would like.
3. Divide into four servings and serve or save for later.

Nutrition: Calories 214 Carbs 35g Fat 6g Protein 9g

Corn and Red Bean Salad

Preparation Time: 15 Minutes
Cooking Time: 0 Minutes
Servings: 4
Ingredients:
- Chopped Romaine lettuce (8 c)
- Barley (1 c.)
- Corn (2 c.)
- Kidney beans (2 cans)
- Chili powder (1 teaspoon.)
- Cashew cream (.25 c.)

Directions:
1. Take out some quart jars and set them out. In a small bowl, whisk the chili powder and cream.
2. Pour a bit of this cream into each jar and then add in some of the kidney beans, corn, and cooked barley.

3. Add in two cups of the romaine and then punch down to fit into the jar well. close the lids and then enjoy.

Nutrition: Calories 303 Carbs 45g Fat 9g Protein 14g

Tabbouleh Salad

Preparation Time: 25 Minutes
Cooking Time: 0 Minutes
Servings: 4
Ingredients:
- Sunflower seeds (4 Tablespoon.)
- Chopped scallions (
- Chopped mint (.25 c.)
- Chopped parsley (1 c.)
- Diced tomato (
- Diced cucumber (.
- Olive oil (1 Tablespoon.)
- Salt
- Pressed garlic cloves (
- Zest and juice of one lemon
- Boiling water (1 c.)
- Couscous (1 c.)

Directions:
1. Put the couscous into a bowl and cover with the boiling water. Cover and set aside.
2. Add the lemon juice and zest to a bowl and stir in the olive oil, salt, and garlic.
3. Put the scallions, mint, parsley, tomato, and cucumber into the bowl and toss to coat with the dressing.
4. Take the plate off the couscous and fluff with the fork. Add this to the vegetables and toss to combine.

Nutrition: Calories 304 Carbs 44g Fat 11g Protein 10g

Cauliflower & Apple Salad

Preparation Time: 25 minutes
Cooking Time: 0 minutes
Servings: 4
Ingredients:
- 3 Cups Cauliflower, Chopped into Florets
- 2 Cups Baby Kale
- 1 Sweet Apple, Cored & Chopped
- ¼ Cup Basil, Fresh & Chopped
- ¼ Cup Mint, Fresh & Chopped
- ¼ Cup Parsley, Fresh & Chopped
- 1/3 Cup Scallions, Sliced Thin
- 2 Tablespoons Yellow Raisins
- 1 Tablespoon Sun Dried Tomatoes, Chopped
- ½ Cup Miso Dressing, Optional
- ¼ Cup Roasted Pumpkin Seeds, Optional

Directions:
1. Combine everything together, tossing before serving.

Interesting Facts: This vegetable is an extremely high source of vitamin A, vitamin B1, B2 and B3.

Nutrition: Calories: 198 Protein: 7 Grams Fat: 8 Grams Carbs: 32 Grams

Corn & Black Bean Salad

Preparation Time: 10 minutes
Cooking Time: 0 minutes

Servings: 6
Ingredients:
- ¼ Cup Cilantro, Fresh & Chopped
- 1 Can Corn, Drained (10 Ounces)
- 1/8 Cup Red Onion, Chopped
- 1 Can Black Beans, Drained (15 Ounces)
- 1 Tomato, Chopped
- 3 Tablespoons Lemon Juice, Fresh
- 2 Tablespoons Olive Oil
- Sea Salt & Black Pepper to Taste

Directions:
1. Mix everything together, and then refrigerate until cool. Serve cold.

Interesting Facts: Whole corn is a fantastic source of phosphorus, magnesium, and B vitamin It also promotes healthy digestion and contains heart-healthy antioxidants. It is important to seek out organic corn in order to bypass all of the genetically modified product that is out on the market.

Nutrition: Calories: 159 Protein: 6.4 Grams Fat: 5.6 Grams Carbs: 23.7 Grams

Spinach & Orange Salad

Preparation Time: 15 minutes
Cooking Time: 0 minutes
Servings: 6
Ingredients:
- ¼ -1/3 Cup Vegan Dressing
- 3 Oranges, Medium, Peeled, Seeded & Sectioned
- ¾ lb. Spinach, Fresh & Torn
- 1 Red Onion, Medium, Sliced & Separated into Rings

Directions:
1. Toss everything together, and serve with dressing.

Interesting Facts: Spinach is one of the most superb green veggies out there. Each serving is packed with 3 grams of protein and is a highly encouraged component of the plant-based diet.

Nutrition: Calories: 99 Protein: 2.5 Grams Fat: 5 Grams Carbs: 13.1 Grams

Red Pepper & Broccoli Salad

Preparation Time: 15 minutes
Cooking Time: 0 minutes
Servings: 2
Ingredients:
- Ounces Lettuce Salad Mix
- 1 Head Broccoli, Chopped into Florets
- 1 Red Pepper, Seeded & Chopped

Dressing:
- 3 Tablespoons White Wine Vinegar
- 1 Teaspoon Dijon Mustard

- 1 Clove Garlic, Peeled & Chopped Fine
- ½ Teaspoon Black Pepper
- ½ Teaspoon Sea Salt, Fine
- 2 Tablespoons Olive Oil
- 1 Tablespoon Parsley, Chopped

Directions:
1. In boiling water, drain the broccoli it on a paper towel.
2. Whisk together all dressing Ingredients
3. Toss Ingredients together before serving.

Interesting Facts: This oil is the main source of dietary fat in a variety of diets. It contains many vitamins and minerals that play a part in reducing the risk of stroke and lowers cholesterol and high blood pressure and can also aid in weight loss. It is best consumed cold, as when it is heated it can lose some of its nutritive properties (although it is still great to cook with – extra virgin is best), many recommend taking a shot of cold oil olive daily! Bonus: if you don't like the taste or texture add a shot to your smoothie.

Nutrition: Calories: 185 Protein: 4g Fat: 14g Carbs: 8g

Lentil Potato Salad

Preparation Time: 35 minutes
Cooking Time: 25 minutes
Servings: 2
Ingredients:
- ½ Cup Beluga Lentils
- 8 Fingerling Potatoes
- 1 Cup Scallions, Sliced Thin
- ¼ Cup Cherry Tomatoes, Halved
- ¼ Cup Lemon Vinaigrette
- Sea Salt & Black Pepper to Taste

Directions:
1. Bring two cups of water to simmer in a pot, adding your lentils. Cook for twenty to twenty-five minutes, and then drain. Your lentils should be tender.
2. Reduce to a simmer, cooking for fifteen minutes, and then drain. Halve your potatoes once they're cool enough to touch.
3. Put your lentils on a serving plate, and then top with scallions, potatoes and tomatoes. Drizzle with your vinaigrette, and season with salt and pepper.

Interesting Facts: Lemons are popularly known as harboring loads of Vitamin C, but are also excellent sources of folate, fiber, and antioxidants. Bonus: Helps lower cholesterol. Double Bonus: Reduces risk of cancer and high blood pressure.

Nutrition: Calories: 400 Protein: 7 Grams Fat: 26 Grams Carbs: 39 Grams

FINGER FOOD

Balls from Beetroot

Preparation Time: 35 minutes
Cooking Time: 0 minutes
Servings: 4
Ingredients:
- 4 sprigs of parsley
- 2 tablespoon walnuts
- 260 g beetroot
- ½ onion
- 1 clove of garlic
- Salt and pepper

Directions:
1. Boil the beetroot, peel and grate coarsely with a kitchen grater.
2. Roast the walnuts and process them into flour in a food processor.
3. Cut the onion into small cubes, peel the garlic clove and mash it with a fork.
4. Wash, shake and chop the parsley.
5. Mix all **Ingredients:** in a bowl and season with salt and a little pepper.
6. Shape into balls of the same size and let stand for a few minutes.
Nutrition: Calories: 239 Fat: 11.4g Carbs: 10.5g Protein: 12.1g Fiber: 3.2g

Polenta Skewers

Preparation Time: 35 minutes
Cooking Time: 0 minutes
Servings: 4
Ingredients:
- ½ avocado
- 10 cherry tomatoes
- 1 mini zucchini
- 150 g corn grits
- 2 tablespoon olive oil
- 1 teaspoon sesame seeds, black
- 10 basil leaves
- 10 toothpicks
- 450 ml vegetable stock
- Salt and pepper

Directions:
1. The day before, bring the corn grits to the boil in the broth and cook for a few minutes, stirring constantly. Pour into a square form and chill until the next day.
2. Cut the polenta into small cubes and fry in a pan in a little olive oil.
3. Wash the zucchini, cut into thin slices and fry in the pan once the polenta is ready.
4. Wash the tomatoes and cut them in half, pluck the basil leaves from the branches.
5. Stone the avocado and cut into thin slices.
6. Skewer a polenta cube, a zucchini, a tomato, a slice of avocado and a basil leaf onto a toothpick. Serve with sesame seeds.
Nutrition: Calories: 259 Fat: 15.4g Carbs: 20.5g Protein: 12.1g Fiber: 3.2g

Börek with Spinach Filling

Preparation Time: 25 minutes
Cooking Time: 0 minutes
Servings: 10
Ingredients:
- 10 yufka sheets
- 2 cloves of garlic
- 1 small onion
- 3 tablespoon soy yogurt
- 4 tablespoon soy milk
- 400 g spin nat
- 3 tablespoons of oil
- 1 pinch of nutmeg
- Salt and pepper

Directions:
1. Wash the spinach, peel the garlic and onion and cut into small cubes.
2. Steam the spinach, onion and garlic in oil in a deep pan.
3. After a few minutes, season with nutmeg, salt and pepper and stir in the yoghurt.
4. Lay out the Yufka leaves and brush with the spinach filling.
5. Roll up and brush with a little milk.
6. Then place on a baking sheet and bake in the oven at 180 degrees Celsius for about 15 minutes.
Nutrition: Calories: 219 Fat: 9.4g Carbs: 10.5g Protein: 11.1g Fiber: 3.2g

Taler With Avocado Cream

Preparation Time: 25 minutes
Cooking Time: 0 minutes
Servings: 5
Ingredients:
- 20 pumpernickels, round
- 1 chilli pepper
- 1 lime
- 2 avocados
- 6 beetroot chips
- 50 g vegan cream cheese
- Salt and pepper

Directions:
1. Cut the chilli pepper lengthways and scrape out the stones.
2. Halve the avocados, core them and scrape the pulp into a blender jar.
3. Add the cream cheese and a little lime juice.
4. Mix a homogeneous cream from the chilli pepper , avocado, lime, cream cheese and a little salt and pepper.
5. Put the little Pumpernickel Taler ready and put a serving of avocado cream on each with a piping bag.
6. Crumble the chips and sprinkle them over the thalers.
Nutrition: Calories: 243 Fat: 10.4g Carbs: 12.5g Protein: 9.1g Fiber: 3.2g

Small Sweet Potato Pancakes

Preparation Time: 20 minutes
Cooking Time: 0 minutes
Servings: 2
Ingredients:
- 1 clove of garlic
- 3 tablespoon wholemeal rice flour
- 1 pinch of nutmeg
- 3 tablespoons of water
- 150 g sweet potato
- 1 pinch of chilli flakes
- 1 teaspoon oil

- Salt

Directions:
1. Peel the garlic clove and mash it with a fork. Peel the sweet potato and grate it into small sticks with a grater.
2. Knead the sweet potato and garlic in a bowl with the rice flour and water, then season with chilli flakes, salt and nutmeg.
3. Heat the oil in a pan and form small buffers.
4. Fry these in the pan on both sides until golden brown.
5. Goes perfectly with tzatziki and other fresh dips.

Nutrition: Calories: 209 Fat: 15.4g Carbs: 10.5g Protein: 8.1g Fiber: 3.2g

Pumpernickel with Avocado

Preparation Time: 10 minutes
Cooking Time: 0 minutes
Servings: 2
Ingredients:
- 6 small slices of pumpernickel
- 1 avocado
- 1 roll of vegan cheese spread
- 1 tablespoon chives
- Salt and pepper

Directions:
1. Halve the avocado, remove the seeds and carefully remove from the skin. Cut into slices and place on a plate.
2. Spread cheese on the bread, then top with avocado and then sprinkle with a little pepper and chopped chives.

Nutrition: Calories: 159 Fat: 9.4g Carbs: 10.5g Protein: 9.1g Fiber: 3.2g

Mushroom Cakes

Preparation Time: 30 minutes
Cooking Time: 0 minutes
Servings: 4
Ingredients:
- 1 bun
- 1 small onion
- 1 clove of garlic
- 500 g mushrooms
- 1 pinch of marjoram
- 2 tablespoons of oil
- 1 tablespoon flaxseed, crushed
- 3 tablespoon soy milk
- Salt and pepper

Directions:
1. Clean the mushrooms and cut into small cubes. Peel the onion and garlic, then also dice.
2. Crumble the bun and mix in a bowl with the mushrooms, garlic and onion.
3. Add marjoram, salt and pepper and fold in the flax seeds as well.
4. Add soy milk so that the mixture sticks well.
5. Heat the oil in a non-stick pan, form small meatballs and fry them until golden brown on both sides.

Nutrition: Calories: 129 Fat: 12.4g Carbs: 11.5g Protein: 9.1g Fiber: 3.2g

Churros With Chocolate

Preparation Time: 35 minutes
Cooking Time: 0 minutes
Servings: 6
Ingredients:
- 2 teaspoons of baking powder
- 1 ¼ cup of flour
- 2 cups of oil
- 1 pinch of salt
- 50 g sugar
- 1 cup of soy milk
- 100 g vegan chocolate
- cinnamon and sugar

Directions:
1. Mix the sugar, baking powder, flour and salt. Then stir in ¾ of the soy milk until a velvety batter is formed.
2. Heat the oil in a saucepan and roll the churro batter into a long line.
3. When the oil is hot, cut the thin roll into pieces with scissors and bake them in the oil until they are evenly golden yellow on all sides.
4. In Zimt and roll sugar and heat the chocolate with the remaining soy milk.

Nutrition: Calories: 209 Fat: 15.4g Carbs: 20.5g Protein: 12.1g Fiber: 3.2g

Zucchini Rolls with Cream Cheese

Preparation Time: 35 minutes
Cooking Time: 0 minutes
Servings: 4
Ingredients:
- 1 tablespoon oil
- 60 g apricots, dried
- 350 g zucchini
- Salt and pepper
- 1 sprig of thyme
- ½ lime

Directions:
1. Turn after a minute and fry the same way on the other side.
2. Let cool on a plate and in the meantime prepare the filling .
3. Let the apricots soak a little and then chop them.
4. Mix with the cream cheese, chopped thyme and a little pepper. Season to taste with salt and prepare.
5. Brush the zucchini slices with some filling and roll up.
6. Add a few squirts of lime juice to serve.

Nutrition: Calories: 235 Fat: 15.4g Carbs: 20.5g Protein: 12.1g Fiber: 3.2g

Skewers of Mozzarella And Tomato

Preparation Time: 15 minutes
Cooking Time: 0 minutes
Servings: 8
Ingredients:
- 1 teaspoon pesto
- 250 g cherry tomatoes
- 250 g vegan mozzarella
- 1 bunch of basil
- 3 tablespoon olive oil

Directions:
1. Wash and prepare the tomatoes.
2. Pluck the basil leaves, cut the mozzarella into small cubes.
3. Mix the pesto with the olive oil in a small bowl.

4.   Prepare wooden skewers and place two tomatoes, two basil leaves and two cubes of mozzarella alternately on the skewers.
5.   Brush with a little pesto to serve.
Nutrition: Calories: 259 Fat: 15.4g Carbs: 20.5g Protein: 12.1g Fiber: 3.2g

Filled Mushrooms

Preparation Time: 55 minutes
Cooking Time: 0 minutes
Servings: 2
Ingredients:
- 30 g pine nuts
- ½ lime
- ½ bunch of basil
- 8 large mushrooms
- 50 ml of water
- 115 g cashew nuts
- 2 tablespoon coconut milk
- Salt and pepper

Directions:
1.   Soak the cashew nuts in water the evening before.
2.   The drain water and fill the cores together with the basil, the coconut milk, the water and the lime juice in a food processor.
3.   Process into a creamy puree.
4.   Clean the mushrooms and brush with the filling.
5.   Then bake in the oven at 180 degrees Celsius for about 15 minutes.
6.   In the meantime, toast the pine nuts in a small non-stick pan.
7.   Sprinkle the pine nuts over the mushrooms to serve.
Nutrition: Calories: 239 Fat: 11.4g Carbs: 10.5g Protein: 11.1g Fiber: 3.2g

Pizza Bites

Preparation Time: 95 minutes
Cooking Time: 0 minutes
Servings: 8
Ingredients:
- 200 g flour
- 1 teaspoon salt
- 180 ml of water
- ½ cubes of yeast
- 1 teaspoon of sugar
- 250 g vegan salami
- 250 g vegan Gouda

Directions:
1.   Mix sugar, flour and salt in a bowl.
2.   Make a well and crumble the yeast into it. Warm the water slightly and gradually pour it into the hollow.
3.   Mix the yeast and let it rise briefly, then work all the Ingredients in the bowl into a smooth dough.
4.   Let rise for 50 minutes, then roll out.
5.   Cut the cheese and salami into thin slices.
6.   Cut rectangles from the dough and cover the lower edge with cheese and salami. Roll up a little, cover again and close the dough.
7.   Bake at 240 degrees Celsius for 10 to 12 minutes.
Nutrition: Calories: 289 Fat: 15.4g Carbs: 20.5g Protein: 12.1g Fiber: 3.2g

Filled Dough Pieces In Carrot Shape

Preparation Time: 30 minutes
Cooking Time: 0 minutes
Servings: 8
Ingredients:
- 400 ml vegetable stock
- 200 g red lentils
- 1 tablespoon almond butter
- 1 pk . Pizza dough
- salt and pepper
- 1 bunch of parsley

Directions:
1.   Do not make funnels out of aluminum paper to hold the pizza dough in the shape of a carrot.
2.   Roll out the dough, cut into strips and wrap around the funnels.
3.   Then bake at 200 degrees Celsius for about 10 minutes until they are golden brown.
4.   In the meantime, bring the broth to the boil and cook the lentils in it.
5.   Season with almond butter, salt and pepper and let cool slightly.
6.   Fill the funnels with lentils and finally put a bunch of parsley on top.
7.   These bites go perfectly with an Easter brunch.
Nutrition: Calories: 229 Fat: 9.4g Carbs: 11.5g Protein: 12.1g Fiber: 3.2g

Cauliflower Nuggets

Preparation Time: 35 minutes
Cooking Time: 0 minutes
Servings: 4
Ingredients:
- 3 tablespoon yeast flakes
- 60 ml soy milk
- ½ cauliflower
- 2 tablespoons of oil
- ½ cup breadcrumbs
- 30 g flour
- Salt and pepper

Directions:
1.   Separate the cauliflower into florets and wash.
2.   Mix the flour, yeast flakes, milk, salt and pepper.
3.   Roll the cauliflower in the mass and then roll in breadcrumbs.
4.   Place on a baking sheet and drizzle with oil.
5.   Bake for about 35 minutes at 200 degrees Celsius, until the cauliflower is cooked through.
Nutrition: Calories: 279 Fat: 15.4g Carbs: 20.5g Protein: 12.1g Fiber: 3.2g

FRUIT SALAD RECIPES

Ambrosia with Pineapple

Preparation Time: 30 Minutes
Cooking Time: 15 Minutes
Servings: 4
Ingredients:
- Orange zest, two teaspoons
- Tofu, soft, pureed, one half cup
- Orange juice, three tablespoons
- Lemon juice, one third cup
- Cornstarch, one tablespoon
- Coconut, unsweetened shredded, one half cup
- Grapes, one cup
- Sugar, three tablespoons
- Strawberries, sliced, one cup
- Orange slices, one cup
- Apples, fresh sliced, one cup
- Pineapple, fresh chopped, one cup

Directions:
1. Use a large-sized bowl to assemble the fruits together and put it in the refrigerator.
2. In a small saucepan, mix together the lemon juice with the cornstarch and keep stirring until they are well mixed.
3. Add in the orange juice and the sugar and place the saucepan over medium-high heat. Cook the mix for five to ten minutes while the mixture gets thicker. Keep stirring constantly.
4. When the mixture is thick, then take the saucepan off of the heat and let it get completely cool.
5. When the mixture in the saucepan has cooled completely, then blends in the orange zest and the pureed tofu.
6. Allow this bowl of mix to rest in the refrigerator for one hour until it becomes chilled. Pour the dressing over the fruit before serving.
Nutrition: Calories: 257 Protein: 8g Fat: 8g Carbs: 44g

Tropical Fruit Salad

Preparation Time: 10 Minutes
Cooking Time: 0 Minutes
Servings: 2
Ingredients:
- Lime juice, one tablespoon
- Kiwi, two
- Dragon fruit, one half of one
- Strawberries, twelve
- Mango, one half of one

Directions:
1. Peel the fruits and chop them into bite-sized pieces. Dump all of the fruit chunks into a large-sized mixing bowl.
2. Drizzle the lime juice over the fruit and toss the fruit gently to coat all of the pieces with the juice. Serve immediately
Nutrition: Calories: 154 Protein: 2g Fat: 1g Carbs: 37g

Fall Fruit with Creamy Dressing

Preparation Time: 25 Minutes
Cooking Time: 0 Minutes
Servings: 4
Ingredients:
Salad
- Pumpkin, raw, shredded, one half cup
- Pomegranate seeds, one half cup
- Grapes, one cup
- Apples, three, cored and cubed
Creamy Dressing
- Cinnamon, one teaspoon
- Lemon juice, one tablespoon
- Almond yogurt, one half cup
Directions:
1. Mix together all of the listed Ingredients for the dressing.
2. In a large-sized bowl, toss the dressing with the shredded raw pumpkin, pomegranate seeds, apples, and the dressing. Serve immediately.
Nutrition: Calories: 161 Protein: 3g Fat: 1g Carbs: 40g

Summertime Fruit Salad

Preparation Time: 15 Minutes
Cooking Time: 0 Minutes
Servings: 6
Ingredients:
- Balsamic vinegar, two teaspoons
- Lemon juice, two tablespoons
- Mint, fresh chopped, one tablespoon
- Blueberries, one cup
- Peaches, fresh, three, peeled and sliced thin
- Strawberries, one pound, cleaned and sliced thin

Directions:
1. Mix together in a medium-sized serving bowl the basil, blueberries, peaches, and strawberries. In a small-sized bowl, mix together the balsamic vinegar and the lemon juice.
2. Pour the liquid dressing over the mixed fruit and toss gently to coat all of the pieces of fruit with the dressing.
3. Serve immediately or keep the salad covered in the refrigerator for no longer than two days.
Nutrition: Calories: 91 Protein: 1g Fat: 6g Carbs: 22g

Cherry Berry Salad

Preparation Time: 10 Minutes
Cooking Time: 0 Minutes
Servings: 6
Ingredients:
- Lemon juice, three tablespoons
- Cardamom, one quarter teaspoon
- Cinnamon, one half teaspoon
- Mint, fresh, three tablespoons
- Blackberries, one cup
- Blueberries, one cup
- Raspberries, one cup
- Cherries, seeded, cut in half, one cup

- Strawberries, cleaned, two cups quartered

Directions:
1. In a small-sized bowl, mix the spices and the lemon juice together well. In a medium-sized bowl, mix the fruits together with the lemon juice and mint mixture.
2. Toss the fruits gently but thoroughly to coat all of the pieces. This will store well in the refrigerator for two to three days.

Nutrition: Calories: 113 Protein: 1g Fat: 1g Carbs: 27g

Fruit Salad with Sweet Lime Dressing

Preparation Time: 15 Minutes
Cooking Time: 0 Minutes
Servings: 9
Ingredients:
Salad
- Mint, fresh chopped, one cup
- Lime juice, two tablespoons
- Kiwi, five, peeled and sliced
- Mangoes, two, peeled and chopped
- Green grapes, one cup cut in half
- Blackberries, one cup
- Blueberries, one cup
- Strawberries, one cup sliced

Sweet Lime Dressing
- Powdered sugar, two tablespoons
- Lime juice, two tablespoons

Directions:
1. Mix together until smooth in a small-sized bowl the powdered sugar and the lime juice.
2. Mix together in a large-sized bowl the fruits, then pour on the dressing and gently toss all of the fruits together well to coat all of the pieces.
3. This will stay good in the refrigerator for no more than one day.

Nutrition: Calories: 50 Protein: 1g Fat: 1g Carbs: 12g

Asian Fruit Salad

Preparation Time: 30 Minutes
Cooking Time: 0 Minutes
Servings: 8
Ingredients:
- Passion fruit, one-half cup (about six of the fruit)
- Papaya, one chopped
- Pineapple, one cup chunked
- Oranges, two separated into segments
- Star fruit, three sliced thin
- Mangoes, two large, peeled and chunked
- Mint, fresh, one-third cup chopped coarse
- Lime juice, one third cup
- Lime zest, one tablespoon
- Ginger, ground, one tablespoon
- Vanilla extract, one tablespoon
- Brown sugar, one half cup
- Water, four cups

Directions:

1. Mix the water and the sugar together in a medium-sized saucepan and put it over a medium to high heat until the sugar is dissolved.
2. Let this simmer for five minutes over a very low heat, so the sugar does not burn. Add in the vanilla extract and the ginger and stir well.
3. Let this cook for ten more minutes. Let the mix cool off the heat until it is room temperature, and then add in the mint, juice, and zest.
4. During the time the sauce is cooling mix together the remainder of the Ingredients in a large-sized bowl.
5. Pour the syrup mixture over the fruit in the bowl and mix gently to coat all pieces with the sauce.
6. Put the bowl in the refrigerator until the fruit is cold then serve.

Nutrition: Calories: 220 Protein: 3g Fat: 1g Carbs: 56g

Mimosa Salad

Preparation Time: 10 Minutes
Cooking Time: 0 Minutes
Servings: 8
Ingredients:
- Mint, fresh, one half cup
- Orange juice, one half cup
- Pineapple, one cup cut into small pieces
- Strawberries, one cup cut into quarters
- Blueberries, one cup
- Blackberries, one cup
- Kiwi, three peeled and sliced

Directions:
1. In a large-sized bowl, mix all of the fruits together and then top with the orange juice and the fresh mint.
2. Toss gently together all of the fruit until they are well mixed.

Nutrition: Calories: 215 Protein: 3g Fat: 1g Carbs: 49g

Honey Lime Quinoa Fruit Salad

Preparation Time: 20 Minutes
Cooking Time: 0 Minutes
Servings: 6
Ingredients:
- Basil, chopped, one tablespoon
- Lime juice, two tablespoons
- Mango, diced, one cup
- Blueberries, one cup
- Blackberries, one cup
- Strawberries, sliced, one and one half cup
- Quinoa, cooked, one cup

Directions:
1. In a large-sized bowl, mix the fruits with the cooked quinoa and mix well.
2. Drizzle on the lime juice and add the chopped basil and mix the fruit gently but thoroughly to coat all of the pieces.

Nutrition: Calories: 246 Protein: 7g Fat: 1g Carbs: 44g

GRAINS AND BEANS

Veggie Barley Bowl

Preparation Time: 10 minutes
Cooking Time: 1 hour 11 minutes
Servings: 8
Ingredients:
- 1 cup barley
- 3 cups low-sodium vegetable broth
- 2 cups sliced mushrooms
- 2 cups broccoli florets
- 1 cup snow peas, trimmed
- ½ cup sliced scallion
- ¼ cup chopped green bell pepper
- ¼ cup chopped red bell pepper
- 1 cup bean sprouts
- ¼ cup soy sauce
- ¼ cup water
- ¼ teaspoon ground ginger
- 1 tablespoon cornstarch, mixed with 2 tablespoons cold water

Directions:
1. In a saucepan over medium heat, place the barley and vegetable stock. Cover and cook for 1 hour.
2. Combine all the vegetables, except for the bean sprouts, in a large pot with the soy sauce, water and ginger. Cook for 5 minutes, stirring constantly.
3. Add the bean sprouts and cook, stirring, for another 5 minutes. Add the cornstarch mixture and cook for about 1 minute, stirring, or until thickened.
4. Remove from the heat. Toss the vegetables with the cooked barley.
5. Serve hot.
Nutrition: calories: 190 fat: 2.6g carbs: 35.7g protein: 5.9g fiber: 6.9g

Indian Lentil Dahl

Preparation Time: 10 minutes
Cooking Time: 25 minutes
Servings: 6
Ingredients:
- 3 cup cooked basmati rice
- 2 tablespoons olive oil (optional)
- 6 garlic cloves, minced
- 2 yellow onions, finely diced
- 1-inch piece fresh ginger, minced
- 2 tomatoes, diced
- 2 tablespoons ground cumin
- 1 tablespoon ground coriander
- 1 tablespoon ground turmeric
- 1 tablespoon paprika
- 4 cups water
- 2 cups uncooked green lentils, rinsed
- 1 teaspoon salt (optional)

Directions:
1. In a large pot, heat the olive oil (if desired) over medium heat. Add the garlic, onions, and ginger. Cook for 3 minutes, or until onions are golden. Add the tomatoes and cook for 2 minutes more, stirring occasionally. Stir in the cumin, coriander, turmeric and paprika.
2. Add the water and lentils. Cover and bring to a boil over high heat. Once boiling, stir and reduce the heat to a simmer. Cook, covered, for 20 minutes, stirring every 5 minutes, or until the lentils are fully cooked and beginning to break down. Season with salt (if desired) and stir.
3. Divide the rice evenly among 6 meal prep containers. Add an equal portion of the dahl to each container. Let cool completely before putting on lids and refrigerating.
Nutrition: calories: 432 fat: 17.2g carbs: 58.8g protein: 10.9g fiber: 8.9g

Kale and Sweet Potato Quinoa

Preparation Time: 10 minutes
Cooking Time: 19 minutes
Servings: 4
Ingredients:
- ¼ cup olive oil (optional)
- 1 yellow onion, diced
- 2 tablespoons ground coriander
- 2 tablespoons ground cumin
- 2 tablespoons mustard powder
- 2 tablespoons ground turmeric
- 2 teaspoons ground cinnamon
- 1 large sweet potato, diced
- 1¼ cup uncooked quinoa
- 4 cups water
- 1 bunch kale, rinsed and chopped
- Salt, to taste (optional)
- Freshly ground black pepper, to taste

Directions:
1. In a large pot, heat the oil (if desired) over medium-high heat. Add the onion and sauté for 3 minutes. Stir in the coriander, cumin, mustard powder, turmeric and cinnamon. Cook for about 1 minute, or until fragrant. Add the sweet potatoes and stir until well coated with the spices.
2. Stir in the quinoa and water. Cover with a lid and bring to a boil over high heat, stirring occasionally. Once the liquid is boiling, remove the lid and reduce the heat to medium-low. Simmer for 15 minutes.
3. Once the water is mostly absorbed and the sweet potato is cooked through, stir in the kale. Remove from the heat and cover with a lid. Let sit for 10 to 15 minutes. The residual heat will cook the kale and the quinoa will absorb the remaining water.
4. Taste and season with salt (if desired) and pepper. Divide evenly among 4 meal prep containers and let cool completely before putting on lids and refrigerating.
Nutrition: calories: 457 fat: 16.2g carbs: 67.9g protein: 10.1g fiber: 12.2g

Brown Rice with Mushrooms

Preparation Time: 15 minutes
Cooking Time: 20 minutes
Servings: 6 to 8

Ingredients:
- ½ pound (227 g) mushrooms, sliced
- 1 green bell pepper, chopped
- 1 onion, chopped
- 1 bunch scallions, chopped
- 2 cloves garlic, minced
- ½ cup water
- 5 cups cooked brown rice
- 1 (16-ounce / 454-g) can chopped tomatoes
- 1 (4-ounce / 113-g) can chopped green chilies
- 2 teaspoons chili powder
- 1 teaspoon ground cumin

Directions:
1. In a large pot, sauté the mushrooms, green pepper, onion, scallions, and garlic in the water for 10 minutes.
2. Stir in the remaining ingredients. Cook over low heat for about 10 minutes, or until heated through, stirring frequently.
3. Serve immediately.

Nutrition: calories: 185 fat: 2.6g carbs: 34.5g protein: 6.1g fiber: 4.3g

Veggie Paella

Preparation Time: 15 minutes
Cooking Time: 52 to 58 minutes
Servings: 4
Ingredients:
- 1 onion, coarsely chopped
- 8 medium mushrooms, sliced
- 2 small zucchinis, cut in half, then sliced ½ inch thick
- 1 leek, rinsed and sliced
- 2 large cloves garlic, crushed
- 1 medium tomato, coarsely chopped
- 3 cups low-sodium vegetable broth
- 1¼ cups long-grain brown rice
- ½ teaspoon crushed saffron threads
- Freshly ground black pepper, to taste
- ½ cup frozen green peas
- ½ cup water
- Chopped fresh parsley, for garnish

Directions:
1. Pour the water in a large wok. Add the onion and sauté for 5 minutes, or until most of the liquid is absorbed.
2. Stir in the mushrooms, zucchini, leek, and garlic and cook for 2 to 3 minutes, or until softened slightly.
3. Add the tomato, broth, rice, saffron, and pepper. Bring to a boil. Reduce the heat and simmer, covered, for 30 minutes.
4. Add the peas and continue to cook for another 5 to 10 minutes. Remove from the heat and let rest for 10 minutes to allow any excess moisture to be absorbed.
5. Sprinkle with the parsley before serving.

Nutrition: calories: 418 fat: 3.9g carbs: 83.2g protein: 12.7g fiber: 9.2g

Vegetable and Wild Rice Pilaf

Preparation Time: 10 minutes
Cooking Time: 48 to 49 minutes
Servings: 6
Ingredients:
- 1 potato, scrubbed and chopped
- 1 cup chopped cauliflower
- 1 cup chopped scallion
- 1 cup chopped broccoli
- 1 to 2 cloves garlic, minced
- 2 tablespoons soy sauce
- 3 cups low-sodium vegetable broth
- 1 cup long-grain brown rice
- 1/3 cup wild rice
- 2 small zucchinis, chopped
- ½ cup grated carrot
- 1/8 teaspoon sesame oil (optional)
- ¼ cup chopped fresh cilantro
- ½ cup water

Directions:
1. Bring the water to a boil in a large saucepan. Add the potato, cauliflower, scallion, broccoli and garlic and sauté for 2 to 3 minutes.
2. Add the soy sauce and cook for 1 minute. Add the vegetable broth, brown rice and wild rice. Bring to a boil. Reduce the heat, cover, and cook for 15 minutes.
3. Stir in the zucchinis. After another 15 minutes, stir in the carrot. Continue to cook for 15 minutes. Stir in the sesame oil (if desired) and cilantro.
4. Serve immediately.

Nutrition: calories: 376 fat: 3.6g carbs: 74.5g protein: 11.8g fiber: 8.1g

Brown Rice with Spiced Vegetables

Preparation Time: 10 minutes
Cooking Time: 16 to 18 minutes
Servings: 6
Ingredients:
- 2 teaspoons grated fresh ginger
- 2 cloves garlic, crushed
- ½ cup water
- ¼ pound (113 g) green beans, trimmed and cut into 1-inch pieces
- 1 carrot, scrubbed and sliced
- ½ pound (227 g) mushrooms, sliced
- 2 zucchinis, cut in half lengthwise and sliced
- 1 bunch scallions, cut into 1-inch pieces
- 4 cups cooked brown rice
- 3 tablespoons soy sauce

Directions:
1. Place the ginger and garlic in a large pot with the water. Add the green beans and carrot and sauté for 3 minutes.
2. Add the mushrooms and sauté for another 2 minutes. Stir in the zucchini and scallions. Reduce the heat. Cover and cook for 6 to 8 minutes, or until the vegetables are tender-crisp, stirring frequently.
3. Stir in the rice and soy sauce. Cook over low heat for 5 minutes, or until heated through.
4. Serve warm.

Nutrition: calories: 205 fat: 3.0g carbs: 38.0g protein: 6.4g fiber:4.4 g

Spiced Tomato Brown Rice

Preparation Time: 10 minutes
Cooking Time: 15 minutes
Servings: 4 to 6
Ingredients:
- 1 onion, diced
- 1 green bell pepper, diced
- 3 cloves garlic, minced
- ¼ cup water
- 15 to 16 ounces (425 to 454g) tomatoes, chopped
- 1 tablespoon chili powder
- 2 teaspoons ground cumin
- 1 teaspoon dried basil
- ½ teaspoon Parsley Patch seasoning, general blend
- ¼ teaspoon cayenne
- 2 cups cooked brown rice

Directions:
1. Combine the onion, green pepper, garlic and water in a saucepan over medium heat. Cook for about 5 minutes, stirring constantly, or until softened.
2. Add the tomatoes and seasonings. Cook for another 5 minutes. Stir in the cooked rice. Cook for another 5 minutes to allow the flavors to blend.
3. Serve immediately.
Nutrition: calories: 107 fat: 1.1g carbs: 21.1g protein: 3.2g fiber: 2.9g

Noodle and Rice Pilaf

Preparation Time: 5 minutes
Cooking Time: 33 to 44 minutes
Servings: 6 to 8
Ingredients:
- 1 cup whole-wheat noodles, broken into 1/8 inch pieces
- 2 cups long-grain brown rice
- 6½ cups low-sodium vegetable broth
- 1 teaspoon ground cumin
- ½ teaspoon dried oregano

Directions:
1. Combine the noodles and rice in a saucepan over medium heat and cook for 3 to 4 minutes, or until they begin to smell toasted.
2. Stir in the vegetable broth, cumin and oregano. Bring to a boil. Reduce the heat to medium-low. Cover and cook for 30 to 40 minutes, or until all water is absorbed.
Nutrition: calories: 287 fat: 2.5g carbs: 58.1g protein: 7.9g fiber: 5.0g

Easy Millet Loaf

Preparation Time: 5 minutes
Cooking Time: 1 hour 15 minutes
Servings: 4
Ingredients:
- 1¼ cups millet
- 4 cups unsweetened tomato juice
- 1 medium onion, chopped
- 1 to 2 cloves garlic

- ½ teaspoon dried sage
- ½ teaspoon dried basil
- ½ teaspoon poultry seasoning

Directions:
1. Preheat the oven to 350°F (180°C).
2. Place the millet in a large bowl.
3. Place the remaining ingredients in a blender and pulse until smooth. Add to the bowl with the millet and mix well.
4. Pour the mixture into a shallow casserole dish. Cover and bake in the oven for 1¼ hours, or until set.
5. Serve warm.
Nutrition: calories: 315 fat: 3.4g carbs: 61.6g protein: 10.2g fiber: 9.6g

Walnut-Oat Burgers

Preparation Time: 5 minutes
Cooking Time: 20 to 30 minutes
Servings: 6 to 8
Ingredients:
- 1 medium onion, finely chopped
- 2 cups rolled oats
- 2 cups unsweetened low-fat soy milk
- 1 cup finely chopped walnuts
- 1 tablespoon soy sauce
- ½ teaspoon dried sage
- ½ teaspoon garlic powder
- ½ teaspoon onion powder
- ½ teaspoon dried thyme
- ¼ teaspoon dried marjoram

Directions:
1. Stir together all the ingredients in a large bowl. Let rest for 20 minutes.
2. Form the mixture into six or eight patties. Cook the patties on a nonstick griddle over medium heat for 20 to 30 minutes, or until browned on each side.
3. Serve warm.
Nutrition: calories: 341 fat: 13.9g carbs: 42.4g protein: 13.9g fiber: 6.8g

Spicy Beans and Rice

Preparation Time: 5 minutes
Cooking Time: 45 minutes
Servings: 4 to 6
Ingredients:
- 1½ cups long-grain brown rice
- 1 (19-ounce / 539-g) can kidney beans, rinsed and drained
- 2 cups chopped onion
- 1 cup mild salsa
- 1 teaspoon ground cumin
- 16 ounces (454 g) tomatoes, chopped
- 3 cups water

Directions:
1. In a pot, bring the water to a boil. Stir in the rice. Bring to a boil again and stir in the remaining ingredients, except for the tomatoes. Return to a boil. Reduce the heat to low. Cover and simmer for 45 minutes.
2. Remove from the heat and stir in the tomatoes. Let sit for 5 minutes, covered.

Nutrition: calories: 386 fat: 7.1g carbs: 71.1g protein: 11.1g fiber: 5.8g

Black-Eyed Peas and Corn Salad

Preparation Time: 30 minutes
Cooking Time: 50 minutes
Servings: 4
Ingredients:
- 2½ cups cooked black-eyed peas
- 3 ears corn, kernels removed
- 1 medium ripe tomato, diced
- ½ medium red onion, peeled and diced small
- ½ red bell pepper, deseeded and diced small
- 1 jalapeño pepper, deseeded and minced
- ½ cup finely chopped cilantro
- ¼ cup plus 2 tablespoons balsamic vinegar
- 3 cloves garlic, peeled and minced
- 1 teaspoon toasted and ground cumin seeds

Directions:
1. Stir together all the ingredients in a large bowl and refrigerate for about 1 hour, or until well chilled.
2. Serve chilled.

Nutrition: calories: 247 fat: 1.8g carbs: 47.6g protein: 12.9g fiber: 11.7g

Indian Tomato and Garbanzo Stew

Preparation Time: 15 minutes
Cooking Time: 50 minutes
Servings: 4 to 6
Ingredients:
- 1 large onion, quartered and thinly sliced
- 1 inch fresh ginger, peeled and minced
- 2 cloves garlic, peeled and minced
- 1 teaspoon curry powder
- 1 teaspoon cumin seeds
- 1 teaspoon black mustard seeds
- 1 teaspoon coriander seeds,
- 1½ pounds (680 g) tomatoes, deseeded and puréed
- 1 red bell pepper, cut into ½-inch dice
- 1 green bell pepper, cut into ½-inch dice
- 3 cups cooked garbanzo beans
- 1 tablespoon garam masala
- 1/3 cup water

Directions:
1. Heat the water in a medium saucepan over medium-low heat. Add the onion, ginger, garlic, curry powder, and seeds to the pan. Sauté for about 10 minutes, or until the onion is tender, stirring frequently.
2. Add the tomatoes and simmer, uncovered, for 10 minutes. Add the peppers and garbanzo beans. Reduce the heat. Cover and simmer for 30 minutes, stirring occasionally. Stir in the garam masala and serve.

Nutrition: calories: 100 fat: 1.2g carbs: 20.9g protein: 5.1g fiber: 7.0g

Simple Baked Navy Beans

Preparation Time: 10 minutes

Cooking Time: 2½ to 3 hours
Servings: 8
Ingredients:
- 1½ cups navy beans
- 8 cups water
- 1 bay leaf
- ½ cup finely chopped green bell pepper
- ½ cup finely chopped onion
- 1 teaspoon minced garlic
- ½ cup unsweetened tomato purée
- 3 tablespoons molasses
- 1 tablespoon fresh lemon juice

Directions:
1. Preheat the oven to 300ºF (150ºC).
2. Place the beans and water in a large pot, along with the bay leaf, green pepper, onion and garlic. Cover and cook for 1½ to 2 hours, or until the beans are softened. Remove from the heat and drain, reserving the cooking liquid. Discard the bay leaf.
3. Transfer the mixture to a casserole dish with a cover. Stir in the remaining ingredients and 1 cup of the reserved cooking liquid. Bake in the oven for 1 hour, covered. Stir occasionally during baking and add a little more cooking liquid if needed to keep the beans moist.
4. Serve warm.

Nutrition: calories: 162 fat: 0.6g carbs: 31.3g protein: 9.1g fiber: 6.4g

Vinegary Black Beans

Preparation Time: 10 minutes
Cooking Time: 2 hours
Servings: 8
Ingredients:
- 1 pound (454 g) black beans, soaked overnight and drained
- 10½ cups water, divided
- 1 green bell pepper, cut in half
- 1 onion, finely chopped
- 1 green bell pepper, finely chopped
- 4 cloves garlic, pressed
- 1 tablespoon maple syrup (optional)
- 1 tablespoon Mrs. Dash seasoning
- 1 bay leaf
- ¼ teaspoon dried oregano
- 2 tablespoons cider vinegar

Directions:
1. Place the beans, 10 cups of the water, and green bell pepper in a large pot. Cook over medium heat for about 45 minutes, or until the green pepper is tendered. Remove the green pepper and discard.
2. Meanwhile, in a different pot, combine the onion, chopped green pepper, garlic and the remaining ½ cup of the water. Sauté for 15 to 20 minutes, or until soft.
3. Add 1 cup of the cooked beans to the pot with vegetables. Mash the beans and vegetables with a potato masher. Add to the pot with the beans, along with the maple syrup (if desired), Mrs. Dash, bay leaf and oregano. Cover and cook over low heat for 1 hour.
4. Drizzle in the vinegar and continue to cook for another hour.

5.	Serve warm.
Nutrition: calories: 226 fat: 0.9g carbs: 42.7g protein: 12.9g fiber: 9.9g

Spiced Lentil Burgers

Preparation Time: 10 minutes
Cooking Time: 43 minutes
Servings: 4
Ingredients:
* ¼ cup minced onion
* 1 clove garlic, minced
* 2 tablespoons water
* 1 cup chopped boiled potatoes
* 1 cup cooked lentils
* 2 tablespoons minced fresh parsley
* 1 teaspoon onion powder
* 1 teaspoon minced fresh basil
* 1 teaspoon dried dill
* 1 teaspoon paprika

Directions:
1.	Preheat the oven to 350ºF (180ºC).
2.	In a pot, sauté the onion and garlic in the water for about 3 minutes, or until soft.
3.	Combine the lentils and potatoes in a large bowl and mash together well. Add the cooked onion and garlic along with the remaining ingredients to the lentil-potato mixture and stir until well combined.
4.	Form the mixture into four patties and place on a nonstick baking sheet. Bake in the oven for 20 minutes. Turn over and bake for an additional 20 minutes.
5.	Serve hot.
Nutrition: calories: 101 fat: 0.4g carbs: 19.9g protein: 5.5g fiber: 5.3g

Pecan-Maple Granola

Preparation Time: 5 minutes
Cooking Time: 50 minutes
Servings: 4
Ingredients:
* 1½ cups rolled oats
* ¼ cup maple syrup (optional)
* ¼ cup pecan pieces
* 1 teaspoon vanilla extract
* ½ teaspoon ground cinnamon

Directions:
1.	Preheat the oven to 300ºF (150ºC). Line a baking sheet with parchment paper.
2.	In a large bowl, stir together all the ingredients until the oats and pecan pieces are completely coated.
3.	Spread the mixture on the baking sheet in an even layer. Bake in the oven for 20 minutes, stirring once halfway through cooking.
4.	Remove from the oven and allow to cool on the countertop for 30 minutes before serving.
Nutrition: calories: 221 fat: 17.2g carbs: 5.1g protein: 4.9g fiber: 3.8g

Bean and Summer Squash Sauté

Preparation Time: 10 minutes
Cooking Time: 15 to 16 minutes
Servings: 4

Ingredients:
* 1 medium red onion, peeled and thinly sliced
* 4 yellow squash, cut into ½-inch rounds
* 4 medium zucchinis, cut into ½-inch rounds
* 1 (15-ounce / 425-g) can navy beans, drained and rinsed
* 2 cups corn kernels
* Zest of 2 lemons
* 1 cup finely chopped basil
* Salt, to taste (optional)
* Freshly ground black pepper, to taste

Directions:
1.	Place the onion in a large saucepan and sauté over medium heat for 7 to 8 minutes. Add water 1 to 2 tablespoons at a time to keep the onion from sticking to the pan.
2.	Add the squash, zucchini, beans, and corn and cook for about 8 minutes, or until the squash is softened.
3.	Remove from the heat. Stir in the lemon zest and basil. Season with salt (if desired) and pepper.
4.	Serve hot.
Nutrition: calories: 298 fat: 2.2g carbs: 60.4g protein: 17.2g fiber: 13.6g

Peppery Black Beans

Preparation Time: 10 minutes
Cooking Time: 33 to 34 minutes
Servings: 4
Ingredients:
* 1 red bell pepper, deseeded and chopped
* 1 medium yellow onion, peeled and chopped
* 2 jalapeño peppers, deseeded and minced
* 4 cloves garlic, peeled and minced
* 1 tablespoon thyme
* 1 tablespoon curry powder
* 1½ teaspoons ground allspice
* 1 teaspoon freshly ground black pepper
* 1 (15-ounce / 425-g)can diced tomatoes
* 4 cups cooked black beans

Directions:
1.	Add the red bell pepper and onion to a saucepan and sauté over medium heat for 10 minutes, or until the onion is softened. Add water 1 to 2 tablespoons at a time to keep the vegetables from sticking to the pan.
2.	Stir in the jalapeño peppers, garlic, thyme, curry powder, allspice and black pepper. Cook for 3 to 4 minutes, then add the tomatoes and black beans. Cook over medium heat for 20 minutes, covered.
3.	Serve immediately.
Nutrition: calories: 283 fat: 1.7g carbs: 52.8g protein: 17.4g fiber: 19.8g

Walnut, Coconut, and Oat Granola

Preparation Time: 15 minutes
Cooking Time: 1 hour 40 minutes
Servings: 4
Ingredients:
* 1 cup chopped walnuts

- 1 cup unsweetened, shredded coconut
- 2 cups rolled oats
- 1 teaspoon ground cinnamon
- 2 tablespoons hemp seeds
- 2 tablespoons ground flaxseeds
- 2 tablespoons chia seeds
- ¾ teaspoon salt (optional)
- ¼ cup maple syrup
- ¼ cup water
- 1 teaspoon vanilla extract
- ½ cup dried cranberries

Directions:

1. Preheat the oven to 250ºF (120ºC). Line a baking sheet with parchment paper.
2. Mix the walnuts, coconut, rolled oats, cinnamon, hemp seeds, flaxseeds, chia seeds, and salt (if desired) in a bowl.
3. Combine the maple syrup and water in a saucepan. Bring to a boil over medium heat, then pour in the bowl of walnut mixture.
4. Add the vanilla extract to the bowl of mixture. Stir to mix well. Pour the mixture in the baking sheet, then level with a spatula so the mixture coat the bottom evenly.
5. Place the baking sheet in the preheated oven and bake for 90 minutes or until browned and crispy. Stir the mixture every 15 minutes.
6. Remove the baking sheet from the oven. Allow to cool for 10 minutes, then serve with dried cranberries on top.

Nutrition: calories: 1870 fat: 115.8g carbs: 238.0g protein: 59.8g fiber: 68.9g

Ritzy Fava Bean Ratatouille

Preparation Time: 15 minutes
Cooking Time: 40 minutes
Servings: 4
Ingredients:

- 1 medium red onion, peeled and thinly sliced
- 2 tablespoons low-sodium vegetable broth
- 1 large eggplant, stemmed and cut into ½-inch dice
- 1 red bell pepper, seeded and diced
- 2 cups cooked fava beans
- 2 Roma tomatoes, chopped
- 1 medium zucchini, diced
- 2 cloves garlic, peeled and finely chopped
- ¼ cup finely chopped basil
- Salt, to taste (optional)
- Ground black pepper, to taste

Directions:

1. Add the onion to a saucepan and sauté for 7 minutes or until caramelized.
2. Add the vegetable broth, eggplant and red bell pepper to the pan and sauté for 10 more minutes.
3. Add the fava beans, tomatoes, zucchini, and garlic to the pan and sauté for an additional 5 minutes.
4. Reduce the heat to medium-low. Put the pan lid on and cook for 15 minutes or until the vegetables are soft. Stir the vegetables halfway through.
5. Transfer them onto a large serving plate. Sprinkle with basil, salt (if desired), and black pepper before serving.

Nutrition: calories: 114 fat: 1.0g carbs: 24.2g protein: 7.4g fiber: 10.3g

Peppers and Black Beans with Brown Rice

Preparation Time: 15 minutes
Cooking Time: 20 minutes
Servings: 4
Ingredients:

- 2 jalapeño peppers, diced
- 1 red bell pepper, seeded and diced
- 1 medium yellow onion, peeled and diced
- 2 tablespoons low-sodium vegetable broth
- 1 teaspoon toasted and ground cumin seeds
- 1½ teaspoons toasted oregano
- 5 cloves garlic, peeled and minced
- 4 cups cooked black beans
- Salt, to taste (optional)
- Ground black pepper, to taste
- 3 cups cooked brown rice
- 1 lime, quartered
- 1 cup chopped cilantro

Directions:

1. Add the jalapeño peppers, bell pepper, and onion to a saucepan and sauté for 7 minutes or until the onion is well browned and caramelized.
2. Add vegetable broth, cumin, oregano, and garlic to the pan and sauté for 3 minutes or until fragrant.
3. Add the black beans and sauté for 10 minutes or until the vegetables are tender. Sprinkle with salt (if desired) and black pepper halfway through.
4. Arrange the brown rice on a platter, then top with the cooked vegetables. Garnish with lime wedges and cilantro before serving.

Nutrition: calories: 426 fat: 2.6g carbs: 82.4g protein: 20.2g fiber: 19.5g

Black-Eyed Pea, Beet, and Carrot Stew

Preparation Time: 15 minutes
Cooking Time: 40 minutes
Servings: 2
Ingredients:

- ½ cup black-eyed peas, soaked in water overnight
- 3 cups water
- 1 large beet, peeled and cut into ½-inch pieces (about ¾ cup)
- 1 large carrot, peeled and cut into ½-inch pieces (about ¾ cup)
- ¼ teaspoon turmeric
- ¼ teaspoon toasted and ground cumin seeds
- 1/8 teaspoon asafetida
- ¼ cup finely chopped parsley
- ¼ teaspoon cayenne pepper
- ¼ teaspoon salt (optional)
- ½ teaspoon fresh lime juice

Directions:

1.   Pour the black-eyed peas and water in a pot, then cook over medium heat for 25 minutes.
2.   Add the beet and carrot to the pot and cook for 10 more minutes. Add more water if necessary.
3.   Add the turmeric, cumin, asafetida, parsley, and cayenne pepper to the pot and cook for an additional 6 minutes or until the vegetables are soft. Stir the mixture periodically. Sprinkle with salt, if desired.
4.   Drizzle the lime juice on top before serving in a large bowl.
Nutrition: calories: 84 | fat: 0.7g | carbs: 16.6g | protein: 4.1g | fiber: 4.5g

Koshari

Preparation Time: 15 minutes
Cooking Time: 2 hours 10 minutes
Servings: 6
Ingredients:
- 1 cup green lentils, rinsed
- 3 cups water
- Salt, to taste (optional)
- 1 large onion, peeled and minced
- 2 tablespoons low-sodium vegetable broth
- 4 cloves garlic, peeled and minced
- ½ teaspoon ground allspice
- 1 teaspoon ground coriander
- 1 teaspoon ground cumin
- 2 tablespoons tomato paste
- ½ teaspoon crushed red pepper flakes
- 3 large tomatoes, diced
- 1 cup cooked medium-grain brown rice
- 1 cup whole-grain elbow macaroni, cooked, drained, and kept warm
- 1 tablespoon brown rice vinegar

Directions:
1.   Put the lentils and water in a saucepan, and sprinkle with salt, if desired. Bring to a boil over high heat. Reduce the heat to medium, then put the pan lid on and cook for 45 minutes or until the water is mostly absorbed. Pour the cooked lentils in the bowl and set aside.
2.   Add the onion to a nonstick skillet, then sauté over medium heat for 15 minutes or until caramelized.
3.   Add vegetable broth and garlic to the skillet and sauté for 3 minutes or until fragrant.
4.   Add the allspice, coriander, cumin, tomato paste, and red pepper flakes to the skillet and sauté for an additional 3 minutes until aromatic.
5.   Add the tomatoes to the skillet and sauté for 15 minutes or until the tomatoes are wilted. Sprinkle with salt, if desired.
6.   Arrange the cooked brown rice on the bottom of a large platter, then top the rice with macaroni, and then spread the lentils over. Pour the tomato mixture and brown rice vinegar over before serving.
Nutrition: calories: 201 fat: 1.6g carbs: 41.8g protein: 6.5g fiber: 3.6g

DRINKS

Banana Weight Loss Juice

Preparation Time: 10 Minutes
Cooking Time: 0 Minutes
Servings: 1
Ingredients:
- Water (1/3 C.)
- Apple (1, Sliced)
- Orange (1, Sliced)
- Banana (1, Sliced)
- Lemon Juice (1 T.)

Directions:
1. Looking to boost your weight loss? The key is taking in less calories; this recipe can get you there.
2. Simply place everything into your blender, blend on high for twenty seconds, and then pour into your glass.

Nutrition: Calories: 289 Total Carbohydrate: 2 g Cholesterol: 3 mg Total Fat: 17 g Fiber: 2 g Protein: 7 g Sodium: 163 mg

Citrus Detox Juice

Preparation Time: 10 Minutes
Cooking Time: 0 Minutes
Servings: 4
Ingredients:
- Water (3 C.)
- Lemon (1, Sliced)
- Grapefruit (1, Sliced)
- Orange (1, Sliced)

Directions:
1. While starting your new diet, it is going to be vital to stay hydrated. This detox juice is the perfect solution and offers some extra flavor.
2. Begin by peeling and slicing up your fruit. Once this is done, place in a pitcher of water and infuse the water overnight.

Nutrition: Calories: 269 Total Carbohydrate: 2 g Cholesterol: 3 mg Total Fat: 14 g Fiber: 2 g Protein: 7 g Sodium: 183 mg

Metabolism Water

Preparation Time: 10 Minutes
Cooking Time: 0 Minutes
Servings: 1
Ingredients:
- Water (3 C.)
- Cucumber (1, Sliced)
- Lemon (1, Sliced)
- Mint (2 Leaves)
- Ice

Directions:
1. At some point, we probably all wish for a quicker metabolism! With the lemon acting as an energizer, cucumber for a refreshing taste, and mint to help your stomach digest, this water is perfect!
2. All you will have to do is get out a pitcher, place all of the ingredients in, and allow the ingredients to soak overnight for maximum benefits!

Stress Relief Detox Drink

Nutrition: Calories: 301 Total Carbohydrate: 2 g Cholesterol: 13 mg Total Fat: 17 g Fiber: 4 g Protein: 8 g Sodium: 201 mg

Preparation Time: 5 Minutes
Cooking Time: 0 Minutes
Servings: 1
Ingredients:
- Water (1 Pitcher)
- Mint
- Lemon (1, Sliced)
- Basil
- Strawberries (1 C., Sliced)
- Ice

Directions:
1. Life can be a pretty stressful event. Luckily, there is water to help keep you cool, calm, and collected! The lemon works like an energizer, the basil is a natural antidepressant, and mint can help your stomach do its job better. As for the strawberries, those are just for some sweetness!
2. When you are ready, take all of the ingredients and place into a pitcher of water overnight and enjoy the next day.

Nutrition: Calories: 189 Total Carbohydrate: 2 g Cholesterol: 73 mg Total Fat: 17 g Fiber: 0 g Protein: 7 g Sodium: 163 mg

Strawberry Pink Drink

Preparation Time: 10 Minutes
Cooking Time: 5 Minutes
Servings: 4
Ingredients:
- Water (1 C., Boiling)
- Sugar (2 T.)
- Acai Tea Bag (1)
- Coconut Milk (1 C.)
- Frozen Strawberries (1/2 C.)

Directions:
1. If you are looking for a little treat, this is going to be the recipe for you! You will begin by boiling your cup of water and seep the tea bag in for at least five minutes.
2. When the tea is set, add in the sugar and coconut milk. Be sure to stir well to spread the sweetness throughout the tea.
3. Finally, add in your strawberries, and you can enjoy your freshly made pink drink!

Nutrition: Calories: 321 Total Carbohydrate: 2 g Cholesterol: 13 mg Total Fat: 17 g Fiber: 2 g Protein: 9 g Sodium: 312 mg

Avocado Pudding

Preparation Time: 10 minutes
Cooking Time: 0 minute
Servings: 8
Ingredients:
- 2 ripe avocados, peeled, pitted and cut into pieces
- 1 tbsp fresh lime juice

- 14 oz can coconut milk
- 80 drops of liquid stevia
- 2 tsp vanilla extract

Directions:
1. Add all ingredients into the blender and blend until smooth.
2. Serve and enjoy.

Nutrition: Calories: 209 Total Carbohydrate: 6 g Cholesterol: 13 mg Total Fat: 7 g Fiber: 2 g Protein: 17 g Sodium: 193 mg

Almond Butter Brownies

Preparation Time: 10 minutes
Cooking Time: 20 minutes
Servings: 4
Ingredients:
- 1 scoop protein powder
- 2 tbsp cocoa powder
- 1/2 cup almond butter, melted
- 1 cup bananas, overripe

Directions:
1. Preheat the oven to 350 F/ 176 C.
1. Spray brownie tray with cooking spray.
2. Add all ingredients into the blender and blend until smooth.
3. Pour batter into the prepared dish and bake in preheated oven for 20 minutes.
4. Serve and enjoy.

Nutrition: Calories: 214 Total Carbohydrate: 2 g Cholesterol: 73 mg Total Fat: 7 g Fiber: 2g Protein: 19 g Sodium: 308 g

Raspberry Chia Pudding

Preparation Time: 3 hours 10 minutes
Cooking Time: 0 minute
Servings: 2
Ingredients:
- 4 tbsp chia seeds
- 1 cup coconut milk
- 1/2 cup raspberries

Directions:
1. Add raspberry and coconut milk in a blender and blend until smooth.
2. Pour mixture into the Mason jar.
3. Add chia seeds in a jar and stir well.
4. Close jar tightly with lid and shake well.
5. Place in refrigerator for 3 hours.
6. Serve chilled and enjoy.

Nutrition: Calories: 189 Total Carbohydrate: 6 g Cholesterol: 3 mg Total Fat: 7 g Fiber: 4 g Protein: 12 g Sodium: 293 mg

Chocolate Fudge

Preparation Time: 10 minutes
Cooking Time: 0 minute
Servings: 12
Ingredients:
- 4 oz unsweetened dark chocolate
- 3/4 cup coconut butter
- 15 drops liquid stevia
- 1 tsp vanilla extract

Directions:
1. Melt coconut butter and dark chocolate.

2. Add ingredients to the large bowl and combine well.
3. Pour mixture into a silicone loaf pan and place in refrigerator until set.
4. Cut into pieces and serve.

Nutrition: Calories: 283 Total Carbohydrate: 10 g Cholesterol: 3 mg Total Fat: 8 g Fiber: 2 g Protein: 9 g Sodium: 271 mg

Quick Chocó Brownie

Preparation Time: 10 minutes
Cooking Time: 2 minutes
Servings: 1
Ingredients:
- 1/4 cup almond milk
- 1 tbsp cocoa powder
- 1 scoop chocolate protein powder
- 1/2 tsp baking powder

Directions:
1. In a microwave-safe mug blend together baking powder, protein powder, and cocoa.
2. Add almond milk in a mug and stir well.
3. Place mug in microwave and microwave for 30 seconds.
4. Serve and enjoy.

Nutrition: Calories: 231 Total Carbohydrate: 2 g Cholesterol: 13 mg Total Fat: 15 g Fiber: 2 g Protein: 8 g Sodium: 298 mg

Simple Almond Butter Fudge

Preparation Time: 15 minutes
Cooking Time: 0 minutes
Servings: 8
Ingredients:
- 1/2 cup almond butter
- 15 drops liquid stevia
- 2 1/2 tbsp coconut oil

Directions:
1. Combine together almond butter and coconut oil in a saucepan. Gently warm until melted.
2. Add stevia and stir well.
3. Pour mixture into the candy container and place in refrigerator until set.
4. Serve and enjoy.

Nutrition: Calories: 198 Total Carbohydrate: 5 g Cholesterol: 12 mg Total Fat: 10 g Fiber: 2 g Protein: 6 g Sodium: 257 mg

Coconut Peanut Butter Fudge

Preparation Time: 1 hour 15 minutes
Cooking Time: 0 minute
Servings: 20
Ingredients:
- 12 oz smooth peanut butter
- 3 tbsp coconut oil
- 4 tbsp coconut cream
- 15 drops liquid stevia
- Pinch of salt

Directions:
1. Line baking tray with parchment paper.
2. Melt coconut oil in a saucepan over low heat.
3. Add peanut butter, coconut cream, stevia, and salt in a saucepan. Stir well.

4. Pour fudge mixture into the prepared baking tray and place in refrigerator for 1 hour.
5. Cut into pieces and serve.
Nutrition: Calories: 189 Total Carbohydrate: 2 g Cholesterol: 13 mg Total Fat: 7 g Fiber: 2 g Protein: 10 g Sodium: 301 mg

Lemon Mousse

Preparation Time: 10 minutes
Cooking Time: 0 minute
Servings: 2
Ingredients:
- 14 oz coconut milk
- 12 drops liquid stevia
- 1/2 tsp lemon extract
- 1/4 tsp turmeric

Directions:
1. Place coconut milk can in the refrigerator for overnight. Scoop out thick cream into a mixing bowl.
2. Add remaining ingredients to the bowl and whip using a hand mixer until smooth.
3. Transfer mousse mixture to a zip-lock bag and pipe into small serving glasses. Place in refrigerator.
4. Serve chilled and enjoy.
Nutrition: Calories: 189 Total Carbohydrate: 2 g Cholesterol: 13 mg Total Fat: 7 g Fiber: 2 g Protein: 15 g Sodium: 321 mg

Chocó Chia Pudding

Preparation Time: 10 minutes
Cooking Time: 0 minutes
Servings: 6
Ingredients:
- 2 1/2 cups coconut milk
- 2 scoops stevia extract powder
- 6 tbsp cocoa powder
- 1/2 cup chia seeds
- 1/2 tsp vanilla extract
- 1/8 cup xylitol
- 1/8 tsp salt

Directions:
1. Add all ingredients into the blender and blend until smooth.
2. Pour mixture into the glass container and place in refrigerator.
3. Serve chilled and enjoy.
Nutrition: Calories: 178 Total Carbohydrate: 3 g Cholesterol: 3 mg Total Fat: 17 g Fiber: g Protein: 9 g Sodium: 297 mg

Spiced Buttermilk

Preparation Time: 5 minutes
Cooking Time: 0 minute
Servings: 2
Ingredients:
- 3/4 teaspoon ground cumin
- 1/4 teaspoon sea salt
- 1/8 teaspoon ground black pepper
- 2 mint leaves
- 1/8 teaspoon lemon juice
- ¼ cup cilantro leaves
- 1 cup of chilled water

- 1 cup vegan yogurt, unsweetened
- Ice as needed

Directions:
1. Place all the ingredients in the order in a food processor or blender, except for cilantro and ¼ teaspoon cumin, and then pulse for 2 to 3 minutes at high speed until smooth.
2. Pour the milk into glasses, top with cilantro and cumin, and then serve.
Nutrition: Calories: 211 Total Carbohydrate: 7 g Cholesterol: 13 mg Total Fat: 18 g Fiber: 3 g Protein: 17 g Sodium: 289 mg

Turmeric Lassi

Preparation Time: 5 minutes
Cooking Time: 0 minute
Servings: 2
Ingredients:
- 1 teaspoon grated ginger
- 1/8 teaspoon ground black pepper
- 1 teaspoon turmeric powder
- 1/8 teaspoon cayenne
- 1 tablespoon coconut sugar
- 1/8 teaspoon salt
- 1 cup vegan yogurt
- 1 cup almond milk

Directions:
1. Place all the ingredients in the order in a food processor or blender and then pulse for 2 to 3 minutes at high speed until smooth.
2. Pour the lassi into two glasses and then serve.
Nutrition: Calories: 392 Fat: 10g Protein: 18g Sugar: 8g

Brownie Batter Orange Chia Shake

Preparation Time: 5 minutes
Cooking Time: 0 minute
Servings: 2
Ingredients:
- 2 tablespoons cocoa powder
- 3 tablespoons chia seeds
- ¼ teaspoon salt
- 4 tablespoons chocolate chips
- 4 teaspoons coconut sugar
- ½ teaspoon orange zest
- ½ teaspoon vanilla extract, unsweetened
- 2 cup almond milk

Directions:
1. Place all the ingredients in the order in a food processor or blender and then pulse for 2 to 3 minutes at high speed until smooth.
2. Pour the smoothie into two glasses and then serve.
Nutrition: Calories: 290 Fat: 11g Protein: 20g Sugar: 9g

Saffron Pistachio Beverage

Preparation Time: 5 minutes
Cooking Time: 0 minute
Servings: 2
Ingredients:
- 8 strands of saffron
- 1 tablespoon cashews

- 1/4 teaspoon ground ginger
- 2 tablespoons pistachio
- 1/8 teaspoon cloves
- 1/4 teaspoon ground black pepper
- 1/4 teaspoon cardamom powder
- 3 tablespoons coconut sugar
- 1/4 teaspoon cinnamon
- 1/8 teaspoon fennel seeds
- 1/4 teaspoon poppy seeds

Directions:
1.   Place all the ingredients in the order in a food processor or blender and then pulse for 2 to 3 minutes at high speed until smooth.
2.   Pour the smoothie into two glasses and then serve.
Nutrition: Calories: 394 Fat: 5g Protein: 12g Sugar: 4g

Mexican Hot Chocolate Mix

Preparation Time: 5 minutes
Cooking Time: 0 minute
Servings: 2
Ingredients:
For the Hot Chocolate Mix:
- 1/3 cup chopped dark chocolate
- 1/8 teaspoon cayenne
- 1/8 teaspoon salt
- 1/2 teaspoon cinnamon
- 1/4 cup coconut sugar
- 1 teaspoon cornstarch
- 3 tablespoons cocoa powder
- 1/2 teaspoon vanilla extract, unsweetened

For **Servings:**
- 2 cups milk, warmed

Directions:
1.   Place all the ingredients of hot chocolate mix in the order in a food processor or blender and then pulse for 2 to 3 minutes at high speed until ground.
2.   Stir 2 tablespoons of the chocolate mix into a glass of milk until combined and then serve.
Nutrition: Calories: 160 Fat: 6g Protein: 26g Sugar: 7g

Pumpkin Spice Frappuccino

Preparation Time: 5 minutes
Cooking Time: 0 minute
Servings: 2
Ingredients:
- ½ teaspoon ground ginger
- 1/8 teaspoon allspice
- ½ teaspoon ground cinnamon
- 2 tablespoons coconut sugar
- 1/8 teaspoon nutmeg
- ¼ teaspoon ground cloves
- 1 teaspoon vanilla extract, unsweetened
- 2 teaspoons instant coffee
- 2 cups almond milk, unsweetened
- 1 cup of ice cubes

Directions:
1.   Place all the ingredients in the order in a food processor or blender and then pulse for 2 to 3 minutes at high speed until smooth.

2.   Pour the Frappuccino into two glasses and then serve.
Nutrition: Calories: 490 Fat: 9g Protein: 12g Sugar: 11g

Cookie Dough Milkshake

Preparation Time: 5 minutes
Cooking Time: 0 minute
Servings: 2
Ingredients:
- 2 tablespoons cookie dough
- 5 dates, pitted
- 2 teaspoons chocolate chips
- 1/2 teaspoon vanilla extract, unsweetened
- 1/2 cup almond milk, unsweetened
- 1 ½ cup almond milk ice cubes

Directions:
1.   Place all the ingredients in the order in a food processor or blender and then pulse for 2 to 3 minutes at high speed until smooth.
2.   Pour the milkshake into two glasses and then serve with some cookie dough balls.
Nutrition: Calories: 240 Fat: 13g Protein: 21g Sugar: 9g

Strawberry and Hemp Smoothie

Preparation Time: 5 minutes
Cooking Time: 0 minute
Servings: 2
Ingredients:
- 3 cups fresh strawberries
- 2 tablespoons hemp seeds
- 1/2 teaspoon vanilla extract, unsweetened
- 1/8 teaspoon sea salt
- 2 tablespoons maple syrup
- 1 cup vegan yogurt
- 1 cup almond milk, unsweetened
- 1 cup of ice cubes
- 2 tablespoons hemp protein

Directions:
1.   Place all the ingredients in the order in a food processor or blender, except for protein powder, and then pulse for 2 to 3 minutes at high speed until smooth.
2.   Pour the smoothie into two glasses and then serve.
Nutrition: Calories: 510 Fat: 18g Protein: 26g Sugar: 12g

Blueberry, Hazelnut and Hemp Smoothie

Preparation Time: 5 minutes
Cooking Time: 0 minute
Servings: 2
Ingredients:
- 2 tablespoons hemp seeds
- 1 ½ cups frozen blueberries
- 2 tablespoons chocolate protein powder
- 1/2 teaspoon vanilla extract, unsweetened
- 2 tablespoons chocolate hazelnut butter
- 1 small frozen banana
- 3/4 cup almond milk

Directions:

1.   Place all the ingredients in the order in a food processor or blender and then pulse for 2 to 3 minutes at high speed until smooth.
2.   Pour the smoothie into two glasses and then serve.
Nutrition: Calories: 195 Fat: 14g Protein: 36g Sugar: 10g

Mango Lassi

Preparation Time: 5 minutes
Cooking Time: 0 minute
Servings: 2
Ingredients:
- 1 ¼ cup mango pulp
- 1 tablespoon coconut sugar
- 1/8 teaspoon salt
- 1/2 teaspoon lemon juice
- 1/4 cup almond milk, unsweetened
- 1/4 cup chilled water
- 1 cup cashew yogurt

Directions:
1.   Place all the ingredients in the order in a food processor or blender and then pulse for 2 to 3 minutes at high speed until smooth.
2.   Pour the lassi into two glasses and then serve.
Nutrition: Calories: 420 Fat: 12g Protein: 23g Sugar: 13g

Mocha Chocolate Shake

Preparation Time: 5 minutes
Cooking Time: 0 minute
Servings: 2
Ingredients:
- 1/4 cup hemp seeds
- 2 teaspoons cocoa powder, unsweetened
- 1/2 cup dates, pitted
- 1 tablespoon instant coffee powder
- 2 tablespoons flax seeds
- 2 1/2 cups almond milk, unsweetened
- 1/2 cup crushed ice

Directions:
1.   Place all the ingredients in the order in a food processor or blender and then pulse for 2 to 3 minutes at high speed until smooth.
2.   Pour the smoothie into two glasses and then serve.
Nutrition: Calories: 432 Fat: 18g Protein: 14g Sugar: 12g

Chard, Lettuce and Ginger Smoothie

Preparation Time: 5 minutes
Cooking Time: 0 minute
Servings: 2
Ingredients:
- 10 Chard leaves, chopped
- 1-inch piece of ginger, chopped
- 10 lettuce leaves, chopped
- ½ teaspoon black salt
- 2 pear, chopped
- 2 teaspoons coconut sugar
- ¼ teaspoon ground black pepper
- ¼ teaspoon salt

- 2 tablespoons lemon juice
- 2 cups of water

Directions:
1.   Place all the ingredients in the order in a food processor or blender and then pulse for 2 to 3 minutes at high speed until smooth.
2.   Pour the smoothie into two glasses and then serve.
Nutrition: Calories: 240 Fat: 4g Protein: 16g Sugar: 3g

Red Beet, Pear and Apple Smoothie

Preparation Time: 5 minutes
Cooking Time: 0 minute
Servings: 2
Ingredients:
- 1/2 of medium beet, peeled, chopped
- 1 tablespoon chopped cilantro
- 1 orange, juiced
- 1 medium pear, chopped
- 1 medium apple, cored, chopped
- 1/4 teaspoon ground black pepper
- 1/8 teaspoon rock salt
- 1 teaspoon coconut sugar
- 1/4 teaspoons salt
- 1 cup of water

Directions:
1.   Place all the ingredients in the order in a food processor or blender and then pulse for 2 to 3 minutes at high speed until smooth.
2.   Pour the smoothie into two glasses and then serve.
Nutrition: Calories: 240 Fat: 4g Protein: 16g Sugar: 3g

Berry and Yogurt Smoothie

Preparation Time: 5 minutes
Cooking Time: 0 minute
Servings: 2
Ingredients:
- 2 small bananas
- 3 cups frozen mixed berries
- 1 ½ cup cashew yogurt
- 1/2 teaspoon vanilla extract, unsweetened
- 1/2 cup almond milk, unsweetened

Directions:
1.   Place all the ingredients in the order in a food processor or blender and then pulse for 2 to 3 minutes at high speed until smooth.
2.   Pour the smoothie into two glasses and then serve.
Nutrition: Calories: 291 Fat: 9g Protein: 17g Sugar: 5g

Chocolate and Cherry Smoothie

Preparation Time: 5 minutes
Cooking Time: 0 minute
Servings: 2
Ingredients:
- 4 cups frozen cherries
- 2 tablespoons cocoa powder
- 1 scoop of protein powder
- 1 teaspoon maple syrup

- 2 cups almond milk, unsweetened

Directions:
1. Place all the ingredients in the order in a food processor or blender and then pulse for 2 to 3 minutes at high speed until smooth.
2. Pour the smoothie into two glasses and then serve.

Nutrition: Calories: 247 Fat: 3g Protein: 18g Sugar: 3g

Strawberry Shake

Preparation Time: 10 minutes
Cooking Time: 10 minutes
Servings: 2
Ingredients:
- 1½ cups fresh strawberries, hulled
- 1 large frozen banana, peeled
- 2 scoops unsweetened vegan vanilla protein powder
- 2 tablespoons hemp seeds
- 2 cups unsweetened hemp milk

Directions:
1. In a high-speed blender, place all the ingredients and pulse until creamy.
2. Pour into two glasses and serve immediately.

Nutrition: Calories: 259 Fat: 3g Protein: 10g Sugar: 2g

Chocolatey Banana Shake

Preparation Time: 10 minutes
Cooking Time: 10 minutes
Servings: 2
Ingredients:
- 2 medium frozen bananas, peeled
- 4 dates, pitted
- 4 tablespoons peanut butter
- 4 tablespoons rolled oats
- 2 tablespoons cacao powder
- 2 tablespoons chia seeds
- 2 cups unsweetened soymilk

Directions:
1. Place all the ingredients in a high-speed blender and pulse until creamy.
2. Pour into two glasses and serve immediately.

Nutrition: Calories: 502 Fat: 4g Protein: 11g Sugar: 9g

Fruity Tofu Smoothie

Preparation Time: 10 minutes
Cooking Time: 10 minutes
Servings: 2
Ingredients:
- 12 ounces silken tofu, pressed and drained
- 2 medium bananas, peeled
- 1½ cups fresh blueberries
- 1 tablespoon maple syrup
- 1½ cups unsweetened soymilk
- ¼ cup ice cubes

Directions:
1. Place all the ingredients in a high-speed blender and pulse until creamy.
2. Pour into two glasses and serve immediately.

Nutrition: Calories 235 Carbohydrates: 1.9g Protein: 14.3g Fat: 18.9g

Green Fruity Smoothie

Preparation Time: 10 minutes
Cooking Time: 10 minutes
Servings: 2
Ingredients:
- 1 cup frozen mango, peeled, pitted, and chopped
- 1 large frozen banana, peeled
- 2 cups fresh baby spinach
- 1 scoop unsweetened vegan vanilla protein powder
- ¼ cup pumpkin seeds
- 2 tablespoons hemp hearts
- 1½ cups unsweetened almond milk

Directions:
1. In a high-speed blender, place all the ingredients and pulse until creamy.
2. Pour into two glasses and serve immediately.

Nutrition: Calories 206 Carbohydrates: 1.3g Protein: 23.5g Fat: 11.9g

Protein Latte

Preparation Time: 10 minutes
Cooking Time: 10 minutes
Servings: 2
Ingredients:
- 2 cups hot brewed coffee
- 1¼ cups coconut milk
- 2 teaspoons coconut oil
- 2 scoops unsweetened vegan vanilla protein powder

Directions:
1. Place all the ingredients in a high-speed blender and pulse until creamy.
2. Pour into two serving mugs and serve immediately.

Nutrition: Calories 483 Carbs: 5.2g Protein: 45.2g Fat: 31.2g

Health Boosting Juices

Preparation Time: 10 minutes
Cooking Time: 15 minutes
Servings: 2
Ingredients for a red juice:
- 4 beetroots, quartered
- 2 cups of strawberries
- 2 cups of blueberries
- Ingredients for an orange juice:
- 4 green or red apples, halved
- 10 carrots
- ½ lemon, peeled
- 1" of ginger
- Ingredients for a yellow juice:
- 2 green or red apples, quartered
- 4 oranges, peeled and halved
- ½ lemon, peeled
- 1" of ginger
- Ingredients for a lime juice:
- 6 stalks of celery

- 1 cucumber
- 2 green apples, quartered
- 2 pears, quartered
- Ingredients for a green juice:
- ½ a pineapple, peeled and sliced
- 8 leaves of kale
- 2 fresh bananas, peeled

Directions:
1. Juice all ingredients in a juicer, chill and serve.

Nutrition: Calories 316 Carbs: 13.5g Protein: 37.8g Fat: 12.2g

Thai Iced Tea

Preparation Time: 5 minutes
Cooking Time: 10 minutes
Servings: 4
Ingredients:
- 4 cups of water
- 1 can of light coconut milk (14 oz.)
- ¼ cup of maple syrup
- ¼ cup of muscovado sugar
- 1 teaspoon of vanilla extract
- 2 tablespoons of loose-leaf black tea

Directions:
1. In a large saucepan, over medium heat bring the water to a boil.
2. Turn off the heat and add in the tea, cover and let steep for five minutes.
3. Strain the tea into a bowl or jug. Add the maple syrup, muscovado sugar, and vanilla extract. Give it a good whisk to blend all the ingredients together.
4. Set in the refrigerator to chill. Upon serving, pour ¾ of the tea into each glass, top with coconut milk and stir.

Tips:
Add a shot of dark rum to turn this iced tea into a cocktail.
You could substitute the coconut milk for almond or rice milk too.

Nutrition: Calories 844 Carbohydrates: 2.3g Protein: 21.6g Fat: 83.1g

Hot Chocolate

Preparation Time: 5 minutes
Cooking Time: 15 minutes
Servings: 2
Ingredients:
- Pinch of brown sugar
- 2 cups of milk, soy or almond, unsweetened
- 2 tablespoons of cocoa powder
- ½ cup of vegan chocolate

Directions:
1. In a medium saucepan, over medium heat gently bring the milk to a boil. Whisk in the cocoa powder.
2. Remove from the heat, add a pinch of sugar and chocolate. Give it a good stir until smooth, serve and enjoy.

Tips:
You may substitute the almond or soy milk for coconut milk too.

Nutrition: Calories 452 Carbs: 29.8g Protein: 15.2g Fat: 30.2g

Chai and Chocolate Milkshake

Preparation Time: 5 minutes
Cooking Time: 15 minutes
Servings: 2 servings
Ingredients:
- 1 and ½ cups of almond milk, sweetened or unsweetened
- 3 bananas, peeled and frozen 12 hours before use
- 4 dates, pitted
- 1 and ½ teaspoons of chocolate powder, sweetened or unsweetened
- ½ teaspoon of vanilla extract
- ½ teaspoon of cinnamon
- ¼ teaspoon of ground ginger
- Pinch of ground cardamom
- Pinch of ground cloves
- Pinch of ground nutmeg
- ½ cup of ice cubes

Directions:
1. Add all the ingredients to a blender except for the ice-cubes. Pulse until smooth and creamy, add the ice-cubes, pulse a few more times and serve.

Tips:
The dates provide enough sweetness to the recipe, however, you are welcome to add maple syrup or honey for a sweeter drink.

Nutrition: Calories 452 Carbs: 29.8g Protein: 15.2g Fat: 30.2g

Colorful Infused Water

Preparation Time: 5 minutes
Cooking Time: 1 hour
Servings: 8 servings
Ingredients:
- 1 cup of strawberries, fresh or frozen
- 1 cup of blueberries, fresh or frozen
- 1 tablespoon of baobab powder
- 1 cup of ice cubes
- 4 cups of sparkling water

Directions:
1. In a large water jug, add in the sparkling water, ice cubes, and baobab powder. Give it a good stir.
2. Add in the strawberries and blueberries and cover the infused water, store in the refrigerator for one hour before serving.

Tips:
Store for 12 hours for optimum taste and nutritional benefits.
Instead of using strawberries and blueberries, add slices of lemon and six mint leaves, one cup of mangoes or cherries, or half a cup of leafy greens such as kale and/or spinach.

Nutrition: Calories 163 Carbs: 4.1g Protein: 1.7g Fat: 15.5g

Hibiscus Tea

Preparation Time: 1 Minute
Cooking Time: 5 minutes
Servings: 2 servings

Ingredients:
- 1 tablespoon of raisins, diced
- 6 Almonds, raw and unsalted
- ½ teaspoon of hibiscus powder
- 2 cups of water

Directions:
1. Bring the water to a boil in a small saucepan, add in the hibiscus powder and raisins. Give it a good stir, cover and let simmer for a further two minutes.
2. Strain into a teapot and serve with a side helping of almonds.

Tips:
As an alternative to this tea, do not strain it and serve with the raisin pieces still swirling around in the teacup.

You could also serve this tea chilled for those hotter days.

Double or triple the recipe to provide you with iced-tea to enjoy during the week without having to make a fresh pot each time.

Nutrition: Calories 139 Carbohydrates: 2.7g Protein: 8.7g Fat: 10.3

Lemon and Rosemary Iced Tea

Preparation Time: 5 minutes
Cooking Time: 10 minutes
Servings: 4 servings
Ingredients:
- 4 cups of water
- 4 earl grey tea bags
- ¼ cup of sugar
- 2 lemons
- 1 sprig of rosemary

Directions:
1. Peel the two lemons and set the fruit aside.
2. In a medium saucepan, over medium heat combine the water, sugar, and lemon peels. Bring this to a boil.
3. Remove from the heat and place the rosemary and tea into the mixture. Cover the saucepan and steep for five minutes.
4. Add the juice of the two peeled lemons to the mixture, strain, chill, and serve.

Tips: Skip the sugar and use honey to taste.
Do not squeeze the tea bags as they can cause the tea to become bitter.

Nutrition: Calories 229 Carbs: 33.2g Protein: 31.1g Fat: 10.2g

Lavender and Mint Iced Tea

Preparation Time: 5 minutes
Cooking Time: 10 minutes
Servings: 8 servings
Ingredients:
- 8 cups of water
- 1/3 cup of dried lavender buds
- ¼ cup of mint

Directions:
1. Add the mint and lavender to a pot and set this aside.
2. Add in eight cups of boiling water to the pot. Sweeten to taste, cover and let steep for ten minutes. Strain, chill, and serve.

Tips:
Use a sweetener of your choice when making this iced tea.
Add spirits to turn this iced tea into a summer cocktail.

Nutrition: Calories 266 Carbs: 9.3g Protein: 20.9g Fat: 16.1g

Pear Lemonade

Preparation Time: 5 minutes
Cooking Time: 30 minutes
Servings: 2 servings
Ingredients:
- ½ cup of pear, peeled and diced
- 1 cup of freshly squeezed lemon juice
- ½ cup of chilled water

Directions:
1. Add all the ingredients into a blender and pulse until it has all been combined. The pear does make the lemonade frothy, but this will settle.
2. Place in the refrigerator to cool and then serve.

Tips:
Keep stored in a sealed container in the refrigerator for up to four days.
Pop the fresh lemon in the microwave for ten minutes before juicing, you can extract more juice if you do this.

Nutrition: Calories: 160 Carbs: 6.3g Protein: 2.9g Fat: 13.6g

Energizing Ginger Detox Tonic

Preparation Time: 15 minutes
Cooking Time: 10 minutes
Servings:
Ingredients:
- 1/2 teaspoon of grated ginger, fresh
- 1 small lemon slice
- 1/8 teaspoon of cayenne pepper
- 1/8 teaspoon of ground turmeric
- 1/8 teaspoon of ground cinnamon
- 1 teaspoon of maple syrup
- 1 teaspoon of apple cider vinegar
- 2 cups of boiling water

Directions:
1. Pour the boiling water into a small saucepan, add and stir the ginger, then let it rest for 8 to 10 minutes, before covering the pan.
2. Pass the mixture through a strainer and into the liquid, add the cayenne pepper, turmeric, cinnamon and stir properly.
3. Add the maple syrup, vinegar, and lemon slice.
4. Add and stir an infused lemon and serve immediately.

Nutrition: Calories 443 Carbs:9.7 g Protein: 62.8g Fat: 16.9g

Warm Spiced Lemon Drink

Preparation Time: 10 minutes
Cooking Time: 2 hours
Servings: 12
Ingredients:
- 1 cinnamon stick, about 3 inches long

- 1/2 teaspoon of whole cloves
- 2 cups of coconut sugar
- 4 fluid of ounce pineapple juice
- 1/2 cup and 2 tablespoons of lemon juice
- 12 fluid ounce of orange juice
- 2 1/2 quarts of water

Directions:
1. Pour water into a 6-quarts slow cooker and stir the sugar and lemon juice properly.
2. Wrap the cinnamon, the whole cloves in cheesecloth and tie its corners with string.
3. Immerse this cheesecloth bag in the liquid present in the slow cooker and cover it with the lid.
4. Then plug in the slow cooker and let it cook on high heat setting for 2 hours or until it is heated thoroughly.
5. When done, discard the cheesecloth bag and serve the drink hot or cold.

Nutrition: Calories 523 Carbohydrates: 4.6g Protein: 47.9g Fat: 34.8g

Soothing Ginger Tea Drink

Preparation Time: 5 minutes
Cooking Time: 2 hours 20 minutes
Servings: 8
Ingredients:
- 1 tablespoon of minced gingerroot
- 2 tablespoons of honey
- 15 green tea bags
- 32 fluid ounce of white grape juice
- 2 quarts of boiling water

Directions:
1. Pour water into a 4-quarts slow cooker, immerse tea bags, cover the cooker and let stand for 10 minutes.
2. After 10 minutes, remove and discard tea bags and stir in remaining ingredients.
3. Return cover to slow cooker, then plug in and let cook at high heat setting for 2 hours or until heated through.
4. When done, strain the liquid and serve hot or cold.

Nutrition: Calories 232 Carbs: 7.9g Protein: 15.9g Fat: 15.1g

Nice Spiced Cherry Cider

Preparation Time: 1 hour 5 minutes
Cooking Time: 3 hours
Servings: 16
Ingredients:
- 2 cinnamon sticks, each about 3 inches long
- 6-ounce of cherry gelatin
- 4 quarts of apple cider

Directions:
1. Using a 6-quarts slow cooker, pour the apple cider and add the cinnamon stick.
2. Stir, then cover the slow cooker with its lid. Plug in the cooker and let it cook for 3 hours at the high heat setting or until it is heated thoroughly.
3. Then add and stir the gelatin properly, then continue cooking for another hour.
4. When done, remove the cinnamon sticks and serve the drink hot or cold.

Nutrition: Calories 78 Carbs: 13.2g Protein: 2.8g Fat: 1.5g

Fragrant Spiced Coffee

Preparation Time: 10 minutes
Cooking Time: 3 hours
Servings: 8
Ingredients:
- 4 cinnamon sticks, each about 3 inches long
- 1 1/2 teaspoons of whole cloves
- 1/3 cup of honey
- 2-ounce of chocolate syrup
- 1/2 teaspoon of anise extract
- 8 cups of brewed coffee

Directions:
1. Pour the coffee in a 4-quarts slow cooker and pour in the remaining ingredients except for cinnamon and stir properly.
2. Wrap the whole cloves in cheesecloth and tie its corners with strings.
3. Immerse this cheesecloth bag in the liquid present in the slow cooker and cover it with the lid.
4. Then plug in the slow cooker and let it cook on the low heat setting for 3 hours or until heated thoroughly.
5. When done, discard the cheesecloth bag and serve.

Nutrition: Calories 136 Fat 12.6 g Carbohydrates 4.1 g Sugar 0.5 g Protein 10.3 g Cholesterol 88 mg

Bracing Coffee Smoothie

Preparation Time: 5 minutes
Cooking Time: 5 minutes
Servings: 1
Ingredients:
- 1 banana, sliced and frozen
- ½ cup strong brewed coffee
- ½ cup milk
- ¼ cup rolled oats
- 1 tsp nut butter

Directions:
1. Mix all the ingredients until smooth.
2. Enjoy your morning drink!

Nutrition: Calories 414 Fat 20.6 g Carbohydrates 5.6 g Sugar 1.3 g Protein 48.8 g Cholesterol 58 mg

Vitamin Green Smoothie

Preparation Time: 5 minutes
Cooking Time: 5 minutes
Servings: 2
Ingredients:
- 1 cup milk or juice
- 1 cup spinach or kale
- ½ cup plain yoghurt
- 1 kiwi
- 1 Tbsp chia or flax
- 1 tsp vanilla

Directions:
1. Mix the milk or juice and greens until smooth. Add the remaining ingredients and continue blending until smooth again.
2. Enjoy your delicious drink!

Nutrition: Calories 397 Fat 36.4 g Carbohydrates 4 g Sugar 1 g Protein 14.7 g Cholesterol 4 mg

Strawberry Grapefruit Smoothie

Preparation Time: 5 minutes

Cooking Time: 5 minutes
Servings: 2
Ingredients:
- 1 banana
- ½ cup strawberries, frozen
- 1 grapefruit
- ¼ cup milk
- ¼ cup plain yoghurt
- 2 Tbsp honey
- ½ tsp ginger, chopped

Directions:
1. Using a mixer, blend all the ingredients.
2. When smooth, top your drink with a slice of grapefruit and enjoy it!
Nutrition: Calories 233 Fat 7.9 g Carbohydrates 3.2 g Sugar 0.1 g Protein 35.6 g Cholesterol 32 m

Inspirational Orange Smoothie

Preparation Time: 5 minutes
Cooking Time: 5 minutes
Servings: 1
Ingredients:
- 4 mandarin oranges, peeled
- 1 banana, sliced and frozen
- ½ cup non-fat Greek yoghurt
- ¼ cup coconut water
- 1 tsp vanilla extract
- 5 ice cubes

Directions:
1. Using a mixer, whisk all the ingredients.
2. Enjoy your drink!
Nutrition: Calories 256 Fat 13.3 g Carbohydrates 0 g Sugar 0 g Protein 34.5 g Cholesterol 78 mg

High Protein Blueberry Banana Smoothie

Preparation Time: 5 minutes
Cooking Time: 5 minutes
Servings: 2
Ingredients:
- 1 cup blueberries, frozen
- 2 ripe bananas
- 1 cup water
- 1 tsp vanilla extract
- 2 Tbsp chia seeds
- ½ cup cottage cheese
- 1 tsp lemon zest

Directions:
1. Put all the smoothie ingredients into the blender and whisk until smooth.
2. Enjoy your wonderful smoothie!
Nutrition: Calories 358 Fat 19.8 g Carbohydrates 1.3 g Sugar 0.4 g Protein 41.9 g Cholesterol 131 mg

Ginger Smoothie with Citrus and Mint

Preparation Time: 5 minutes
Cooking Time: 3 minutes
Servings: 3
Ingredients:
- 1 head Romaine lettuce, chopped into 4 chunks
- 2 Tbsp hemp seeds
- 5 mandarin oranges, peeled
- 1 banana, frozen
- 1 carrot
- 2-3 mint leaves
- ½ piece ginger root, peeled
- 1 cup water
- ¼ lemon, peeled
- ½ cup ice

Directions:
1. Put all the smoothie ingredients in a blender and blend until smooth.
2. Enjoy!
Nutrition: Calories 101 Fat 4 g Carbohydrates 14 g Sugar 1 g Protein 2 g Cholesterol 3 mg

Strawberry Beet Smoothie

Preparation Time: 5 minutes
Cooking Time: 50 minutes
Servings: 2
Ingredients:
- 1 red beet, trimmed, peeled and chopped into cubes
- 1 cup strawberries, quartered
- 1 ripe banana
- ½ cup strawberry yoghurt
- 1 Tbsp honey
- 1 Tbsp water
- Milk, to taste

Directions:
1. Sprinkle the beet cubes with water, place on aluminum foil and put in the oven (preheated to 204°C). Bake for 40 minutes.
2. Let the baked beet cool.
3. Combine all the smoothie ingredients.
4. Enjoy your fantastic drink.
Nutrition: Calories 184 Fat 9.2 g Carbohydrates 1 g Sugar 0.4 g Protein 24.9 g Cholesterol 132 mg

Peanut Butter Shake

Preparation Time: 5 minutes
Cooking Time: 5 minutes
Servings: 2
Ingredients:
- 1 cup plant-based milk
- 1 handful kale
- 2 bananas, frozen
- 2 Tbsp peanut butter
- ½ tsp ground cinnamon
- ¼ tsp vanilla powder

Directions:
1. Use a blender to combine all the ingredients for your shake.
2. Enjoy it!
Nutrition: Calories 184 Fat 9.2 g Carbohydrates 1 g Sugar 0.4 g Protein 24.9 g Cholesterol 132 mg

DESSERTS

Apple Crumble

Preparation Time: 20 minutes
Cooking Time: 25 minutes
Servings: 6
Ingredients:
- For the filling
- 4 to 5 apples, cored and chopped (about 6 cups)
- ½ cup unsweetened applesauce, or ¼ cup water
- 2 to 3 tablespoons unrefined sugar (coconut, date, sucanat, maple syrup)
- 1 teaspoon ground cinnamon
- Pinch sea salt
- For the crumble
- 2 tablespoons almond butter, or cashew or sunflower seed butter
- 2 tablespoons maple syrup
- 1½ cups rolled oats
- ½ cup walnuts, finely chopped
- ½ teaspoon ground cinnamon
- 2 to 3 tablespoons unrefined granular sugar (coconut, date, sucanat)

Directions:
1. Preparing the Ingredients.
2. Preheat the oven to 350°F. Put the apples and applesauce in an 8-inch-square baking dish, and sprinkle with the sugar, cinnamon, and salt. Toss to combine.
3. In a medium bowl, mix together the nut butter and maple syrup until smooth and creamy. Add the oats, walnuts, cinnamon, and sugar and stir to coat, using your hands if necessary. (If you have a small food processor, pulse the oats and walnuts together before adding them to the mix.)
4. Sprinkle the topping over the apples, and put the dish in the oven.
5. Bake for 20 to 25 minutes, or until the fruit is soft and the topping is lightly browned.
Nutrition: Calories 195 Fat 7 g Carbohydrates 6 g Sugar 2 g Protein 24 g Cholesterol 65 mg

Cashew-Chocolate Truffles

Preparation Time: 15 minutes
Cooking Time: 0 minutes
Servings: 12
Ingredients:
- 1 cup raw cashews, soaked in water overnight
- ¾ cup pitted dates
- 2 tablespoons coconut oil
- 1 cup unsweetened shredded coconut, divided
- 1 to 2 tablespoons cocoa powder, to taste

Directions:
1. Preparing the Ingredients.
2. In a food processor, combine the cashews, dates, coconut oil, ½ cup of shredded coconut, and cocoa powder. Pulse until fully incorporated; it will resemble chunky cookie dough. Spread the remaining ½ cup of shredded coconut on a plate.
3. Form the mixture into tablespoon-size balls and roll on the plate to cover with the shredded coconut. Transfer to a parchment paper–lined plate or baking sheet. Repeat to make 12 truffles.
4. Place the truffles in the refrigerator for 1 hour to set. Transfer the truffles to a storage container or freezer-safe bag and seal.
Nutrition: Calories 160 Fat 1 g Carbohydrates 1 g Sugar 0.5 g Protein 22 g Cholesterol 60 mg

Banana Chocolate Cupcakes

Preparation Time: 20 minutes
Cooking Time: 20 minutes
Servings: 1
Ingredients:
- 3 medium bananas
- 1 cup non-dairy milk
- 2 tablespoons almond butter
- 1 teaspoon apple cider vinegar
- 1 teaspoon pure vanilla extract
- 1¼ cups whole-grain flour
- ½ cup rolled oats
- ¼ cup coconut sugar (optional)
- 1 teaspoon baking powder
- ½ teaspoon baking soda
- ½ cup unsweetened cocoa powder
- ¼ cup chia seeds, or sesame seeds
- Pinch sea salt
- ¼ cup dark chocolate chips, dried cranberries, or raisins (optional)

Directions:
1. Preparing the Ingredients.
2. Preheat the oven to 350°F. Lightly grease the cups of two 6-cup muffin tins or line with paper muffin cups.
3. Put the bananas, milk, almond butter, vinegar, and vanilla in a blender and purée until smooth. Or stir together in a large bowl until smooth and creamy.
4. Put the flour, oats, sugar (if using), baking powder, baking soda, cocoa powder, chia seeds, salt, and chocolate chips in another large bowl, and stir to combine. Mix together the wet and dry ingredients, stirring as little as possible. Spoon into muffin cups, and bake for 20 to 25 minutes. Take the cupcakes out of the oven and let them cool fully before taking out of the muffin tins, since they'll be very moist.
Nutrition: Calories 295 Fat 17 g Carbohydrates 4 g Sugar 0.1 g Protein 29 g Cholesterol 260 mg

Minty Fruit Salad

Preparation Time: 15 minutes
Cooking Time: 5 minutes
Servings: 4
Ingredients:
- ¼ cup lemon juice (about 2 small lemons)
- 4 teaspoons maple syrup or agave syrup
- 2 cups chopped pineapple
- 2 cups chopped strawberries
- 2 cups raspberries

- 1 cup blueberries
- 8 fresh mint leaves

Directions:
Preparing the Ingredients.
1. Beginning with 1 mason jar, add the ingredients in this order:
2. 1 tablespoon of lemon juice, 1 teaspoon of maple syrup, ½ cup of pineapple, ½ cup of strawberries, ½ cup of raspberries, ¼ cup of blueberries, and 2 mint leaves.
3. Repeat to fill 3 more jars. Close the jars tightly with lids.
4. Place the airtight jars in the refrigerator for up to 3 days.
Nutrition: Calories 339 Fat 17.5 g Carbohydrates 2 g Sugar 2 g Protein 44 g Cholesterol 100 mg

Mango Coconut Cream Pie

Preparation Time: 20 minutes
Cooking Time: 30 minutes
Servings: 8
Ingredients:
- For the crust
- ½ cup rolled oats
- 1 cup cashews
- 1 cup soft pitted dates
- For the filling
- 1 cup canned coconut milk
- ½ cup water
- 2 large mangos, peeled and chopped, or about 2 cups frozen chunks
- ½ cup unsweetened shredded coconut

Directions:
1. Preparing the Ingredients.
2. Put all the crust ingredients in a food processor and pulse until it holds together. If you don't have a food processor, chop everything as finely as possible and use ½ cup cashew or almond butter in place of half the cashews. Press the mixture down firmly into an 8-inch pie or springform pan.
3. Put the all filling ingredients in a blender and purée until smooth (about 1 minute). It should be very thick, so you may have to stop and stir until it's smooth.
4. Pour the filling into the crust, use a rubber spatula to smooth the top, and put the pie in the freezer until set, about 30 minutes. Once frozen, it should be set out for about 15 minutes to soften before serving.
5. Top with a batch of Coconut Whipped Cream scooped on top of the pie once it's set. Finish it off with a sprinkling of toasted shredded coconut.
Nutrition: Calories 545 Fat 39.6 g Carbohydrates 9.5 g Sugar 3.1 g Protein 43 g Cholesterol 110 mg

Cherry-Vanilla Rice Pudding (Pressure cooker)

Preparation Time: 5 minutes
Cooking Time: 30 minutes
Servings: 4-6
Ingredients:
- 1 cup short-grain brown rice
- 1¾ cups nondairy milk, plus more as needed

- 1½ cups water
- 4 tablespoons unrefined sugar or pure maple syrup (use 2 tablespoons if you use a sweetened milk), plus more as needed
- 1 teaspoon vanilla extract (use ½ teaspoon if you use vanilla milk)
- Pinch salt
- ¼ cup dried cherries or ½ cup fresh or frozen pitted cherries

Directions:
1. Preparing the Ingredients. In your electric pressure cooker's cooking pot, combine the rice, milk, water, sugar, vanilla, and salt.
2. High pressure for 30 minutes. Close and lock the lid, and select High Pressure for 30 minutes.
3. Pressure Release. Once the **Cooking Time:** is complete, let the pressure release naturally, about 20 minutes. Unlock and remove the lid. Stir in the cherries and put the lid back on loosely for about 10 minutes. Serve, adding more milk or sugar, as desired.
Nutrition: Calories 420 Fat 27.4 g Carbohydrates 2 g Sugar 0.3 g Protein 46.3 g Cholesterol 98 mg

Lime in the Coconut Chia Pudding

Preparation Time: 10 minutes
Cooking Time: 20 minutes
Servings: 4
Ingredients:
- Zest and juice of 1 lime
- 1 (14-ounce) can coconut milk
- 1 to 2 dates, or 1 tablespoon coconut or other unrefined sugar, or 1 tablespoon maple syrup, or 10 to 15 drops pure liquid stevia
- 2 tablespoons chia seeds, whole or ground
- 2 teaspoons matcha green tea powder (optional)

Directions:
1. Preparing the Ingredients.
2. Blend all the ingredients in a blender until smooth. Chill in the fridge for about 20 minutes, then serve topped with one or more of the topping ideas.
3. Try blueberries, blackberries, sliced strawberries, Coconut Whipped Cream, or toasted unsweetened coconut.
Nutrition: Calories 381 Fat 17.1 g Carbohydrates 4.1 g Sugar 0.6 g Protein 50.6 g Cholesterol 358 mg

Mint Chocolate Chip Sorbet

Preparation Time: 5 minutes
Cooking Time: 0 minute
Servings: 1
Ingredients:
- 1 frozen banana
- 1 tablespoon almond butter, or peanut butter, or other nut or seed butter
- 2 tablespoons fresh mint, minced
- ¼ cup or less non-dairy milk (only if needed)
- 2 to 3 tablespoons non-dairy chocolate chips, or cocoa nibs
- 2 to 3 tablespoons goji berries (optional)

Directions:
1. Preparing the Ingredients.

2. Put the banana, almond butter, and mint in a food processor or blender and purée until smooth.
3. Add the non-dairy milk if needed to keep blending (but only if needed, as this will make the texture less solid). Pulse the chocolate chips and goji berries (if using) into the mix so they're roughly chopped up.
Nutrition: Calories 299 Fat 16 g Carbohydrates 3 g Sugar 6 g Protein 38 g Cholesterol 108 mg

Peach-Mango Crumble (Pressure cooker)

Preparation Time: 10 minutes
Cooking Time: 6 minutes
Servings: 4-6
Ingredient:
- 3 cups chopped fresh or frozen peaches
- 3 cups chopped fresh or frozen mangos
- 4 tablespoons unrefined sugar or pure maple syrup, divided
- 1 cup gluten-free rolled oats
- ½ cup shredded coconut, sweetened or unsweetened
- 2 tablespoons coconut oil or vegan margarine

Directions:
1. Preparing the Ingredients. In a 6- to 7-inch round baking dish, toss together the peaches, mangos, and 2 tablespoons of sugar. In a food processor, combine the oats, coconut, coconut oil, and remaining 2 tablespoons of sugar. Pulse until combined. (If you use maple syrup, you'll need less coconut oil. Start with just the syrup and add oil if the mixture isn't sticking together.) Sprinkle the oat mixture over the fruit mixture.
2. Cover the dish with aluminum foil. Put a trivet in the bottom of your electric pressure cooker's cooking pot and pour in a cup or two of water. Using a foil sling or silicone helper handles, lower the pan onto the trivet.
3. High pressure for 6 minutes. Close and lock the lid, and select High Pressure for 6 minutes.
4. Pressure Release. Once the **Cooking Time:** is complete, quick release the pressure. Unlock and remove the lid.
5. Let cool for a few minutes before carefully lifting out the dish with oven mitts or tongs. Scoop out portions to serve.
Nutrition: Calories 275 Fat 19 g Carbohydrates 19 g Sugar 4 g Protein 14 g Cholesterol 60 mg

Zesty Orange-Cranberry Energy Bites

Preparation Time: 10 minutes
Cooking Time: 15 minutes
Servings: 12
Ingredients:
- 2 tablespoons almond butter, or cashew or sunflower seed butter
- 2 tablespoons maple syrup, or brown rice syrup
- ¾ cup cooked quinoa
- ¼ cup sesame seeds, toasted
- 1 tablespoon chia seeds
- ½ teaspoon almond extract, or vanilla extract

- Zest of 1 orange
- 1 tablespoon dried cranberries
- ¼ cup ground almonds

Directions:
1. Preparing the Ingredients.
2. In a medium bowl, mix together the nut or seed butter and syrup until smooth and creamy. Stir in the rest of the ingredients, and mix to make sure the consistency is holding together in a ball. Form the mix into 12 balls.
3. Place them on a baking sheet lined with parchment or waxed paper and put in the fridge to set for about 15 minutes.
4. If your balls aren't holding together, it's likely because of the moisture content of your cooked quinoa. Add more nut or seed butter mixed with syrup until it all sticks together.
Nutrition: Calories 493 Fat 33 g Carbohydrates 8 g Sugar 9 g Protein 47 g Cholesterol 135 mg

Almond-Date Energy Bites

Preparation Time: 5 minutes
Cooking Time: 15 minutes
Servings: 24
Ingredients:
- 1 cup dates, pitted
- 1 cup unsweetened shredded coconut
- ¼ cup chia seeds
- ¾ cup ground almonds
- ¼ cup cocoa nibs, or non-dairy chocolate chips

Directions:
1. Purée everything in a food processor until crumbly and sticking together, pushing down the sides whenever necessary to keep it blending. If you don't have a food processor, you can mash soft Medjool dates. But if you're using harder baking dates, you'll have to soak them and then try to purée them in a blender.
2. Form the mix into 24 balls and place them on a baking sheet lined with parchment or waxed paper. Put in the fridge to set for about 15 minutes. Use the softest dates you can find. Medjool dates are the best for this purpose. The hard dates you see in the baking aisle of your supermarket are going to take a long time to blend up. If you use those, try soaking them in water for at least an hour before you start, and then draining.
Nutrition: Calories 171 Fat 4 g Carbohydrates 7 g Sugar 7 g Protein 22 g Cholesterol 65 mg

Pumpkin Pie Cups (Pressure cooker)

Preparation Time: 5 minutes
Cooking Time: 6 minutes
Servings: 4-6
Ingredients:
- 1 cup canned pumpkin purée
- 1 cup nondairy milk
- 6 tablespoons unrefined sugar or pure maple syrup (less if using sweetened milk), plus more for sprinkling
- ¼ cup spelt flour or whole-grain flour
- ½ teaspoon pumpkin pie spice

- Pinch salt

Directions:
1. Preparing the Ingredients. In a medium bowl, stir together the pumpkin, milk, sugar, flour, pumpkin pie spice, and salt. Pour the mixture into 4 heat-proof ramekins. Sprinkle a bit more sugar on the top of each, if you like. Put a trivet in the bottom of your electric pressure cooker's cooking pot and pour in a cup or two of water. Place the ramekins onto the trivet, stacking them if needed (3 on the bottom, 1 on top).
2. High pressure for 6 minutes. Close and lock the lid, and select High Pressure for 6 minutes.
3. Pressure Release. Once the **Cooking Time:** is complete, quick release the pressure. Unlock and remove the lid. Let cool for a few minutes before carefully lifting out the ramekins with oven mitts or tongs. Let cool for at least 10 minutes before serving.
Nutrition: Calories 152 Fat 4 g Carbohydrates 4 g Sugar 8 g Protein 18 g Cholesterol 51 mg

Coconut and Almond Truffles

Preparation Time: 15 minutes
Cooking Time: 0 minutes
Servings: 8
Ingredients:
- 1 cup pitted dates
- 1 cup almonds
- ½ cup sweetened cocoa powder, plus extra for coating
- ½ cup unsweetened shredded coconut
- ¼ cup pure maple syrup
- 1 teaspoon vanilla extract
- 1 teaspoon almond extract
- ¼ teaspoon sea salt

Directions:
1. Preparing the Ingredients.
2. In the bowl of a food processor, combine all the ingredients and process until smooth. Chill the mixture for about 1 hour.
3. Roll the mixture into balls and then roll the balls in cocoa powder to coat.
4. Serve immediately or keep chilled until ready to serve.
Nutrition: Calories 126 Fat 5 g Carbohydrates 13 g Sugar 7 g Protein 5 g Cholesterol 0 mg

Fudgy Brownies(Pressure cooker)

Preparation Time: 10 minutes
Cooking Time: 5 minutes
Servings: 4-6
Ingredients:
- 3 ounces dairy-free dark chocolate
- 1 tablespoon coconut oil or vegan margarine
- ½ cup applesauce
- 2 tablespoons unrefined sugar
- 1/3 cup whole-grain flour
- ½ teaspoon baking powder
- Pinch salt

Directions:
1. Preparing the Ingredients. Put a trivet in your electric pressure cooker's cooking pot and pour in a cup or two of two of water. Select Sauté or Simmer. In a large heat-proof glass or ceramic bowl, combine the chocolate and coconut oil. Place the bowl over the top of your pressure cooker, as you would a double boiler. Stir occasionally until the chocolate is melted, then turn off the pressure cooker. Stir the applesauce and sugar into the chocolate mixture. Add the flour, baking powder, and salt and stir just until combined. Pour the batter into 3 heat-proof ramekins. Put them in a heat-proof dish and cover with aluminum foil. Using a foil sling or silicone helper handles, lower the dish onto the trivet. (Alternately, cover each ramekin with foil and place them directly on the trivet, without the dish.)
2. High pressure for 6 minutes. Close and lock the lid, and select High Pressure for 5 minutes.
3. Pressure Release. Once the **Cooking Time:** is complete, quick release the pressure. Unlock and remove the lid.
4. Let cool for a few minutes before carefully lifting out the dish, or ramekins, with oven mitts or tongs. Let cool for a few minutes more before serving.
5. Top with fresh raspberries and an extra drizzle of melted chocolate.
Nutrition: Calories 256 Fat 29 g Carbohydrates 1 g Sugar 0.5 g Protein 11 g Cholesterol 84 mg

Chocolate Macaroons

Preparation Time: 10 minutes
Cooking Time: 15 minutes
Servings: 8
Ingredients:
- 1 cup unsweetened shredded coconut
- 2 tablespoons cocoa powder
- 2/3 cup coconut milk
- ¼ cup agave
- pinch of sea salt

Directions:
1. Preparing the Ingredients.
2. Preheat the oven to 350°F. Line a baking sheet with parchment paper. In a medium saucepan, cook all the ingredients over -medium-high heat until a firm dough is formed. Scoop the dough into balls and place on the baking sheet.
3. Bake for 15 minutes, remove from the oven, and let cool on the baking sheet.
4. Serve cooled macaroons or store in a tightly sealed container for up to
Nutrition: Calories 371 Fat 15 g Carbohydrates 7 g Sugar 2 g Protein 41 g Cholesterol 135 mg

Chocolate Pudding

Preparation Time: 5 minutes
Cooking Time: 0 minutes
Servings: 1
Ingredients:
- 1 banana
- 2 to 4 tablespoons nondairy milk
- 2 tablespoons unsweetened cocoa powder
- 2 tablespoons sugar (optional)
- ½ ripe avocado or 1 cup silken tofu (optional)

Directions:

1. Preparing the Ingredients.
2. In a small blender, combine the banana, milk, cocoa powder, sugar (if using), and avocado (if using). Purée until smooth. Alternatively, in a small bowl, mash the banana very well, and stir in the remaining ingredients.
Nutrition: Calories 537 Fat 26 g Carbohydrates 13 g Sugar 16 g Protein 54 g Cholesterol 152 mg

Lime and Watermelon Granita

Preparation Time: 15 minutes
Cooking Time: 0 minutes
Servings: 4
Ingredients:
- 8 cups seedless -watermelon chunks
- juice of 2 limes, or 2 tablespoons prepared lime juice
- ½ cup. brown sugar
- strips of lime zest, for garnish

Directions:
1. Preparing the Ingredients.
2. In a blender or food processor, combine the watermelon, lime juice, and sugar and process until smooth. You may have to do this in two batches. After processing, stir well to combine both batches.
3. Pour the mixture into a 9-by-13-inch glass dish. Freeze for 2 to 3 hours. Remove from the freezer and use a fork to scrape the top layer of ice. Leave the shaved ice on top and return to the freezer.
4. In another hour, remove from the freezer and repeat. Do this a few more times until all the ice is scraped up. Serve frozen, garnished with strips of lime zest.
Nutrition: Calories 281 Fat 20 g Carbohydrates 14 g Sugar 9 g Protein 11 g Cholesterol 32 mg

Coconut-Banana Pudding

Preparation Time: 4 minutes
Cooking Time: 5 minutes
Servings: 4
Ingredients:
- 3 bananas, divided
- 1 (13.5-ounce) can full-fat coconut milk
- ¼ cup organic cane sugar
- 1 tablespoon cornstarch
- 1 teaspoon vanilla extract
- 2 pinches sea salt
- 6 drops natural yellow food coloring (optional)
- Ground cinnamon, for garnish

Directions:
1. Preparing the Ingredients.
2. Combine 1 banana, the coconut milk, sugar, cornstarch, vanilla, and salt in a blender. Blend until smooth and creamy. If you're using the food coloring, add it to the blender now and blend until the color is evenly dispersed.
3. Transfer to a saucepot and bring to a boil over medium-high heat. Immediately reduce to a simmer and whisk for 3 minutes, or until the mixture thickens to a thin pudding and sticks to a spoon.
4. Transfer the mixture to a container and allow to cool for 1 hour. Cover and refrigerate overnight to set.

When you're ready to serve, slice the remaining 2 bananas and build individual servings as follows: pudding, banana slices, pudding, and so on until a single-serving dish is filled to the desired level. Sprinkle with ground cinnamon.
Nutrition: Calories 170 Fat 4 g Carbohydrates 34 g Sugar 14g Protein 9 g Cholesterol 14 mg

Spiced Apple Chia Pudding

Preparation Time: 5 minutes
Cooking Time: 0 minutes
Servings: 1
Ingredients:
- ½ cup unsweetened applesauce
- ¼ cup nondairy milk or canned coconut milk
- 1 tablespoon chia seeds
- 1½ teaspoons sugar
- Pinch ground cinnamon or pumpkin pie spice

Directions:
1. Preparing the Ingredients.
2. In a small bowl, stir together the applesauce, milk, chia seeds, sugar, and cinnamon. Enjoy as is, or let sit for 30 minutes so the chia seeds soften and expand.
Nutrition: Calories 145 Fat 4 g Carbohydrates 19 g Sugar 9 g Protein 2 g Cholesterol 26 mg

Caramelized Pears with Balsamic Glaze

Preparation Time: 5 minutes
Cooking Time: 15 minutes
Servings: 4
Ingredients:
- 1 cup balsamic vinegar
- ¼ cup plus 3 tablespoons brown sugar
- ¼ teaspoon grated nutmeg
- pinch of sea salt
- ¼ cup coconut oil
- 4 pears, cored and cut into slices

Directions:
1. Preparing the Ingredients.
2. In a medium saucepan, heat the balsamic vinegar, ¼ cup of the brown sugar, the nutmeg, and salt over medium-high heat, stirring to thoroughly incorporate the sugar. Allow to simmer, stirring occasionally, until the glaze reduces by half, 10 to 15 minutes.
3. Meanwhile, heat the coconut oil in a large sauté pan over medium-high heat until it shimmers. Add the pears to the pan in a single layer. Cook until they turn golden, about 5 minutes. Add the remaining 3 tablespoons brown sugar and continue to cook, stirring occasionally, until the pears caramelize, about 5 minutes more.
4. Place the pears on a plate. Drizzle with balsamic glaze and serve.
Nutrition: Calories 237 Fat 5 g Carbohydrates 7 g Sugar 0.4 g Protein 31 g Cholesterol 101 mg

Salted Coconut-Almond Fudge

Preparation Time: 5 minutes
Cooking Time: 0 minutes
Servings: 12
Ingredients:

- ¾ cup creamy almond butter
- ½ cup maple syrup
- 1/3 cup coconut oil, softened or melted
- 6 tablespoons fair-trade unsweetened cocoa powder
- 1 teaspoon coarse or flaked sea salt

Directions:
1. Preparing the Ingredients.
2. Line a loaf pan with a double layer of plastic wrap. Place one layer horizontally in the pan with a generous amount of overhang, and the second layer vertically with a generous amount of overhang.
3. In a medium bowl, gently mix together the almond butter, maple syrup, and coconut oil until well combined and smooth. Add the cocoa powder and gently stir it into the mixture until well combined and creamy.
4. Pour the mixture into the prepared pan and sprinkle with the sea salt. Bring the overflowing edges of the plastic wrap over the top of the fudge to completely cover it. Place the pan in the freezer for at least 1 hour or overnight, until the fudge is firm.
5. Remove the pan from the freezer and lift the fudge out of the pan using the plastic-wrap overhangs to pull it out. Transfer to a cutting board and cut into 1-inch pieces.

Nutrition: Calories 297 Fat 20.3 g Carbohydrates 4 g Sugar 5 g Protein 21 g Cholesterol 80 mg

Caramelized Bananas

Preparation Time: 5 minutes
Cooking Time: 10 minutes
Servings: 2
Ingredients:
- 2 tablespoons vegan margarine or coconut oil
- 2 bananas, peeled, halved crosswise and then lengthwise
- 2 tablespoons dark brown sugar, demerara sugar, or coconut sugar
- 2 tablespoons spiced apple cider
- Chopped walnuts, for topping

Directions:
1. Preparing the Ingredients.
2. Melt the margarine in a nonstick skillet over medium heat. Add the bananas, and cook for 2 minutes. Flip, and cook for 2 minutes more.
3. Sprinkle the sugar and cider into the oil around the bananas, and cook for 2 to 3 minutes, until the sauce thickens and caramelizes around the bananas. Carefully scoop the bananas into small bowls, and drizzle with any remaining liquid in the skillet. Sprinkle with walnuts.

Nutrition: Calories: 413 Fat: 13g Saturated fat: 4g Cholesterol: 98mg Sodium: 432mg Carbohydrates: 64g Fiber: 5g Protein: 37g

Mixed Berries and Cream

Preparation Time: 10 minutes
Cooking Time: 0 minutes
Servings: 4
Ingredients:
- two 15-ounce cans full-fat coconut milk
- 3 tablespoons agave
- ½ teaspoon vanilla extract
- 1 pint fresh blueberries
- 1 pint fresh raspberries
- 1 pint fresh strawberries, sliced

Directions:
1. Preparing the Ingredients.
2. Refrigerate the coconut milk overnight. When you open the can, the liquid will have separated from the solids. Spoon out the solids and reserve the liquid for another purpose.
3. In a medium bowl, whisk the agave and vanilla extract into the coconut solids. Divide the berries among four bowls. Top with the coconut cream. Serve immediately.

Nutrition: Calories: 468 Total fat: 19g Saturated fat: 9g Cholesterol: 51mg Sodium: 1041mg Carbohydrates: 53g Fiber: 8g Protein: 23g

"Rugged" Coconut Balls

Preparation Time: 15 minutes
Cooking Time: 0 minute
Servings: 8
Ingredients:
- 1/3 cup coconut oil melted
- 1/3 cup coconut butter softened
- 2 oz coconut, finely shredded, unsweetened
- 4 Tbsp coconut palm sugar
- 1/2 cup shredded coconut

Directions:
1. Combine all ingredients in a blender.
2. Blend until soft and well combined.
3. Form small balls from the mixture and roll in shredded coconut.
4. Place on a sheet lined with parchment paper and refrigerate overnight.
5. Keep coconut balls into sealed container in fridge up to one week.

Nutrition: Calories: 247 Total Fat: 7g Saturated Fat: 2g Cholesterol: 17mg Sodium: 563mg Carbohydrates: 33g Fiber: 3g Protein: 12g

Almond - Choco Cake

Preparation Time: 45 minutes
Cooking Time: 32 minutes
Servings: 8
Ingredients:
- 1 1/2 cups of almond flour
- 1/3 cup almonds finely chopped
- 1/4 cup of cocoa powder unsweetened
- Pinch of salt
- 1/2 tsp baking soda
- 2 Tbsp almond milk
- 1/2 cup Coconut oil melted
- 2 tsp pure vanilla extract
- 1/3 cup brown sugar (packed)

Directions:
1. Preheat oven to 350 F.
2. Line 9" cake pan with parchment paper, and grease with a little melted coconut oil; set aside.
3. Stir the almond flour, chopped almonds, cocoa powder, salt, and baking soda in a bowl.
4. In a separate bowl, stir the remaining ingredients.

5. Combine the almond flour mixture with the almond milk mixture and stir well.
6. Place batter in a prepared cake pan.
7. Bake for 30 to 32 minutes.
8. Remove from the oven, allow it to cool completely.
9. Store the cake-slices a freezer, tightly wrapped in a double layer of plastic wrap and a layer of foil. It will keep on this way for up to a month.
Nutrition: Calories: 460 Total Fat: 32g Saturated Fat: 23g Cholesterol: 223mg Sodium: 902mg Carbohydrates: 16g Fiber: 5g Protein: 29g

Banana-Almond Cake

Preparation Time: 15 minutes
Cooking Time: 45 minutes
Servings: 8
Ingredients:
- 4 ripe bananas in chunks
- 3 Tbs honey or maple syrup
- 1 tsp pure vanilla extract
- 1/2 cup almond milk
- 3/4 cup of self-raising flour
- 1 tsp cinnamon
- 1 tsp baking powder
- 1 pinch of salt
- 1/3 cup of almonds finely chopped
- Almond slices for decoration

Directions:
1. Preheat the oven to 400 F (air mode).
2. Oil a cake mold; set aside.
3. Add bananas into a bowl and mash with the fork.
4. Add honey, vanilla, almond, and stir well.
5. In a separate bowl, stir flour, cinnamon, baking powder, salt, the almonds broken, and mix with a spoon.
6. Combine the flour mixture with the banana mixture, and stir until all ingredients combined well.
7. Transfer the mixture to prepared cake mold and sprinkle with sliced almonds.
8. Bake for 40-45 minutes or until the toothpick inserted comes out clean.
9. Remove from the oven, and allow the cake to cool completely.
10. Cut cake into slices, place in tin foil, or an airtight container, and keep refrigerated up to one week.
Nutrition: Calories: 301 Total fat: 8g Saturated Fat: 1g Cholesterol: 99mg Sodium: 808mg Carbohydrates: 21g Fiber: 4g Protein: 26g

Banana-Coconut Ice Cream

Preparation Time: 15 minutes
Cooking Time: 0 minutes
Servings: 6
Ingredients:
- 1 cup coconut cream
- 1/2 cup Inverted sugar
- 2 large frozen bananas (chunks)
- 3 Tbsp honey extracted
- 1/4 tsp cinnamon powder

Directions:
1. In a bowl, whip the coconut cream with the inverted sugar.

2. In a separate bowl, beat the banana with honey and cinnamon.
3. Incorporate the coconut whipped cream and banana mixture; stir well.
4. Cover the bowl and let cool in the refrigerator over the night.
5. Stir the mixture 3 to 4 times to avoid crystallization.
6. Keep frozen 1 to 2 months.
Nutrition: Calories: 257 Total Fat: 4g Saturated Fat: 0g Cholesterol: 33mg Sodium: 819mg Carbohydrates: 37g Fiber: 7g Protein: 20g

Coconut Butter Clouds Cookies

Preparation Time: 15 minutes
Cooking Time: 10 minutes
Servings: 8
Ingredients:
- 1/2 cup coconut butter softened
- 1/2 cup peanut butter softened
- 1/2 cup of granulated sugar
- 1/2 cup of brown sugar
- 2 Tbsp chia seeds soaked in 4 tablespoons water
- 1/2 tsp pure vanilla extract
- 1/2 tsp baking soda
- 1/4 tsp salt
- 1 cup of all-purpose flour

Directions:
1. Preheat oven to 360 F.
2. Add coconut butter, peanut butter, and both sugars in a mixing bowl.
3. Beat with a mixer until soft and sugar combined well.
4. Add soaked chia seeds and vanilla extract; beat.
5. Add baking soda, salt, and flour; beat until all ingredients are combined well.
6. With your hands, shape dough into cookies.
7. Arrange your cookies onto a baking sheet, and bake for about 10 minutes.
8. Remove cookies from the oven and allow to cool completely.
9. Sprinkle with icing sugar and enjoy your cookies.
10. Place cookies in an airtight container and keep refrigerated up to 10 days.
Nutrition: Calories: 731 Total Fat: 26g Saturated Fat: 17g Cholesterol: 169mg Sodium: 1167mg Carbohydrates: 56g Fiber: 5g Protein: 45g

Chocomint Hazelnut Bars

Preparation Time: 5 minutes
Cooking Time: 15 minutes
Servings: 8
Ingredients:
- 1/2 cup coconut oil, melted
- 4 Tbsp cocoa powder
- 1/4 cup almond butter
- 3/4 cup brown sugar - (packed)
- 1 tsp vanilla extract
- 1 tsp pure peppermint extract
- pinch of salt
- 1 cup shredded coconut
- 1 cup hazelnuts sliced

Directions:
1. Chop the hazelnuts in a food processor; set aside.
2. Fill the bottom of a double boiler with water and place it on low heat.
3. Put the coconut oil, cacao powder, almond butter, brown sugar, vanilla, peppermint extract, and salt in the top of a double boiler over hot (not boiling) water and constantly stir for 10 minutes.
4. Add hazelnuts and shredded coconut to the melted mixture and stir together.
5. Pour the mixture in a dish lined with parchment and freeze for several hours.
6. Remove from the freezer and cut into bars.
7. Store in airtight container or freezer bag in a freezer.
8. Let the bars at room temperature for 10 to 15 minutes before eating.
Nutrition: Calories: 186 Total Fat: 4g Saturated Fat: 0g Cholesterol: 33mg Sodium: 783mg Carbohydrates: 23g Fiber: 6g Protein: 19g

Coco-Cinnamon Balls

Preparation Time: 10 minutes
Cooking Time: 5 minutes
Servings: 12
Ingredients:
- 1 cup coconut butter softened
- 1 cup coconut milk canned
- 1 tsp pure vanilla extract
- 3/4 tsp cinnamon
- 1/2 tsp nutmeg
- 2 Tbsp coconut palm sugar (or granulated sugar)
- 1 cup coconut shreds

Directions:
1. Combine all ingredients (except the coconut shreds) in a heated bath - bain-marie.
2. Cook and stir until all ingredients are soft and well combined.
3. Remove bowl from heat, place into a bowl, and refrigerate until the mixture firmed up.
4. Form cold coconut mixture into balls, and roll each ball in the shredded coconut.
5. Store into a sealed container, and keep refrigerated up to one week.
Nutrition: Calories: 213 Fat: 6g Fiber: 13g Carbs: 16g Protein: 22g

Chocolate and Avocado Pudding

Preparation Time: 3 hours and 10 minutes
Cooking Time: 0 minute
Servings: 1
Ingredients:
- 1 small avocado, pitted, peeled
- 1 small banana, mashed
- 1/3 cup cocoa powder, unsweetened
- 1 tablespoon cacao nibs, unsweetened
- 1/4 cup maple syrup
- 1/3 cup coconut cream

Directions:
1. Add avocado in a food processor along with cream and then pulse for 2 minutes until smooth.
2. Add remaining ingredients, blend until mixed, and then tip the pudding in a container.
3. Cover the container with a plastic wrap; it should touch the pudding and refrigerate for 3 hours.
4. Serve straight away.
Nutrition: Calories: 87 Cal Fat: 7 g Carbs: 9 g Protein: 1.5 g Fiber: 3.2 g

Chocolate Avocado Ice Cream

Preparation Time: 1 hour and 10 minutes
Cooking Time: 0 minute
Servings: 2
Ingredients:
- 4.5 ounces avocado, peeled, pitted
- 1/2 cup cocoa powder, unsweetened
- 1 tablespoon vanilla extract, unsweetened
- 1/2 cup and 2 tablespoons maple syrup
- 13.5 ounces coconut milk, unsweetened
- 1/2 cup water

Directions:
1. Add avocado in a food processor along with milk and then pulse for 2 minutes until smooth.
2. Add remaining ingredients, blend until mixed, and then tip the pudding in a freezer-proof container.
3. Place the container in a freezer and chill for freeze for 4 hours until firm, whisking every 20 minutes after 1 hour.
4. Serve straight away.
Nutrition: Calories: 80.7 Cal Fat: 7.1 g Carbs: 6 g Protein: 0.6 g Fiber: 2 g

Watermelon Mint Popsicles

Preparation Time: 8 hours and 5 minutes
Cooking Time: 0 minute
Servings: 8
Ingredients:
- 20 mint leaves, diced
- 6 cups watermelon chunks
- 3 tablespoons lime juice

Directions:
1. Add watermelon in a food processor along with lime juice and then pulse for 15 seconds until smooth.
2. Pass the watermelon mixture through a strainer placed over a bowl, remove the seeds and then stir mint into the collected watermelon mixture.
3. Take eight Popsicle molds, pour in prepared watermelon mixture, and freeze for 2 hours until slightly firm.
4. Then insert popsicle sticks and continue freezing for 6 hours until solid.
5. Serve straight away
Nutrition: Calories: 90 Cal Fat: 0 g Carbs: 23 g Protein: 0 g Fiber: 0 g

Mango Coconut Chia Pudding

Preparation Time: 2 hours and 5 minutes
Cooking Time: 0 minute
Servings: 1
Ingredients:
- 1 medium mango, peeled, cubed
- 1/4 cup chia seeds

- 2 tablespoons coconut flakes
- 1 cup coconut milk, unsweetened
- 1 1/2 teaspoons maple syrup

Directions:
1. Take a bowl, place chia seeds in it, whisk in milk until combined, and then stir in maple syrup.
2. Cover the bowl with a plastic wrap; it should touch the pudding mixture and refrigerate for 2 hours until the pudding has set.
3. Then puree mango until smooth, top it evenly over pudding, sprinkle with coconut flakes and serve.

Nutrition: Calories: 159 Cal Fat: 9 g Carbs: 17 g Protein: 3 g Fiber: 6 g

Brownie Energy Bites

Preparation Time: 1 hour and 10 minutes
Cooking Time: 0 minute
Servings: 2
Ingredients:
- 1/2 cup walnuts
- 1 cup Medjool dates, chopped
- 1/2 cup almonds
- 1/8 teaspoon salt
- 1/2 cup shredded coconut flakes
- 1/3 cup and 2 teaspoons cocoa powder, unsweetened

Directions:
1. Place almonds and walnuts in a food processor and pulse for 3 minutes until the dough starts to come together.
2. Add remaining ingredients, reserving ¼ cup of coconut and pulse for 2 minutes until incorporated.
3. Shape the mixture into balls, roll them in remaining coconut until coated, and refrigerate for 1 hour.
4. Serve straight away

Nutrition: Calories: 174.6 Cal Fat: 8.1 g Carbs: 25.5 g Protein: 4.1 g Fiber: 4.4 g

Strawberry Coconut Ice Cream

Preparation Time: 5 minutes
Cooking Time: 0 minute
Servings: 4
Ingredients:
- 4 cups frouncesen strawberries
- 1 vanilla bean, seeded
- 28 ounces coconut cream
- 1/2 cup maple syrup

Directions:
1. Place cream in a food processor and pulse for 1 minute until soft peaks come together.
2. Then tip the cream in a bowl, add remaining ingredients in the blender and blend until thick mixture comes together.
3. Add the mixture into the cream, fold until combined, and then transfer ice cream into a freezer-safe bowl and freeze for 4 hours until firm, whisking every 20 minutes after 1 hour.
4. Serve straight away.

Nutrition: Calories: 100 Cal Fat: 100 g Carbs: 100 g Protein: 100 g Fiber: 100 g

Salted Caramel Chocolate Cups

Preparation Time: 5 minutes
Cooking Time: 2 minutes
Servings: 12
Ingredients:
- ¼ teaspoon sea salt granules
- 1 cup dark chocolate chips, unsweetened
- 2 teaspoons coconut oil
- 6 tablespoons caramel sauce

Directions:
1. Take a heatproof bowl, add chocolate chips and oil, stir until mixed, then microwave for 1 minute until melted, stir chocolate and continue heating in the microwave for 30 seconds.
2. Take twelve mini muffin tins, line them with muffin liners, spoon a little bit of chocolate mixture into the tins, spread the chocolate in the bottom and along the sides, and freeze for 10 minutes until set.
3. Then fill each cup with ½ tablespoon of caramel sauce, cover with remaining chocolate and freeze for another 2salt0 minutes until set.
4. When ready to eat, peel off liner from the cup, sprinkle with sauce, and serve.

Nutrition: Calories: 80 Cal Fat: 5 g Carbs: 10 g Protein: 1 g Fiber: 0.5 g

Chocolate Peanut Butter Energy Bites

Preparation Time: 1 hour and 5 minutes
Cooking Time: 0 minute
Servings: 4
Ingredients:
- 1/2 cup oats, old-fashioned
- 1/3 cup cocoa powder, unsweetened
- 1 cup dates, chopped
- 1/2 cup shredded coconut flakes, unsweetened
- 1/2 cup peanut butter

Directions:
1. Place oats in a food processor along with dates and pulse for 1 minute until the paste starts to come together.
2. Then add remaining ingredients, and blend until incorporated and very thick mixture comes together.
3. Shape the mixture into balls, refrigerate for 1 hour until set and then serve.

Nutrition: Calories: 88.6 Cal Fat: 5 g Carbs: 10 g Protein: 2.3 g Fiber: 1.6 g

Mango Coconut Cheesecake

Preparation Time: 4 hours and 10 minutes
Cooking Time: 0 minute
Servings: 4
Ingredients:
For the Crust:
- 1 cup macadamia nuts
- 1 cup dates, pitted, soaked in hot water for 10 minutes

For the Filling:
- 2 cups cashews, soaked in warm water for 10 minutes
- 1/2 cup and 1 tablespoon maple syrup

- 1/3 cup and 2 tablespoons coconut oil
- 1/4 cup lemon juice
- 1/2 cup and 2 tablespoons coconut milk, unsweetened, chilled

For the Topping:
- 1 cup fresh mango slices

Directions:
1. Prepare the crust, and for this, place nuts in a food processor and process until mixture resembles crumbs.
2. Drain the dates, add them to the food processor and blend for 2 minutes until thick mixture comes together.
3. Take a 4-inch cheesecake pan, place date mixture in it, spread and press evenly, and set aside.
4. Prepare the filling and for this, place all its ingredients in a food processor and blend for 3 minutes until smooth.
5. Pour the filling into the crust, spread evenly, and then freeze for 4 hours until set.
6. Top the cake with mango slices and then serve.

Nutrition: Calories: 200 Cal Fat: 11 g Carbs: 22.5 g Protein: 2 g Fiber: 1 g

Rainbow Fruit Salad

Preparation Time: 10 minutes
Cooking Time: 0 minute
Servings: 4
Ingredients:

For the Fruit Salad:
- 1 pound strawberries, hulled, sliced
- 1 cup kiwis, halved, cubed
- 1 1/4 cups blueberries
- 1 1/3 cups blackberries
- 1 cup pineapple chunks

For the Maple Lime Dressing:
- 2 teaspoons lime zest
- 1/4 cup maple syrup
- 1 tablespoon lime juice

Directions:
1. Prepare the salad, and for this, take a bowl, place all its ingredients and toss until mixed.
2. Prepare the dressing, and for this, take a small bowl, place all its ingredients and whisk well.
3. Drizzle the dressing over salad, toss until coated and serve.

Nutrition: Calories: 88.1 Cal Fat: 0.4 g Carbs: 22.6 g Protein: 1.1 g Fiber: 2.8 g

Cookie Dough Bites

Preparation Time: 4 hours and 10 minutes
Cooking Time: 0 minute
Servings: 18
Ingredients:
- 15 ounces cooked chickpeas
- 1/3 cup vegan chocolate chips
- 1/3 cup and 2 tablespoons peanut butter
- 8 Medjool dates pitted
- 1 teaspoon vanilla extract, unsweetened
- 2 tablespoons maple syrup
- 1 1/2 tablespoons almond milk, unsweetened

Directions:
1. Place chickpeas in a food processor along with dates, butter, and vanilla and then process for 2 minutes until smooth.
2. Add remaining ingredients, except for chocolate chips, and then pulse for 1 minute until blends and dough comes together.
3. Add chocolate chips, stir until just mixed, then shape the mixture into 18 balls and refrigerate for 4 hours until firm.
4. Serve straight away

Nutrition: Calories: 200 Cal Fat: 9 g Carbs: 26 g Protein: 1 g Fiber: 0 g

Dark Chocolate Bars

Preparation Time: 1 hour and 10 minutes
Cooking Time: 2 minutes
Servings: 12
Ingredients:
- 1 cup cocoa powder, unsweetened
- 3 Tablespoons cacao nibs
- 1/8 teaspoon sea salt
- 2 Tablespoons maple syrup
- 1 1/4 cup chopped cocoa butter
- 1/2 teaspoons vanilla extract, unsweetened
- 2 Tablespoons coconut oil

Directions:
1. Take a heatproof bowl, add butter, oil, stir, and microwave for 90 to 120 seconds until melts, stirring every 30 seconds.
2. Sift cocoa powder over melted butter mixture, whisk well until combined, and then stir in maple syrup, vanilla, and salt until mixed.
3. Distribute the mixture evenly between twelve mini cupcake liners, top with cacao nibs, and freeze for 1 hour until set.
4. Serve straight away

Nutrition: Calories: 100 Cal Fat: 9 g Carbs: 8 g Protein: 2 g Fiber: 2 g

Almond Butter, Oat and Protein Energy Balls

Preparation Time: 1 hour and 10 minutes
Cooking Time: 3 minutes
Servings: 4
Ingredients:
- 1 cup rolled oats
- ½ cup honey
- 2 ½ scoops of vanilla protein powder
- 1 cup almond butter
- Chia seeds for rolling

Directions:
1. Take a skillet pan, place it over medium heat, add butter and honey, stir and cook for 2 minutes until warm.
2. Transfer the mixture into a bowl, stir in protein powder until mixed, and then stir in oatmeal until combined.
3. Shape the mixture into balls, roll them into chia seeds, then arrange them on a cookie sheet and refrigerate for 1 hour until firm.
4. Serve straight away

Nutrition: Calories: 200 Cal Fat: 10 g Carbs: 21 g Protein: 7 g Fiber: 4 g

Chocolate and Avocado Truffles

Preparation Time: 1 hour and 10 minutes
Cooking Time: 1 minute
Servings: 18
Ingredients:
- 1 medium avocado, ripe
- 2 tablespoons cocoa powder
- 10 ounces of dark chocolate chips

Directions:
1. Scoop out the flesh from avocado, place it in a bowl, then mash with a fork until smooth, and stir in 1/2 cup chocolate chips.
2. Place remaining chocolate chips in a heatproof bowl and microwave for 1 minute until chocolate has melted, stirring halfway.
3. Add melted chocolate into avocado mixture, stir well until blended, and then refrigerate for 1 hour.
4. Then shape the mixture into balls, 1 tablespoon of mixture per ball, and roll in cocoa powder until covered.
5. Serve straight away.
Nutrition: Calories: 59 Cal Fat: 4 g Carbs: 7 g Protein: 0 g Fiber: 1 g

Coconut Oil Cookies

Preparation Time: 10 minutes
Cooking Time: 10 minutes
Servings: 15
Ingredients:
- 3 1/4 cup oats
- 1/2 teaspoons salt
- 2 cups coconut Sugar
- 1 teaspoons vanilla extract, unsweetened
- 1/4 cup cocoa powder
- 1/2 cup liquid Coconut Oil
- 1/2 cup peanut butter
- 1/2 cup cashew milk

Directions:
1. Take a saucepan, place it over medium heat, add all the ingredients except for oats and vanilla, stir until mixed, and then bring the mixture to boil.
2. Simmer the mixture for 4 minutes, mixing frequently, then remove the pan from heat and stir in vanilla.
3. Add oats, stir until well mixed and then scoop the mixture on a plate lined with wax paper.
4. Serve straight away.
Nutrition: Calories: 112 Cal Fat: 6.5 g Carbs: 13 g Protein: 1.4 g Fiber: 0.1 g

Express Coconut Flax Pudding

Preparation Time: 5 minutes
Cooking Time: 15 minutes
Servings: 4
Ingredients:
- 1 Tbsp coconut oil softened
- 1 Tbsp coconut cream
- 2 cups coconut milk canned
- 3/4 cup ground flax seed
- 4 Tbsp coconut palm sugar (or to taste)

Directions:
1. Press SAUTÉ button on your Instant Pot
2. Add coconut oil, coconut cream, coconut milk, and ground flaxseed.
3. Stir about 5 - 10 minutes.
4. Lock lid into place and set on the MANUAL setting for 5 minutes.
5. When the timer beeps, press "Cancel" and carefully flip the Quick Release valve to let the pressure out.
6. Add the palm sugar and stir well.
7. Taste and adjust sugar to taste.
8. Allow pudding to cool down completely.
9. Place the pudding in an airtight container and refrigerate for up to 2 weeks.
Nutrition: Calories: 140 Fat: 2g Fiber: 23g Carbs: 22g Protein: 47g

Full-flavored Vanilla Ice Cream

Preparation Time: 5 minutes
Cooking Time: 20 minutes
Servings: 8
Ingredients:
- 1 1/2 cups canned coconut milk
- 1 cup coconut whipping cream
- 1 frozen banana cut into chunks
- 1 cup vanilla sugar
- 3 Tbsp apple sauce
- 2 tsp pure vanilla extract
- 1 tsp Xanthan gum or agar-agar thickening agent

Directions:
1. Add all ingredients in a food processor; process until all ingredients combined well.
2. Place the ice cream mixture in a freezer-safe container with a lid over.
3. Freeze for at least 4 hours.
4. Remove frozen mixture to a bowl and beat with a mixer to break up the ice crystals.
5. Repeat this process 3 to 4 times.
6. Let the ice cream at room temperature for 15 minutes before serving.
Nutrition: Calories: 342 Fat: 15g Fiber: 11g Carbs: 8g Protein: 10g

Irresistible Peanut Cookies

Preparation Time: 5 minutes
Cooking Time: 25 minutes
Servings: 8
Ingredients:
- 4 Tbsp all-purpose flour
- 1 tsp baking soda
- pinch of salt
- 1/3 cup granulated sugar
- 1/3 cup peanut butter softened
- 3 Tbsp applesauce
- 1/2 tsp pure vanilla extract

Directions:
1. Preheat oven to 350 F.
2. Combine the flour, baking soda, salt, and sugar in a mixing bowl; stir.
3. Add all remaining ingredients and stir well to form a dough.

4. Roll dough into cookie balls/patties.
5. Arrange your cookies onto greased (with oil or cooking spray) baking sheet.
6. Bake for about 8 to 10 minutes.
7. Let cool for at least 15 minutes before removing from tray.
8. Remove cookies from the tray and let cool completely.
9. Place your peanut butter cookies in an airtight container, and keep refrigerated up to 10 days.
Nutrition: Calories: 211 Fat: 18g Fiber: 20g Carbs: 17g Protein: 39g

Murky Almond Cookies

Preparation Time: 10 minutes
Cooking Time: 15 minutes
Servings: 12
Ingredients:
- 4 Tbsp cocoa powder
- 2 cups almond flour
- 1/4 tsp salt
- 1/2 tsp baking soda
- 5 Tbsp coconut oil melted
- 2 Tbsp almond milk
- 1 1/2 tsp almond extract
- 1 tsp vanilla extract
- 4 Tbsp corn syrup or honey

Directions:
1. Preheat oven to 340 F degrees.
2. Grease a large baking sheet; set aside.
3. Combine the cocoa powder, almond flour, salt, and baking soda in a bowl.
4. In a separate bowl, whisk melted coconut oil, almond milk, almond and vanilla extract, and corn syrup or honey.
5. Combine the almond flour mixture with the almond milk mixture and stir until all ingredients incorporate well.
6. Roll tablespoons of the dough into balls, and arrange onto a prepared baking sheet.
7. Bake for 12 to 15 minutes.
8. Remove from the oven and transfer onto a plate lined with a paper towel.
9. Allow cookies to cool down completely and store in an airtight container at room temperature for about four days.
Nutrition: Calories: 508 Fat: 12g Fiber: 9g Carbs: 24g Protein: 40g

Orange Semolina Halva

Preparation Time: 15 minutes
Cooking Time: 5 minutes
Servings: 12
Ingredients:
- 6 cups fresh orange juice
- Zest from 3 oranges
- 3 cups brown sugar
- 1 1/4 cup semolina flour
- 1 Tbsp almond butter (plain, unsalted)
- 4 Tbsp ground almond
- 1/4 tsp cinnamon

Directions:

1. Heat the orange juice, orange zest with brown sugar in a pot.
2. Stir over medium heat until sugar is dissolved.
3. Add the semolina flour and cook over low heat for 15 minutes; stir occasionally.
4. Add almond butter, ground almonds, and cinnamon, and stir well.
5. Cook, frequently stirring, for further 5 minutes.
6. Transfer the halva mixture into a mold, let it cool and refrigerate for at least 4 hours.
7. Keep refrigerated in a sealed container for one week.
Nutrition: Calories: 285 Fat: 28g Fiber: 7g Carbs: 34g Protein: 23g

Seasoned Cinnamon Mango Popsicles

Preparation Time: 15 minutes
Cooking Time: 0 minute
Servings: 6
Ingredients:
- 1 1/2 cups of mango pulp
- 1 mango cut in cubes
- 1 cup brown sugar (packed)
- 2 Tbsp lemon juice freshly squeezed
- 1 tsp cinnamon
- 1 pinch of salt

Directions:
1. Add all ingredients into your blender.
2. Blend until brown sugar dissolved.
3. Pour the mango mixture evenly in popsicle molds or cups.
4. Insert sticks into each mold.
5. Place molds in a freezer, and freeze for at least 5 to 6 hours.
6. Before serving, un-mold easy your popsicles placing molds under lukewarm water.
Nutrition: Calories: 423 Fat: 2g Fiber: 0g Carbs: 20g Protein: 33g

Strawberry Molasses Ice Cream

Preparation Time: 20 minutes
Cooking Time: 0 minute
Servings: 8
Ingredients:
- 1 lb. strawberries
- 3/4 cup coconut palm sugar (or granulated sugar)
- 1 cup coconut cream
- 1 Tbsp molasses
- 1 tsp balsamic vinegar
- 1/2 tsp agar-agar
- 1/2 tsp pure strawberry extract

Directions:
1. Add strawberries, date sugar, and the balsamic vinegar in a blender; blend until completely combined.
2. Place the mixture in the refrigerator for one hour.
3. In a mixing bowl, beat the coconut cream with an electric mixer to make a thick mixture.
4. Add molasses, balsamic vinegar, agar-agar, and beat for further one minute or until combined well.
5. Keep frozen in a freezer-safe container (with plastic film and lid over).

Nutrition: Calories: 110 Fat: 31g Fiber: 18g Carbs: 15g Protein: 12g

Strawberry-Mint Sorbet

Preparation Time: 10 minutes
Cooking Time: 5 minutes
Servings: 6
Ingredients:

- 1 cup of granulated sugar
- 1 cup of orange juice
- 1 lb. frozen strawberries
- 1 tsp pure peppermint extract

Directions:
1. Add sugar and orange juice in a saucepan.
2. Stir over high heat and boil for 5 minutes or until sugar dissolves.
3. Remove from the heat and let it cool down.
4. Add strawberries into a blender, and blend until smooth.
5. Pour syrup into strawberries, add peppermint extract and stir until all ingredients combined well.
6. Transfer mixture to a storage container, cover tightly, and freeze until ready to serve.
Nutrition: Calories: 257 Fat: 13g Fiber: 37g Carbs: 11g Protein: 8g

Keto Chocolate Brownies

Preparation Time: 15 minutes
Cooking Time: 15 minutes
Servings: 4
Ingredients:

- ¼ t. of the following:
- salt
- baking soda
- ½ c. of the following:
- sweetener of your choice
- coconut flour
- vegetable oil
- water
- ¼ c. of the following:
- cocoa powder
- almond milk yogurt
- 1 tbsp. ground flax
- 1 t. vanilla extract

Directions:
1. Bring the oven to 350 heat setting.
2. Mix the ground flax, vanilla, yogurt, oil, and water; set to the side for 10 minutes.
3. Line an oven-safe 8x8 baking dish with parchment paper.
4. After 10 minutes have passed, add coconut flour, cocoa powder, sweetener, baking soda, and salt.
5. Bake for 15 minutes; make sure that you placed it in the center. When they come out, they will look underdone.
6. Place in the refrigerator and let them firm up overnight.
Nutrition: Calories: 208 Fat: 3g Fiber: 4g Carbs: 7g Protein: 27g

Chocolate Fat Bomb

Preparation Time: 5 minutes
Cooking Time: 0 minutes

Servings: 14
Ingredients:

- 1 tbsp. liquid sweetener of your choice.
- ¼ c. of the following:
- coconut oil, melted
- cocoa powder
- ½ c. almond butter

Directions:
1. Mix the ingredients in a medium bowl until smooth. Pour into the candy molds or ice cube trays.
2. Put in the freezer to set.
3. Store in freezer.
Nutrition: Calories: 241 Fat: 2g Fiber: 16g Carbs: 9g Protein: 22g

Vanilla Cheesecake

Preparation Time: 3 hours 20 minutes
Cooking Time: 0 minute
Servings: 10
Ingredients:

- 1 tbsp. vanilla extract,
- 2 ½ tbsp. lemon juice
- ½ c. coconut oil
- 1/8 t. stevia powder
- 6 tbsp. coconut milk
- 1 ½ c. blanched almonds soaked

Crust:

- 2 tbsp. coconut oil
- 1 ½ c. almonds

Directions:
For the Crust:
1. In a food processor, add the almonds and coconut oil and pulse until crumbles start to form.
2. Line a 7-inch springform pan with parchment paper and firmly press the crust into the bottom.
3. For the Sauce:
4. Bring a saucepan of water to a boil and soak the almonds for 2 hours. Drain and shake to dry.
5. Next, add the almonds to the food processor and blend until completely smooth.
6. Add vanilla, lemon, coconut oil, stevia, and coconut milk and blend until smooth.
7. Pour over the crust and freeze overnight or for a minimum of 3 hours.
8. Serve and enjoy.
Nutrition: Calories: 267 Fat: 13g Fiber: 14g Carbs: 17g Protein: 10g

Chocolate Mousse

Preparation Time: 5 minutes
Cooking Time: 0 minute
Servings: 2
Ingredients:

- 6 drops liquid stevia extract
- ½ t. cinnamon
- 3 tbsp. cocoa powder, unsweetened
- 1 c. coconut milk

Directions:
1. On the day before, place the coconut milk into the refrigerator overnight.
2. Remove the coconut milk from the refrigerator; it should be very thick.
3. Whisk in cocoa powder with an electric mixer.

4. Add stevia and cinnamon and whip until combined.
5. Place in individual bowls and serve and enjoy.
Nutrition: Calories: 130 Fat: 5g Fiber: 3g Carbs: 6gProtein: 7g

Peanut Butter Energy Bars

Total time: 5 hours 20 minutes
Ingredients
- 1/2 cup cranberries
- 12 Medjool dates, pitted
- 1 cup roasted almond
- 1 tablespoon chia seeds
- 1 1/2 cups oats
- 1/8 teaspoon salt
- 1/4 cup and 1 tablespoon agave nectar
- 1/2 teaspoon vanilla extract, unsweetened
- 1/3 cup and 1 tablespoon peanut butter, unsalted
- 2 tablespoons water

Directions:
1. Place an almond in a food processor, pulse until chopped, and then transfer into a large bowl.
2. Add dates into the food processor along with oats, pour in water, and pulse for dates are chopped.
3. Add dates mixture into the almond mixture, add chia seeds and berries and stir until mixed.
4. Take a saucepan, place it over medium heat, add remaining butter and remaining ingredients, stir and cook for 5 minutes until mixture reaches to a liquid consistency.
5. Pour the butter mixture over date mixture, and then stir until well combined.
6. Take an 8 by 8 inches baking tray, line it with parchment sheet, add date mixture in it, spread and press it evenly and refrigerate for 5 hours.
7. Cut it into sixteen bars and serve.

Black Bean Brownie Pops

Total time: 47 minutes
Ingredients
- 3/4 cup chocolate chips
- 15 ounce cooked black beans
- 1 tablespoon maple syrup
- 5 tablespoons cacao powder
- 1/8 teaspoon sea salt
- 2 tablespoons sunflower seed butter

Directions:
1. Place black beans in a food processor, add remaining ingredients, except for chocolate, and pulse for 2 minutes until combined and the dough starts to come together.
2. Shape the dough into twelve balls, arrange them on a baking sheet lined with parchment paper, then insert a toothpick into each ball and refrigerate for 20 minutes.
3. Then meat chocolate in the microwave for 2 minutes, and dip brownie pops in it until covered.
4. Return the pops into the refrigerator for 10 minutes until set and then serve.

Caramel Brownie Slice

Total time: 4 hours

Ingredients
For the Base:
- ¼ cup dried figs
- ½ cup cacao powder
- ½ cup pecans
- ½ cup walnuts

For the Caramel Layer:
- ¼ teaspoons sea salt
- 3 Tablespoons coconut oil
- 5 Tablespoons water

For the Chocolate Topping:
- 1/3 cup agave nectar
- ½ cup cacao powder
- ¼ cup of coconut oil
- 1 cup dried dates

Directions:
1. Prepare the base, and for this, place all its ingredients in a food processor and pulse for 3 to 5 minutes until the thick paste comes together.
2. Take an 8 by 8 inches baking dish, grease it with oil, place base mixture in it and spread and press the mixture evenly in the bottom, and freeze until required.
3. Prepare the caramel layer, and for this, place all its ingredients in a food processor and pulse for 2 minutes until smooth.
4. Pour the caramel into the prepared baking dish, smooth the top and freeze for 20 minutes.
5. Then prepare the topping and for this, place all its ingredients in a food processor, and pulse for 1 minute until combined.
6. Gently spread the chocolate mixture over the caramel layer and then freeze for 3 hours until set.
7. Serve straight away.

Snickers Pie

Total time: 4 hours
Ingredients
For the Crust:
- 12 Medjool dates, pitted
- 1 cup dried coconut, unsweetened
- 5 tablespoons cocoa powder
- 1/2 teaspoon sea salt
- 1 teaspoon vanilla extract, unsweetened
- 1 cup almonds

For the Caramel Layer:
- 10 Medjool dates, pitted, soaked for 10 minutes in warm water, drained
- 3 teaspoons vanilla extract, unsweetened
- 3 teaspoons coconut oil
- 3 tablespoons almond butter, unsalted

For the Peanut Butter Mousse:
- 3/4 cup peanut butter
- 2 tablespoons maple syrup
- 1/2 teaspoon vanilla extract, unsweetened
- 1/8 teaspoon sea salt
- 28 ounces coconut milk, chilled

Directions:
1. Prepare the crust, and for this, place all its ingredients in a food processor and pulse for 3 to 5 minutes until the thick paste comes together.

2.   Take a baking pan, line it with parchment paper, place crust mixture in it and spread and press the mixture evenly in the bottom, and freeze until required.
3.   Prepare the caramel layer, and for this, place all its ingredients in a food processor and pulse for 2 minutes until smooth.
4.   Pour the caramel on top of the prepared crust, smooth the top and freeze for 30 minutes until set.
5.   Prepare the mousse and for this, separate coconut milk and its solid, then add solid from coconut milk into a food processor, add remaining ingredients and then pulse for 1 minute until smooth.
6.   Top prepared mousse over caramel layer, and then freeze for 3 hours until set.
7.   Serve straight away.

Matcha Coconut Cream Pie

Total time: 5 minutes
Ingredients
For the Crust:
- 1/2 cup ground flaxseed
- 3/4 cup shredded dried coconut
- 1 cup Medjool dates, pitted
- 3/4 cup dehydrated buckwheat groats
- 1/4 teaspoons sea salt

For the Filling:
- 1 cup dried coconut flakes
- 4 cups of coconut meat
- 1/4 cup and 2 Tablespoons coconut nectar
- 1/2 Tablespoons vanilla extract, unsweetened
- 1/4 teaspoons sea salt
- 2/3 cup and 2 Tablespoons coconut butter
- 1 Tablespoons matcha powder
- 1/2 cup coconut water

Directions:
1.   Prepare the crust, and for this, place all its ingredients in a food processor and pulse for 3 to 5 minutes until the thick paste comes together.
2.   Take a 6-inch springform pan, grease it with oil, place crust mixture in it and spread and press the mixture evenly in the bottom and along the sides, and freeze until required.
3.   Prepare the filling and for this, place all its ingredients in a food processor, and pulse for 2 minutes until smooth.
4.   Pour the filling into prepared pan, smooth the top, and freeze for 4 hours until set.
5.   Cut pie into slices and then serve.

Chocolate Peanut Butter Cake

Total time: 5 minutes
Ingredients
For the Base:
- 1 tablespoon ground flaxseeds
- 1/8 cup millet
- 3/4 cup peanuts
- 1/4 cup and 2 tablespoons shredded coconut unsweetened
- 1 teaspoon hemp oil
- 1/2 cup flake oats

For the Date Layer:
- 1 tablespoon ground flaxseed
- 1 cup dates
- 1 tablespoon hemp hearts
- 2 tablespoons coconut
- 3 tablespoons cacao

For the Chocolate Layer:
- 3/4 cup coconut flour
- 2 tablespoons and 2 teaspoons cacao
- 1 tablespoon maple syrup
- 8 tablespoons warm water
- 2 tablespoons coconut oil
- 1/2 cup coconut milk
- 2 tablespoons ground flaxseed

For the Chocolate Topping:
- 7 ounces coconut cream
- 2 1/2 tablespoons cacao
- 1 teaspoon agave

For Assembly:
- 1/2 cup almond butter

Directions:
1.   Prepare the crust, and for this, place all its ingredients in a food processor and pulse for 3 to 5 minutes until the thick paste comes together.
2.   Take a loaf tin, grease it with oil, place crust mixture in it and spread and press the mixture evenly in the bottom and along the sides, and freeze until required.
3.   Prepare the date layer, and for this, place all its ingredients in a food processor and pulse for 2 minutes until smooth.
4.   Prepare the chocolate layer, and for this, place flour and flax in a bowl and stir until combined.
5.   Take a saucepan, add remaining ingredients, stir until mixed and cook for 5 minutes until melted and smooth.
6.   Add it into the flour mixture, stir until dough comes together, and set aside.
7.   Prepare the chocolate topping, place all its ingredients in a food processor and pulse for 3 to 5 minutes until smooth.
8.   Press date layer into the base layer, refrigerate for 1 hour, then press chocolate layer on its top, finish with chocolate topping, refrigerate for 3 hours and serve.

Strawberry Mousse

Total time: 20 minutes
Ingredients
- 8 ounces coconut milk, unsweetened
- 2 tablespoons honey
- 5 strawberries

Directions:
1.   Place berries in a blender and pulse until the smooth mixture comes together.
2.   Place milk in a bowl, whisk until whipped, and then add remaining ingredients and stir until combined.
3.   Refrigerate the mousse for 10 minutes and then serve.

Blueberry Mousse

Total time: 20 minutes

Ingredients
* 1 cup wild blueberries
* 1 cup cashews, soaked for 10 minutes, drained
* 1/2 teaspoon berry powder
* 2 tablespoons coconut oil, melted
* 1 tablespoon lemon juice
* 1 teaspoon vanilla extract, unsweetened
* 1/4 cup hot water

Directions:
1. Place all the ingredients in a food processor and process for 2 minutes until smooth.
2. Set aside until required.

Chocolate Raspberry Brownies

Total time: 4 hours
Ingredients
For the Chocolate Brownie Base:
* 12 Medjool Dates, pitted
* 3/4 cup oat flour
* 3/4 cup almond meal
* 3 tablespoons cacao
* 1 teaspoon vanilla extract, unsweetened
* 1/8 teaspoon sea salt
* 3 tablespoons water
* 1/2 cup pecans, chopped

For the Raspberry Cheesecake:
* 3/4 cup cashews, soaked, drained
* 6 tablespoons agave nectar
* 1/2 cup raspberries
* 1 teaspoon vanilla extract, unsweetened
* 1 lemon, juiced
* 6 tablespoons liquid coconut oil

For the Chocolate Coating:
* 2 1/2 tablespoons cacao powder
* 3 3/4 tablespoons coconut Oil
* 2 tablespoons maple syrup
* 1/8 teaspoon sea salt

Directions:
1. Prepare the crust, and for this, place all its ingredients in a food processor and pulse for 3 to 5 minutes until the thick paste comes together.
2. Take a 6-inch springform pan, grease it with oil, place crust mixture in it and spread and press the mixture evenly in the bottom and along the sides, and freeze until required.
3. Prepare the cheesecake topping, and for this, place all its ingredients in a food processor and pulse for 2 minutes until smooth.
4. Pour the filling into prepared pan, smooth the top, and freeze for 8 hours until solid.
5. Prepare the chocolate coating and for this, whisk together all its ingredients until smooth, drizzle on top of the cake and then serve.

Brownie Batter

Total time: 5 minutes
Ingredients
* 4 Medjool dates, pitted, soaked in warm water
* 1.5 ounces chocolate, unsweetened, melted
* 2 tablespoons maple syrup

* 4 tablespoons tahini
* ½ teaspoon vanilla extract, unsweetened
* 1 tablespoon cocoa powder, unsweetened
* 1/8 teaspoon sea salt
* 1/8 teaspoon espresso powder
* 2 to 4 tablespoons almond milk, unsweetened

Directions:
1. Place all the ingredients in a food processor and process for 2 minutes until combined.
2. Set aside until required.

Double Chocolate Orange Cheesecake

Total time: 4 hours
Ingredients
For the Base:
* 9 Medjool dates, pitted
* 1/3 cup Brazil nuts
* 2 tablespoons maple syrup
* 1/3 cup walnuts
* 2 tablespoons water
* 3 tablespoons cacao powder

For the Chocolate Cheesecake:
* 1/2 cup cacao powder
* 1 1/2 cups cashews, soaked for 10 minutes in warm water, drained
* 1/3 cup liquid coconut oil
* 1 teaspoon vanilla extract, unsweetened
* 1/3 cup maple syrup
* 1/3 cup water

For the Orange Cheesecake:
* 2 oranges, juiced
* 1/4 cup maple syrup
* 1 cup cashews, soaked for 10 minutes in warm water, drained
* 1 teaspoon vanilla extract, unsweetened
* 2 tablespoons coconut butter
* 1/2 cup liquid coconut oil
* 2 oranges, zested
* 4 drops of orange essential oil

For the Chocolate Topping:
* 3 tablespoons cacao powder
* 3 drops of orange essential oil
* 2 tablespoons liquid coconut oil
* 3 tablespoons maple syrup

Directions:
1. Prepare the base, and for this, place all its ingredients in a food processor and pulse for 3 to 5 minutes until the thick paste comes together.
2. Take a cake tin, place crust mixture in it and spread and press the mixture evenly in the bottom, and freeze until required.
3. Prepare the chocolate cheesecake, and for this, place all its ingredients in a food processor and pulse for 2 minutes until smooth.
4. Pour the chocolate cheesecake mixture on top of the prepared base, smooth the top and freeze for 20 minutes until set.
5. Then prepare the orange cheesecake and for this, place all its ingredients in a food processor, and pulse for 2 minutes until smooth

6.   Top orange cheesecake mixture over chocolate cheesecake, and then freeze for 3 hours until hardened.
7.   Then prepare the chocolate topping and for this, take a bowl, add all the ingredients in it and stir until well combined.
8.   Spread chocolate topping over the top, freeze the cake for 10 minutes until the topping has hardened and then slice to serve.

Coconut Ice Cream Cheesecake

Total time: 3 hours
Ingredients
For the First Layer:
- 1 cup mixed nuts
- 3/4 cup dates, soaked for 10 minutes in warm water
- 2 tablespoons almond milk

For the Second Layer:
- 1 medium avocado, diced
- 1 cup cashew nuts, soaked for 10 minutes in warm water
- 3 cups strawberries, sliced
- 1 tablespoon chia seeds, soaked in 3 tablespoons soy milk
- 1/2 cup agave
- 1 cup melted coconut oil
- 1/2 cup shredded coconut
- 1 lime, juiced

Directions:
1.   Prepare the first layer, and for this, place all its ingredients in a food processor and pulse for 3 to 5 minutes until the thick paste comes together.
2.   Take a springform pan, place crust mixture in it and spread and press the mixture evenly in the bottom, and freeze until required.
3.   Prepare the second layer, and for this, place all its ingredients in a food processor and pulse for 2 minutes until smooth.
4.   Pour the second layer on top of the first layer, smooth the top, and freeze for 4 hours until hard.
5.   Serve straight away.

Lemon Cashew Tart

Total time: 3 hours 15 minutes
Ingredients
For the Crust:
- 1 cup almonds
- 4 dates, pitted, soaked in warm water for 10 minutes in water, drained
- 1/8 teaspoon crystal salt
- 1 teaspoon vanilla extract, unsweetened

For the Cream:
- 1 cup cashews, soaked in warm water for 10 minutes in water, drained
- 1/4 cup water
- 1/4 cup coconut nectar
- 1 teaspoon coconut oil
- 1 teaspoon vanilla extract, unsweetened
- 1 lemon, Juiced
- 1/8 teaspoon crystal salt

For the Topping:
- Shredded coconut as needed

Directions:
1.   Prepare the cream and for this, place all its ingredients in a food processor, pulse for 2 minutes until smooth, and then refrigerate for 1 hour.
2.   Then prepare the crust, and for this, place all its ingredients in a food processor and pulse for 3 to 5 minutes until the thick paste comes together.
3.   Take a tart pan, grease it with oil, place crust mixture in it and spread and press the mixture evenly in the bottom and along the sides, and freeze until required.
Pour the filling into the prepared tart, smooth the top, and refrigerate for 2 hours until set.
Cut tart into slices and then serve.

Peppermint Oreos

Total time: 2 hours
Ingredients
For the Cookies:
- 1 cup dates
- 2/3 cup brazil nuts
- 3 tablespoons carob powder
- 2/3 cup almonds
- 1/8 teaspoon sea salt
- 3 tablespoons water

For the Crème:
- 2 tablespoons almond butter
- 1 cup coconut chips
- 2 tablespoons melted coconut oil
- 1 cup coconut shreds
- 3 drops of peppermint oil
- 1/2 teaspoon vanilla powder

For the Dark Chocolate:
- 3/4 cup cacao powder
- 1/2 cup date paste
- 1/3 cup coconut oil, melted

Directions:
1.   Prepare the cookies, and for this, place all its ingredients in a food processor and pulse for 3 to 5 minutes until the dough comes together.
2.   Then place the dough between two parchment sheets, roll the dough, then cut out twenty-four cookies of the desired shape and freeze until solid.
3.   Prepare the crème, and for this, place all its ingredients in a food processor and pulse for 2 minutes until smooth.
4.   When cookies have harden, sandwich crème in between the cookies by placing dollops on top of a cookie and then pressing it with another cookie.
5.   Freeze the cookies for 30 minutes and in the meantime, prepare chocolate and for this, place all its ingredients in a bowl and whisk until combined.
6.   Dip frouncesen cookie sandwich into chocolate, at least two times, and then freeze for another 30 minutes until chocolate has hardened.
7.   Serve straight away.

Key Lime Pie

Total time: 3 hours 15 minutes
Ingredients

For the Crust:
- ¾ cup coconut flakes, unsweetened
- 1 cup dates, soaked in warm water for 10 minutes in water, drained

For the Filling:
- ¾ cup of coconut meat
- 1 ½ avocado, peeled, pitted
- 2 tablespoons key lime juice
- ¼ cup agave

Directions:
1. Prepare the crust, and for this, place all its ingredients in a food processor and pulse for 3 to 5 minutes until the thick paste comes together.
2. Take an 8-inch pie pan, grease it with oil, pour crust mixture in it and spread and press the mixture evenly in the bottom and along the sides, and freeze until required.
3. Prepare the filling and for this, place all its ingredients in a food processor, and pulse for 2 minutes until smooth.
4. Pour the filling into prepared pan, smooth the top, and freeze for 3 hours until set.
5. Cut pie into slices and then serve.

Chocolate Mint Grasshopper Pie

Total time: 4 hours 15 minutes
Ingredients
For the Crust:
- 1 cup dates, soaked in warm water for 10 minutes in water, drained
- 1/8 teaspoons salt
- 1/2 cup pecans
- 1 teaspoons cinnamon
- 1/2 cup walnuts

For the Filling:
- ½ cup mint leaves
- 2 cups of cashews, soaked in warm water for 10 minutes in water, drained
- 2 tablespoons coconut oil
- 1/4 cup and 2 tablespoons of agave
- 1/4 teaspoons spirulina
- 1/4 cup water

Directions:
1. Prepare the crust, and for this, place all its ingredients in a food processor and pulse for 3 to 5 minutes until the thick paste comes together.
2. Take a 6-inch springform pan, grease it with oil, place crust mixture in it and spread and press the mixture evenly in the bottom and along the sides, and freeze until required.
3. Prepare the filling and for this, place all its ingredients in a food processor, and pulse for 2 minutes until smooth.
4. Pour the filling into prepared pan, smooth the top, and freeze for 4 hours until set.
5. Cut pie into slices and then serve.

Oatmeal Raisin Muffins

Total time: 45 minutes
Ingredients
- 2½ cups rolled oats
- ½ cup oat flour
- 1 teaspoon baking powder
- ½ teaspoon baking soda
- 1 teaspoon salt
- 1 tablespoon cinnamon
- ½ teaspoon ground nutmeg
- 4 ripe bananas, mashed
- 1 apple, grated
- ½ cup almond milk
- 3 teaspoons vanilla extract
- ½ cup raisins
- ½ cup chopped walnuts

Directions:
1. Preheat your oven to 350 degrees F.
2. Whisk the dry ingredients in a mixing bowl, and wet ingredients in a separate bowl.
3. Beat the two mixtures together until smooth.
4. Fold in apples, walnuts and raisins, give it a gentle stir.
5. Line a muffin tray with muffin cups and evenly divide the muffin batter among the cups.
6. Bake for nearly 35 minutes and serve.

Fudge Popsicles

Total time: 2 hours 10 minutes
Ingredients
- 1 cup almond milk
- 3 ripe bananas
- 3 tablespoon cocoa powder
- 1 tablespoon almond butter

Directions:
1. In a blender, blend all the ingredients for popsicles until smooth.
2. Divide the popsicle blend into the popsicle molds.
3. Insert the popsicles sticks and close the molds.
4. Place the molds in the freezer for 2 hours to set.
5. Serve.

Strawberry Coconut Popsicles

Total time: 2 hours 10 minutes
Ingredients
- 2 medium bananas, sliced
- 1 can coconut milk
- 1 cup strawberries
- 3 tablespoons maple syrup

Directions:
1. In a blender, blend all the ingredients for popsicles until smooth.
2. Divide the popsicle blend into the popsicle molds.
3. Insert the popsicles sticks and close the molds.
4. Place the molds in the freezer for 2 hours to set.
5. Serve.

Green Popsicle

Total time: hours 10 minutes
Ingredients
- 1 ripe avocado, peeled and pitted
- 1 cup fresh spinach

- 1 can (13.5 ounce) full fat coconut milk
- ¼ cup lime juice
- 2 tablespoons maple syrup
- 1 teaspoon vanilla extract

Directions:
1. In a blender, blend all the ingredients for popsicles until smooth.
2. Divide the popsicle blend into the popsicle molds.
3. Insert the popsicles sticks and close the molds.
4. Place the molds in the freezer for 2 hours to set.
5. Serve.

Peach Popsicles

Total time: 2 hours 10 minutes
Ingredients
- 2½ cups peaches, peeled and pitted
- 2 tablespoons agave
- ¾ cup coconut cream

Directions:
1. In a blender, blend all the ingredients for popsicles until smooth.
2. Divide the popsicle blend into the popsicle molds.
3. Insert the popsicles sticks and close the molds.
4. Place the molds in the freezer for 2 hours to set.
5. Serve.

Coconut Fat Bombs

Total time: 1 hour 11 minutes
Ingredients
- 1 can coconut milk
- ¾ cup coconut oil
- 1 cup coconut flakes
- 20 drops liquid stevia

Directions:
1. In a bowl combine all the ingredients.
2. Melt in a microwave for 1 minute.
3. Mix well then divide the mixture into silicone molds.
4. Freeze them for 1 hour to set.
5. Serve.

Apple Pie Bites

Total time: 1 hour 10 minutes
Ingredients
- 1 cup walnuts, chopped
- ½ cup coconut oil
- ¼ cup ground flax seeds
- ½ ounce freeze dried apples
- 1 teaspoon vanilla extract
- 1 teaspoon cinnamon
- Liquid stevia, to taste

Directions:
1. In a bowl add all the ingredients.
2. Mix well then roll the mixture into small balls.
3. Freeze them for 1 hour to set.
4. Serve.

Mojito Fat Bombs

Total time: 1 hour 11 minutes
Ingredients
- ¾ cup hulled hemp seeds
- ½ cup coconut oil
- 1 cup fresh mint
- ½ teaspoon mint extract
- Juice & zest of two limes
- ¼ teaspoon stevia

Directions:
1. In a bowl, combine all the ingredients.
2. Melt in the microwave for 1 minute.
3. Mix well then divide the mixture into silicone molds.
4. Freeze them for 1 hour to set.
5. Serve.

Protein Fat Bombs

Total time: 1 hour 10 minutes
Ingredients
- 1 cup coconut oil
- 1 cup peanut butter, melted
- ½ cup cocoa powder
- ¼ cup plant-based protein powder
- 1 pinch of salt
- 2 cups unsweetened shredded coconut

Directions:
1. In a bowl, add all the ingredients except coconut shreds.
2. Mix well then make small balls out of this mixture and place them into silicone molds.
3. Freeze for 1 hour to set.
4. Roll the balls in the coconut shreds
5. Serve.

Chocolate Peanut Fat Bombs

Total time: 1 hour 11 minutes
Ingredients
- ½ cup coconut butter
- 1 cup plus 2 tablespoons peanut butter
- 5 tablespoons cocoa powder
- 2 teaspoons maple syrup

Directions:
1. In a bowl, combine all the ingredients.
2. Melt them in the microwave for 1 minute.
3. Mix well then divide the mixture into silicone molds.
4. Freeze them for 1 hour to set.
5. Serve.

Carrot Flaxseed Muffins

Total time: 30 minutes
Ingredients
- 2 tablespoons ground flax
- 5 tablespoons water
- ¾ cup almond milk
- ¾ cup applesauce
- ½ cup maple syrup
- 1 teaspoon vanilla extract
- 1½ cups whole wheat flour
- ½ cup rolled oats
- 1 teaspoon baking soda

- 1½ teaspoon baking powder
- ¼ teaspoon ground ginger
- 1 teaspoon salt
- 1 teaspoon cinnamon
- 1 cup grated carrot

Directions:

1. Whisk flaxseed with water in a bowl and leave it for 10 minutes
2. Preheat your oven to 350 degrees F.
3. Separately, whisk together the dry ingredients in one bowl and the wet ingredients in another bowl.
4. Beat the two mixtures together until smooth.
5. Fold in flaxseed and carrots, give it a gentle stir.
6. Line a muffin tray with muffin cups and evenly divide the muffin batter among the cups.
7. Bake for 20 minutes and serve.

Banana Walnut Muffins

Total time: 28 minutes

Ingredients

- 4 large pitted dates, boiled
- 1 cup almond milk
- 2 tablespoons lemon juice
- 2½ cups rolled oats
- 1 teaspoon baking powder
- 1 teaspoon baking soda
- 1 teaspoon cinnamon
- ¼ teaspoon nutmeg
- ⅛ teaspoon salt
- 1½ cups mashed banana
- ¼ cup maple syrup
- 1 tablespoon vanilla extract
- 1 cup walnuts, chopped

Directions:

1. Preheat your oven to 350 degrees F.
2. Separately, whisk together the dry ingredients in one bowl and the wet ingredients in another bowl.
3. Beat the two mixtures together until smooth.
4. Fold in walnuts and give it a gentle stir.
5. Line a muffin tray with muffin cups and evenly divide the muffin batter among the cups.
6. Bake for 18 minutes and serve.

2 WEEKS MEAL PLAN

Day	Breakfast	Lunch	Dinner	Dessert/snacks
1	Gingerbread Waffles	Chickpea Sunflower Sandwich	Black Bean Burgers	Express Coconut Flax Pudding
2	Oatmeal & Peanut Butter Breakfast Bar	Pesto Quinoa with White Beans	Dijon Maple Burgers	Pumpkin Pie Cups
3	Easy Hummus Toast	White Bean and Artichoke Sandwich	Bok Choy Salad	Banana-Coconut Ice Cream
4	Blueberry French Toast Breakfast Muffins	Rainbow Taco Boats	Garlic Zucchini and Cauliflower	Nice Spiced Cherry Cider
5	Avocado Toast with White Beans	Green Bean Casserole	Herbed Beets	Full-flavored Vanilla Ice Cream
6	Sweet Pomegranate Porridge	Roasted Vegetables	Spinach and Pear Salad	Strawberry Coconut Ice Cream
7	Vegan Breakfast Biscuits	Loaded Kale Salad	Steamed Cauliflower	Roasted Almond Protein Salad
8	Orange French Toast	Mediterranean Pizza	Olives and Mango Mix	Dark Chocolate Bars
9	Coffee Smoothie	Pumpkin Risotto	Marinara Broccoli	Mimosa Salad
10	Berries and Banana Smoothie Bowl	Black Bean and Quinoa Salad	Red Onion, Avocado and Radishes Mix	Mixed Berries and Cream
11	Carrot Cake Oats	Spicy Peanut Soba Noodles	Sage Walnuts and Radishes	Pear Lemonade
12	Dairy-Free Coconut Yogurt	Tahini Broccoli	Curried Apple	Brownie Energy Bites
13	Mint Chocolate Green Protein	Garden Pasta Salad	Cajun and Balsamic Okra	Beetroot Hummus
14	Cinnamon Rolls with Cashew Frosting	Jamaican Jerk Tofu Wrap	Plant Based Keto Lo Mein	Skewers of Mozzarella And Tomato

APPENDIX : RECIPES INDEX

Lovely Parsnip & Split Pea Soup 51
Low-fat Stuffed Mushrooms 93

M

Mango Agua Fresca 96
Mango and Leeks Meatballs 64
Mango Coconut Cheesecake 194
Mango Coconut Chia Pudding 193
Mango Coconut Cream Pie 187
Mango Lassi 180
Maple Bagel Spread 93
Maple Dijon Burgers 48
Maple Dijon Dressing 129
Maple Flavoured Oatmeal 30
Marinara Broccoli 60
Marinated Mushrooms 148
Marinated Mushrooms 93
Masala Popcorn 149
Matcha Coconut Cream Pie 200
Matcha Limeade 97
Mediterranean Hummus Pizza 47
Mediterranean Hummus Pizza 80
Mediterranean Pizza 32
Medley of Mushroom Soup 122
Metabolism Water 176
Mexican Hot Chocolate Mix 179
Mexican Lentil Soup 49
Mexican Soup 121
Mimosa Salad 168
Mint Chocolate Chip Sorbet 187
Mint Chocolate Green Protein Smoothie 19
Mint Chocolate Protein Smoothie 20
Minted Peas 81
Minty Fruit Salad 186
Minutes Vegetarian Pasta 85
Minutes Vegetarian Pasta 88
Miso Ramen 72
Miso Spaghetti Squash 81
Mixed Berries and Cream 191
Mixed Grain Salad 161
Mocha Chocolate Shake 180
Moist Banana Bread 123
Mojito Fat Bombs 204
Molasses Tahini Sauce 136
Mongolian Seitan 53
Moroccan Vegetable Stew 116
Moroccan Vermicelli Vegetable Soup 116
Murky Almond Cookies 197
Mushroom & Broccoli Soup 110
Mushroom Cakes 165
Mushroom Steaks 100
Mushrooms Sandwich 34
Mustard Beets 59

N

Nacho Cheese Sauce 131
Nacho Cheese Sauce 149
Nacho Kale Chips 148
Nice Spiced Cherry Cider 184

No-Bake Chewy Granola Bars 14
Nooch Popcorn 152
Noodle and Rice Pilaf 171
Noodles with Sticky Tofu 73
Not-Tuna Salad 162
Nourishing Curried Lentil and Sweet Potato
Bowl 76
Nutty Stuffed Squash 74

O

Oatmeal & Peanut Butter Breakfast Bar 15
Oatmeal Raisin Muffins 203
Oatmeal with Berries 125
Oats with Chia 22
Olive and White Bean Pasta 69
Olives and Mango Mix 60
Omelet with Chickpea Flour 27
One Pan Spicy Rice 32
Onion & Mushroom Tart with a Nice Brown
Rice Crust 28
Onion and Tomato Bowls 65
Onion Gravy with Red Onion 135
Orange French Toast 17
Orange Semolina Halva 197
Orange Walnut Pasta 68
Oven-Dried Grapes 152

P

Pad Thai Bowl 45
Paprika Sweet Potato 106
Parsley Green Beans 59
PB&J Oats 127
Peach & Chia Seed Breakfast Parfait 14
Peach Popsicles 204
Peach-Mango Crumble (Pressure cooker) 188
Peanut Butter Energy Bars 199
Peanut Butter Granola 27
Peanut Butter Shake 185
Pear Lemonade 183
Pecan Pumpkin Spice Oatmeal 125
Pecan-Maple Granola 173
Peppered Pinto Beans 62
Peppermint Oreos 202
Peppers and Black Beans with Brown Rice 174
Peppers Bowl 105
Peppery Black Beans 173
Perfect Breakfast Shake 28
Perfect Polenta with a Dose of Cranberries &
Pears 28
Pesto and White Bean Pasta 62
Pesto Pea Soup 119
Pesto Quinoa with White Beans 39
Pineapple Mint Salsa 131
Pizza Bites 166
Plant Based Keto Lo Mein 85
Polenta Skewers 164
Pomegranate and Pears Salad 66
Pomegranate Overnight Oats 25
Potato Chips 151

Printed by Libri Plureos GmbH in Hamburg,
Germany